BEFORE THE
PHARAOHS

pg 221 = 1, 2, 3

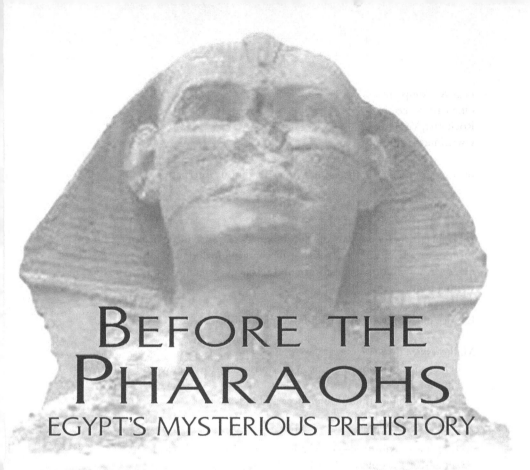

BEFORE THE PHARAOHS

EGYPT'S MYSTERIOUS PREHISTORY

Edward F. Malkowski

Bear & Company
Rochester, Vermont

Bear & Company
One Park Street
Rochester, Vermont 05767
www.InnerTraditions.com

Bear & Company is a division of Inner Traditions International

Library of Congress Cataloging-in-Publication Data

Malkowski, Edward F.
  Before the pharaohs : Egypt's mysterious prehistory / Edward F. Malkowski.
    p. cm.
  Includes bibliographical references and index.
  ISBN 978-159143048-3
  ISBN 1-59143-048-8
    1. Egypt—Civilizaton—To 332 B.C. 2. Civilization, Ancient.
  3. Prehistoric peoples.   I. Title.
  DT61.M293 2005
  932'.011—dc22

                                                                    2005022780

Printed and bound in the United States

10 9 8 7

Text design and layout by Priscilla Baker
This book was typeset in Sabon, with Avenir, Papyrus, and Basilea used as display typefaces

The illustration in figure 6.1 is used with the permission of Palladium Books, Inc., which holds the copyright and reserves all rights worldwide.

The photograph in figure 8.3 and illustrations in figures 8.4 and 11.5 are used with the permission of the copyright holder, Garber Communications/ Steiner Books.

To correspond with the author of this book, send a first-class letter to the author c/o Inner Traditions • Bear & Company, One Park Street, Rochester, VT 05767, and we will forward the communication.

CONTENTS

ACKNOWLEDGMENTS

This book is dedicated to John Anthony West, to whom I extend a very special thanks. In many respects, his work has forged a new generation of Egyptologists and historians, of which I am one.

I also want to express my gratitude to Christopher Dunn for his brilliant insights into the technologies of ancient Egypt; Dr. Thomas Brophy, for his astute observations into the level of knowledge of the prehistoric peoples of North Africa; and Dr. Robert Schoch and Colin Reader, for their continuing research into the origins of the Great Sphinx of Egypt. To these men and all the others in the following pages, we who search for truth in history owe a debt of gratitude.

I would like to thank the following people for permitting me to use photographs and illustrations in this book:

> Jon Bodsworth of The Egypt Archive Web site (figures 1.3, 1.6, 4.2 [bottom], 4.4, 4.5, and 11.3)
>
> John Anthony West (figure 1.2)
>
> Colin Reader (figures 1.4, 2.1)
>
> Christopher Dunn (figures 4.2 [top], 4.6, 6.3, 6.4)
>
> Jimmy Dunn (figures 4.7 and 4.8)
>
> Thomas Brophy (figures 4.9 and 4.12)
>
> Dorothy Norton (figure 4.10)
>
> Bruce Bradley (figure 9.1)

Olga Soffer (figures 9.2 and 9.3)

John Opsopaus, from The Pythagorean Tarot Web site (figure 10.2)

Tony Ford (figure 12.2)

Martin Gray (figure 12.3)

Every effort has been made to trace the ownership of all illustrative material reproduced in this book. Should any error or omission in acknowledgment have been made, the author offers his apologies and will make the necessary corrections in future editions.

PREFACE

In primary and secondary schools, history is taught as dates and facts. From an early age we learn that civilization began on the Mesopotamian Plain five thousand years ago, then spread throughout the rest of the world. Twenty-five hundred years after the birth of civilization, the classical Greek state emerged as the progenitor of the modern world, solely responsible for the birth of philosophy, science, and mathematics—or so we are taught. Thanks to a rather provocative professor, I discovered that this view of the origin of Western civilization was more interpretation than it was historical fact, and that history—particularly ancient history—is more theory than anything else. As a result, I have devoted the past twenty-five years to investigating unanswered questions concerning ancient history, and will continue to do so for the remaining years of my life.

Pursuing the truth of what actually happened so long ago is a quest I find endlessly intriguing. At its heart is the same mystery everyone wants solved: Who are we and where did we come from? These two questions are ultimately the driving force behind all philosophy and religion as well as the scientific disciplines. Investigating them requires a certain amount of insight into the intricacies of human behavior as much as it does deductive logic. Knowing what motivated ancient peoples, and how they viewed the world around them, is just as important as determining where they lived and what they ate.

Even though the social sciences are relatively new disciplines, after 150 years of scholarship there exists a profusion of historical and archaeological research available to everyone. All this data has led to various theories describing "what really happened" during the most ancient of times. Some of those claims are in striking opposition to the established ideas regarding the timeline for civilization's development. Among them is the supposition that civilization had achieved a high level of sophistication more than *ten thousand* years ago. Defending such a theory would, of course, require extraordinary evidence. As a skeptic I was surprised to discover that extraordinary evidence does, in fact, exist.

I first learned of this in 1993 as I watched Charlton Heston narrate the NBC special presentation *The Mystery of the Sphinx*, based on the research of John Anthony West and Boston University geologist Dr. Robert Schoch. According to the documentary, the Sphinx was carved thousands of years before the birth of dynastic Egypt. I noted with interest the harsh reaction from the Egyptology community to West and Schoch's conclusions. Why was there such outrage? For me, it was obvious that West and Schoch had touched a nerve, and that mainstream ideas about the origins of mankind and of civilization were teetering on the brink of change. So-called crackpot theorists with unsubstantiated claims are typically ignored by the academic mainstream, but West and Schoch were receiving a Super Bowl of attention. Fascinated by the story, I decided to begin my own investigation into what West and Schoch's opponents claimed was missing from their argument: namely, the existence of evidence that mankind had achieved a level of civilization capable of building such a precision-crafted structure well before 3000 B.C. Geologists, archaeologists, and historians have been investigating prehistory for many years, which has resulted in volumes of analysis and opinion. Essentially there were two kinds of evidence available: the physical, or archaeological, and the historical—what the ancient people themselves reported about their history. I wanted to survey the data and see for myself what evidence existed and how it might explain West and Schoch's conclusion concerning the age of the Sphinx.

What I found out is that there is a wealth of evidence attesting to a high level of civilization in ancient Egypt. Yet there is little to go on in deducing the events that spurred its creation. It is unlikely that Egyptian civilization suddenly erupted from a primitive hunter-gatherer society into a sophisticated, centralized state; yet historians have been hard-pressed to explain what seems to have been an abrupt emergence of advanced social organization and technology. Some have argued that Egypt's development was influenced by invasions of cultures from other regions, but there is evidence that contradicts this theory. In this book,

I hope to demonstrate that the emergence of pharaonic Egypt was a result of indigenous efforts. Furthermore, I aim to show that there is substantial and convincing archaeological and historical evidence that the beginnings of Egyptian civilization occurred thousands of years before what is traditionally believed.

In one sense, the remains of ancient Egypt can be compared to a crime scene that has gone unnoticed for years, weathered by the forces of nature, and whose witnesses have long since passed away. Since moving objects around can mask clues as to what happened, when police investigators arrive at a crime scene, they prefer that everything remain as it was when the offense occurred. They need as many clues as possible in their search for the perpetrator. In some cases there are plenty of clues; in others there are not, and the crime may go unsolved for years and sometimes, unfortunately, indefinitely. If enough facts can be established through deduction, an explanation of all the evidence leads the sleuth to a theoretical conclusion as to "whodunit." It serves as the basis for further investigation and, hopefully, apprehension of the person who committed the crime.

Investigating prehistory is not all that different from investigating a crime scene, but it takes place on a much broader scale. The greater the evidence, the greater the possibility that researchers can ascertain what happened when, and who was involved. As do police investigators, archaeologists and other historical researchers prefer that the evidence discovered remain in situ—in its original place when discovered—and untouched by human hands. This reveals irrefutable facts that are essential for the formation of a viable theory.

However, in the formulation of theory, the interpretation of evidence may be problematic. Physical evidence and historical facts are often viewed with a certain bias. This bias is a set of assumptions an individual brings to the evaluation of evidence. For example, researchers who believe civilization has only recently achieved technical sophistication will tend to disregard any evidence to the contrary, sometimes no matter how strong. One way to work around this bias is to consider expert analysis from other disciplines.

It is with this multidisciplinary approach—drawing from astronomy, engineering, geology, and dental anthropology, as well as insights from other historians—that I address the question of the origins of Egyptian civilization. We will explore artifacts, which include everything from skeletal remains to stone vases, temples, and other monuments, that are considered primary pieces of evidence. Among these are the pyramids of Egypt, especially the Great Pyramid, and the mysterious megaliths of Nabta Playa, which have been dated to approximately 5000 B.C.E. These are observable structures, facts that have been visited and revisited by researchers over the years. The relentless mystery is that as yet no one, in my opinion, has explained the historical context that surrounds this seemingly anachronistic and anomalistic evidence in a satisfactory way. According to orthodox history, the technology associated with such structures could not possibly have existed so long ago.

In science, without speculation there can be no hypothesis. And without a hypothesis to test or investigate, there can be no theories—all of which are subject to argument from various perspectives. Since scientists and researchers are human, science itself often takes on the dualistic nature of mankind; opposite forces work together in a cooperative battle of ideas, a scientific yin and yang. With speculation come new ideas and theories, which are often viewed initially as the whims of the uninformed. But over time, new ideas with merit survive, are synthesized into the growing body of scientific knowledge, and often, much later, become a standard of thought in their own right.

It is my belief that sincere and dedicated researchers have found enough anomalies and anachronisms regarding the rise of Egyptian civilization to warrant a new interpretation of the evidence, and possibly a new history of mankind. As a whole, their work is greater than the sum of its parts in painting a more thorough picture of Egypt's prehistory, as you will discover in *Before the Pharaohs*.

INTRODUCTION

One of the principal questions that historians seek to answer is how civilization began. With the rise of the university system, with its measured and meticulous research specialists, billions of dollars have been spent over the past five generations in digging up the past. As a result, Western society has undergone a drastic revision of its understanding of history. The result of ongoing search for physical evidence of life long ago now paints a very different picture of history from what our forefathers accepted two hundred years ago.

But there are really two different histories; researchers subject to different political and philosophical persuasions argue over interpretations of the evidence. One version is common knowledge, taught to us from an early age, and we accept it as fact. Those responsible for our educational institutions consider the other version maverick at best. As a result, researchers who engage in the latter may be called irresponsible and speculative, and are charged with misinterpreting the evidence. In a search for truth, when significant portions of the story are missing, the interpretation is often determined by the interpreter's underlying philosophy. With today's news-breaking discoveries about our past, the evidence seldom speaks for itself.

Before the Pharaohs searches deep into the past of the Nile Valley and reveals a culture that predates what most historians consider the birth of Egyptian civilization by many thousands of years. Egypt has always been enthralling to the ancient-history enthusiast, and for good reason. Although Mesopotamia is considered the cradle of civilization,

1

the Nile Valley has been an archaeological wellspring of temples, monuments, artifacts, and insights into our ancient past for more than a hundred years. It still is today. Over the last two decades, independent as well as some academic researchers have postulated that an older, more advanced civilization once existed from which the Egyptians inherited their ways. But the evidence has always been too mysterious and subtle, and the advanced culture never identified satisfactorily enough, for traditional academics to accept this theory.

Forty years ago, the prominent Egyptologist and chair of the Egyptology department at the University of London, Walter Bryan Emery, believed in the possibility of an older Egyptian civilization. A lifelong veteran of archaeological fieldwork, which included excavations at Sakkara's Archaic Cemetery and discovery of the "mummified zoo," he considered the possibility of the influence of another culture on Egyptian as well as Mesopotamian society. In his 1961 book *Archaic Egypt,* Emery writes that modern scholars tend to ignore the possibility that a more advanced community from a yet-to-be-discovered area emigrated to the Nile Valley, where they were subjugated by the indigenous people. Vast tracts of the Middle East, the region of the Red Sea, and the East African coast remain unexplored. According to Emery, such a possibility must not be entirely dismissed. Indeed, he believes that the existence of another culture whose achievements were passed on independently to Egypt and Mesopotamia would best explain the common features of, as well as the fundamental differences between, these two civilizations. Although his "dynastic race" idea has come into disfavor by Egyptologists, seen as a racist idea and robbing Egypt of its heritage, the evidence indicates that the idea is nearly irrefutable. Where it fails is that his dynastic race was not indigenous to Egypt. I argue that a dynastic race indeed existed, but that it was indigenous to the Nile Valley, and that the resurgence of civilization in this region in 3000 B.C.E. is directly attributable to their knowledge, skills, and leadership.

One of the biggest mysteries of prehistory has always been the sudden appearance of anatomically modern man, referred to as Cro-Magnon, in western Europe. We are his descendants in some way, scientists claim, although his disappearance, at the end of the ice age around 10,000 B.C.E., is as much a mystery as his origins. In this book we will investigate evidence that not only explains Cro-Magnon's origin and demise, but also links his existence to dynastic Egypt and the ancient culture of the Mediterranean.

The pages that follow examine the evidence put forth by some of today's best researchers and most astute minds, bringing together unrelated research and completing the jigsaw puzzle of our most ancient history. From the multifarious megaliths of Nabta Playa to Egypt's Great Sphinx, the perplexing internal structures of the Great Pyramid, the oral traditions of ancient Egypt, the cyclopean temples of the Mediterranean, and even the connections between ancient Egypt and the ancient Mayans of Mexico and Central America, I assert that there is finally cumulative proof from various fields that a culture existed that was as advanced in many areas of knowledge as we are today. This book is also a history of today's historians, who are painting a new picture of our ancient past.

RAINY DAYS FOR THE EGYPTIAN SPHINX

Old Evidence, New Observations

With its grand monuments and golden treasures, Egypt has long been the shining star of interest in the study of ancient civilizations. No other culture of antiquity has been studied to such an extent as the land of the Nile. And no other civilization has left so much to study. From Cairo to Memphis, to the biblical city of Ramses, to the structures on the Giza plateau, ancient engineers and architects planned and built cities of stone that rival our own modern accomplishments. Also to its credit are finer achievements, such as the birth of modern medicine under Imhotep—priest, physician, and chief architect of the third dynasty from 2687–2668 B.C.E. He diagnosed and treated tuberculosis, gallstones, appendicitis, gout, and arthritis, as well as more than two hundred other diseases.[1] He also performed surgery and practiced dentistry a hundred years or more before the great pyramids were constructed. For three thousand years, Egypt was the finest culture brought forth by mankind.

During the last century, through various disciplines, Egyptologists have painstakingly constructed the history of ancient Egypt. Although Napoleon's engineers, surveyors, astronomers, and artists conducted

4

a systematic examination of the Giza plateau in 1798, the first comprehensive work was carried out by Sir John Gardner Wilkinson (1797–1875), during the late 1820s and 1830s. Later came Sir William Matthew Flinders Petrie (1853–1942), who conducted meticulous excavations at Giza between 1880 and 1883 and was responsible for creating the modern methodology of archaeology. During the past one hundred years, Egyptian civilization has captured the public's interest, and as a result has become its own field of study, called Egyptology.

The Conventional View of Ancient Egyptian Civilization

Egyptologists have divided ancient Egyptian history into several key periods: the predynastic period (5500–3000 B.C.); the early dynastic period (3000–2650 B.C.); the Old Kingdom (2650–2152 B.C.E.); the Middle Kingdom (1986–1759 B.C.E.); the New Kingdom (1539–1069 B.C.E.), and the Late Period (664–332 B.C.E.), with three "Intermediate" periods, one each before the Middle, New, and Late kingdoms. (See Timeline of Egypt's Periods and Dynasties, page 6.)

About six miles west of Cairo, the Giza plateau, a part of the ancient Memphis necropolis, stand the oldest and most famous structures ever built by man, the three Great Pyramids. Also on the plateau there are eight smaller pyramids, four valley temples, three mortuary temples, three procession ways, several boat pits, and numerous *mastabas* (rectangular tombs). Here also stands the largest statue ever carved by man, the Great Sphinx, which will be a major focus of our discussion of Egypt's origins. It faces due east and is linked to the Great Pyramid by a causeway. The three large pyramids are believed to have been sacred monuments and tombs for the Old Kingdom's fourth-dynasty pharaohs: Khufu (reigned 2589–2566 B.C.E.), his son Khafre (2520–2494 B.C.E.), and Khafre's son Menkaure (2490–2472 B.C.E.). The Giza area remains a rich archaeological site, still being researched by various universities and researchers as well as independent Egyptologists and historical investigators.

Although flavored with a dash of mystery, as is all of prehistory, a consensus of scholars explains that the land of the Nile was united as a kingdom under Menes, considered the first king of the first dynasty, just before the third millennium B.C.E. However, in the Turin Kings list—a unique papyrus dating to the nineteenth dynasty (1295–1186 B.C.E.), written in the ancient Egyptian hieratic script, and discovered in Thebes in 1822 by the Italian explorer Bernardino Drovetti—Menes follows a

TIMELINE OF EGYPT'S PERIODS AND DYNASTIES

Predynastic Period	(5500–3100 B.C.)		**Second Intermediate Period**	
			15th Dynasty	(1674–1567 B.C.)
Early Dynastic Period			16th Dynasty	(1684–1567 B.C.)
1st Dynasty	(2920–2770 B.C.)		17th Dynasty	(1650–1539 B.C.)
2nd Dynasty	(2770–2650 B.C.)			
			New Kingdom	
Old Kingdom			18th Dynasty	(1539–1295 B.C.)
3rd Dynasty	(2650–2575 B.C.)		19th Dynasty	(1295–1186 B.C.)
4th Dynasty	(2575–2467 B.C.)		20th Dynasty	(1186–1069 B.C.)
5th Dynasty	(2465–2323 B.C.)			
6th Dynasty	(2323–2152 B.C.)		**Third Intermediate Period**	
			21st Dynasty	(1070–945 B.C.)
First Intermediate Period			22nd Dynasty	(945–712 B.C.)
7th Dynasty	(2152–2160 B.C.)		23rd Dynasty	(828–725 B.C.)
8th Dynasty	(2159–2130 B.C.)		24th Dynasty	(725–715 B.C.)
9th Dynasty	(2130–2080 B.C.)		25th Dynasty	(712–657 B.C.)
10th Dynasty	(2080–2040 B.C.)			
			Late Dynastic Period	
Middle Kingdom			26th Dynasty	(664–525 B.C.)
11th Dynasty	(1986–1937 B.C.)		27th Dynasty	(525–404 B.C.)
12th Dynasty	(1937–1759 B.C.)		28th Dynasty	(404–399 B.C.)
13th Dynasty	(1759–1633 B.C.)		29th Dynasty	(399–380 B.C.)
14th Dynasty	(1786–1603 B.C.)		30th Dynasty	(380–343 B.C.)
			31st Dynasty	(343–332 B.C.)

list of gods or demigods who ruled before him. The Palermo Stone, an inscribed block of basalt twenty-five centimeters high discovered by Sir Flinders Petrie in 1900, dated to approximately 3000 B.C.E., also contains the names of these kings and dynasties (the more familiar Greek names are in parentheses): Geb, Ausar (Osiris), Setekh (Seth), Hor (Horus), Djehuty (Thoth), Maa't, and again Hor (Horus). Without historical verification, these kings have been relegated to myth. Although conventional Egyptian history begins at 3000 B.C.E. with the uniting of people in the Nile Valley under Menes, important records exist indicating a substantial history prior to Menes.

At the close of the ice age around 10,000 B.C.E., global weather patterns shifted. As a result, the increasingly arid climate of North Africa gave birth to the Sahara Desert, which has been continually expanding.

According to modern Egyptology, primitive peoples, forced to move by the increasing dryness of West Africa, migrated east to the Nile Valley during the last quarter of the fourth millennium B.C.E. to begin Egyptian civilization. With them came their religious beliefs and their mythology. The growing population in the valley created a unique circumstance that enabled early Egyptians to band together for the common good and a common goal. A large labor supply and bountiful harvests led to overall prosperity, and the kings of early dynasties ordered the construction of public projects that included pyramids, temples, tombs, and a colossal statue of a lion with a king's head known as the Great Sphinx.

The Great Sphinx

The Great Sphinx is an enduring, enigmatic icon of ancient civilization. Its name is derived from the Greek word *sphingo* or *sphingein,* which means to strangle or to bind tight. Although no one knows what the earliest Egyptians called it, during the latter half of the second millennium B.C.E. it was referred to as Hor-em-akht (Horus in the Horizon), as Bw-How (Place of Horus), and also as Ra-horakhty (Ra of Two Horizons).

The feline form was revered in ancient Egypt, and the lion in particular has a long association with the king. According to excavation leader Dr. Alain Zivie, pharaonic inscriptions suggest lions were bred in special areas and buried in sacred cemeteries, but none had ever been found until he and his team found one in 2001. This mummified lion was discovered in the tomb of a woman believed to be King Tutankhamun's wet nurse, buried about 1430 B.C.E. Analysis of the wear on the lion's teeth indicates that it lived to be very old and was likely a captive animal.

A cult devoted to the Egyptian cat goddess Bastet was dominant in the area of the Nile Delta. Most likely evolving out of an even older lion cult, the cat cult dates back to approximately 3200 B.C.E. Bastet was first mentioned during the second dynasty. A fifth-dynasty temple inscription proclaims, "Bastet, lady of Ankh-taui," along with her earliest known depiction. Carving a gigantic cat with the head of a king would have been a likely expression of religion for the megabuilders of the fourth dynasty in 2500 B.C.E.

The Sphinx was excavated and carved from the limestone that permeates the Giza plateau. Two hundred forty-one feet long and sixty-five feet tall, this sculpted lion with a human face sits in a rectangular hollow. The area around the Sphinx was dug out, or quarried, in order to carve the lion's image. Only its head and the uppermost portions of its back are above the surface of the plateau; the hollow it sits in is referred to as the Sphinx ditch, enclosure, or quarry. The limestone rock removed from this area was used to build a temple directly east of the Sphinx, as well as another known as the Valley Temple. Most Egyptologists contend that this occurred during the Old Kingdom's fourth dynasty (2575–2467 B.C.E.). With no evidence to the contrary, current Egyptology accepts this as the most probable scenario.

The Challenge from John Anthony West

While living in London during the early 1970s, the American writer John Anthony West read a novel by Isha Schwaller entitled *Her-Bak*. Although West was unimpressed by the author's writing style, he was intrigued by her frequent references to the symbolist works of her late husband, the hermeticist and independent Egyptologist René Schwaller de Lubicz. The book's unique portrayal of ancient Egypt fascinated West, so for eight weeks he visited the British Museum to read Schwaller's work, a French dictionary at his side as it had yet to be translated into

Photo courtesy of Space.com

Fig. 1.1. Aerial view of the Sphinx complex

English. When he finished, he was thoroughly convinced that Schwaller had revealed an untold story of ancient Egypt, particularly its philosophy and the symbolic way it was expressed in its art and architecture.

Although the works of Schwaller focused on ancient Egyptian culture and architecture with a symbolic interpretation of Egyptian society, his assertion that the Sphinx was weathered by water roused West's curiosity. During the 1970s, West, still unaware of any English translations of Schwaller's works, concentrated his efforts on bringing a symbolist view of Egypt to the English-speaking world. In 1978, West published *Serpent in the Sky*, introducing Schwaller's view of ancient Egyptian wisdom—which held that symbolism captures absolute truths that can be accessed and understood only through indirect means. (See chapter 10 for a detailed explanation.)

West, now a self-proclaimed Egyptologist and independent researcher, teamed up with the geologist Dr. Robert M. Schoch, of Boston University, in 1990 to investigate the possibility that the Egyptian Sphinx was carved, at least in part, *before* 2500 B.C.E. West, as did Schwaller, believed the weathering of the Sphinx and its enclosure was caused by erosion from rainwater. This would have had to occur before the third millennium B.C.E.—before North Africa became a desert. Schoch, a scientist and skeptic, initially believed that he would be able to convince West of the error of his unconventional views concerning the Sphinx and its associated structures.[2]

> I found that West had a very extreme idea that the Sphinx was thousands of years older than the Egyptologists thought. I thought this was a long shot, but I thought that, maybe, West was onto something. I thought it was improbable, but it was worth looking at further. I am a curious type of person.[3]

Schoch and West visited Egypt in early 1991 to study the erosion on the Sphinx and the Giza plateau. A detailed survey of its features led Schoch to believe there was more to the story than established history was able to explain.

Observations at Giza: April 1991

At Giza, Schoch observed that the Sphinx and the Valley Temple had been constructed in two stages and had undergone repair, even during ancient times. He also ascertained that the Sphinx temple, and possibly the Valley

Temple, was constructed from limestone blocks quarried from the Sphinx enclosure, which provided the room for sculptors to carve its body. If true, this would mean that the temple structures must be as old as the Sphinx itself. Later, the ancient Egyptians faced these temples with ashlars, carved smooth stones made of Aswan granite. Schoch's observations of the facings and underlying limestone blocks led him to believe that the core blocks in both temples were exposed to the elements and underwent considerable weathering before the ashlars were applied.

Where the Valley Temple's walls have been stripped of their facings, an irregular surface is visible. This uneven surface, "higgledy-piggledy," as Schoch refers to it, is apparently a result of the ancient Egyptians cutting back and smoothing out the weathered walls before applying the granite facings.[4] It looks "higgledy-piggledy" because they did not take off enough of the weathered surface to make it perfectly smooth. In various places, the backside of the granite blocks was cut to fit the bumpy patterns of the wall. In this way, they matched the granite blocks to the shape of the irregular weathering patterns on the core limestone blocks they intended to reface. For Schoch, it was apparent that the weathering of the structures was already substantial even in ancient times.

Schoch observed that there were four distinct types of weathering exhibited in the geologic area in and around the Sphinx: rainwater, wind, flaking, and disintegration (also referred to as dissolution). Weathering from rainwater, Schoch concluded, is visible on the body of the Sphinx and on its enclosure walls. Where the water erosion occurred on the walls, there is a rolling and undulating profile to the rock. This water erosion is well developed and prominent within the enclosure. There are also vertical crevices where the flowing water followed joints and faults in the rock.[5]

Weathering from wind, distinctly different from rain-induced erosion, is also evident on the Giza structures and probably began, Schoch believes, during Old Kingdom times (2650–2152 B.C.E.). The faces carved on tombs and statues are still clearly visible; however, softer rock layers have been gouged out from wind and sand, resulting in a deeply eroded "wind-tunnel" characteristic. Various Old Kingdom tombs and structures south and west of the Sphinx, carved from the same layers of limestone as its body, are exemplary of wind erosion.

One way to envision wind erosion is to think of the limestone bedrock as a layer cake. Each alternating layer of cake and icing represents hard and soft layers of stone. When the cake is cut in half, its profile is exposed and the layers are clearly visible. If you run your finger along a cake layer, the cake doesn't give. However, running your finger along an icing layer, representing the soft stone, results in a horizontally "scooped-out" look. Such is the nature of wind erosion on hard and soft rock layers.

The third type of erosion that has affected the rock surfaces is known as flaking. The flaking apparent on the Sphinx and temple structures occurred relatively recently (within the last two hundred years) as a result of modern causes: acid rain and air pollution. A fourth type of weathering, dissolution, exists only in a few, cavernlike structures, such as tombs, because of the evaporation cycle that occurs in these enclosed spaces. The condensation and evaporation of water in the atmosphere covers the rock with a very fine coating of mineral crystals, giving the rock's surface in these areas the appearance of melted wax.

In some cases, the four different types of weathering may be difficult to distinguish, with some types overlain by another; but in general, the different forms of weathering are clear and distinct from one another. What Schoch perceives as precipitation-induced weathering is the oldest prevalent type of weathering on the Giza plateau. It is significant only on the oldest structures at Giza, such as the Sphinx body and its enclosure

Photo courtesy of John Anthony West

Fig. 1.2. Western wall of the Sphinx enclosure

walls. In many places, wind erosion is superimposed on water-worn rock. Presumably, he concludes, the major portion of this precipitation-induced weathering occurred prior to North Africa becoming a desert.

In support of this observation are the mud-brick mastabas on the Sakkara plateau, ten miles south of Giza. Unquestionably dated to the first and second dynasties (2920–2650 B.C.E.), these structures do not exhibit evidence of water erosion such as is seen in the Sphinx enclosure. Like these mastabas, Giza's Old Kingdom tombs (2650–2152 B.C.E.) show obvious signs of wind erosion but are devoid of signs suggesting water erosion. For these reasons, Schoch concluded that the severe water erosion, as seen on the Great Sphinx and its associated structures, predate Old Kingdom times and likely predate dynastic times altogether.

Beginning with the ancient Egyptians themselves and continuing to the present, the Sphinx has undergone a number of repair campaigns—during the Old Kingdom in 2500 B.C.E.; in New Kingdom times in 1400 B.C.E.; during the twenty-sixth dynasty, 664–525 B.C.E.; and also during the Greco-Roman era, between 300 B.C.E. and 400 C.E.[6] During these repairs, the ruler often excavated the Sphinx enclosure from the sands that would fill its surrounding hollow when left unattended for a few decades. After each excavation, repair blocks were often mortared to the weathered body in an attempt to restore the sculpture to its original outlines. According to Schoch, the earliest repair to its surface was performed using what appears to be an Old Kingdom–style masonry technique. If true, it would be another argument in favor of an earlier date for the Sphinx.

Seismic Surveys

The surface of limestone rock looks solid, but it is actually soft and porous, from a geologic perspective. Once rock is cut out, it begins to weather, and the degree or depth of weathering below the surface correlates precisely with how long that rock has been exposed to the elements.

In this process of weathering, which is deterioration, rock becomes softer. Some of its particles dissolve and it becomes a weaker rock. How deeply the weathering penetrates into the rock below its surface depends on the type of rock, but also—very important—how long it has been exposed to the elements. Seismic refraction, the charting of geologic features through the use of sound waves, enables geologists to map the boundary between weak, deteriorated rock and the underlying hard limestone. By locating how far down the rock is deteriorated, an estimate can be made as to how long ago the excavation ocurred. When rock is quarried, the remaining (unquarried) rock is exposed to the elements and starts to weather. Over time, the weathering sinks farther into the remaining rock. How deep the weathering is in the remaining rock provides an estimate as to how long ago the quarrying was performed.

With permission from the Egyptian Antiquities Organization, Schoch, with the assistance of the seismologist Dr. Thomas Dobecki, performed a seismic refraction survey to get a picture of the Sphinx enclosure's subsurface weathering. The results indicated that the weathering below the surface is not uniform, which strongly suggests, according to Schoch, that the enclosure was not quarried all at once. By estimating when the least weathered area was excavated, and thereby first exposed, he could estimate the minimum age of the Sphinx.

The survey indicated that in front and along the sides of the Sphinx, the weathering beneath the surface measures from six feet to eight feet in depth. However, along the back (west) side, the limestone had been weathered to a depth of only four feet—a finding that was completely unexpected. If the Sphinx was carved out all at once, it is reasonable to assume that the surrounding limestone would generally show the same depth of weathering.[7]

One interpretation of these unexpected results is that only the sides and front of the Sphinx initially were carved, so that it projected as an outcropping with its rear still part of the natural rock. Schoch believes a likely scenario is that its rear was initially carved only to the level of the upper terrace, which today remains immediately west of the Sphinx within the enclosure.

According to the Egyptian Egyptologist Selim Hassan, originally the Sphinx was to be viewed from the front only, so that its temple, which is in front of it, appeared to be a pedestal on which the Sphinx sat. An alternative theory is that the rear of the Sphinx was cut from the bedrock during the original carving, but only by a narrow passage that was later widened.

To determine accurately when the rear of the Sphinx was freed from the bedrock and establish a chronology of the possible widening of the passage at the enclosure's west wall, more work would have to be performed. But it is clear that the limestone floor behind the Sphinx's rear, which was seismically tested in April 1991, was exposed later, possibly during Khafre's time. In other words, once the front and sides of the

Sphinx were carved, the limestone floors adjacent to these three sides began to weather, but what would later be the limestone floor behind its rear was still protected by a thick layer of solid rock.

It also may be the case that Khafre repaired the Sphinx and its temples in 2500 B.C.E., and that at that time the back of the Sphinx was carved, thereby separating its body from the enclosure wall. Since the base of its rear had been weathered and repaired with limestone blocks during Khafre's reign, it is unlikely that the Sphinx's rear was carved anytime later. If the New Kingdom restorations during the eighteenth dynasty (1539–1295 B.C.E.) were responsible for freeing the Sphinx's rear, then it would not be possible to account for the four feet of sub-surface weathering, as the enclosure has been filled with sand for much of the time since. Schoch believes Khafre uncovered the limestone floor behind the Sphinx that was sampled in the 1991 seismic survey and that in 2500 B.C.E., the limestone floor on the western, back end began to weather.

Fig. 1.3. Frontal view of the Sphinx

Photo courtesy of Jon Bodsworth

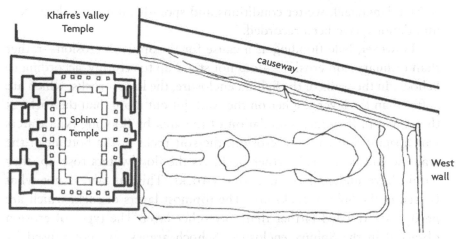

*Fig. 1.4. Layout of the Sphinx and its enclosure
(from an illustration by Colin Reader)*

Based in part on his analysis of the evidence that the weathering of the limestone floor surrounding the Sphinx is 50 to 100 percent deeper at the front and sides of the Sphinx than at the rear, Schoch provides one estimate of the date of the carving of the front and sides of the Sphinx and another for the rear. Simply stated, the floor in the back of the Sphinx was weathered to a depth of only four feet, while the front was weathered to a depth of eight feet; this suggests that the front of the Sphinx is twice as old as the back. Schoch estimates that the rear floor of the enclosure was first exposed in 2500 B.C.E., and that the exposure of the front and side floors of the enclosure (and the initial Sphinx carving) must have occurred between 7000 and 5000 B.C.E.[8]

According to Schoch, this is an estimate, and since weathering rates are not constant, the initial carving may be even older. If the Sphinx was heavily weathered by precipitation at an early period in its existence, Schoch argues that it may have been carved prior to the last great period of major precipitation in the Nile Valley, between ten thousand and five thousand years ago.

Floodwaters or Rain?

Egypt experienced a period of unpredictable flooding during this era of rainfall, often referred to as the Nabtian Pluvial. It has also been postulated that sporadic heavy rains along the Nile may have lasted as late as 2350 B.C.E. Even during historical times (when humanity had a written language), wetter conditions and sporadic, unusually high Nile inundations have been recorded.

However, Nile flooding as a cause for the Sphinx's erosion—rather than ordinary rain erosion—does not stand up to scrutiny, according to Schoch. In the walls of the Sphinx enclosure, the lowest rocks, which are softer than the layers higher on the wall, jut out more than the rocks at the very top. If sudden inundation of the area by flooding Nile waters was a significant cause of erosion, the soft rocks at the bottom of the walls would be eroded farther back. As the floodwaters rose up, they would have undercut the uppermost rocks. This, in fact, is not what is seen in the Sphinx enclosure. The topmost layers of rock, which are harder, are receded farther than any other layer. The types of erosion observed in the Sphinx enclosure, Schoch argues, are not caused by floodwaters. "It is clearly rain, precipitation, causing these erosional features," Schoch says. For him, the weathered profile of the enclosure walls is obvious evidence of rain erosion: "This is a classic, textbook example of what happens to a limestone wall when you have rains beating down on it for thousands of years."[9]

This type of weathering—rain erosion—is found in only one area of the Giza plateau: on the Sphinx and on the walls of its enclosure.

Schoch's Conclusion

On the basis of Egypt's climatic history, one could argue that the Sphinx was carved in very early dynastic times, 2920–2650 B.C.E., or in the predynastic period during the late fourth millennium and third millennium B.C.E. However, because of the seismic data and the severe weathering on the Sphinx itself, its enclosure, and its associated temples (which were refaced during the Old Kingdom, 2650 to 2152 B.C.E.), Schoch concluded that the Sphinx carving was likely performed several thousand years before its generally accepted date of 2500 B.C.E. As noted previously, based on the evidence he observed, Schoch estimates that the colossal sculpture was initially carved around 7000 to 5000 B.C.E., and perhaps even earlier.

Schoch recognizes that one of the difficulties many people have with his conclusions is historians' lack of a cultural and archaeological context that could account for the Sphinx's carving before the third millennium B.C.E. Today there is little to suggest that a culture capable of carving such a large statue and temple existed at that time. But it could also be the case that the known predynastic settlements are not representative of the more sophisticated culture responsible for the Sphinx's carving. It is possible that other cultural remains exist but have not been found; they could be buried deep under the Nile alluvium. Furthermore, a higher sea level since ten thousand years ago may have submerged vast expanses of land along the Mediterranean coast that were inhabited by early cultures.

Schoch argues that evidence of sophisticated cultures in other regions during this era, such as the eastern Mediterranean, *have* been discovered, implying that it is possible for such a culture to have existed. The prehistoric city-style settlements of Jericho and Çatalhöyük attest to the fact that organized cultures prior to 5000 B.C.E. were capable of sophisticated projects. The people of Çatalhöyük built with mud brick and timber, creating a domestic scene not all that different from today's home. Their homes included a kitchen and living and sleeping quarters, as well as a storage area. Artfully decorated religious shrines were also discovered, indicating that within their culture there existed complex symbolism and religious tradition.

Jericho's original builders date back to the ninth millennium B.C.E. Possibly used for flood protection, a large stone wall and tower with interior stairs were built to the west of the city. These structures are dated from 8000 B.C.E. In the center of the tower, the steps were built from huge stone slabs, similar to the construction techniques seen in towers in European medieval castles. Schoch suggests that the Sphinx complex would not have been an isolated phenomenon in the Neolithic world. Other megalithic structures were being built around the Mediterranean as early as ten thousand years ago.

The Reaction: Arguing for a Younger Sphinx

Before a formal presentation of West and Schoch's findings, news leaked out to the press of their work and preliminary conclusions. Egyptologists were infuriated. One called their work "an American hallucination. West is an amateur. There is no scientific basis for any of this," and suggested that they were "exploiting the monuments of Egypt for personal gains." Another well-respected Egyptologist referred to them as "ignorant and insensitive."[10]

In Chicago, on February 7, 1992, at the American Association for the Advancement of Science's annual meeting, Schoch and West presented their case to several hundred scientists, who included Egyptologists and geologists. Dr. Schoch's evidence and associated theory to explain the data was not well received by the Egyptology community. Afterward, Egyptologist Mark Lehner's reaction was one of disbelief. He was still waiting to see the hardcore data that the weathering of the Sphinx was, in fact, rainwater induced:

> I didn't see any evidence. I saw many slides and, yes, this drasti-
> cally undulating profile of what we call Member II of the Sphinx.
> But I didn't see any data that convinced me one way or another
> that [the Sphinx erosion] is, in fact, rain induced. Our reaction is,
> if it was built by a civilization or a culture that existed *that* much
> earlier, where is the other evidence of this culture? Where? Show
> me a potshard. Show me a tomb. Show me an inscription. Show me
> any other piece of sculpture. Show me any archaeological site that
> dates to this period.[11]

The author and historian Dr. Paul William Roberts was at the conference, representing one of Canada's leading investigative journals. In his opinion, John West was an academic's worst nightmare. Out of nowhere came this man with a theory. It was well thought out, coher-ently described, beautifully written, and well presented. Furthermore, it was full of irrefutable data. According to Roberts, "If they'd allowed John West to be on the podium, and not be kept off the podium because he does not have degrees behind his name, they would have had an even more devastating attack. And they would have been less able to defend. As it was, they were unable to respond to what Dr. Schoch said."[12] It was a difficult day for traditional Egyptologists. As a result of Schoch's presentation, 275 of the attending geologists offered to assist Schoch and West with their project.

Later that year, BC Video entered into an agreement with the West-Schoch team to produce a video. This led to the 1993 NBC documen-tary entitled *The Mystery of the Sphinx*, hosted by Charlton Heston, for which West was awarded an Emmy for "best research." Since then, the argument over the weathering evidence of the Sphinx has escalated into a battle over evidence interpretation.

Zahi Hawass, secretary general of the Supreme Council of Antiquities in Egypt and director of the Giza Pyramids Excavation, refuses to con-sider the idea. He asserts that any alternative explanation of the Sphinx's carving should be ignored and suggests that it is "not good to argue; then the theory can die."[13] The Egyptologist and author of *Riddles of the Sphinx* Paul Jordan explains this position: "If you are going to make the Sphinx much older, as some people—like Dr. Schoch—would like to do, well then, you have really done some violence to the whole view of Egyptian civilization as we have painstakingly built it up."[14]

The heart of the matter for these Egyptologists is that an older Sphinx questions the conventional wisdom concerning when and how civilization developed in the Nile Valley. If true, it forces Egyptologists to rethink their traditional story as to exactly who the dynastic Egyptians were and where they came from, culturally as well as geographically. It seems they would prefer not to do that.

In a critique of Schoch's research published in *Archeology Magazine*, Zahi Hawass and Mark Lehner reject Schoch's claims and direct their attack toward the television documentary *The Mystery of the Sphinx*. Yet Schoch contends that this popular documentary was never intended to take the place of the fifteen comprehensive academic articles he has published on the subject.[15] Hawass and Lehner's argument for a younger Sphinx asserts that its present condition is representative of past, non-rainwater-induced weathering. They state, "Ancient and modern weathering on the Sphinx are, for the most part, the same ball game."[16] They discuss the variations in limestone quality layered in the rock, and claim that the flaking of the stone is the cause for the erosion, past and present. Schoch's opinion is that this flaking is superficial weathering and is due to modern-day pollution, acid deposition, salt deposited by water tables from a nearby village, and the damming of the Nile.

In response to Hawass and Lehner's fevered rebuttal, Schoch writes that he is simply trying to explain the geologic data he has studied and observed:

> In presenting the hypothesis that initial carving of the Great Sphinx of Giza may predate its traditional attribution, it appears that I have stirred up much controversy within the Egyptological-archaeological community. I have no desire to be the proponent of a controversial hypothesis; I am simply advocating a tentative assumption that, in my opinion, best fits the evidence.[17]

Dr. Schoch's purpose was not to be dogmatic in his assertion that the Sphinx was carved thousands of years before the first Egyptian dynasty, but rather simply to present a testable hypothesis regarding the age of the Sphinx.

Salt as the Source of Erosion

During the early 1980s, while mapping the Sphinx geology, Dr. K. Lal Gauri observed that sand, which had been removed from the walls of the Sphinx enclosure, although dry at the surface, was soaked with water a few inches into the ground.[18] He also noticed that the bedrock, which was in contact with the sand, was also soaked with water. Two years later, Gauri, along with George Holdren and Willard Vaughan, suggested in a scientific paper that much of the Sphinx's deterioration was due to the salt content of the rock and how it reacts with air moisture. Since the water table lies many feet below the surface, they argued, the source of the water must be from the air.

Gauri found there are two major water-soluble salts in the limestone from which the Sphinx was carved: gypsum and halite. A less stable type of water-soluble salt, calcium sulfite, also exists, but he could not determine whether it occurs in the rock or exists in the water. Gypsum and halite were present in all the samples studied.

According to Gauri's theory, over the centuries the Sphinx's burial in desert sand resulted in the migration of salts from the depth of the bedrock toward its outer layers. During this long burial, the rock must have become wet to a considerable depth and, after being exposed to the sun, the drying process brought these salts to the surface. This chemical weathering, through the reaction of salt and water, results in a flaking away of the stone, called exfoliation. It is clearly visible and a continuing manner of erosion today.

This type of erosion occurs through the formation of dew at night on the surface of the rock, which dissolves salts in the surface layer of rock. This thin layer of salty water is then drawn into the rock's pores. After the sun rises, the temperature increases and evaporates the water, leaving behind the salt. As crystals form in these pores, they exert pressure that forces a thin layer of surface rock to flake away.

Gauri contends that the Sphinx and its enclosure have been and are subject to extremely rapid weathering, pointing out that since the beginning of the twentieth century, there has been significant deterioration. The limestone is so soft in some places because of salt exfoliation that you can crumble the stone with your fingertips. The flaking of the stone is so advanced that it produces giant potato chip–like flakes. Gauri maintains that the weathering and erosion of the Sphinx and its enclosure walls are the result of this type of chemical weathering, and that a redating of the Sphinx is unnecessary.

Gauri suggests that the deep fissures in the west and south walls of the Sphinx enclosure represent faults in the rock that originated when a shift of the whole plateau caused the rock strata to tilt, millions of years ago. They were widened into cavities or channels by the hydraulic circulation of the underground water. Later, they were exposed when the Sphinx enclosure was excavated. A related theory, proposed by Hawass and Lehner, is that subsurface water movements, during Eocene times, caused the fissures to open as the water table dropped.

Hawass and Lehner accept Gauri's conclusions and have argued, in various articles throughout the 1990s, for a Sphinx carving date in the mid–second millennium B.C.E. Their argument rests on the assertion that the Sphinx's present weathering and rate of erosion are indications of its past weathering. They believe that ancient and modern weathering on the Sphinx is, for the most part, the same.

Schoch's Rebuttal to Salt Exfoliation

Schoch does recognize that salt exfoliation is an important current weathering factor on the Giza plateau. But this alone, he contends, does not account for all of the weathering features seen on the Sphinx and its enclosure. More specifically, it does not account for the more intense erosion seen on the western end of the Sphinx enclosure. Schoch observes that other researchers have focused on the current weathering methods of the Sphinx, particularly the damage caused by mobilized salts; although these studies are of importance in attempting to halt current erosion, he says, these studies may be irrelevant when attempting to determine the origin of ancient weathering on the Sphinx. He argues that one cannot extrapolate present, modern weathering rates back into the distant past of the Giza plateau. Schoch believes that air pollution, acid rain, rising water tables because of encroaching settlement, and automobile exhaust may be affecting the structures on the Giza plateau in a detrimental manner, and that the processes of modern erosion are not the same as the ancient processes in every—and particularly this—case.

Schoch argues that salt exfoliation will have its maximum effect on the Sphinx under extremely arid conditions and when its structures are exposed to the elements. However, when buried under a layer of sand, the Sphinx and its enclosure are protected from this type of erosion. Furthermore, the flaking of the rock should affect all limestone surfaces on the Giza plateau. Yet no other surface shows the same type of weathering profile as seen in the Sphinx enclosure. Salt crystal growth is indeed damaging the Sphinx and other structures during the present day, but it does not explain the ancient weathering patterns observed on the Sphinx's body and in its enclosure. These specific types of erosion, Schoch maintains, are from rainwater and occur virtually nowhere else on the Giza plateau.

As for the fissures noted above, Schoch points out that the limestone rock at Giza is "crisscrossed" with fractures or joints that date back millions of years. Some of them may be due to geologic faulting, but not all have opened up as fissures everywhere on the Giza plateau. Schoch argues that vertical fissures, like those on the Sphinx enclosure wall, can be produced only by water, primarily precipitation, and do bear on the age of the Sphinx. Precipitation runoff follows the path of least resistance and works its way into weak joints and fractures. This type of erosion is visible on the western wall of the Sphinx enclosure and the western portion of the southern wall. Schoch asserts that fissures in these areas have been caused by substantial rainwater runoff. The eastern portion of the southern wall, where the fissures are much less extreme, and the eastern portion of the enclosure have not taken the brunt of the runoff. Schoch distinguishes naturally occurring joints from open fissures developed only through weathering processes, though his critics do not.[19]

Observations by David Coxill

In November 1997, David Coxill, a British urban planner and a fellow of the Geological Society of London, visited Egypt and the Giza plateau to better understand the heated controversy over the age of the Sphinx. Trained as a geologist, Coxill has published research papers on the Ostracoda of the southwest Atlantic and books relating to the mining history of Shropshire. His observations of the Giza plateau were published in an article entitled "Riddle of the Sphinx."[20]

As did geological researchers before him, Coxill observed that the limestone from which the Sphinx was carved was the ancient sediment from a warm, shallow, carbonate-rich sea during the Eocene epoch, fifty million years ago. The Sphinx monument and surrounding enclosure were carved from two layers, called members, of the formation of limestone deposits. The hardest limestone, known as Member III, forms the head of the Sphinx, while the remainder of the body and the surrounding area are composed of Member II, a softer and more porous type of limestone. Member I is a very hard layer that comprises the lower portion of the Sphinx.

The head of the Sphinx, which is composed of hard limestone (Member III), is almost devoid of erosion features. Markings that do exist on it are called, in geological terms, current bedding. *Current bedding* refers to sets of striated markings that indicate the prevailing direction and angle of rest of sedimentary deposition. In contrast, Member II represents thin beds of limestone, called laminars, which are highly jointed and deeply weathered. Both layers (Members II and III) from which the Sphinx was carved come from subhorizontal strata (layers of rock angled near but not exactly at 180 degrees).

Subvertical joints (joints near but not perfectly vertical) of Member II are characteristic of the surrounding enclosure and the Sphinx itself, although to a lesser extent, and are natural fissures in the rock. They were formed by the contraction of sediments when they were undergoing the process of becoming rock and are not tectonic faults related to earthquakes. Some joints are open at the top, and narrow, and gradually close farther down the vertical profile of the enclosure wall; these joints exist in the Sphinx's body also. Coxill observed that these weaknesses in the rock have been selectively, and thereby progressively, exploited by the erosional forces of nature—in other words, rainfall.

The layers of sedimentary limestone that compose the Sphinx's body are eroded with a relatively smooth, rolling appearance, with alternating areas that stand out and recede.

Generally, harder layers stand out and softer layers recede. A rounded "cove" appearance is prominent on the surrounding enclosure walls, where they have substantially receded. Paradoxically, just below the Sphinx's neck, both the harder and softer layers have receded more than similar areas in Member II near the base of the Sphinx body. According to Coxill, this indicates that the upper layers have been exposed longer.

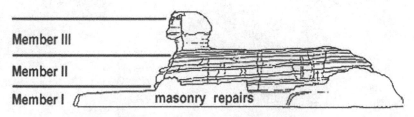

Fig. 1.5. Rock strata of the Sphinx
(from an illustration by Mark Lehner)

As for the agents responsible for these weathering features, Coxill believes it is important to make deductions based on the observable evidence, and not to assume that the present Sahara Desert is responsible. If sand and wind were responsible for the erosion, then sharp, angular contacts between the alternating layers would be expected. However, this is not observable. Instead, it is smooth and rolling. Joints open up at the top and narrow farther down the rock. The greatest erosion, if wind was the cause, would be expected at the base of the Sphinx body and surrounding enclosure. There, and just below the neck of the monument, the force of a sand-blasting wind would be most powerful. Because of protective stone blocks from ancient repairs, erosion at the base of the Sphinx's body is difficult to interpret. However, this is not the case for the surrounding enclosure. It shows more extensive erosion, not associated with wind, and is characteristic of water cascading over the sides of the monument and the surrounding enclosure. This same style of weathering is also visible in the limestone blocks that were used to build the Valley Temple. Yet they are absent from other monuments assigned to the Old Kingdom (2650–2152 B.C.E.). Coxill sees that this is where the controversy lies and asks: How can this be explained, and what are the implications for archaeology?

Photo courtesy of Jon Bodsworth

Fig. 1.6. Water eroson of the south wall of the Sphinx enclosure

If not regularly excavated, within decades the Sphinx enclosure fills with desert sand. Napoleon found the Sphinx in the same condition as did Thutmose IV between 1425 and 1417 B.C.E.: buried up to its neck. It was last cleared in 1925. To Coxill, this explains why the features from water erosion were not destroyed by the blowing wind and why the Sphinx has survived to the present day with significant repair to its base. For most of the Sphinx's history, a blanket of sand has covered these weathering features and, in essence, has been protecting them. If the Sphinx had been situated on higher ground, this would not have been the case.

Coxill also believes that the theory put forth by Boston University's Farouk El Baz—that the Sphinx was a *yardang* (an outcrop of rock, a ridge formed by wind erosion from a dried-up riverbed)—is unlikely. Only its head could have been a natural outcrop; the rest, Coxill maintains, had to be excavated. He refutes the yardang theory and suggests that the whole of the Sphinx is a natural rock outcrop, showing weathering profiles that existed prior to its carving. If it was originally a yardang, with weathering already present, then its carving would have, at least, removed the rolling, undulating profile now seen on the body.

As for salt exfoliation as the primary cause for erosion, Coxill believes this also is unlikely. Coxhill agrees with Schoch's observation that condensation affects all the monuments in the Giza complex, but very rarely do they show the same type of weathering features as do the Sphinx, its enclosure, and the stone blocks of the Valley Temple. Furthermore, these features require intense weathering to form their present profile. As does Schoch, Coxill believes that erosion from condensation and evaporation is simply too mild and insignificant in an arid climate to have produced these effects.

Coxill thinks that fluctuations in the water table below the Sphinx structures could not have led to fissures that are wider at the top (which, as noted above, Hawass and Lehner have argued). Coxill also disagrees with Gauri's suggestion that the smooth roundness of the weathered profile of the layers is due to gradational differences in the hardness of the strata; Coxill believes that gradational differences do not account for variations in the weathering profile within the Member II rock or the presence of open fissures.

He also disagrees with James Harrell's 1994 theory that Nile flooding and occasional rainfall produced wet sands, which led to the Sphinx's visible erosion. This theory is not acceptable, according to Coxill, as floodwaters would have produced a wave-cut "bench and notch" effect. This kind of erosion begins by the formation of a notch in the wall, which initiates the formation of a wave-cut platform that extends inward. This would certainly be seen today in the Sphinx enclosure if flooding was the cause, yet this is not evident. Furthermore, if Nile flooding had caused the Sphinx's erosion, this still would not satisfactorily explain the presence of erosion features higher up the Sphinx's body and enclosure walls.

Coxill believes that the region's *karst topography* (a limestone landscape in which cavities, sinkholes, and natural fissures are produced by percolating groundwaters and in which there is no surface runoff) could explain weathering in the lower areas of the Sphinx and its enclosure, but not the smoothness and rolling quality at the top.

Coxill's Conclusions

By a process of elimination, Coxill believes that only rainfall explains the weathering features visible on the Sphinx and its enclosure. Floodwaters, fluctuating groundwater, or salt exfoliation cannot explain the visible evidence. This, of course, raises the question as to when it last rained in Egypt with sufficient intensity and over a long enough period to produce the erosion we see today.

With the rapid retreat of glaciers at the end of the last ice age, a dramatic rise in sea level occurred between 13,000 and 9500 B.C.E. This was accompanied by torrential rain and, in Egypt, Nile floods. As the temperate zone worked its way north, a dry period followed between 9500 and 7000 B.C.E. From 7000 to 3000 B.C.E., a period of moderate rainfall prevailed. With this climate history and, taking into account Schoch and Dobecki's seismic survey, Coxill agrees with a seven thousand-year-old date for the Sphinx. He does caution, however, that dates should be as conservative as possible until conclusive evidence comes to light. Geologists are not sure at what rate rocks erode, so it is risky to assume it is constant.

One thing is certain, according to Coxill: the Sphinx is clearly older than the traditional date of 2500 B.C. He believes this date is given more by its association with Khafre's complex than by proof. He also believes the Sphinx's origins are more complex than has been previously considered. It is undeniable that the techniques and tools used by the Egyptians in Old Kingdom construction are a mystery.

THE WEIGHT OF GEOLOGIC EVIDENCE
Erosion and the Age of the Sphinx

Not all geologists agree with Schoch's conclusion that the Sphinx was originally carved between 7000 and 5000 B.C.E. The British geologist Colin Reader provides a date much more palatable to traditional Egyptologists. Reader, with an honors degree in geological engineering from London University, links civil engineering with geology, and has considerable experience in the study of the historical development of archaeological sites. He also has a deep interest in the Giza plateau. In August 1999, he wrote an unpublished paper, Khufu Knew the Sphinx: A Reconciliation of the Geological and Archaeological Evidence for the Age of the Sphinx and a Revised Sequence of Development for the Giza Necropolis. Two years later, he published "A Geomorphological Study of the Giza Necropolis, with Implications for the Development of the Site."[1]

Reader's first study, as the subtitle suggests, is intended to reconcile the highly criticized conclusions of Dr. Schoch. He reviews the geology, geomorphology, and surface hydrology of the Giza necropolis and puts forth a revised sequence of the Giza plateau development. In his study, he considers the development of ancient Egyptian stone masonry, reconciles the geological and archaeological evidence, and places the

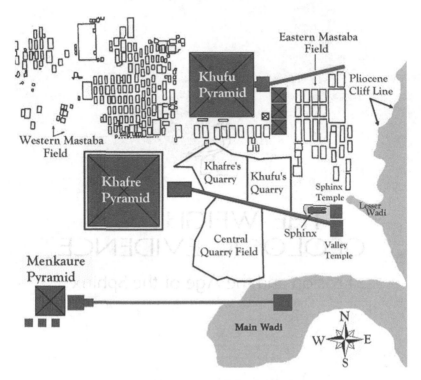

*Fig. 2.1. Structures of the Giza plateau
(from an illustration by Colin Reader)*

carving of the Sphinx within the context of the first or second dynasty (2920–2650 B.C.E.).

Some Egyptologists argue that the Sphinx was carved from a single block of limestone that remained after quarrying stone blocks for Khufu's pyramid (2609–2584 B.C.E.). Others believe that it was as an essential part of Khafre's mortuary complex, thought to have been built during the fourth dynasty (2575–2467 B.C.E.), and that the Sphinx site was dictated by the layout of adjacent buildings: the Sphinx Temple, the Valley Temple, and Khafre's causeway. Reader rejects both of these hypotheses. The notion that the Sphinx was carved from a single block of limestone assumes, as noted previously, that the ground level was above the head of the Sphinx but was reduced through extensive quarrying. Reader believes this major site modification conflicts with the archaeological evidence—the "quarry-block hypothesis" neglects the influence of natural geologic processes on the development of the Giza plateau.

According to Reader, the placement of the Sphinx was determined by the topography of the plateau. Evidence suggests that the plateau's landscape features were the result of natural geologic processes; for example, between seven and two million years ago, the advance of the Mediterranean Sea inundated the Giza area. Its progress was halted by a southeastern dip of Upper Mokattam (native Cairo) limestone, as well as a number of cliffs to the north and east. This resulted in the formation of the plateau.

Reader also believes there are other features indicating that the Sphinx's location was determined by site topography, and that the head of the Sphinx was carved from an elevated body of rock. South of Giza there was a *wadi* (a stream or channel of water) known as the "main

Fig. 2.2. Reader's Giza topography. (1) The Sphinx, (2) main wadi, (3) lesser wadi, (4) central quarry, (5) Khafre's quarry, (6) Khufu's quarry, (7) eastern mastaba field, (8) western mastaba field. Arrows indicate cliff line.

wadi." Between this wadi and the Sphinx, the original profile of the ground inclines to the north and west toward the Sphinx. North of the Sphinx there is a rock face where a number of tombs were cut out. The weathering of this rock, and its continuity with the cliff line (a defining feature of the eastern edge of the plateau), indicates the rock face is a naturally eroded feature. Reader refers to the rock face as the northern bank of a second and smaller wadi, known as the "lesser wadi." Where the western wall of the Sphinx enclosure meets a retaining wall (which supports a modern road), part of the southern bank of the lesser wadi may still exist. Here, the rock that defines the top of the western Sphinx exposure drops sharply beneath accumulated sand. The resulting depression is filled with modern masonry. Its profile is rounded, suggesting it is a natural feature rather than the result of quarrying.

As a whole, these landscape features indicate that the east end of Khafre's mortuary complex was determined by the local topography. Originally, the ground rose from the main wadi in the south to a high point near the Sphinx. Rock from which the Sphinx was to be carved was isolated from the northern extension of the plateau (where Khufu's pyramid was built) by erosion along the lesser wadi. The resulting portion of rock, separated from a main formation through erosion, is capped by hard strata (Member III) and is likely to have preserved the steep profile of the cliff line on its east side. As a consequence, the area where the Sphinx was carved may have been particularly prominent when viewed from the Nile Valley.

Debating Member II Erosion

Much of the debate concerning the age of the Sphinx focuses on the erosion of the Member II, or porous limestone, layer of rock, the most widely distributed layer of rock within the enclosure. Reader examined this layer and established that three principal features characterize the present deterioration of the Member II limestone in the Sphinx enclosure: subhorizontal (between thirty and forty degrees from horizontal) degradation, subvertical (between thirty and forty degrees from vertical) degradation, and rock that has receded at the top of the exposures.[2] Based on the division of these features, the exposed layers of rock can be divided into four areas: the Sphinx's body, the eastern end of the southern exposure, the western end of the southern exposure, and the western exposure.

On the body of the Sphinx, a large portion of the Member I and lower Member II layers of rock is obscured by masonry that was used to repair its profile. Several restorations were carried out, with the earliest thought to date from the Old Kingdom (2650–2152 B.C.E.) and the latest completed on May 25, 1998.

The exposed upper layer of the Sphinx is dominated by rounded subhorizontal weathering. Reader considers this to be the result of differential degradation of the exposed strata. Less durable areas recede from the original Sphinx profile. There are relatively few subvertical weathering features other than the "main fissure," which cuts through the body of the Sphinx slightly forward of the Sphinx's hindquarters. Those that do exist are generally poorly defined and limited in extent.

At the east end of the southern exposure, subhorizontal degradation of weaker layers is evident. These layers have receded somewhat from the original carved profile. However, the profile of the Sphinx's face is preserved almost in its original form, possibly as a result of re-carving.

Reader observed that the southern exposure shows subvertical erosion becoming progressively more frequent and extensive to the west. At the extreme west end, subvertical features are more deeply incised than those to the east and those on the Sphinx's face.

In the western exposure, subhorizontal erosion in less durable layers is more distinct than elsewhere. More durable layers have also been substantially eroded. The frequency of subvertical degradation along the western exposure is also greater and more pronounced than elsewhere, which has led to the development of a rounded lateral profile—the "coved" appearance Schoch describes in his analysis. In places, these features combine in a branching pattern indicating that even minor discontinuities in the exposed rock layer have been exploited by the weather. When compared with the reconstruction of the original cut profile, the uppermost units have receded considerably.

In summary, according to Reader, it is evident that much of the Sphinx's body and the east end of the southern exposure exhibit moderate deterioration that is characterized by subhorizontal deterioration and limited erosion of the enclosure walls. Comparing the same types of rock at different locations within the Sphinx enclosure, it is visible that the erosion of the enclosure walls in the west has been more intense. They are deeply incised with subhorizontal and subvertical erosion, even the most durable layers of rock. Reader considers this distribution of the intensity of erosion, with respect to the age of the Sphinx, particularly significant. It indicates that the water came from one direction determined by the terrain and slope of the plateau. According to Reader's analysis, the visible erosion is explainable by rainfall runoff, called sheet wash, that flowed across open ground during the first three dynasties (2920–2575 B.C.E.) as a result of brief but violent storms. Running water as such can be very damaging and helps to explain the more intense weathering on the weaker layers such as Member II. This allows assumption of a much later date for the carving of the Sphinx, possibly around 3000 B.C.E.

Rainfall Runoff

As mentioned previously, Egypt has not always been a desert. Although arid conditions have dominated since 2350 B.C.E., more humid periods are known to have existed. Temperate conditions between 7000 and 5000 B.C.E., to which Schoch attributes the weathering of the Sphinx, are separated from later, more arid conditions by a transitional phase. During this transition, seasonal rains occasionally interrupted increasingly arid conditions. At that time, the Giza plateau was sparsely covered with vegetation, so heavy rainfall would quickly saturate the ground and excess water would flow on the surface in the direction of the Nile Valley. In Colin Reader's opinion, the momentum from the running water was capable of inflicting substantial erosion. As an example, he cites the Valley Temple, which has been significantly eroded.

During severe storms, Reader asserts that rainfall runoff from the Giza plateau flowed toward the lower-lying areas in the east. Much of the water would have made its way to the Sphinx and spilled over the western wall, eroding the exposed limestone and selectively following any joints exposed along the face of the rock. A minimal amount of water would have flowed over the eastern wall. Although the east and west exposures of the Sphinx complex are the same age, weathering of the west wall is more pronounced. Reader argues that the west wall obviously took the brunt of the runoff.

According to Reader, when the erosive potential of rainfall runoff is considered in addition to groundwater movement, chemical weathering (rainfall and humidity), and salt exfoliation (flaking), a comprehensive interpretation of erosion within the Sphinx enclosure is possible. Rainfall runoff, Reader maintains, must be included with the other factors in order to explain the overall erosion in general as well as the intense erosion in the western part of the enclosure.

The Sphinx Temple

Most Egyptologists agree that the Sphinx and its temple were likely built at the same time, because the stone blocks used for the temple's construction were quarried from the Sphinx enclosure. The distribution of fossils in the stone that composes the temple is the same as that found in the Sphinx enclosure. This suggests that both the Sphinx and its temple predate Khufu's work on the site. In addition, the architectural style of the Sphinx temple, referred to as cyclopean, is different from Khufu's structures. Huge stones weighing between six and ten tons were used to create the structure. However, two other sources of evidence appear to conflict with dating the Sphinx prior to Khufu: the excavation of numerous pieces of fourth-dynasty (2575–2467 B.C.E.) pottery within the Sphinx enclosure and the discovery of fourth-dynasty pottery and hammerstones in the immediate area. Older artifacts have not been found.

Previous excavations within the Sphinx enclosure uncovered a limestone block resting upon debris containing numerous pieces of fourth-dynasty pottery. And immediately north of the Sphinx temple, evidence indicates that an area quarried in the Member I layer of rock occurred during the fourth dynasty. Mark Lehner and Zahi Hawass date this quarry work to the fourth dynasty based on recovered artifacts that include hammerstones and pottery.

However, there is also evidence that suggests this fourth-dynasty work was only an incomplete stage of construction and cannot be used to officially date the construction of either the Sphinx or its temple. The German Egyptologist Herbert Ricke identified a seam of rock that runs through the stone masonry in all four corners of the Sphinx temple, marking the outside of its walls in the first phase of construction. The north and south colonnades of the temple, he asserts, were added *later,* when the interior was repaired with granite sheathing. To construct this addition, parts of the north and south walls were pushed back and large limestone blocks added to the outside. Ricke argues that some abandoned blocks, apparently from this second phase of construction, are those under which the fourth-dynasty pottery was found. Although Ricke does not address the time period that separates fourth-dynasty work from the previous construction, it is evident that the two projects occurred during different climatic periods. The contrast of weathering on the stone indicates they were separated by a significant span of time.

More evidence comes from a fourth-dynasty quarry face from

durable Member I rock identified by Lehner. Since the time of the fourth dynasty (2575 B.C.E.), this rock face has been subject to the elements, yet it depicts only slight degradation. Interestingly, the same Member I layers exposed elsewhere in the Sphinx enclosure show more severe deterioration. According to Reader, this contrast in weathering at the western limit of the fourth-dynasty quarrying is striking. Rock exposures beyond the quarry are heavily weathered. Reader believes that, generally, the more intense weathering of the Member I rock in some areas can be explained only by dating the Sphinx's construction and the first phase of its temple to a time before Khufu's work on the Giza plateau (2589–2566 B.C.E.)—when the exposed limestone was subject to erosion by surface water runoff.

Reader concludes that Khafre's fourth-dynasty construction within the Sphinx complex was a second phase of construction. As noted above, modifications were made to the temple's north and south walls, together with some quarrying of Member I limestone to the immediate north. Since these alterations occurred after Khufu's quarrying, the newly exposed rock was not subject to erosion by rainfall runoff. Therefore, they do not show the same pattern of heavy weathering apparent elsewhere in the Sphinx enclosure.

Khafre's Causeway and Mortuary Temple

Khafre's causeway runs along a ridge of exposed bedrock with masonry pavement placed at its east end linking the low-lying Valley Temple to the mortuary temple and enclosed pyramid courtyard. It is believed to have been a processional route for the funeral cortege. On its northern shoulder, bedrock is exposed beneath the pavement, suggesting that the masonry is a single course of stone blocks and was likely used to provide a consistent gradient along the causeway. The eastern portion of the causeway runs along the Sphinx complex's southern exposure. Therefore, according to Reader, these two features have a common alignment, which rarely happens by chance. This increases the likelihood that these two structures were constructed at the same time: In other words, if the Sphinx predates Khufu's complex, and the causeway was built at the same time as the Sphinx, then the causeway must also predate Khufu. Further support is available from the geographic relationship between the causeway and the two quarries created during Khufu's reign.

Traditional Egyptologists' series of development calls for Khafre's causeway and the Sphinx (2589–2566 B.C.E.) being developed after Khufu's quarrying and construction. If this is correct, Khafre's quarrying would not have been limited to the extent of the causeway; thus Reader questions why Khafre's workers would stop, move a number of yards south, and start a new quarry. It makes little sense. According to Reader this would have served no apparent purpose. He is convinced that the causeway and the Sphinx were constructed at the same time.

The Great Sphinx, the temples to the east, and the pyramids to the west are connected by Khafre's causeway. Khafre's temple consists of two distinct elements, characterized by different architectural styles. The remains of the temple closer to Khafre's pyramid consist of square blocks of masonry, moderately sized. In contrast, the east end of the temple consists of large cyclopean-style masonry. Furthermore, the temple is constructed on an elevated site, with the ground sloping sharply to the east and moderately to the west. In the area of cyclopean architecture, there is little open space within the structure's interior. In many areas, the cyclopean-style masonry is heavily weathered, with much of the deterioration running across the exposed faces of adjoining blocks. According to Reader, the likely scenario is that the deterioration occurred after the masonry was put into place.

In light of the area's topography, Reader observed that the eastern area of Khafre's temple, what he refers to as the "proto-mortuary temple," benefits from a more prominent position than even Khafre's pyramid. This dominant position on the western horizon, as well as its distinct primitive architecture and association with the causeway, suggests that this portion of Khafre's temple may also predate Khufu's structures.

Ten miles south of Giza is Sakkara, which was part of the Old Kingdom's capital during the first dynasty and the second dynasty (2920–2650 B.C.E.). At Sakkara there exists a plateau where the earliest Egyptian step pyramid was built as well as numerous mastabas and other structures. The earliest part of the complex was built at the edge of the escarpment overlooking the Nile Valley. Topography, it seems, was one of the primary factors in laying out Sakkara, as well as the pre-Khufu structures at Giza. Reader suggests that Khafre's causeway may have been aligned the way it was simply to connect the prominent sites of the Sphinx and the proto-mortuary temple.

In conclusion, Reader believes that a number of structures on the Giza plateau predate Khufu's development: the proto-mortuary temple, the causeway, the Sphinx, and the Sphinx's temple. With the intense weathering on the western side of the Sphinx enclosure, and the rate at which erosion occurs, it is also his opinion that they predate the fourth dynasty.

The Giza Sun Cult

For any pre-fourth-dynasty buildings to have been preserved during Khufu's extensive construction on Giza, those structures must have had some type of significance, religious or otherwise. Possibly, they were an important part of a temple or cult. The evidence so far suggests only a general date for the construction of these pre-Khufu structures. A better resolution may be found in the use of stone in ancient Egyptian architecture.

The culture that developed prior to the fourth dynasty must have already had experience in stone masonry. The earliest known use of stone construction in ancient Egypt is from predynastic times—the Coptos statues, for example, found in the early 1900s at the town of Coptos, twenty-seven miles north of modern Luxor. Later, in the construction of tombs, stone blocks were first used at Helwan, fifteen miles south of Cairo, during the first and second dynasties (2920–2650 B.C.E.). According to the Palermo Stone, the last pharaoh of the second dynasty, Khasekhemwy, used stone in construction, consistent with the earliest known stone masonry in Egypt.

Between the first and third dynasties, artifacts recovered from the southern region of Giza provide evidence of the area's importance. In *Archaic Egypt,* Emery refers to the discovery of a large but ruined royal monument at Giza. He believed it to be the tomb of Uadji, a consort of a first-dynasty king. Other evidence that associates early dynasties with Giza include inscriptions on a flint bowl bearing the name of the first king of the second dynasty, Hotepsekhemui; and jar seals that bear the name of a later second-dynasty king, Neteren. Furthermore, Covington's Tomb, a large paneled brick mastaba excavated by Dow Covington on a high point in the ridge southeast of the Third Pyramid, probably of the second-dynasty reign of Khasekhemwy (2734–2707 B.C.E.), provides evidence of Giza's continued use into the third dynasty.

In Egyptian mythology, the lion is regarded as the guardian of sacred places. How or when this conception arose is unknown, but it likely dates to the remote past. The Heliopolis priests incorporated the lion into their sun worship. It was possibly revered as the guardian of the gates to the underworld on the eastern and western horizons.

Colin Reader uses the known history of stone masonry to establish a development sequence for the Giza necropolis. In predynastic Egypt, the site where the Sphinx was eventually carved may have achieved local importance, possibly as a gathering place for worship. Reader puts forth a theory that an outcrop of rock, from which the Sphinx was carved, resembled a lion's head and was linked to sun worship. This justified the construction of its own cult temple. It would have been built from reeds or mud brick directly in front of the outcrop of rock. Dedicated to the setting sun, a second temple would have been built so it occupied a prominent position on a small hill when viewed from the Nile Valley.

However, the idea of a lone lion's head with no body does not fit well into Egyptian iconography. Reader believes that as the stone masonry techniques developed during the later part of the early dynasties, the Egyptians decided to "liberate" the body of the lion from the rock. This led to the carving of the Sphinx, possibly with the head of a lion, and the construction of stone temples to the rising and setting sun: the Sphinx and the proto-mortuary temples.

Reader sees the presence of these two temples as a reflection of a principal belief of ancient Egypt: duality with respect to the sun god. The god manifested itself in the nature of the rising and setting of the sun. According to Herbert Ricke and Siegfried Schott, this duality was incorporated into the architecture of the Sphinx, its temple, and the proto-mortuary temple as a solar-cult complex. They interpreted the Sphinx and the two temples as the result of two separate cults, one on the east and the other from the west. The temples were used for rituals dedicated to the rising and setting sun. In the proto-mortuary temple (known as Khafre's temple), a long and narrow chamber runs deep into the core of the building. Ricke believes it was built for the two barques (boats) of the sun god, south for the day and north for the night. Perhaps as a processional route, the alignment between the Sphinx and the proto-mortuary temple was established as a link for the elevated sites along the southern end of the Sphinx enclosure.

When Khufu selected a site for his complex, Reader argues, he chose Giza since the site was already established by the solar cult. His choice explains the Egyptian name for Giza, which means "the pyramid that is the place of sunrise and sunset." When Djedfre, Khufu's eldest son, succeeded Khufu, the name of the sun god Ra was integrated into the royal cartouche. By the reign of Khafre, Khufu's younger son, the idea that the pharaoh was the earthly expression of the sun god developed further. Then Khafre incorporated the existing solar-cult complex into his own, perhaps to strengthen his association with the sun cult. To accomplish this, he built the Valley Temple, modified the Sphinx temple, constructed a covered processional along the existing causeway, and integrated the proto-mortuary temple into his own temple. Reader also believes that Khafre may have been responsible for the earliest repairs to the Sphinx's body and for recarving the Sphinx's head into that of a human form, but not to produce a likeness of Khafre.

Reader's Conclusion

Reader concludes that the excavation of the Sphinx enclosure, the Sphinx's carving, and the construction of the Sphinx temple occurred before Khafre's fourth-dynasty projects. It is his opinion that water erosion on the Giza plateau, as well as its structures, demonstrates that this is the case. The geographic relationships among Khafre's causeway, the Sphinx, and Khufu's quarries provide additional evidence.

As for the "wet-sand theory" put forth by James Harrell to explain the erosion of the Sphinx, Reader believes it does not stand up to scrutiny and is largely untenable. And although K. Lal Gauri's observation that salt exfoliation is a significant erosional feature is accurate, it does not account for all visible erosion within the Sphinx enclosure.

Reader is in agreement with Schoch that water was a prominent force of weathering, but disagrees with Schoch's assessment that the Sphinx was constructed seven thousand to nine thousand years ago. Reader believes it was built within a few hundred years of dynastic times, around 3000 B.C.E. He believes the relative weakness of the Upper Mokattam limestone, from which the Sphinx was carved, along with the prevailing climatic conditions, makes it conceivable that intense weathering could have developed within a shorter period of time.

Although arid conditions were predominant during the early dynasties, conditions were generally not as dry as today's. With less arid conditions, chemical weathering likely resulted in the leaching of soluble salts from the exposed rock. As this soluble component was removed from the rocks, the potential for further chemical weathering was reduced, according to Reader.

The exposed rock that was not subjected to rainfall runoff weathered as a result of leaching, the process by which soluble materials in the soil or rock (salts, nutrients, other chemicals or contaminants) are washed into a lower layer or are dissolved and carried away by water. However, in the western area of the Sphinx enclosure, heavy seasonal rainfall runoff removed much of the weathered limestone, exposing comparatively unweathered rock. Given the soluble component of newly exposed rocks, which is significant, this type of erosion likely promoted a renewed phase of chemical weathering and leaching, which accelerated the deterioration process. Reader believes that these particularly aggressive and repetitive weathering conditions in the western area of the enclosure could have developed over a relatively short time period, in geologic terms.

He argues that the Giza plateau was developed in association with the development of sun worship in ancient Egypt, based upon the erosion's intensity in the western area of the Sphinx enclosure as well as the known use of stone in ancient Egyptian architecture. Accordingly, Reader tentatively places the quarrying of the Sphinx enclosure, the construction of its associated temples, and its carving around 3000 B.C.

Although the origins of the Sphinx as a cultural icon are unclear, based on the sequence of development, Reader proposes that the concept of the man-headed lion was an evolutionary one that began during the Early Dynastic Period. The lion was associated with solar worship, and, by the fourth dynasty, the pharaoh became associated with the sun god. This is the reason for recarving the Sphinx's head into that of the divine king. This recarving may have occurred during Khafre's reign.

Reader looks to the Egyptologist and author Jaromir Malek for a degree of support for his sequence of Giza development. In Malek's book *In the Shadow of the Pyramids,* he writes that the official dogma concerning the king's relationship with the gods was redefined during the fourth dynasty. The pharaoh was made part of the new religious system with the creator and sun god Re. The rise in popularity of the sun god led to its recognition as the primary god of the Old Kingdom (2650–2152 B.C.E.) and is reflected in royal names and titles. Malek observes that Khafre's inclusion of the Sphinx, its temple, and the use of the hieroglyphic symbols for "to rise" and "Re" in his royal name support Reader's assertion that Khafre achieved a redefinition of the king's relationship with the gods.

The Weight of Geologic Evidence

Based on an analysis of weathering throughout the Giza plateau, as well as information gathered though a seismic survey of the Sphinx's enclosure floor, Robert Schoch set forth a theory explaining that the Sphinx was carved between 7000 and 5000 B.C.E. According to his theory, rainwater beating down over the Sphinx and its enclosure walls left unambiguous signs of water erosion. In the late 1990s, Colin Reader conducted his own geologic investigation of the Sphinx and the Giza plateau. Although he does not dispute that rainfall was a factor in its erosion, Reader argues that the primary source was rainfall runoff cascading over the edge of the Sphinx enclosure. Furthermore, he argues that sufficient rainstorms existed during the early part of the second millennium B.C.E. to justify a carving date for the Sphinx between 3000 and 2500 B.C.E.

However unpopular and contrary to traditional Egyptologists' opinions, Schoch and Reader's conclusions about the weathering of the Sphinx have never been proved incorrect. Although they disagree on the particulars and the rate of erosion, Schoch and Reader agree on the cause.

Wind and chemical weathering do exist within the Sphinx complex. But without erosion from rainwater, any explanation falls short of the visible evidence. Since the Sphinx was carved from stone, the weight of geologic evidence should not be ignored. Obviously, the Sphinx would have to have existed when rain or rainfall runoff could deteriorate its surface. With this conclusion in mind, the question, then, is when was there sufficient rain to inflict the erosion visible on the Sphinx and its enclosure? A geologic history of the region provides a climatic context.

THE GREEN SAHARA
A Climatic Context for the Sphinx

Today, Egypt's Western Desert lies within the extremely arid region of the eastern Sahara. It currently receives less than one centimeter of rainfall per decade, leaving it barren and uninhabitable. However, there is widespread evidence indicating that the Sahara's climate has fluctuated greatly since the end of the ice age, especially in Mali and Niger. Long ago in those countries, standing water formed lakes that existed over a considerable period of time. Analysis of these ancient lake sediments shows that, at one time, high beach levels existed near Lake Chad, indicative of a wetter climate. According to climate researchers, this "wet" Saharan environment occurred between 8000 and 6000 B.C.E., and affected all of North and East Africa.

The increase in wetter weather created new grasslands that lasted until 2500 B.C. As a result, migrating herders from adjacent lands to the northeast brought their domesticated sheep to Africa. Sheep bones have been found in numerous places, and, according to archaeologists, their presence in the archaeological record coincides with the beginning of a grassland ecosystem. Archaeologists have also discovered cultural remains indicating that people lived near the ancient lakes and rivers of Mali, Niger, and Chad. Bone tools, particularly harpoons, have been found across a wide area stretching from the Nile Valley to the central

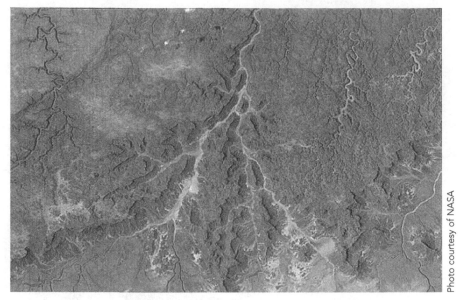

Photo courtesy of NASA

*Fig. 3.1. Evidence of an ancient river system in Algeria
as seen from orbit*

Sahara in Niger, Mali, and Chad. Artifacts have also been found around Lake Turkana in northern Kenya. Most archaeologists conclude that between 6000 and 4000 B.C.E. pastoral people increasingly occupied the entire region, such as the Tin–Torha in Libya, the Meniet in the Hoggar Mountains of Algeria, and the Adrar Bous in the Tenere Desert in Niger. According to the radiocarbon dating of artifacts, the pastoral cultures migrated from the northeast to the southwest.[1]

The archaeologist Fred Wendorf calculated that there were three major eras of rain in the eastern Sahara prior to 2500 B.C.E. According to Wendorf, evidence of these rainy eras is seen in the massive silt deposits that remain from seasonal playas, or temporary lakes, from which over one hundred radiocarbon dates have been obtained. These three episodes of high precipitation were separated by periods of extreme aridity from 5300 to 5100 B.C.E. and 4700 to 4500 B.C.E., with the water table falling to the same (or lower) level at which it is today. During these intervening arid periods, playa silts were extensively eroded and, in some cases, sand dunes filled in the hollows of the drained lake basins. The megalithic structures and sandstone circles at Nabta Playa, in southern Egypt, discussed in depth in the next chapter, were placed in sediments that had accumulated between 5000 and 4700 B.C.E.[2]

Prehistoric settlements, such as Nabta, reveal repeated occupation over several thousand years, especially during the summer rains, when water was plentiful for large groups of people and their animals. From charcoal and ostrich eggshells, radiocarbon dates tell of larger communities existing between 6100 and 6000 B.C.E. One excavated village contained more than eighteen houses, arranged in straight lines, with deep, walk-in wells—a task obviously requiring significant labor. One well Wendorf excavated was twelve feet wide and nine feet deep, large enough to enable life in the desert throughout the year. He believes the construction of these wells is possibly the first sign of an emerging social structure that later designed and built the Nabta megalithic complex around 5000 B.C.E.[3]

However, the rains did not last. A southerly shift of the monsoon around 2800 B.C.E. once again rendered the Nabta area extremely arid

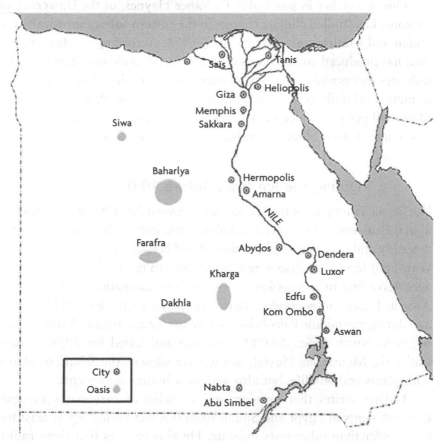

Fig. 3.2. Map of Egypt's cities and oases

and uninhabitable. At this time, an exodus from the Nubian Desert (the eastern region of the Sahara Desert in northeast Africa, between the Nile and the Red Sea) south to Upper Egypt may have stimulated social differentiation and cultural complexity in this area, and movement toward the Nile Valley where a source of fresh water was available.[4]

Climatically, what happened between 10,000 and 2500 B.C.E. in the Sahara Desert is an important factor in supporting (or not) an early date for the carving of the Sphinx. Although it is impossible to know exactly what happened during prehistoric times, a number of researchers have been studying this epoch for the last thirty years and have composed a plausible scenario of its changing climate. There is a vast amount of data available from western Egypt and northern Sudan, including more than five hundred published radiocarbon dates and various geological archives.

One researcher in particular, C. Vance Haynes, of the University of Arizona, has studied climate change in the eastern Sahara (northwestern Sudan and southwestern Egypt) since 1973. According to Haynes, this area has produced consistent evidence of climatic change. The evidence indicates distinctive changes from extreme aridity (less than half an inch of annual rainfall) to semiarid conditions (with more than eleven inches of rainfall per year).[5] A climatic history of the region reveals the Sahara has bounced from blossoms to barrenness and back several times.

During the Ice Age: Before 10,000 B.C.E.

During the latter part of the last ice age, between 20,000 and 10,000 years ago, the eastern Sahara was uninhabited and extremely arid. Although a few early and middle Paleolithic sites (dated between 100,000 and 40,000 years ago) have been discovered, none dates to the final stages of the ice age. According to archaeologists, the earliest occupation in the Darb El Arba'in Desert, in southwest Egypt, occurred more than 70,000 years ago during the middle Paleolithic, before the ice age began. A wet climate began in North Africa 50,000 years ago and lasted for 20,000 years. Called the Mousterian Pluvial, this wet era allowed the Sahara to bloom with plants and wildlife, but also with new human settlements.

Haynes writes that uranium-series testing of carbonates suggests that sediments in Egypt and Sudan from this wet period are at least ten times older than other tests indicate. He also believes that these radiocarbon ages that have been taken over the last twenty-five years should be used as minimum values, since the possibility exists that they were chemically altered through numerous later periods of rain. According to Haynes, if a significant wet period existed in the eastern Sahara during that time twenty thousand to ten thousand years ago, it should contain archaeological evidence of a human presence, since people naturally migrate to fertile lands. However, no such evidence exists.[6]

During the final years of the ice age, intense winds blew across an extremely arid Sahara. Sand dunes stretched from central to northern Sudan. According to optical dates, from seventeen thousand to eleven thousand years ago the howling wind deposited sand in the region of the Selima Sand Sheet. Dunes also formed at Nabta Playa, the Great Sand Sea, and Wadi Bakht in the Gilf Kebir.[7] As a result, the environment changed drastically. River systems were eradicated and the wind scoured out hollows across the land. However, at the end of the ice age, archaeological and geological evidence suggests wetter conditions began to prevail.

Summer Rains: 8000 to 5000 B.C.E.

As the climate grew more humid around 8000 B.C.E., rainfall turned low-lying areas into lakes and playas. With the onset of this "Neolithic pluvial," the region we now know as Egypt became an extension of the Sahelian savanna. The area offered pastoralists and animals new habitable lands. According to Haynes, during that time, the area received a minimum of eleven inches of rainfall annually and possibly as much as twenty-four. Between 7000 and 4000 B.C.E., when the leading edge of monsoon rains covered a significant portion of Africa's interior, a "pluvial maximum"—when rainfall was at its peak—developed, turning the desert green with life.[8]

Some records indicate that the onset of rains began at Bîr Kiseiba around 10,000 B.C.E., but in many other areas, including Abu Ballas in south-central Egypt, they came a thousand years later. Nonetheless, by 7500 B.C.E., rising water tables were able to support lakes in the Sudan. Archaeologists have discovered sediments from these ancient lakes that include sand, mud, freshwater carbonates, sulfate layers, salts, and plant fossils. Pollen analysis indicates that a sparsely wooded steppe developed in the Selima Oasis area with *Acacia*, *Commiphora*, and *Maerua* trees throughout the land. Also growing were perennials such as *Tribulus*, *Blepharis*, and members of the Chenopodiaceae–Amaranthaceae families.

Today these flowering plants are found at Ennedi, Darfur, and other places where sufficient moisture allows them to flourish. The Nile-fed lake of Bîrket Qarun also rose during this period, and in southern Egypt basins filled with rainwater. In other areas where rainfall was heavier, lakes and swamps existed. Radiocarbon-dated charcoal from prehistoric campfires attests to the increasing humidity and cooling temperatures.

Evidence from the Gilf Kebir region reflects a semiarid to arid climate that was dominated by hare, gazelle, and rodents. Remains discovered at Dahkla include hartebeest, gazelle, horse, hippopotamus, bovids, elephant, ostrich, and fish. Rhinoceros bones have been found at Merga, and elephant, antelope, wild cats, and giraffe at Abu Ballas. Since giraffes eat the leaves, buds, and twigs of acacia trees and other plants, it can be assumed that across the region sufficient trees were available to support their diet.

By 7300 B.C.E., the Wadi Howar was active in northern Sudan and flowed into the Nile River. Near Gebel Rahib, conditions sustained cool, freshwater lakes with a depth of twelve to thirty feet. Nabta Playa, as well as Umm Dabadib along the Libyan plateau, also experienced a wet climate before 7400 B.C.E. Mud accumulated along the Wadi Tushka and at other locations in the Great Sand Sea south of Siwa. By 7100 B.C.E., springs and artesian lakes existed in Khârga and Dahkla.

Playas

A playa is a shallow, short-lived lake that forms where water drains into a basin with no outlet to the sea but later evaporates, leaving a flat plain formed from mud. Playas are common features in desert regions and are among the flattest landforms in the world. The formation of these temporary lakes at Nabta and Kiseiba was periodic, with alternating intervals of aridity. The distribution of silt and clay sediments from playas depict scattered heavy rainfalls and ensuing flash floods. Three distinctive cultures recognized within the seventh millennium B.C.E. lend credence to these alternating climates. Animal remains (including large bovids and possibly domesticated cattle) indicate pastoralism may have been practiced locally. Other playas near the Bîr Kiseiba Oasis were occupied between 8000 and 6200 B.C.E.

Radiocarbon dates in the Kiseiba region indicate a dry period between 6200 and 6100 B.C.E., while an extremely arid interval in the Nabta region occurred around 6500 B.C.E. According to archaeolo-

gists, prehistoric artifacts were stirred up during that time by contract-
ing and expanding clays within the playa sediments. Clay-covered
storage pits discovered at Nabta suggest the area became wet again
after 6100 B.C.E. However, by 5900 B.C.E., another arid period set in,
and it lasted for two hundred years before the next wet phase began.[9]

Sedimentary deposits provide evidence of a climate with considerable rainfall, up to twelve inches annually. Some playa basins have
retained the remnants of shorelines; others are covered with rounded
beach gravel. Unlike the active playas of North America, which have a
smooth floor of hardened and cracked mud, those in the Arba'in have
been eroded in various degrees by the wind. Some contain yardangs
(outcrops of rock) standing several meters above the playa floor. Others
have been so severely eroded that no yardangs remain, and a few have
been scoured to the bedrock.[10]

Playa sediments were created from the erosion of bedrock by sheet-
wash (water flowing across the land). Typically, these sediments are
composed of sandstone, shale, and windblown sand. Where exposed
through excavation, sandstone *facies* (stratified rock distinguished from
the surrounding rock by its appearance) are distinct from rounded
beach gravel. In deeper parts of the basin, they grade into muddy sand
and clay. Flakes and curls of mud indicate brief intervals of extreme
aridity during this rainy period. Few fossils remain, but what does exist
consists mainly of poorly preserved bones of game animals, domestic
cattle, sheep, or goats, and a few snail shells.[11]

Playas in the northern Egyptian oases were active until 5000 B.C.E.
In the Siwa Oasis, the Hatiet Um El-Hiyus Playa was active through
5900 B.C.E. but began to dry out from its high point during the sixth
millennium B.C.E. The evidence from these playas indicates that between
8000 and 5000 B.C.E. the climate conditions alternated between arid
and wet. Although wet periods lasted for several hundred years, making
the region habitable, the overall climate was mostly dry.

Lakes

Swamplike conditions existed between 6400 and 5000 B.C.E. in northern
Sudan, with shallow lakes peppering the dunes west of the Nile Valley.
Waterways, near Naga Hamra, Gebel Nageru, and Wadi Howar, supported a diversity of animals that included crocodile, hippopotamus, land
tortoise, domesticated cattle, elephant, rhinoceros, warthog, giraffe, and
several varieties of fish. Aquatic animal fossils, such as hippopotamus,

crocodile, and fish, indicate that waterways existed, and that some were connected to the Nile.

Lake sediments in northern Sudan have enabled geologists to reconstruct a detailed picture of the environment. Pollen records from core samples in the Selima Oasis, the Oyo Depression, and El-'Atrun indicate that a steep foliage incline existed in the eastern Sahara between 6500 and 5000 B.C.E.[12] A zone of plant life stretched across a five-hundred-kilometer-wide belt in northwest Sudan, from wooded savannas near El-'Atrun to sparse steppes at Selima. Farther south, pollen from shallow, rain-fed lakes tells of the existence of tall acacia grass, which requires fifteen to twenty inches of annual rainfall. Also during this time, the Oyo Depression supported a deep freshwater lake surrounded by savanna-style plant life.

To the south of Egypt, in northwestern Sudan near an extinct tributary of the Nile, lake deposits consist of thin, alternating layers of chemical precipitates and rich organic mud. These deposits provide detailed information concerning the region's prehistoric climate. They contain pollen, diatoms (unicellular algae), invertebrate remains, and useful stable (nonradioactive) isotopes* indicating that conditions ranged from tropical savanna woodlands to grasslands.[13]

An interesting feature about this region is that, according to Haynes, archaeological sites are located on the bedrock or earlier Pleistocene beds. As a result, there is no stratigraphic connection to the deposits that occurred between 10,000 and 3000 B.C.E. What this means is that there is no way to construct a chronology of human occupation, since the bedrock has been there for millions, perhaps billions, of years. Cultural deposits found on dunes were lowered to the bedrock or earlier Pleistocene beds through erosion during extremely arid times that were laced between the wet periods. This erosion left low domes of sand littered with artifacts and hearthstones. Although radiocarbon dates of hearths and ostrich eggshells provide the time periods of occupation, they do not date the lake beds themselves.

In dating the Egyptian and Sudanese lake beds, Haynes relied upon the radiocarbon ages of organic matter found in mud: carbonate precipitates, snail shells, and, in rare cases, charcoal fragments. In one instance, at the lake bed's base, he found one- to two-centimeter-thick charcoal deposits of burnt reeds resting on windblown sand. However,

---

*An istotope is one of several forms of an element having the same atomic number but differing atomic masses.

dispersed charcoal may have been redeposited and, Haynes believes, should be used only as a maximum possible age of the deposit. Ages of the lowest level of charcoal found in the soil are the most reliable and at Selima, the base layer of charcoal was from two distinct ages, 7700 and 6500 B.C.E.[14] According to Haynes, the remnants of an early lake still existed before the rise of a second lake. This second lake also had a base layer of charred reeds, likely burned by prehistoric pastoralists to provide better access to the rising lake water.

Reasonable estimates of the age of these ancient lakes have been obtained from radiocarbon dating of various kinds of sediments. However, in some cases, the estimates may be slightly too old because of redeposition of sediments from earlier lake beds or other factors that complicate age estimates. With this in mind, researchers have dated the beginning of Saharan pluvial conditions between 9000 and 7880 B.C.E.

What can be surmised is that evidence from the Sudanese and Egyptian lake beds indicate that the beginning of the Sahara's pluvial conditions began about 7880 and ended around 5490 B.C.E. The first wet phase began about 7800 B.C.E., with a second wet phase occurring around 6900 B.C.E. There is also evidence that a third phase existed between 5490 and 5220 B.C.E. Between these wet phases the climate returned to being relatively dry.

Rivers

Traversing 4,132 miles, the Nile River is the longest in the world. It is actually made up of two rivers, the Blue Nile and the White Nile. The Blue Nile is the primary headstream of the Nile and flows from northwest Ethiopia to Sudan. The White Nile rises from Lake Victoria, then flows north and westward through Uganda, Lake Kyoga, and Lake Albert. Both rivers meet in Sudan to form what is commonly known as the Nile River.

High *strandlines* (discoloration where water once rose) along the White Nile indicate that between 6500 and 6000 B.C.E., flooding occurred ten feet above today's flood line. Several wadis flowed into the Nile, including the Wadi Howar, across north-central Sudan, and the Wadi Melik, which flowed from 5700 to 4000 B.C. Humid conditions along the Nile Valley resulted in deposits of silt, mud, and gravel before 3000 B.C. Nile flooding between 6200 and 4600 B.C.E. created high lake levels in El Faiyûm, a province in Upper Egypt, and discharged a considerable amount of freshwater into the Mediterranean Sea.

The Selima Sand Sheet

A flat, sand-covered, 40,000-square-kilometer area called the Selima Sand Sheet is the heart of the eastern Sahara. It is also the heart of the desert's aridity on the Egyptian-Sudanese border. In his analysis of the sand sheet, Dr. Haynes divided it into four main depositional age groups: A through D, from the oldest to the youngest. Strata A and C are composed of sand and gravel deposits formed under less arid conditions. Stratum A, which is the oldest, has the best-developed soil. Sediments of stratum A contain artifacts from the Acheulian culture, which is attributed to *Homo erectus* between 1.5 million and 300,000 years ago.[15] Stratum C, in some cases, may be remnants of A that have undergone iron reduction from groundwater in low areas. However, some of stratum C is as young as 70,000 to 90,000 years and contains Middle Paleolithic artifacts. Strata B and D are sand sheets deposited under extremely arid conditions.[16] The red stratum B, older than 300,000 years, exhibits stronger soil-building progress and is more hardened than the light brown D stratum of the Holocene age, which is between 9000 B.C.E. and the present.[17]

As suggested above, these layered sheets of sand show evidence of soil formation in varying degrees. This "soil building," referred to as *pedogenesis,* occurs when wet, very small amounts of clay and carbonates present in the sand serve as a binding, cohesive substance. Over a long period of time, sand can be converted into soil when subjected to moisture. Haynes divides the layered sheets of sand into five stages of pedogenesis, 0 through 4, as follows:

Stage 0: No cohesion; will not stand as a vertical wall when it is excavated.

Stage 1: Adequate cohesion to stand as a vertical wall when trenched, but no soil structure exists.

Stage 2: Adequate cohesion with weak, medium-prismatic structure. The cracks between soils are so fine that little or no cracking pattern emerges upon scraping away the overlying sand with stage 0 pedogenesis. Layers are distinct within each soil.

Stage 3: No primary sedimentary features because of disturbance of layers by plant root activity, animal burrowing, and trampling by people and animals. Soil colors become redder and browner.

Stage 4: Redder than Stage 3, with a stronger structure; apparently older.

According to Haynes, stage 3 pedogenesis soils in the sand sheet are clearly the product of wetter climates. Those developed in stratum D often contain prehistoric cultural artifacts. Stages 0, 1, and 2 appear to be products of the frequency and intensity of rainfall. As a result, they do not necessarily have chronological significance. In other words, rain may have penetrated the upper layer of sand and converted a stage 0 to a stage 1 by allowing a slight degree of cohesion.

A team from Oxford used optically simulated luminescence (OSL) to date the Selima Sand Sheet. Sands with stage 2 pedogenesis provided ages of 3,380 and 4,640 years old; sands with stage 3 pedogenesis provided ages of 15,690 and 19,220, suggesting that the infilling of the Selima Sand Sheet occurred during the late glacial maximum, which was fifteen thousand to twenty thousand years ago.[18]

Sedimentary deposits were followed by soil formation during the wet phases between 7800 and 3000 B.C. This means that the prehistoric lake and playa sequences correlate with periods of wetness and soil formation and not with evolution of the Selima Sand Sheet. The formation of the Selima Sand Sheet occurred only with the extreme dryness of the ice age, and after 3000 B.C.E., when the region's climate returned to extreme aridity.

Fossil shells of the large land snail, found in stage 3 surface soils in northwestern Sudan, provide evidence of at least twelve inches of annual precipitation during the late stage of this Neolithic Pluvial. Radiocarbon ages determined on the organic fraction of the snail shells range from 4500 B.C.E. at the north end of the study area, to later than 1100 B.C.E. at the south end, indicative of a retreating forest-savanna during the final stages of the pluvial period in northwestern Sudan. Fossil evidence from the Selima Sand Sheet, which was initially formed during the ice age, also suggests that a wet period occurred between 8000 and 5000 B.C.E.

Return of the Desert: 5000 B.C.E. to the Present

Wet and humid conditions prior to 5000 B.C.E. established an ecosystem consisting of seasonal grassy plains, shrubs, and trees. Flora was especially concentrated in wadis, lakes, and springs, which attracted animals and people. Later, the environment became generally semiarid across southern Egypt and northern Sudan as the rain belt moved farther and farther south. The continuance of wet conditions varied by location, with some areas drying up more quickly than others. Lakes that were supported by groundwater typically persisted longer than rain-fed playas. Plant life diminished as aridity set in. According to pollen studies, climate aridity progressed rapidly after the sixth millennium B.C.E. The edge of the rain belt migrated 250 kilometers south at an estimated rate of thirty-six kilometers every hundred years—equivalent to one degree of latitude every three hundred years. Plants and animals, over much of the region, were eventually either destroyed or confined to small pockets of livable land.[19]

Playas in the northern Egyptian oases dried up around 5000 B.C.E. and their basins filled in with windblown sand. The Hatiet Um El-Hiyus Playa, in the Siwa Oasis, was active through 5900 B.C.E., but began to dry out from its high point during the sixth millennium B.C.E.

The Nile flowed at high stage through 4600 B.C.E., but was lower with only occasional high stages thereafter. Intermittent floods and low flow stages resulted in the deposition of sediments, oxidized layers, and calcareous "oozes" along the Nile cone (the area of Mediterranean Sea at the river's mouth). After 4500 B.C.E. lake levels in Faiyûm dropped fifty feet, surged to higher levels around 3800–3700 B.C.E., and waned again from 3700 to 1700 B.C. Along the Nile's higher reaches, tributaries stopped flowing altogether around the fifth millennium B.C. The Wadi Melik ran dry around 4000 B.C.E. Flows from Wadi Howar diminished significantly. Areas west of the Nile Valley and the Faiyûm region are generally recognized as arid from 5000 to 4500 B.C.E. After 4500 B.C.E., savanna flora diminished, allowing Saharan elements to dominate. By 4000 B.C.E., a full desert flora was in place in most areas of southern Egypt, excluding some oases, wadis, and the region of the Gilf Kebir. Through 3000 B.C.E., water was still seasonally available, allowing the growth of rich vegetation, comparable to the modern gallery forests of Tibesti and Hoggar.[20]

Aridity may have slightly lessened during the fourth millennium B.C.E., with annual rainfall around six inches, but the climate continued to deteriorate. Plant fossils suggest that the climate through 2000 B.C.E. became increasingly more arid, with estimated annual rainfall of less than four inches.

Many locations in southern Egypt seem to have been abandoned around 4000 B.C.E. The main period of settlement in the Gilf Kebir region lasted from 4000 to 3000 B.C.E.; other playas, such as Wadi Bakht and Ard El-Akhdar, continued to exist through 3000 B.C.E. and then abruptly stopped. However, sand dunes that dammed up the playas may have been breached, possibly by a hundred-year storm of great magnitude.

Similar patterns of climate change existed in northern Sudan, although conditions were generally wetter than those in southern Egypt. Some lakes and playas in northern Sudan dried up by 5000 B.C.E. In the Laquiya and Tageru areas, many lakes dried up around 4500 B.C.E. Some lakes in the general region of Merga remained active at 4900 B.C.E. Playas at Laquiya Umran were still active around 4100 B.C.E., and some hearths in Wadi Sahl, near Laquiya Arba'in, date to 2700 B.C. Playas and *slack-water environments* (areas unaffected by currents, that is, still water) along Wadi Howar and Wadi Mansourab waned after 5000 B.C.E. and ended sometime before 2800 B.C.E.[21]

Investigations at Selima suggest that the lake endured intense evaporation between 5000 and 4000 B.C.E., resulting in the formation of a saltwater lake around 4400 B.C.E. Plant life, established in the region, persisted until 4000 B.C.E. Isotopic measurements on mollusks indicate that dry conditions prevailed around 3600 B.C.E. As local rainfall dwindled and the climate became progressively more arid, the lake at Selima diminished in size and disappeared around 2000 B.C.E. At Oyo, four hundred kilometers south, similar changes were occurring. A deep lake persisted until 5000 B.C.E., but diminished in size and became saline. By 4600 B.C.E. the deciduous savanna-woodlands began to deteriorate. Between 4000 and 2500 B.C.E., the acacia thorn and scrub grasslands replaced the existing subtropical Sudanese and Sahelian savannas. After 2900 B.C.E., windblown sands covered Oyo's lakeside.[22]

The Great Sand Sea, south of Siwa, also underwent a trend toward eventual aridness. Analysis of playa sediments suggests that arid periods interrupted wet conditions through the fifth millennium B.C.E. The deposition of windblown sands indicates a minor arid climate around 4300 B.C.E., before the sand dunes were, again, partially inundated with water and stabilized by plant life (around 2780 B.C.E.). After 2700 B.C.E. the area remained extremely arid. Evidence of hand-dug wells at playa sites near Siwa suggests that similar dry conditions had set in around the same time.

By 5000 B.C.E., many rain-fed playas in Egypt had vanished. Most were significantly desiccated, due to drought, by 3500 B.C.E., and plant life began to disappear as early as 5600 B.C.E. After 3900 B.C.E., many playa basins were literally filled with sand. At Nabta Playa alternating layers of forest and windblown sands indicate that arid periods interrupted more humid conditions between 5700 and 3800 B.C.E.

In the Kiseiba region, a wet climate may have lasted a little longer. Playas near Bîr Kiseiba appear to have existed through 3400 B.C.E., possibly as a result of buried groundwater between the layers of sands. Water supplies dwindled at Abu Ballas through 4300 B.C.E., after which windblown sands buried the playa mud. The Dahkla Oasis experienced a similar drying trend after 4500 B.C.E.[23]

In the Khârga basin's southern region at Shurafa Hill, between 6000 and 5000 B.C.E., intensive winds removed significant amounts of surface sediment. The depth of the erosion likely kept pace with the lowering of the water table, although other factors were likely involved. After 3000 B.C.E., extensive sand dunes began to cover many of the inhabited sites.

In the Sudan, around 2800 B.C.E., the flow of Wadi Howar diminished and its lakes evaporated, marking the official end of the general wet period in northwest Nubia. By 2500 B.C.E., even the desert scrub grasslands disappeared from most of southern Egypt and northern Sudan, excluding some oases and wadis. A lack of vegetation allowed sands to overtake most of the region. Arid to extremely arid conditions were established across the region by 2500 B.C.E. The lakes at Selima dried up around 2000 B.C.E., and at El-'Atrun and the region of Gebel Tageru around 1600 B.C.E. Dated archaeological finds indicate that these desert regions were abandoned. After 4000 B.C.E., hand-dug wells signal that the onset of arid conditions influenced human activities. By 2075 B.C.E., the Wadi Howar, a southern tributary of the Nile, was dry, and north-central Sudan had become a waterless desert.

The modern Sahara desert is now nearly lifeless, with populations limited to the hardiest of desert plants and animals. The once semiarid habitable environment of southern Egypt and northern Sudan has dried up since 4500 B.C.E., and is now dominated by the wind.

Climate Summary

Egypt's Arba'in Desert and surrounding region has been arid, receiving less than half an inch of rain per year for the last fifteen thousand to twenty thousand years. However, as described above, wetter conditions prevailed between 7000 and 4000 B.C.E., with rainwater averaging more than twelve inches per year and possibly as much as twenty-four.

Yet, the region was drought-prone because of the rains' seasonal nature. Scanty, steppe-style desert plants provided enough vegetation for animal and human life between 6500 and 1000 B.C.E. As the area became increasingly more arid and isolated from monsoonal rains, the availability of surface water became an ongoing problem. Lakes and rivers dried up and wind erosion prevailed. This climatic scenario is also supported by a geologic history of Nile flooding. According to Robert J. Wenke, in "Egypt: Origins of Complex Societies," Nile flood levels were high from 6800 B.C.E. through 3800 B.C.E. After that, however, flood levels were low, except for brief wet periods around 3400 B.C.E. and 2500 B.C.E.[24]

With a "green" Sahara existing between 7000 and 4000 B.C.E. and rains reaching as much as twenty-four inches per year, one can argue that Egypt's Sphinx was originally carved shortly after 7000 B.C. Although contrary to traditional opinion, this would allow enough time for the rock in the western wall to erode through rainfall. It would also agree with Schoch's findings. However, rates of erosion are, at best, estimates about which scientists often disagree. This raises the question of how fast rock erodes.

Erosion and the Sphinx

All land surfaces can be considered hill slopes even if they have no incline (a flat surface has a "slope" of zero degrees). In most cases, the erosion of a slope can be considered a system that links together weathering (the breakdown of rock), hill slope processes (such as mass wasting of solid rock and the movement of loose rock and soil downslope by either gravity or running water), and erosion, which typically occurs from rivers in valley bottoms.

Rainfall is the source of water erosion. Whether the water infiltrates the ground depends on rainfall intensity and the rate of infiltration allowed by surface conditions. Where rainfall intensity exceeds the infiltration capacity of the soil, shallow water flows over the land. This "saturation" overflow occurs mainly at the base of slopes and in concavities. The ground becomes saturated during prolonged rain by a combination of infiltration, the downslope flow within the soil, and groundwater flow. Once the soil is saturated, its infiltration capacity is zero, so any additional rain cannot soak in. When this occurs, it is stored on the surface or becomes overland flow.

Water that infiltrates the ground becomes either soil moisture or groundwater (the top of the saturated zone is the top of the water table). Just above the water table there is the capillary fringe, where water is drawn up from the water table by capillary action, referred to as "discontinuous saturation." The water table is not level and follows the shape of the surface—higher under hills, lower in valleys. Because of this, both soil moisture and groundwater can flow from high to lower elevations, although these flows are usually very slow. A typical flow rate for clean sand is around ten meters a day. The main contribution of these flows to slope erosion is the removal of material in solution.

Water flowing overland, whether in a channel or moving across an open plain, transports sediment down a slope. This results in sheet wash, rills, and gullies. Sheet wash is, as the name suggests, a sheet of water flowing across a surface. It is the uniform removal of soil without the development of visible water channels, and is the least apparent of erosion types. Rills occur when sheet wash concentrates into many small but conspicuous channels. Gullies occur when sheet wash and/or rills concentrate into larger flows. Sheet wash is aided by rain-splash erosion—in which raindrops detach particles from the surface—and is most effective in dry regions that lack protective vegetation. In all cases, the movement of soil and rock particles by flowing water is erosion.

Significant overland flows occur where infiltration is low and rainfall intensity high. Infiltration is affected greatly by the presence of vegetation, which promotes water absorption by maintaining an open soil structure. For this reason, *Hortonian flows* (flows that do not drain into channels or gullies) occur mainly in arid regions with poor vegetation cover. These areas are subject to rare but intense thunderstorms, such as in the southwestern United States, as well as in areas of northern Africa. In these places, intense rain may last only a few minutes, but significant erosion can occur.

Erosion in Perspective

More than twenty-five years of geological and archaeological investigations in the extremely arid regions of southwestern Egypt and northwestern Sudan demonstrate that wet conditions existed in these areas beginning around 8000 B.C.E. At that time, the eastern Sahara changed from an extremely arid, lifeless desert dominated by wind erosion to a semiarid savanna that attracted plants and animals. This life-supporting climate continued and gradually deteriorated until the beginning of the third millennium B.C.E., when the current episode of extreme aridity ensued. This prehistoric wet period can further be broken down into a sequence of three phases. The first existed from 8000 to 6200 B.C.E.; the second, 6100 to 5900 B.C.E.; and a third, from 5700 to 2600 B.C.E.

Both Schoch and Reader agree on rain as a primary source of the Sphinx's erosion. However, Reader does not fully agree with Schoch's scenario. According to Reader, it is not necessary to place a carving date of the Sphinx prior to 5000 B.C.E. He believes that the rains were heavy enough during this last wet phase to account for the visible erosion. Furthermore, he believes that rainfall runoff and sheet wash, and not direct rainfall, were the source of the water erosion on the Sphinx's western enclosure wall. Any exposed rock would suffer from runoff following the rains and would be heavily eroded. Once the rock from the west of the Sphinx was quarried during the fourth dynasty, the potential for runoff erosion of the enclosure walls ended. So the Sphinx was carved, at least, before 2500 B.C.E.

The walls of the Sphinx enclosure exhibit erosion to a depth of three feet and at its greatest point to a depth of over six and a half feet.[25] So, the pertinent question is, how long did it take for this erosion to occur?

According to geology textbooks, the lowering of ground through water erosion is generally a slow process. The rate at which rock erodes depends upon the type of rock. In general, igneous and metamorphic rock erodes 0.5–7.0 mm every 1,000 years; sandstone, 16–34 mm every 1,000 years; and limestone, 22–100 mm every 1,000 years.

TABLE 3.1 EROSION RATES FOR ROCK (in inches)		
Type	Per 1,000 years	Per 10,000 years
igneous/metamorphic	0.002–0.28	.02–2.8
sandstone	0.24–1.34	2.4–13.4
limestone	0.87–3.94	8.7–39.4

Although there is no available data for erosion rates on the Giza plateau, geologists have studied the erosion of rock formations around the world. One of the most well-known erosional features in North America is the Grand Canyon. Geologists have calculated that it is six million years old. Since it is six thousand feet deep at its deepest point, this means that every one million years, the rock, which defines the canyon, erodes a thousand feet. In other words, every year for the past six million years the Colorado River has eroded the underlying bedrock 0.001 foot, which is 0.012 inch per year. If we applied this rate of erosion to the Sphinx's enclosure walls, it would take three thousand years to erode three feet and six thousand years to erode six. However, one would expect the steady force of the Colorado River to erode rock at a faster rate than either rainfall or sheet wash from rainstorms.

All running water gathers and transports particles of soil and fragments of rock. Every stream carries material, received from its tributaries or from its own banks, suspended or rolling along its bottom. These particles strike against the bedrock of the stream's channel and literally grind away the surface; they eventually settle out along the channel or get transported out to sea. In this way, the Mississippi River has been reducing the underlying bedrock at the rate of one foot every nine thousand years, which is .0013 inch per year. If the Sphinx's enclosure walls eroded as the same rate as the Mississippi River's foundations, it would take twenty-eight thousand years for three feet of erosion and fifty-six thousand for six feet. (Of course, a large-volume river has a lot more erosional force than periodic rain erosion or sheet wash, so this is not a comparison of like phenomena.)

In studying the Wutach *catchment* (a geographical area where water collects) in the southeastern region of Germany's Black Forest, European geologists Philippe Morel, Friedhelm von Blackenburg, Mirjam Schaller, Matthias Hinderer, and Peter Kubik calculated the rate of erosion for sandstone at 9–14 mm every 1,000 years; granite, 27–37 mm every 1,000 years; and limestone 70–90 mm (which is $2^3/_4$–$3^1/_2$ inches) every 1,000 years.[26] Using three inches as an average rate for limestone erosion every 1,000 years (.003 inch per year) it would take twelve thousand years for the Sphinx enclosure to erode three feet and twenty-four thousand for six feet.

According to the geologists John Stone and Paulo Vasconcelos, erosion rates in Australia vary with climate and the character of the rock formation, as well as the local landscape. Chlorine-36 measurements on calcite from limestone outcrops around the continent indicate that erosion rates from rainfall vary from one meter every million years, in the arid interior, to 150 meters every million years, in the highlands of Papua New Guinea. That's a range of one millimeter (0.03937 inch) to 150 millimeters (six inches) every thousand years. According to these rates, it would take anywhere between six thousand and one million years to erode the Sphinx enclosure walls three feet and between twelve thousand and two million years to erode six feet.[27]

Furthermore, Stone and Vasconcelos concluded that limestone erosion rates are well correlated with average annual rainfall at values close to those predicted by the equilibrium solubility of calcite. In other words, the more it rains, the greater the rate of erosion in limestone rock.

Geologists Ari Matmon, Ezra Zilberman, and Yehouda Enzel, in their study of tectonic activity in the Galilee region of Israel, were able to provide the first estimated rates of landscape-forming processes. According to their study, limestone erosion occurred at a rate of approximately 29 meters every million years, which is 0.029 millimeter (0.00114 inch) per year. At this rate, it would take the enclosure wall 32,000 years to erode three feet and 64,000 years to erode six feet.[28]

One instance where rock rapidly erodes is at Niagara Falls. According to geologists, the falls have receded 11.4 kilometers in 12,400 years, a very fast average rate of nearly one meter per year. However, the rate of erosion has decreased recently because of the erosion-resistant limestone caprock the falls flow over. This limestone layer begins approximately one-half kilometer north of Rainbow Bridge. However, as the falls continue to erode southward, the erosion rate will, again, increase when it reaches another soft layer of rock near Navy Island.

Niagara Falls is actually composed of three falls: the American Falls, between Prospect Point and Luna Island; the Bridal Veil Falls, between Luna Island and Goat Island; and the Horseshoe (Canadian) Falls, between Goat Island and Table Rock. Rock characteristics vary among these different areas. In general, the natural bedrock at the falls is composed of soft shale and limestone. Over the years, the continual flow of water has caused large sections of bedrock to break away and remain at the base of the cataracts. The soft shale erodes faster than limestone, undermining its stability. However, today the American Falls has no regular mode of collapse. The present amount of water flowing over the American Falls is insufficient to erode the *dolostone talus* (slope formed by rock debris) at the base of the falls. (Dolostone is similar to limestone, but is composed mostly of the mineral dolomite.) The current rate of erosion at the American Falls is estimated at one-quarter inch per year—250 inches (twenty feet) every thousand years. The water flow, which is regulated at a minimum level of 10 percent of the estimated 100,000 cubic feet per second during the summer (half that during winter), is insufficient to cause major erosion.

TABLE 3.2 EROSION RATES PER 1,000 YEARS (in inches)
FOR VARIOUS GEOGRAPHIC AREAS[29]

	Minimum	Maximum	Average
Galilee	–	–	0.001
Mississippi	–	–	1.3
Wutach	2.75	3.5	2.0
Australia	0.04	6.0	3.02
Grand Canyon	–	–	12.0
Giza (Schoch)	16	29	22.5
Giza (traditional)	–	–	72.0
Niagara (American Falls)	–	–	250.0

As various as they may be, environmental influences will always play a role in physical and chemical weathering rates. Records shows physical weathering is most pronounced in cool, humid climates, because of water's characteristic to freeze and thaw. On the other hand, rates for chemical weathering are driven by temperature and water supply. As a result, chemical weathering is most pronounced in hot, humid regions. Since water is a large factor in chemical weathering, and also erosion when particles are moved away, weathering rates and erosion are slowest in arid environments, precisely what Stone and Vasconcelos found in their Australian study. It is also why rivers produce some of the greatest erosion rates.

There is a well-documented correlation of annual rainfall and temperature with weathering and erosion. This correlation serves as a principle for understanding what types of erosion can be expected in various climates. In regions where rainfall and temperature are both relatively high—for example, a tropical rainforest—chemical weathering (the breakdown of rocks resulting from chemical reactions between the minerals in the rocks and substances in the environment such as water, oxygen, and weakly acidic rainwater) is strongest and a predominant feature of exposed rock. At the other extreme, where both temperature and rainfall are relatively low, mechanical weathering is predominant and may be slight to moderate depending on the rainfall. Mechanical weathering is the process by which frost action, salt-crystal growth, absorption of water, and other physical processes break down a rock to fragments, involving no chemical change. Temperate latitudes

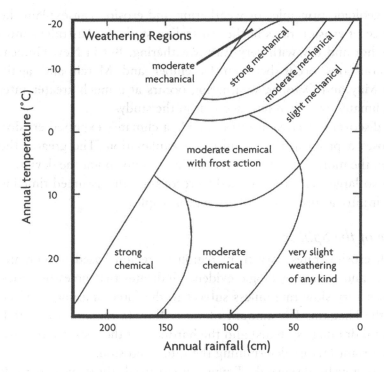

Fig. 3.3. Weathering regions according to temperature and rainfall (from Geological Sciences Department, California State Polytechnic University)

in North America and Europe are good examples of regions that experience prominent mechanical weathering, although in some areas annual rainfall may exceed fifty inches.

In extremely arid areas, one would expect to find only very slight weathering of any kind. What would be expected is erosion from airborne particles by way of windstorms. North Africa and the Middle East are good examples of this type of erosion, and the desert region that stretches from northern Mexico into the southwestern United States illustrates this as well.

Geologists seldom try to generalize about rates of weathering and erosion because weathering and erosion vary in each climate, and perhaps in microclimates within each climate. There is also the type of rock and terrain to consider. However, for a given area, one would expect a certain range of weathering and erosion that would be consistent with the model presented in figure 3.3. Substantial deviations from those ranges suggest that the climate was different in the past.

The geologic principles of weathering and erosion can explain the wide range of erosion rates in the Australian study. In Australia's interior, it is hot and dry with very little weathering. But in New Guinea, where monsoons occur between December and March and again between May and October, weathering occurs at a much greater rate. Several climates are taken into account in the study.

The discovery of erosion rates outside a climate's expected erosion range poses a problem that requires an explanation. The greater the deviation, the more difficult it is to explain. At some point the deviation becomes so large that one is forced to reconsider the assumed timeline to bring it into accordance with known principles.

The Age of the Sphinx

Although erosion rates vary from region to region based on climate, rock type, and terrain, geologic evidence indicates that limestone rock erodes at a very slow rate unless subject to the force of a mighty river, such as the Niagara. The amount of water flow (a function of rainfall and natural drainage systems) and the hardness of the rock are the two most important factors determining the rate of erosion.

As previously discussed, Egypt experienced three wet periods between 8000 and 2600 B.C.E. Yet the rainfall during these wet periods averaged just enough—twelve to twenty-four inches annually—to turn the climate from arid to semiarid, resulting in a landscape similar to the southwest region of North America: dry, but wet enough to allow plant and animal life to flourish.

I argue that we can use geologists' knowledge of erosion to answer the question of the Sphinx's age. From the studies conducted by Gauri, and later confirmed by Schoch and other researchers, the rock where the Sphinx was carved consists of alternating layers of hard and soft limestone. As would be expected, the softer limestone has eroded to a greater degree than the harder layers. However, the hard layers, especially at the top of the west enclosure wall, also show significant weathering. To explain this, Schoch postulates that the erosion occurred over many thousands of years, specifically from rainfall. Reader argues that it occurred relatively quickly, during Egypt's early-dynastic times (2920–2650 B.C.E.), because of sporadic and severe thunderstorms that resulted in sheet wash rolling across the plain and over the edge of the enclosure.

Given the known climate of Egypt for the past ten thousand years, it is highly probable the temperature and rainfall characteristics of the area fall into the region, noted in figure 3.3 (see page 61), where "very slight weathering of any kind" would be expected. The average rate of limestone erosion, drawn from table 3.2 on page 60 (excluding the Giza plateau and Niagara Falls), is three and a half inches every thousand years. Using this average, it would take ten thousand years for the Sphinx's western enclosure wall to erode three feet and twenty thousand years for it to erode six feet. Although it would be incorrect to assume that this is actually the case, these figures support Schoch's conclusion that rock weathers slowly, and that the Great Sphinx of Egypt eroded in this manner. He believes that the Sphinx is at least seven thousand years old—which, he says, is a conservative estimate.

If Reader's scenario is correct—that the erosion occurred at a faster pace—how many thunderstorms would be necessary to cause the observed degradation? What amount of water, and during what length of time, would be needed to flow down the plain and over the top of the enclosure wall? Although Giza did experience rainfall during early and predynastic times, the climatic evidence suggests that these rainy periods were moderate and not long-lived.[30]

The alternative to either Schoch's or Reader's theory is that the conventional view is correct, and the observed erosion occurred during the fourth and fifth dynasties, between about 2500 and 2350 B.C.E., a period of 150 years. This calls for an erosion rate of one-quarter inch per year—nearly identical to the current erosion rate of Niagara's American Falls. If this is true, then the real mystery is not Schoch's or Reader's geological analysis of the Sphinx and the Giza plateau, but the unidentified forces that caused the limestone rock of the Sphinx enclosure to break down so rapidly.

WHAT CULTURE, WHEN?

A Massive Contextual Problem Solved

According to traditional Egyptologists, there exists a massive problem with a Sphinx carving date prior to the fourth dynasty (2575–2467 B.C.E.). There is no evidence that the tools and know-how to carve such a large statue existed prior to that time. Furthermore, the headdress of the Sphinx is clearly a fourth-dynasty fashion. The lack of evidence of a sufficiently advanced culture to produce an artifact is referred to as a problem of cultural context. In his investigation, Colin Reader attempts to provide an early-dynastic context (2920–2650 B.C.E.) for the Sphinx's carving. However, Schoch's Sphinx, it seems, was carved by an unknown civilization several thousand years before the first Egyptian ever shaped a copper chisel. Thus, Schoch's theory on the age of the Sphinx is apparently without a cultural context. This is the subject we will investigate in this chapter.

Evidence certainly exists for early-dynastic activity on the Giza plateau. Although substantial development is generally considered to have begun with the fourth dynasty, as Reader points out, there are published archaeological findings to indicate activity prior to that time. In the late 1800s, four ceramic jars were discovered at the foot of the Great Pyramid. At first they were believed to be from the first dynasty (2920–2770 B.C.E.). Later, however, Bodil Mortensen determined them to be typical of the late-predynastic Maadi period (approximately 3500 to 3050 B.C.E.). Mortenson also argued that they were from a burial rather than a settlement site, since the jars were found intact.

Reader points out that the discovery of pre-fourth-dynasty artifacts on the Giza plateau has to be considered in the context of the fourth-dynasty development. Unarguably, fourth-dynasty use of Giza was substantial. Most of the available land was quarried or built upon. Both of these activities were destructive acts, and likely involved the removal of earlier structures and the clearing of debris. Therefore, the remains from earlier inhabitants were probably dumped in open, vacated quarries or in other areas outside the area of construction. During the 1970s, the Austrian Egyptologist Karl Kromer found such a dump site south of Giza filled with relics from predynastic (5500–3100 B.C.E.) as well as early-dynastic (2920–2650 B.C.E.) times. Further study of Kromer's site indicates that instead of a single settlement, there were several. Sand blew into the hollowed area and separated the layers of early Egyptian litter. Others have criticized the dating of various objects Kromer found, but excavated jar seals are generally agreed upon as predynastic.

Cultural Context: Is There More Than One?

If Schoch is accurate concerning the dating of the limestone floor of the Sphinx enclosure—that it was first exposed to the air at least seven thousand years ago—could there be more than one cultural context? The best evidence for such a culture to have existed is the relative sophistication with which Egyptian civilization first appeared. Most scholars argue that during predynastic times, the Egyptians endeavored to invent and develop the magnificent stone technology found at the step pyramid at Sakkara and the various structures on the Giza plateau. Other researchers, such as John Anthony West, insist that what is interpreted as a development is really a legacy. West argues that the Egyptians who built the pyramids and other structures on the Giza plateau were the benefactors of another, older culture.

The controversy and debate lies in the advanced level of stoneware and stoneworking techniques discovered in some of the earliest sites of Egyptian civilization, such as Sakkara and Giza, and not found in sites from any later era in Egyptian history. (Much of this magnificent stoneware is on exhibit in the Cairo Museum and in the Petrie Museum of Egyptian Archaeology in London.) A primitive people with the technology to manufacture sophisticated stoneware, such as hollowed-out granite vases, is indeed a mystery deserving explanation.

According to the Egyptologist Walter Emery, the stone vessels of Egypt's archaic period (3100–2650 B.C.E.) were perhaps the Egyptians' greatest method for artistic expression. No other country, at that time or since, has achieved such precision. While the quality varied, stoneware was manufactured in vast quantities and with astonishing aesthetic design and technique.[1] Every type of available stone was used. Specimens, dated to the first (2920–2770 B.C.E.) and second (2770–2650 B.C.E.) dynasties, have been found that are made from diorite, schist, alabaster, volcanic rock, serpentine, steatite, breccia, marble, limestone, mottled black-and-white porphyritic rock, purple porphyry, red jasper, obsidian quartz, dolomite, rock crystal, and basalt. Even with our modern industrial knowledge, we have yet to reproduce such items with the techniques or machinery they employed. Furthermore, stoneware such as this has not been found from any later era in Egyptian history. It seems, then, that the skills necessary to produce such meticulously crafted items were somehow lost.

Magnificent Stoneware: Evidence of a Preexisting Culture

From predynastic times through the Old Kingdom, evidence exists that the ancient Egyptians had a well-developed technology for working with stone. Based on recovered artifacts, the earliest Egyptians used tube drills, saws (reciprocating as well as circular), and lathes to cut and shape stone into items of household use. Museums around the world display examples of early Egyptian stoneware that depict the unique features of their manufacture. They were made from a variety of materials, ranging from soft stone, such as alabaster, to the hardest known rock, granite. These museum pieces are some of the finest artifacts ever found, and, ironically, are from a very early period of Egyptian civilization. Many were found in and around Djoser's step pyramid at Sakkara.

Djoser's step pyramid, built during the third dynasty, around 2630 B.C.E., is believed to be the oldest stone pyramid in Egypt, and the first pyramid ever built. Apparently it is also the only place where these types of stone housewares have been found in quantity, although Sir Flinders Petrie, a late-nineteenth-century investigator, found fragments of similar bowls at Giza. Much of the stoneware is inscribed with symbols from the earliest kings of the predynastic era. Some have argued, because of the primitive style of the inscriptions, that it is unlikely that those who fashioned the bowls also made those signatures. It is possible that pre-dynastic Egyptians acquired the stoneware some time after it was made and then marked it with their sign of ownership.

In the center of open bowls and plates, where the angle of the cut changes rapidly, one can see a clean, narrow, and perfectly circular line made by the tip of a cutting tool. Unmistakably, these tool marks were from lathe manufacturing (rotating an item on two spindles so the reduction of material is even on all sides). Soft stone is relatively simple to machine and can be worked with simple tools and abrasives; however, the level of precision used in manufacturing these items rivals twentieth-century industry. Delicate vases, made of brittle stone such as schist, were finished, turned, and polished to a flawless, paper-thin edge. One nine-inch bowl, hollowed out with a three-inch opening at its top, was flawlessly turned so that it balances perfectly on a rounded and tipped bottom. This tip is the size of an egg's rounded point, requiring a symmetrical wall thickness without any substantial error.

Elegant items made from granite indicate not only an accomplished level of skill, but perhaps an advanced level of technology as well. Pieces made from granite, porphyry, or basalt cores were hollowed out with a narrow and flared opening, some of which have a long neck.

Sir Flinders Petrie, in his 1883 book *The Pyramids and Temples of Gizeh,* suggests that the lathe was as familiar an instrument in the fourth dynasty as it is in the modern workshop. Diorite bowls and vases of the Old Kingdom frequently show great technical skill and were likely turned on a lathe. One piece Petrie found at Giza shows that the method employed was true lathe turning for the removal of mate-rial and not a process of grinding. The bowl had been knocked off its centering and recentered imperfectly. The old turning did not quite turn out, so there are two surfaces belonging to different centers meeting in a cusp. A grinding or rubbing process that pressed on the surface could not produce such an appearance.

Another interesting detail, visible in Petrie's fragment No. 15, is the bowl's spherical circumference. To accomplish this, the bowl must have been cut by a tool sweeping an arc from a fixed center while the bowl rotated. The center, or hinge, of the tool was in the axis of the lathe to create the general surface of the bowl, right up to its edge. However, since a lip was desired on the finished product, the centering of the tool was shifted with exactly the same radius of its arc and a fresh cut was made

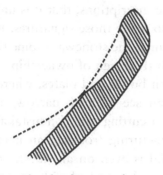

Fig. 4.1. Sketch of Petrie's fragment No. 15

to create a lip on the bowl. According to Petrie, this was certainly not a result of chance. The exact circularity of the curves, their equality, and the cusp left where they meet tell a tale of precision manufacturing. It was not rounded off, as would certainly be the case if it was done by hand. It is physical proof of the rigidly mechanical method of striking the curves.

Tube Drilling

Ancient Egyptian craftspeople also used a tube drill to hollow out holes. A tube drill is a hollowed cylinder with teeth on one end. It worked based on the same principle as an apple-coring tool: by applying pressure with it against a solid material and rotating it, a cylindrical core was cut through the object by the drill's teeth and then removed. Tubular drills varied in thickness from one-quarter inch to five inches in diameter and from one-thirtieth to one-fifth inch thick.[2] A two-inch-diameter hole is the smallest yet found in granite, although larger examples exist. At El Bersheh, a platform of limestone rock was dressed down (shaped into the desired form) by cutting it away with eighteen-inch tube drills.[3] According to Petrie, the circular grooves that occasionally intersect prove it was done merely to remove the rock. In 1996, a piece of granite with spiral grooves on its visible portions was displayed in the Cairo Museum. The grooves were at a regular depth and spacing, obvious signs they had been created by a tube drill. They likely would not have been so consistent if made by abrasive slurry (a mixture of finely ground sand and water that wears away material—for example, rubbing compound to remove light scratches in a finish).

A tube drill was also used to hollow out the sarcophagus in the king's chamber of the Great Pyramid. Despite polishing of the finished product, tube-drill markings were left on the top, inside the sarcophagus on its east side. Judging by the radius of the cut, less than two inches, masons made numerous holes, each of which was several inches deep.

Near the Sphinx, in the overhead door lintels of the Valley Temple, a tube drill was used to bore holes through granite. Evidence of tube drilling is still visible in most of the temple's doorways. One theory is that these holes were used to hold in place long vertical shafts that rotated and served as door hinges.

Tube drilling is a specialized method that likely did not develop without the need for a large hole. Furthermore, making a bit strong enough to drill through granite is not a simple or primitive task. Petrie believed that to create a tool to remove hard rock, bronze tube drills were set with jeweled points. Of course this implies that mining, metallurgy, and bit manufacturing, not to mention generations of experience with grinding materials and rotational manufacturing techniques, must have occurred long before the structures on the Giza plateau were erected.

Stone Saws

The ancient Egyptians also used stone saws. An example of this is at Giza, where blocks of basalt were cut to make paving stones. Evidence of the use of paving stones is visible on the east side of the Great Pyramid. Paving stones were placed on top of limestone blocks, which were prefit to the underlying bedrock. Apparently, the blocks were cut level after being placed on the ground. They are irregular in thickness, and sometimes rounded on the bottom side. A close-up view of an abandoned cut, where the worker began cutting in the wrong place, shows the cut is crisp and parallel to the edge (see fig. 4.2 on page 70). The quality of this incision requires that the blade be held steady while cutting occurs. Several other places exist where "over cuts" like this are visible. To the north of these over-cut blocks, there are several more with nearly identical cuts within thirty feet.

In yet another nearby area, there are long saw cuts through very hard rock. In most cases, the cuts are consistent, smooth, and parallel. There is no trace of "blade wobble," which happens when a long, hand-pulled saw begins to cut into a hard material. One possibility is that the blade was held firmly in place by the rock above it. The sarcophagus in the king's chamber of the Great Pyramid was cut with a very large saw, perhaps eight or nine feet long. Marks left from its use were discovered and described by

Photo courtesy of Christopher Dunn

Photo courtesy of Jon Bodsworth

Fig. 4.2. Top: stone blocks at Giza; bottom: closeup of saw marks

Petrie. He also described a perceptible error in cutting. The sawing was off the mark for several inches before the workers noticed and backed out the saw. A green stain in the sides of the cuts, as well as grains of sand left in grooves, indicate the saw blades were made from bronze.[4]

Petrie studied numerous examples of stonework. One of the more unusual items was his artifact No. 6, a slice of diorite bearing equally distant and regular grooves of circular arcs, parallel to one another. Although the grooves were nearly polished away by cross grinding, they are still slightly visible. According to Petrie, the only feasible explanation for this is that they were produced by a circular saw.

The cutting of hard materials by using a soft substance, such as copper, wood, and horn, with a hard powder applied to it, has been a common method throughout history. Powder sticks were used in this way to wear away stone when scraped over its surface. Many assumed that the Egyptians used this method out of necessity. Although this method sufficed for alabaster and other soft stones, Petrie argues that the early Egyptians did not use this technique with harder rock. He suggests that the cutting and shaping of hard rock

> such as granite, diorite, basalt, etc., was by means of bronze tools; these were set with cutting points, far harder than the quartz which was operated on. The material of these cutting points is yet undetermined; but only five substances are possible: beryl, topaz, chrysoberyl, corundum or sapphire, and diamond. The character of the work would certainly seem to point to diamond as being the cutting jewel; and only the considerations of its rarity in general, and its absence from Egypt, interfere with this conclusion, and render the tough uncrystallized corundum the more likely material.[5]

In his remarks concerning the mechanical methods of the Egyptians, Petrie concluded that they were acquainted with a cutting jewel far harder than quartz, and used this jewel as a sharp-pointed graver. From diorite bowls with fourth-dynasty inscriptions, fragments of which he found at Giza, as well as the scratches on polished granite of Ptolemaic age at San, Petrie had no doubt that the makers of these objects used complex saws and drills. Hieroglyphs were incised with a free-cutting point. They were not scraped or ground out, but plowed through with rough

Fig. 4.3. Petrie's artifact No. 6

edges to the line. The fact that some lines were only 1/150 inch wide is evidence that the cutting point must have been much harder than quartz and tough enough not to splinter with an edge only 1/200 inch in width. Petrie and his team did not hesitate to accept that the engraved lines that were cut in hard stone were accomplished by jewel-point tools.

Additionally, saw cuts in the surfaces of diorite, with grooves as deep as 1/100 inch, are far more likely to have been produced by fixed jewel points in a saw than by the friction of a loose powder. The deep grooves are almost always regular, uniform in depth, and equidistant. Though no jewel-tipped blades have yet been found, the saw cuts on these surfaces are almost irrefutable evidence that the Egyptians used jewel-tipped saws.

Eyes of the Pharaohs

Sophisticated techniques were not limited to stoneware. Other works of precision and artistic brilliance were also performed in preparation for funerals. Most everyone is familiar with the extravagant way in which the Egyptians entombed their dead with a bounty of goods for the afterlife. Grave goods also included statues, carved as lifelike representations of the people they honored. Some of these statues had truly remarkable eyes, fashioned in such a way that they seem to follow an onlooker as he or she walks in front of the statue. Examples of such statues, from the fourth and fifth dynasties (2575–2323 B.C.E.), are on display at the Louvre in Paris and the Egyptian Museum in Cairo.

One additional statue containing these unique stylized eyes, the Ka statue of King Auib-rê Hor, appeared in the thirteenth dynasty of the Middle Kingdom, around 1750 to 1700 B.C.E. Other statues were discovered in the mastabas of Sakkara. As did the production of unique stoneware, the manufacture of these magical eyes disappeared from Egyptian civilization after the thirteenth dynasty.[6]

During the late 1990s, Jay Enoch, from the School of Optometry at the University of California at Berkeley, and Vasudevan Lakshminarayanan from the School of Optometry at the University of Missouri at St. Louis re-created the optical attributes of these "eyes of the pharaoh" in order to better understand their unique properties. For comparison, and to gauge the success of their work, they took photographs of the "seated scribe," a statue discovered at Sakkara and dated to 2475 B.C.E. on display at the Louvre.

Fig. 4.4. The "seated scribe"— from a fifth dynasty tomb at Sakkara

Fig. 4.5. Statue of fourth dynasty prince Rahotep exhibits typically stylized eyes

Photo courtesy of Jon Bodsworth

Photo courtesy of Jon Bodsworth

Enoch and Lakshminarayanan observed that the front area of the eye was composed of a very hard form of quartz crystal fashioned into a flat cornea of fine optical quality. The iris was painted to resemble the living human iris. In the center, at the rear of the cornea lens, a small, concave curve was either drilled or ground to match the pupil aperture of the human eye. It formed a concave lens of high negative refractive power. The front surfaces of the cornea had considerable positive refractive power, but much weaker than the rear element. A resin was used to attach the lens element to the white part of the eye. The rear of the cornea lens had two optical zones. One was peripheral and flat, the other, a distinct negative curve. Both were centered on each other. These were centered on the front area of the cornea's surface, which had a convex or positive curve, possibly in order to form a multifocal element.

Using a stack of washers placed on white paper, Enoch and Lakshminarayanan created a model simulating the front part of the eyes. Above the washers a twenty-diopter spherical lens was placed three quarters of an inch above the hole. Another three quarters of an inch above this, a larger (twenty-six diopter) spherical lens was suspended. The distances from the plane of the washers to each lens were less than the focal length of either of the two lens elements. So, if an observer rotated forty degrees to sixty degrees in any direction about either lens, the holes (pupils) appeared to move with the observer. In this way, Enoch and Lakshminarayanan created a model simulating the magical eyes of the pharaohs.[7]

In their model, they observed that foreshortening in the meridian of rotation about the washer's hole (the eye's pupil) was greatest when viewed through the more powerful concave lens. In other words, if one moves to the side, the aperture becomes more elliptical in appearance, with the observed width of the hole decreasing in the direction of increasing rotation. They also discovered that this effect was not noticed perpendicular to the direction of rotation by the observer—a well-known cosine effect. According to Enoch and Lakshminarayanan, the same foreshortening effect is readily observed and photographed in the Egyptian statues.

According to their results, both the front and rear surfaces of the Egyptian lenses contribute to the perceived movement of the pupil as the observer rotates about the statue. Furthermore, the movement will be in the same direction. In this way, the pupil appears to move with the observer and becomes progressively foreshortened in the direction of the observer's movement. As it is in the Egyptian statues, the perceived motion caused by the rear element is most significant and different from the normal prismatic qualities of lenses. The combined effect of the two lenses is greater than that of either lens alone.

Enoch and Lakshminarayanan concluded that this optical "following" effect of the statue's eyes was duplicated in the laboratory and was recorded, although not well displayed, in their photographs. (These effects, easily seen by the observer, were difficult to photograph.) Amazingly, the ancient Egyptian lenses were of better quality than the duplications. In their final analysis, Enoch and Lakshminarayanan conclude that because of the performance quality and design complexity, it is highly doubtful that the lenses used to re-create eye structures in ancient Egyptian statues were the first lenses created, despite the fact that they are forty-six hundred years old.[8]

An Expert Machinist's Deposition

Those of us who are not engineers or machinists can only imagine the difficulty and skill in planning and constructing the precision-built items previously described. Christopher Dunn, a senior manager at Danville Metal Stamping in Illinois, has been involved with construction and manufacturing techniques for almost thirty years and is well qualified to comment on the difficulties of precision. Most of his career has been spent working with machinery that manufactures precision parts for jet engines, and has included nonconventional methods such as laser processing and electrical discharge machining. He is not an Egyptologist, archaeologist, or historian, yet is fascinated by the evidence left behind by the Egyptians. He has visited Egypt several times, studied many of the perplexing artifacts, and come to his own conclusion that an advanced system of manufacturing existed in early Egypt. According to Dunn, there is evidence of other nonconventional machining methods, as well as more sophisticated conventional sawing, lathe, and milling practices. "Undoubtedly," Dunn says, "some of the artifacts that Petrie was studying were produced using lathes."[9] There is also evidence of clearly defined lathe tool marks on some sarcophagus (stone coffin) lids.

Dunn believes that the Great Pyramid leads a long list of artifacts that have been misunderstood and misinterpreted over the years by archaeologists. They have promoted theories and methods based on a collection of tools from which they struggle to replicate even the simplest aspects of Egyptian work. According to Dunn, the Cairo Museum contains enough evidence, once properly analyzed, to prove that the ancient Egyptians used highly sophisticated manufacturing methods, in spite of the fact that these tools have not yet been found. The museum's Old Kingdom (2650–2152 B.C.E.) collection is full of vases, bowls, large lidded boxes, and statues—carved from schist, diorite, granite, and obsidian—that defy simple answers as to how ancient sculptors carved this hard igneous rock with such precision. For generations, the focus has centered on the nature of the cutting tools used. However, while he was in Egypt in February 1995, Dunn discovered evidence that raises this question: "What guided the cutting tool?"[10]

The lathe is the father of all machine tools in existence. As discussed above, Petrie discovered evidence showing not only that lathes were used, but also that they performed tasks considered impossible without highly specialized techniques, such as cutting concave and convex spherical radii without splintering the material.

According to traditional theory, the ancient Egyptians used hardened copper tools in quarrying and carving. Having worked with copper on numerous occasions, including the hardened variety, Dunn found this idea ridiculous. Certainly, copper can be hardened by striking it repeatedly or even by bending it. However, after a specific hardness has been reached, the copper begins to split and break apart. This is why, when working with copper, it has to be periodically annealed, or softened, to keep it in one piece. However, despite the strength of the hardened copper, it will not cut granite. The hardest copper alloy in existence today is beryllium copper. There is no evidence to suggest that the ancient Egyptians possessed it. If they did, it is still not hard enough to cut granite. According to traditional historians, copper was the only metal available at the time the Great Pyramid was built. Consequently, it would follow that all work sprang from the ability to use this basic metal. Dunn believes there is more to the metal story, that it may be an incorrect assumption to think that copper was the only metal available to the ancient Egyptians. A little-known fact about the pyramid builders is that they were iron makers as well. According to Ian Lawton and Chris Ogilvie-Herald's *Giza: The Truth,* in 1837, during the Howard Vyse excavations, an iron plate twelve by four inches and an eighth inch thick was discovered embedded in cement in one of the shafts leading into the king's chamber. The iron plate was embedded so deep in the masonry that it had to be removed by blasting the outer two tiers of stones. Upon removal, it was forwarded to the British Museum along with certificates of authenticity.

Primitive tools discovered through archaeological excavation are considered contemporaneous with the artifacts of the same period. Yet during this period in Egyptian history, these artifacts were produced in prolific numbers with no tools surviving to explain their creation. According to Dunn, the tools found cannot be explained in simple terms and do not fully represent the "state of the art" evident in the artifacts. The tools displayed by Egyptologists as instruments for the creation of many of these incredible artifacts are physically incapable of reproducing them. After viewing these engineering marvels, and then being shown a trivial collection of copper tools at the Cairo Museum, Dunn is bemused and frustrated.[11]

Granite Boxes of the Serapeum

To the northwest of Djoser's step pyramid at Sakkara there is a gallery of tombs built into tunneled rock dedicated to the Apis bull. The Greek geographer Strabo (63 B.C.E.–22 C.E.) wrote, after visiting Egypt, that the apis bulls were buried in an underground chamber, called the Serapeum, at the end of a paved avenue flanked by 140 stone sphinxes.

Fig. 4.6. Serapeum stone box

Photo courtesy of Christopher Dunn

The site is constantly being buried by windblown sand and was difficult to visit even during Strabo's time. For centuries, these tombs were lost; then in 1850, the twenty-nine-year-old Frenchman Auguste Mariette found the head and paws of a stone sphinx jutting from the sand.

Inside the Serapeum, chambers with ceilings nearly twenty-five feet high and floors five feet lower than the main floor were carved into both sides of a main corridor. These open rooms are where the massive stone sarcophagi for the Apis bulls once stood. Each sarcophagus was carved from a single block of granite, and each lid weighed many tons. Several sarcophagi still exist within the Serapeum today.

In 1995 Dunn, armed with a six-inch precision straightedge, inspected the interior and exterior surfaces of two sarcophagi. The twenty-seven-ton lid of one the sarcophagi, and the inside surface of the granite box on which it sat, was precisely square to .00005 inch— 5/100,000 of an inch. He also verified that its corners were precise to 5/32 of an inch.[12] According to Dunn, replicating the precision of the granite boxes in the Serapeum would be extremely difficult even today. The smooth, perfectly flat surfaces and the tight, perfectly square corners left him in awe. The granite box found in the Great Pyramid has the same characteristics as the boxes in the Serapeum. Yet these boxes are assigned to Egypt's eighteenth dynasty, over a thousand years after Egyptian stoneworking was supposed to be in decline. Since their dating is based on pottery found nearby and not on the boxes themselves, Dunn believes it is reasonable to speculate that the boxes are not correctly dated. Their stonework has left marks of careful and remarkable manufacturing methods. It is unmistakable and irrefutable. He believes that the artifacts he measured in Egypt "are the smoking gun that proves, without a shadow of a doubt, that a higher civilization than what we have been taught existed in ancient Egypt. The evidence is cut into the stone."[13]

Theory and Evidence

Petrie's analysis of ancient Egyptian stoneworking techniques over a hundred years ago, and Dunn's most recently, offers an explanation of how the ancient Egyptians crafted stone in building their temples, pyramids, and other objects. Tube drills, saws, jewelry bits, and the machinery to hold them steady and apply rotational torque gave them the means to accomplish such feats. They also had lathes, which could turn and polish granite, schist, and basalt, and the means to cut accurate parallel limestone joints with remarkable flatness over large surface areas, apparently a mastered technique before the casing of the Great Pyramid. More mysteriously, they had the knowledge and technology to lift, maneuver, and delicately place enormous blocks of stone weighing many tons, as well as the means to quarry and move millions of blocks over a long period of time.

In order to accomplish this, they also had to be well organized and motivated and possess administrative skill and wealth. The Giza development was an enormous, multigenerational public project, which was the largest, most ambitious, and longest-term construction program in the history of mankind. The massive project included all facets of civil engineering, architecture, surveying, personnel, and materials management. There also would have had to be a leadership so effective that the undertaking of such an immense program, and all the personal sacrifices required, would have been possible to sustain.

The perpetual question for many people, myself included, has been whether or not the Egyptians had help during the infancy of their civilization. Traditional Egyptologists claim that they did not, that primitive tribes, under the increasing sands and hostility of the Sahara Desert, moved to the Nile Valley, organized themselves, and invented all the tools, techniques, and philosophies of Egyptian civilization. Yet it seems unlikely that primitive tribes could do so much in the span of a thousand years. Nevertheless, without any other indications of sophisticated knowledge, this inventionist approach to Egyptian civilization has endured. However, there is an unusual archaeological site a hundred miles west of the Nile—Nabta Playa—with evidence that profoundly challenges this conclusion.

Prehistoric Astronomy in the Sahara

The Western Sahara was uninhabitable during the latter part of the ice age (ten thousand to twenty thousand years ago). But as the ice melted, climatic changes brought renewed life to this arid land. Summer rains moved out of the central part of the continent and into Egypt. As a result, numerous seasonal lakes, or playas, were formed. One such lake, known as Nabta, one of the largest in southern Egypt, became the focal point of an unknown culture beginning ten thousand years ago. Pastoralists, along with their cattle, entered the Nabta area during the summer looking for plush pastures. Living the life of nomads, they moved away in the winter but returned to Nabta the next summer.

In 1973, while traveling through the Western Desert from Bir Sahara east to Abul Simbel, archaeologists Fred Wendorf and Romauld Schild decided to stop for a rest. A hundred kilometers west of the Nile Valley, they discovered a large ancient lake basin with hundreds of Stone Age camps. Among the finds were grave mounds that included offerings of butchered cattle, goats, and sheep, as well as groups of megalithic structures and alignments of upright stones. Because of the obvious nature of these tumuli, or ancient burial mounds, they named the basin Valley of the Sacrifices. Yet the significance of these megaliths would not be recognized for nearly twenty years. In 1992, Wendorf and Schild began to realize that the Nabta megaliths and stelae (upright stone slabs typically used as grave markers) played a role in the spiritual and religious life of those inhabiting Egypt's southwestern desert so long ago.

Six groups of stones, extending across the ancient basin, contained a total of twenty-four megaliths. Like the spokes on a wheel, each alignment radiates outward from a unique, complex structure. Astonishingly, these megaliths span twenty-five hundred meters in a north–south direction. In the north, there are ten preserved burial mounds made from broken sandstone blocks along the west bank of a shallow wadi. This northern group of megaliths ends in a small stone circle atop a rounded hill. This stone circle has been identified as a calendar. It contains two lines of stone sights consisting of pairs of narrow, upright slabs positioned to the north where the sun rose at the summer solstice, which was the beginning of the rainy season six thousand years ago.

According to Wendorf and Schild, this astronomical date—the summer solstice, 4000 B.C.E.—corresponds to the time the device was last used. The dates and archaeological artifacts attributed to the site indi-

Photo courtesy of Jimmy Dunn

Fig. 4.7. Calendar circle at Nabta Playa

cate that the Ru'at El Baqar people, Stone Age cattle herders who lived in the region seven thousand years ago, erected the Valley of Sacrifices burial mounds. In Africa, it is the earliest known ceremonial center that marks the beginning of complex societies.[14]

South of the valley there is a low, elongated hill with two smaller parallel rises. On the northernmost hill, a six-hundred-meter alignment of once upright sandstone megaliths, some of which weighed several tons, now appears as a cluster of broken rocks. University of Colorado astronomy professor John McKim Malville established that the line of megaliths was actually composed of three sublines aimed at the point where the brightest star of the Big Dipper, Ursa Majoris, rose between 6,700 and 6,000 years ago. In the area south of the first line, several other lines of upright stones have been recognized and mapped. The first is a 250-meter-long double alignment of stone blocks aiming at the point where the brightest stars in Orion's belt rose between 6,170 and 5,800 years ago. The second line of stones is slightly shorter and stands a bit farther away from the other two. It points to the position of Sirius, Canis Majoris, 6,800 years ago.[15]

Past the long alignment of stones are two more sets of clusters, composed of whole and broken sandstone blocks in various sizes. Some weigh several tons. They are placed over two flat clay rises. At the south end of the largest set is a large sandstone quarry where the blocks were extracted from the ground.

Photo courtesy of Jimmy Dunn

Fig. 4.8. Complex Structure A, the "sculptured cow"

Originally, Wendorf and Schild believed they had found gigantic, undisturbed tombs. However, a few years later, they opened three of the alleged graves and found almost nothing. Interestingly, all three revealed enormous pits excavated in the clay below. This led to the discovery of a mushroom-shaped sandstone rock formed by the desert winds long before the clay sediments were deposited. The rock was slightly sculpted to form a mysterious crude protrusion on its northern side. Afterward, the pit was filled with its original clay. A piece of charcoal from one of the pits was radiocarbon-dated to five thousand six hundred years old.[16]

Centered upon a small hill, the largest group of megaliths contained what Wendorf and Schild call a "treasure."[17] A large sandstone block weighing more than a ton was slightly shaped and polished. Its general form very loosely resembles a cow. This unusual central structure, designated Complex Structure A, seems to form the starting point of the alignments, with its long axis pointing to the north. They found this "sculpted cow" buried six feet below the ground and blocked in place by two smaller slabs. In 1997 Wendorf and Schild used theodolite and differential Global Positioning System measurements to map the megaliths. They also discovered two more megalithic alignments that radiated from the vicinity of Structure A.[18]

A twelve-foot-diameter circle of small standing slabs contained four sets of uprights, which may have been used for sight-lines along the horizon. They estimate that the azimuth for the first rays of the summer solstice sun six thousand years ago would have been 63.2 degrees. This means the sun would have risen through the slots created by the circle's upright stones. Furthermore, because of Nabta's proximity to the Tropic of Cancer, the rising sun may have had additional importance. About three weeks before and after the summer solstice, the sun crosses the zenith and casts no shadows, often regarded as a significant event.[19]

Wendorf and Schild concluded that the symbolic richness and spatial awareness seen in the Nabta complex may have developed from an adaptation by nomadic peoples to the stresses of life in the harsh desert environment. The ceremonial complex must be at least as old as the beginning of extremely arid conditions four thousand eight hundred years ago. This places Nabta's construction before most of the megalithic sites in Great Britain, Brittany, and elsewhere in Europe. Within five hundred years or so after the abandonment of the Nabta Playa region by the people who erected the megaliths, the Sakkara step pyramid was built (approximately 2650 B.C.E.). Wendorf and Schild believe that the exodus, five thousand years ago, from Nabta Playa and the Nubian Desert could have hastened the development of predynastic Egyptian culture. When these nomadic groups arrived in the Nile Valley, they were better organized than the valley natives and possessed a more complex cosmology than the inhabitants they encountered.[20]

Some scholars believe Wendorf is forcing a pattern onto the stones without sufficient evidence and argue that the site needs further study. They claim that while Wendorf's ideas are interesting, they are lacking a cultural context, and should be kept at the level of speculation. Other sites in the Eastern Desert, such as El Badari, that also date from the period around 5000 B.C.E. contain no megalithic structures with alignments. The Nabta Playa stone complex is an anomaly and a mystery. However, in the late 1990s, an astrophysicist from the University of Colorado decided to investigate further.

A "User-Friendly" Star-Viewing Diagram

The ongoing research and breaking story of Nabta Playa was front-page news within the scientific community and attracted the interest of Dr. Thomas G. Brophy, a former research associate at the Laboratory for Atmospheric and Space Physics at the University of Colorado and a veteran of the U.S. and Japanese space programs, including the NASA Voyager project. Brophy corresponded with Dr. Wendorf and visited Nabta Playa to investigate it firsthand. In 2002, he published his conclusions in a book titled *The Origin Map*.

To properly grasp the significance of his findings requires a basic understanding of the phenomenon known as precession of the equinoxes. Over a period of approximately 25,900 years, the Earth's axis of rotation varies between an angle of 20.4 degrees and 26.2 degrees. This slow change in the angle of the Earth's axis causes the apparent position of the stars to change over time. Today, Polaris is referred to as the North Star because it remains stationary above the North Pole, and all other stars appear to move around the Earth. In 3000 B.C.E., the North Star was Thuban, and two thousand years from now it will be Alrai.

This slow change in the angle of the Earth's axis also causes the constellations of the zodiac to change their position in the night sky relative to the vernal (spring) equinox. Known as precession, this phenomenon causes the zodiac constellations to appear to be moving backward as the arrow of time proceeds forward, moving to the next constellation approximately every 2,150 years. In our time, each April twenty-first

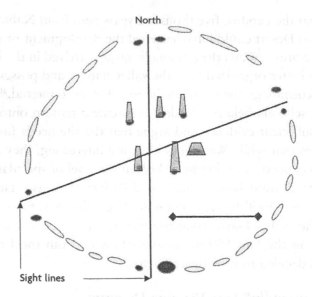

*Fig. 4.9. Calendar circle megaliths
(from Thomas Brophy,* The Origin Map)

the sun rises into the constellation of Pisces. Within a few hundred years it will rise on that date into the constellation of Aquarius. Before the Common Era, between 2000 B.C.E. and 1 C.E., the sun rose on the twenty-first of April into the constellation of Aries. After 25,900 years, each zodiac constellation will have had its turn positioned in the eastern sky as the sun rises on the equinox.

What Brophy discovered was that the calendar circle at Nabta Playa was more than a calendar (see figure 4.9). It was also a star-viewing diagram. Three of the six stones in the center of the circle diagramed the stars of Orion's belt as it appeared on the meridian at the summer solstice between 6400 and 4900 B.C.E. In other words, if a person stood at the north end of the meridian sight line and looked down on the stone diagram, he or she would see a representation of Orion's belt as it appeared in the sky just before sunrise.[21] During the year 6400 B.C.E., Orion's belt moved along the meridian fifty minutes before the summer solstice sunrise, then faded into the predawn twilight—the first and only time this occurred precisely on the summer solstice at Nabta Playa. However, after 4900 B.C.E., the constellation of Orion appeared in the sky on the meridian at sunset, ending the applicability of the stone diagram.

In precise terms, the heliacal culmination at the summer solstice in

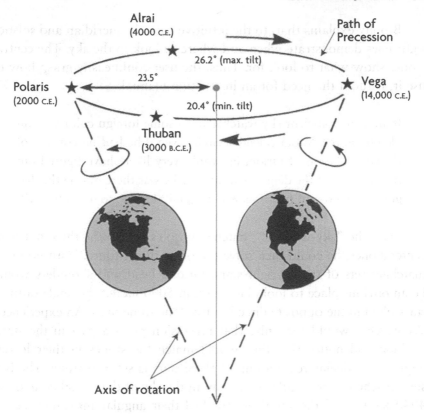

Fig. 4.10. Precession of the equinoxes
(courtesy of Dorothy Norton)

6400 B.C.E. marked the beginning of the diagram's relevance and the achronal culmination at the winter solstice in 4900 B.C.E., its end. In other words, it was a valid point of reference at Orion's first appearance of the year, just before sunrise, when the constellation was at its highest altitude and passed the meridian—the *heliacal culmination*. Its relevance ended when its last appearance of the year was after sunset—the *achronal culmination*.[22]

The other three stones chart Orion's head and shoulders as they appeared on the summer solstice meridian, at sunset, during the years around 16,500 B.C.E.—symmetrically opposite Orion's belt stars in 5000 B.C. According to Brophy, both dates are the maximum and minimum of Orion's tilt angle in the sky. In other words, the stone diagram depicts the time, location, and tilting behavior of the constellation of Orion through its celestial cycle. More important, it illustrates how to visually understand the pattern of stones.[23]

Brophy explains that, to the intuitive user, the meridian and solstice sight lines demonstrate when and where to look in the sky. The central stones show what to look for. Thus, the user could easily grasp how to use it, without the need for an instruction manual.

> If an astute, ancient sky-watcher from some foreign culture stumbled upon the Nabta calendar circle, even if he had no concept of the constellation of Orion, he would very likely have figured out the meaning of the diagram, as long as he was there during the diagram's window of functionality from 6400 B.C.E. to 4900 B.C.E.[24]

Once the "sky-watcher" matched Orion's belt to the three northern center stones, he could then solve the other three stones. With no other matching sets of three bright stars, Orion's head and shoulders would be an obvious place to look. However, in 5000 B.C.E., the angle of these stars tilted in the opposite direction from the stone map. An experienced sky-watcher would recognize that precession plays a part in the stars' position and notice that they would match the stones in their lowest angle. A particular relationship of these stars is set into stone. The belt stars reached their angular minimum in the sky at the vernal equinox in 4940 B.C.E., and the shoulders reached their angular maximum at the autumn equinox in 16,500 B.C.E. As Brophy explains, this is represented by the stone map:

> Thus with winter solstice heliacal culmination and summer solstice achronal culmination, the head and shoulders diagram in the stones is the converse of the Orion's belt diagram, and both are congruent with the solstice and meridian sight lines in the stone calendar circle.[25]

Brophy also points out that the largest stone of the circle represents the brightest star in the Orion constellation, Betelgeuse.

In 16,500 B.C.E., the star diagram was equally a user-friendly design mirroring the image visible in 5000 B.C.E. But how could someone living in the year 5000 B.C.E., without the aid of a modern computer to simulate the sky in 16,500 B.C.E., possibly figure out this half of the diagram?

One possibility is that since these early residents of Nabta Playa built precise, long-distance megalith alignments to rising stars, they knew that

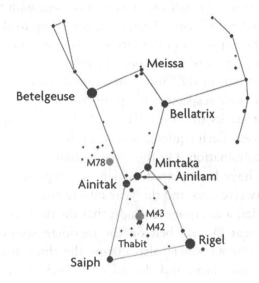

Fig. 4.11. Stars of the constellation Orion

a star's rising position in the sky changed over time. Since they had the ability to mark east to within 0.02 degree, it is reasonable to conclude that they were aware of precession, even with the naked eye.[26] Although the positions of stars change very slowly over time, this stellar precession is observable within the span of a human life. However difficult, it would not have been impossible for them to deduce the maximum tilt as it is represented in the stones. Fred Wendorf and others have argued the importance of the solar zenith, that the ancients tracked the sunrise angle throughout the year as indicated in the stone circle. With that knowledge, it is not much of a stretch to assume they were able to conceptualize the long-term tilting of Orion from the sunrise solstices in summer to winter. Another possibility is that astronomical observations were passed from generation to generation through cultural tradition. As a result, later peoples could have designed the calendar circle in 5000 B.C.E. and built into their model a knowledge of precession gained over centuries.[27]

The eastern half of the outer circle of the stone calendar is a semicircle but the western half is not. Instead, it appears to be adjusted and scaled to fit the Orion congruencies. In 4940 B.C.E., Orion's right shoulder would be on the edge of the solstice sight-line window. At that time, Orion would be in the middle of its ascent to a northern culmination. Conceptually increased, it would match the size of the figure on the ground. Likewise, in 16,500 B.C.E., it would be halfway down its descent with the ground figure size conceptually decreased. Therefore, according to Brophy, it is possible that the different scales of the Orion figure have meaning.

A corroborating aspect of this interpretation is that the location of each three-stone set within the circle corresponds to their stars' altitude in the sky on their respective diagram-matching dates. Another possibility is that it marks the constellation at its extremes, the spring and autumn equinoxes. Each equinox is halfway between a star's northern and southern culmination. On the circular half of the stone structure, twelve stones have been placed, which may represent a partition of the zodiac into twelve ages and the year into twelve months.[28]

Brophy concludes, and argues strongly, that the three northernmost center stones represent Orion's belt on the meridian solstice between 6400 B.C.E. and 4900 B.C.E. He also claims the three southernmost stones represent Orion's head and shoulders in 16,500 B.C.E., despite the fact that this idea is troubling to some scholars. The lack of evidence for human activity at Nabta Playa in 16,500 B.C.E. requires that the megalithic circle not be that old.

If that is not strange enough, there is an even stranger coincidence in Brophy's analysis. At the previous time, when Orion's belt was at its descending equinox, Earth's axis was near a minimum obliquity, close to 22.5 degrees. This, in fact, is the latitude of Nabta Playa in the year 31,330 B.C.E., according to Berger's celestial pole model. At this time, Orion's belt also matched the stone diagram, congruent on the meridian fifteen minutes before summer solstice sunrise. Brophy does not claim the Nabta Playa megaliths to be that old, but the strange coincidence of the diagram repeating, and being accurate at an even older age, can add to our appreciation of the stone calendar and may contribute to our understanding of its design and use as we gather more data.[29]

In a 1998 investigation, Wendorf and Schild reported that other evidence suggests very ancient activity at Nabta Playa. For some unknown reason, the inhabitants were able to locate and excavate "table rocks" more than six feet below the surface, which would have been visible only in the remote past, before being covered by sediments. It is also possible that these buried rocks were somehow previously marked in a way similar to how they were marked in 5000 B.C.E. According to Brophy, whether or not the stone diagram at Nabta Playa is the earliest astronomically aligned stone circle, it is one of the most elegantly and artfully designed. Furthermore, in his opinion as an astrophysicist, "the design of this star diagram in the calendar circle stones is wonderfully simple and clear."[30] But what is unique about Nabta Playa—what most other megalithic alignments fall short in—is that it represents more than one coordinate.

A simple megalith alignment typically represents one coordinate in the sky. As a result, at any given time several stars will rise near the alignment marker. So, when hundreds or thousands of years separate us from the date the megalith was erected, several bright stars will have passed a given declination as they proceed through the sky. This brings into doubt the validity of a proposed alignment. It is for this reason that simple stellar alignments have been considered uncertain in rigorous archaeoastronomy.

The addition of a second coordinate, the right ascension at spring equinox heliacal rising, removes this uncertainty at Nabta Playa and allows for a very accurate two-dimensional star map. According to Brophy, that is precisely what the Nabta megalithic complex is. Additionally, each star alignment is marked with a simultaneous alignment to a northerly marker star, Vega. It was a logical star to use, as it was the brightest star in the north.[31]

A Star Chart in Three Dimensions

Another set of upright stones was placed five hundred meters south of the calendar circle. With the accuracy of the Nabta star chart, Brophy wondered if the ancient astronomers had left behind even more information to decipher. However, since the three upright stones were such long and nonuniform distances from the calendar stones, their role in the map was not so obvious. He first considered that the distances represented the brightness of Orion's stars. However, Betelgeuse is brighter than the belt stars, as well as Bellatrix, which is nearly the same brightness as Ainilam. Thus, visual brightness did not fit. The next logical step would be to verify if the distances on the ground represented the actual distance in space, from Earth to the stars. This was unlikely, but just for fun Brophy looked up the astrophysical distances from Earth to these stars, using data from the Hipparcos Space Astronomy satellite. Brophy found that one of the stars did match the megalith pattern. In this case, one meter was equivalent to 0.799 light-year.[32]

According to the Hipparcos tables, if the distance between the standing stones and the calendar circle represents the distance between Orion's various stars and Earth, the stone corresponding to the star Meissa should have been placed farther out. However, the head of

Orion—actually a number of stars—is what the megalith alignments signify, and not necessarily the star Meissa. The Ainilam megalith is too far out, according to Hipparcos measurement, but it is also the most uncertain. Its actual distance from Earth has been narrowed only to within a large range.

Brophy replotted the distances with Ainilam, Ainitak, and Mintaka at one standard error from their measured values. Using the errors quoted by Hipparcos, all three stars were within a standard error of their corresponding megaliths! "This is more than astonishing," Brophy writes, "since star distances are difficult to measure and have been erroneous until recently."[33] If the distances are not a coincidence, and if representing these distances was the intention of the Nabta megalith builders, then much of our understanding of prehistoric civilization needs to be reconsidered.

According to Brophy, if the southern megaliths represent distance, it was likely that the northern megaliths represent the speed at which the stars are moving away from Earth (called radial velocity)—if the builders were thinking like astrophysicists. They were. According to Brophy's calculations, one meter at Nabta represents 0.0290 km/sec. The velocities at which Betelgeuse and Bellatrix are moving away from Earth are just right for their respective megaliths, and Ainilam is correct to within 2 km/sec. Although the stars Ainitak and Mintaka are moving too slowly for their megalith markers, radial velocity measurements for these stars are considered uncertain, with no standard error estimate for Ainitak.[34]

The velocity at which Vega is moving away from Earth does not match its megalith marker (the distance is too short), but the distance is within a standard error of Vega's radial velocity. However, this star is a special case because it is actually moving *toward* Earth, and on the autumn equinox, it may be consistent with the other markers. According to Brophy, this is yet a further level of significance of the megalithic map. It corroborates that the northern megalith placements do, in fact, indicate velocities.

A Planetary Systems Map?

Brophy continued looking at the site and noticed that each alignment had a primary stone, probably representing the primary star, plus secondary stones. The obvious question he considered, given the arrangement of stones, was whether the other megaliths in each line represented planets or companion stars. Although the hypothesis is not

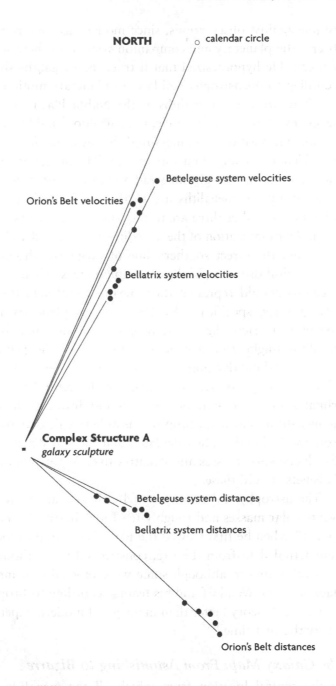

NORTH ○ calendar circle

● Betelgeuse system velocities

Orion's Belt velocities ●●

Bellatrix system velocities

Complex Structure A
galaxy sculpture

Betelgeuse system distances

Bellatrix system distances

Orion's Belt distances

*Fig. 4.12. Overhead view of Nabta Playa megaliths
(from Thomas Brophy and Paul Rosen, "Satellite imagery measures of the
astronomically aligned megaliths at Nabta Playa")*

testable against observations, since modern astronomers are unable to observe the planetary and companion systems of these stars, the physics of it can. He hypothesized that if true, the megaliths should be placed according to the astrophysical laws of planetary motion.

There are many megaliths at the Nabta Playa site. In addition to the stones of the calendar circle, Fred Wendorf and his team determined the original positions and measured the locations for twenty-three others, which are arranged into six groups. The designers of the site placed upright stones in straight lines radiating outward from a central point. Three groups of megaliths are to the north-northeast of this central point and the other three are to the south-southeast (see figure 4.9).

If the organization of the megaliths represented a planetary systems map, then the direct southern line of megaliths should represent the mean orbital distances of the companion stars. Their northern velocity megaliths should represent their mean orbital velocities. By applying some physics, specifically Kepler's laws of planetary motion, to the megaliths in each alignment, Brophy demonstrated that the satellite megaliths might represent actual satellites of the primary stars. The physics of orbital dynamics provides that the square of the mean orbital velocity is proportional to the mass of the central star divided by the orbital distance. So with the velocities and distances already available in the megalithic star map, Brophy was able to calculate the stars' masses. From the Nabta data, he calculated that the star Betelgeuse had a value of eighteen solar masses and Bellatrix five. As the other data confirmed his beliefs, so did these.

The astrophysical estimates of Betelgeuse are between twelve and twenty solar masses and roughly ten for Bellatrix. Brophy was "nearly floored" when he first viewed the plot. The megalith location markers were actual data from the site, constructed seven thousand years ago or possibly longer, although some were repositioned into their correct placements by Wendorf and his team. According to Brophy, "[T]hey fit the physical theory better than many good modern experiments fit their theory the first time."[35]

The Galaxy Map: From Astonishing to Bizarre

At the central location from which all the megaliths radiate, there is a "complex structure" that itself consists of several megaliths. A single upright marks the center, while several others form an oval a few meters across. There are at least thirty other similar megalithic constructions in the vicinity. Archaeologists were unable to develop a clear definition of what these structures were, so they simply refer to them as "complex structures" with the central one named Complex Structure A.

At first, these structures were believed to be the graves of elite chieftains, but excavations of structures A and B provided no remains, human or animal, or grave goods of any kind. What the excavation team did find was bizarre. The surface complex structures marked sculptures carved onto the bedrock eight to twelve feet below the surface.[36]

Brophy examined the original sketch of the bedrock sculpture under Complex Structure A, drawn by Marek Puszkarski, and the sketch from Schild and Krolik's *The Holocene Settlement of the Egyptian Sahara;* he found that the coordinates of Complex Structure A marked the central point of all megalith alignments.[37] Over this map, he superimposed the location of the sun and the galactic center correlated to the direction of the spring equinox's heliacal rising of the galactic center in 17,700 B.C.E. Again, it was a match:

> Astonishing as it may be, the bedrock sculpture underneath "Complex Structure A" at Nabta Playa appears to be an accurate depiction of our Milky Way Galaxy, as it was oriented astronomically at a specific time: vernal equinox heliacal rising of the Galactic Center in 17,700 B.C.E.[38]

A galactic center is the central region of a galaxy characterized by high densities of stars and, according to some astronomers, may contain a super-massive black hole. The Milky Way's galactic center is not visible to the naked eye at this time, but may have been, ages ago, because of bursts of particles and electromagnetic radiation. According to Paul LaViolette in *Earth Under Fire,* a major galactic core outburst occurred sixteen thousand years ago, with visible effects spanning several thousand years.

A recently discovered small galaxy called the Sagittarius Dwarf galaxy is a satellite to our own Milky Way. According to Brophy, it quite possibly is represented in the correct place on the sculpture, as are the Milky Way's galactic spiral arms. Brophy also claims that recent astrophysical analysis of the shape and location of this dwarf galaxy indicates that it is a better fit with the Nabta sculpture than the Electronic Sky drawing published in *Monthly Notices of the Royal Astronomical Society.*[39]

Archaeologists also excavated Complex Structure B, forty-five meters southeast of Complex Structure A, and were again disappointed to find no remains or grave goods. What they found was a large, oddly shaped, tilted, lumpy, oval sculpture cut directly onto the bedrock. It was almost twice as big as the Milky Way galaxy sculpture under Complex Structure A. According to Brophy, it is likely a sculpture of the Andromeda galaxy, our nearest galaxy.

The Andromeda galaxy is a large elliptical galaxy twice as big as our own. Together with our galaxy, it is the dominant member of the local group of smaller galaxies. It was created with the same scale as the Milky Way galaxy sculpture.

According to Brophy, the distance and direction to the Andromeda galaxy sculpture appears consistent with the coordinate system defined by the vertical notches cut into the Milky Way galaxy sculpture. Based on the available drawings of the sculpture, its plane appears consistent with the Milky Way galaxy plane, as it was on the spring equinox sunrise for the northern culmination of the galactic center in 10,909 B.C.E. It also appears consistent with a projection from a coordinate system rotated 90 degrees within that plane.

He also believes that the sculpted stone could be a representation of the cosmological "big bang" representing the age of our solar system (six billion years). The distance from the sun's position to the edge of the sculpture is six billion light-years, according to scale. Another possibility is that the creators of the map intended the sculpture's diameter of curvature to represent the current age of the universe, which is twelve billion years. A third possibility is that it represents a current universe age of six billion years, which would mean our models are in error by a factor of two. Whatever the case, the cosmological significance of the sculpture is further corroborated.

Brophy also believes the stone may represent a declination window for the galactic center as viewed from Nabta Playa, looking to the east and up: "Except for the angular protrusion on one corner, the four curved, angle cornered sides may match a shape defined by two lines of declination on the sides, and on the top and bottom by two lines of right ascension."[40]

So the shape of the sculpture, as it was placed facing outward from the sun's location on the galaxy sculpture, forms a "declination window" for the galactic center. It appears to have been carefully oriented so that this declination window subtends the full range of motion of the declinations of the galactic center. In other words, the sculpture marks the apparent motion of the galactic center throughout the full 25,900-year precession cycle. A line from the sun's representation to the actual galactic center passes though the window for a period of about three hours every day, starting forty minutes or so after its rise above the horizon.

Further confirmation of cosmological significance appears to be the orientation of the angular protrusion on the "cow stone" (Complex Structure A). It was placed so that the protrusion pointed in the direction of what astrophysicists call the "least velocity direction of the cosmic background radiation dipole." This would occur at the spring equinox heliacal rising of the galactic center in 17,700 B.C.E. In other words, it pointed in the direction, cosmologically, from which we came. Conceptually it can be interpreted as pointing toward the big bang of creation.

Brophy also puts forth the idea that the cosmological cow sculpture, being very close to one Planck length thick, doubles as a Planck-scale sculpture. (The *Planck length* is a fundamental length in physics and a constant of nature, and is derived from Planck's constant, the universal gravitation constant, and the speed of light. It is a size smaller than that which all known physics breaks down.) By applying the scaling law built into the Nabta megalith design, the inverse natural log of the prime number seventy-nine produces a scale that could represent only objects much larger than the known universe. But by reversing the scale so that the relationship is micro to macrocosm, extremely small things can be represented—0.505 meter is equivalent to one Planck length.

A Cultural Context for Astronomy

For some, the evidence and theory put forth by Brophy are outrageous, unbelievable, or just a coincidence. But what is the probability of this being a natural coincidence? According to Brophy, in a method developed by Schaefer in 1986, the probability that seven stars align with megaliths is less than 2 in 1,000,000. Strikingly, that is more than a thousand times as certain as the usual three standard deviations requirement for accepting a scientific hypothesis as valid. Even by conservative estimates, these are by far the most certain ancient megalithic astronomical alignments known in the world.

Understanding the origins of the Nabta Playa's astronomically aligned megaliths seems a near impossible task. No texts from this ancient culture have ever been found, nor is it likely they will be, since these people thrived long before the dawn of the written word. Why would nomadic herdsman be so interested in watching the night sky? Navigation is a likely answer, but with the precision in which they constructed the Nabta Playa star diagram, certainly there must be more to it, especially if Brophy's insights into the "complex structures" are correct. Alignments to equinoxes and solstices for religious or agricultural purposes are understandable in the context of primitive societies. However, a star chart that captures not only the movement of constellations, but also the distance and speed of its member stars, is surely an anachronism. This knowledge is mysterious to most of us today, even in our world of wristwatches and atomic clocks.

Of particular interest for this book is the fact that there is a link from the culture of Nabta Playa to Egyptian civilization. In a 1998 research paper, Wendorf and Schild noted that several elements of the Old Kingdom culture might have come from the Nabta.[41] The role of cattle in representing wealth, power, and authority, as well as in religious symbolism, is likely a carryover from more herdsman-oriented times. There are also the use of astronomical knowledge and ways of predicting solar events in early dynastic times. Egyptians used "decan stars" and star groups to measure time in one-hour intervals. (Decans subdivided the calendar into ten-day periods, with the start of a new ten-day period signaled by the brief appearance of a decan star at dawn. Twelve decan stars rose in the course of one night—hence, the division of half of each day into twelve hours.) They also depicted star groups in their art and architecture, and aligned a ritual shaft in the Great Pyramid to Orion's belt. Furthermore, the constellation Orion, which they referred to as Sahu, signified great importance in their cosmology. It was associated with their primary god, Osiris. Brophy believes that the culture and knowledge evident in the Nabta calendar circle influenced and maintained some continuity in Old Kingdom Egypt.

For most of us, astronomy is a complex science we know little about, a discipline relegated to the halls of a university or a planetarium. We regard time as a clock on a wall, and forget that those who keep the "official" time, such as the U.S. Naval Observatory, watch the skies and make slight adjustments accordingly. The role of such officials is to "determine the positions and motions of celestial bodies, motions of the Earth, and precise time." Although it is easy to assume keeping time is a modern habit, it is really quite ancient. It also seems to be a universal trait of culture and civilization.

KEEPING TIME

Remembering the Forgotten Science of Astrology

History as we know it began near the start of the third millennium B.C.E. with the advent of writing. But records of another kind—stories told of the times before written history—point to the existence of a prehistoric Egyptian culture reaching far back into the remote past. Furthermore, Egypt is not alone in having a culture that predates written history, for there are other cultures, such as the Sumerians of the Mesopotamian Valley, the Vedas of the Indus Valley, and the Maya in Central America, whose cultural traditions include stories of their earliest beginnings. This epoch before history for which there exist only stories, or oral histories, is commonly referred to by historians as the Age of Myth.

What these mythologies refer to has been, for the most part, a matter of educated guessing ever since academics and amateur enthusiasts alike began to take an interest in their meaning. Are they nothing more than silly stories to amuse? Are they religious narratives? Or are they something more? The answers to these questions are not easily answered, as an understanding of the worldview of their prehistoric authors is required. But what we do know is that mythology typically involves the heavenly bodies, predominantly those of the nighttime sky.

These myths have traditionally been viewed as religious expressions, attempts to provide purpose and a sense of history to human existence. But some scholars claim that these myths have been greatly misunderstood, and may actually be a scientific language for expressing beliefs concerning humanity and nature: not a technical language such as we have today, but a unique and symbolic form that accomplishes what science is really all about—explaining the processes of nature and the universe.

Those who espouse such a theory suggest that there may be a common origin for the astronomical and religious opinions of various cultures, particularly those who live in close proximity to one another. As we explore the claim that the Egyptians were the benefactors of a pre-existing sophisticated culture, an understanding of the possibile role of mythology played in those times serves to paint a picture of prehistory, not in the traditional sense of who lived where and when kingdoms were established, but rather of the intelligence and sophistication of the era. If the megaliths of Nabta Playa were indeed the product of sophisticated astronomical knowledge, other evidence should corroborate that.

Measuring the Hours

A system for keeping time has been in existence since around 2000 B.C.E., when the ancient Egyptians calculated the hours of the night based on stellar observations. During the Middle Kingdom, it was developed further. By 1870 B.C.E., rising stars were replaced by their culminations. Although some evidence suggests an even earlier date, by 1300 B.C.E. daytime hours were measured through the use of a gnomon, a sundial-type device that used shadow length as an indicator of the passage of time. At Abydos, in the cenotaph of Seti I, a funerary text (religious "spells" and other needed information buried with the deceased to help navigate the afterlife) covers the entire subject of time measurement. From astronomical calculations, the text was dated to the nineteenth century B.C.E. In this text, daytime hours were calculated using a shadow stick, a device with an upright post connected to a horizontal arm for scaling. It came with instructions. The stick was aligned east to west and was moved at noon so that the upright was facing due east in the morning and due west in the afternoon. Since shadow changes in length as well as angle, the upright would need to have been widened, possibly by a T-bar, so the shadow would always fall on the scale.

The Seti diagram featured a clock that directly measured eight hours, although the text is clear that from sunup to sunup there were twenty-four hours in a full day. The twelve hours of the night were measured according to decan stars. The ancient Egyptians selected a succession of thirty-six bright stars whose rising was separated from each other by ten-day intervals. Two hours before noon and another two in the late afternoon when the device was inoperative provide for the twenty-four hours a day. Later, the Thutmosid shadow stick measured ten hours directly.

During the reign of Amunhotep I (1527–1506 B.C.E.), with the invention of the water clock came the capability of dividing the night into twelve seasonal hours. It could operate in twilight as well as in full darkness, probably equalizing the hours of the day and night from this time forward.[1]

Although these sundial devices were a functional way of keeping time during daily life, a much older methodology rooted in a more ancient astronomy tradition continued into the Common Era. As we have seen from the Nabta Playa calendar circle, this method utilizes the cyclical movement of stars in the sky.

Measuring the Ages

For us, paper calendars and digital clocks mark time by the second and months by the week. Longer periods of time are arranged metrically—decades, centuries, and millennia—constructs of contemporary civilization.

For the ancients, as it is for us, keeping time through a short duration was never a problem. As it has always been, the rising of the sun marks each day, each lunar cycle marks one month, and the four seasons mark one year. But how did ancient peoples count the years?

The Julian Calendar

In 527 C.E., the Roman abbot Dionysius Exiguus instituted our calendar convention of "A.D." (Anno Domini Nostri Jesu Christi—Year of Our Lord Jesus Christ). The year 0, according to this convention, estimates the year in which Jesus Christ was born. Prior to the sixth century C.E., Western civilization followed a different standard, instituted by the Roman emperor Julius Caesar in the year 46 B.C.E.

In that year, Sosigenes of Alexandria (an Egyptian astronomer and mathematician of Greek descent) consulted with the emperor to reform the Roman calendar and achieve a more manageable and accurate structure. In order to compensate for past error, he added ninety days to the year 46 B.C.E. He also changed the number of days in the months to attain an accurate 365-day year. For year 0 in this new order of time, he chose 4713 B.C.E. and started the clock on January first—a strange choice. Why 4713 B.C.E.? Why not start fresh with year 0 being, perhaps, Julius Caesar's birthday, or when he became emperor, or the founding of Rome?

Because of his wealth and prominence, Julius Caesar likely studied at the Pythagorean School of Sacred Geometry as a part of his required education. Pythagoras espoused an ideal reality based on "perfect solids," which could also explain the movement of the stars and planets. With this in mind, it is well within reason that Caesar was displaying his Pythagorean knowledge and honoring Egyptian astrology if, from the Egyptian's perspective, that year was cosmologically significant. It was, and a very special year indeed. Here's why.

The rising and setting stars Aldebaran (in the constellation Taurus) and Antares (in the constellation Scorpio) were situated on the horizon at midnight on January 1, 4713 B.C.E. At this time, Antares was rising in the east and Aldebaran was setting in the west. Antares was fourteen minutes from the horizon. Also at that time, the sun was at a celestial longitude of 14 degrees (13 degrees, 43 minutes) into the constellation Aquarius. And the moon's velocity, which is not constant and varies between 11 and 15 degrees, was 14 degrees (13 degrees, 59 minutes) per day. On day 0, year 0, these important celestial bodies were converging on the number fourteen Accordingly, fourteen is the sacred number of Osiris—an important god in Egyptian cosmology.

In addition to Aldebaran and Antares, Saturn played a crucial role in the selection of this date. It was in conjunction with the most sacred star in Egypt, Sirius, 19 minutes away and 19 degrees in its own sign. The sun, whose birth is what was being celebrated on that day, was in Saturn's sign of Aquarius. Julius Caesar chose January 1, 4713 B.C.E., as the start of his calendar to honor the birth of the sun at the Giza plateau. But at the same time, he honored the Roman festival of Saturnalia. For Caesar, that year, so long ago (even by Romans standards), seems to have been an obvious and logical choice.[2]

Precession of the Equinoxes

The Greek astronomer Hipparchus (190–120 B.C.E.) was an ambitious scientist. During his life, he observed and cataloged over a thousand stars, calculating and recording their latitude, longitude, and magnitude. Hipparchus also observed lunar eclipses and compared his results with those of Timocharis (who lived 150 years prior) regarding Spica, a bright star near the ecliptic (the great imaginary circle on the celestial sphere that contains the plane of the earth's orbit, called the plane of the ecliptic). By measuring the distance between Spica and the center of the moon during an eclipse, Hipparchus could calculate the variance of longitude between the sun (which would be 180 degrees from the moon) and Spica, thereby solving for the star's exact longitude. What he found was that its longitude had increased two degrees since the days of Timocharis.

In subsequent studies, Hipparchus also noticed that the sun, in its annual movement, would come to its original observation point slightly before its original position in relation to the stars. As a result, he concluded that equinoxes would occur slightly earlier with each successive year. From his discovery, we derive the term "precession of equinoxes." In Hipparchus's day, the vernal (spring) equinox would have occurred at a point between the constellations of Aries and Pisces. And since the precession moves very slowly, it would have been nearly the same at the birth of Christ, but not for much longer. The astrological age of Pisces was about to begin.[3]

It is in this measurement of time through the stars that ancient cultures measured the long periods of time we call ages. There can be little doubt that the early Christians' secret sign of the fish was born of this grand clock. Their Lord, God, and Savior was born on the eve of the age of Pisces (the fish) and sacrificed as a lamb (or ram—Aries). He was a fisher of men, and those he caught (actual fishermen) he turned into disciples and taught them to be fishers of men. Miraculously, on the Mount of Olives, he fed a multitude by multiplying two fish (a common zodiac sign for Pisces) and five loaves of bread. Even the story of Mary's virgin birth echoes Piscean polarity through its opposite sign of Virgo. As it turned out, early Christians' selection of the fish was an apt symbol to convey the idea of a new god who would reign throughout the age of Pisces.

A perplexing question is: Was the knowledge of equinox precession and zodiac ages disseminated and accepted that quickly from the time of Hipparchus to the life of Christ? Or were early Christians perhaps using a more common, ancient body of knowledge that was endowed with the concept of stellar movements?

Flight of the Phoenix

When Julius Caesar decided to reform the Roman calendar, he chose Sosigenes of Alexandria for a reason. The Egyptians possessed the only wholly reliable calendar in the ancient world. In fact, they had two that were far superior to anything known to the Babylonians. One was a 365-day calendar (twelve months of thirty days each), which included five additional feast days, and a Sothis calendar. The other consisted of 365.25 days, based on the helical rising of the star Sothis (Sirius). The Egyptians knew that the two calendars would be out of step with each other after 1,461 years and that they would have to make adjustments accordingly. Resetting the calendar to correlation with the sun involved the legend of the Phoenix, its death and rebirth.[4]

The legend holds that there is only one Phoenix. At the end of its life, it returns to its birthplace in the Arabian Desert between the Nile River and the Red Sea. Once there, it burns itself to death (the glow of dawn), then rises from the ashes. Although told in mythical fashion, it was clearly a way of conveying an astronomical truth—that the sun doesn't really die each day but disappears and reappears because the Earth spins about its axis.

Gilgamesh, the Flood, and Myth as Science

The farther back we trace history, the fewer available documents there are to measure the level of ancient knowledge. It is unclear at what level of precision ancient cultures could track the stars, and whether or not they noticed the precession of the equinox. What is clear is that ancient peoples closely watched the night sky and could track the sun and moon with relative precision, and that celestial objects played a large role in their mythology. Many scholars believe there is more to ancient myths than moral fables and strange tales. The question must be asked: Did the ancients really believe the stars in the sky were gods, which is the traditional view, or were they using a stylized language to disseminate information concerning the keeping of time?

To answer that question we must first define what we mean by "gods." The way in which ancient texts have been translated and interpreted imposes a modern view of what a god is, omnipotent and omnipresent. However, it is unlikely that the ancients held that view. Within the context of their stories, a god can also be interpreted as a principle or function of nature. The difficulty in interpreting what a god is lies in the symbolic nature of the language used by ancient cultures. In his text

Theurgia, or *The Egyptian Mysteries,* the Greek philosopher Iamblichus (250–325) explains the traditions of ancient Egyptian priests. He reveals that what seems to be the worship of a pantheon of gods is really a description of how nature works. Specific principles of nature such as digestion, respiration, and reproduction are personified by gods. For example, after mummification, the stomach and upper intestines were placed into a canopic jar in the shape of the god Anubis, who was portrayed as a jackal-headed man. Anubis represents the principle of digestion because it can eat rotten meat without becoming ill.

Thus, it should come as no surprise that to many researchers the oldest written story known to man, the *Epic of Gilgamesh,* seems to be more about the heavens than the actual life and times of the man himself. According to the Sumerian records, Gilgamesh was one of the earliest kings of Uruk. Although the Sumerians first recorded the story of Gilgamesh as early as the first half of the second millennium B.C.E., it is likely its origin is much older. Its popularity in ancient times was unmatched by any other story. Hurrians, Hittites, Assyrians, and Babylonians rehearsed it in various ways throughout ancient times.

In the *Epic of Gilgamesh,* Enkidu (the wild man, hairy and of enormous strength) is seduced by a harlot and learns the ways of man. This lures him into the city, where he encounters Gilgamesh in a fierce battle that rocks the community house and damages the doorpost. Gilgamesh, after subduing him, decides he is worthy of friendship. Together they plan an expedition to the great forest to slay the terrible monster Humbaba, whom the god Enlil (the god of storm or god of air) appointed as the forest's guardian: the *Epic of Gilgamesh* states that "Enlil has appointed him as a terror to mortals. His roaring is the Great Flood. His mouth is fire, His breath is death!"

Humbaba was called a god in the text, with *hum* meaning "creator" or "father" and Humbaba meaning "the guardian of the cedar of paradise." This corresponds to the Elamitic god Humba or Humban, who shares the title "prevalent" and "strong" with the planets Mercury and Jupiter and with Procyon (Alpha Canis Minoris).

Humbaba is a "god of the intestines." His head is made from intestines, and a single winding line, except for the eyes, designs his face. History of science professors Giorgio de Santillana and Hertha von Dechend, the authors of *Hamlet's Mill: An Essay on Myth and the Frame of Time,* believed that Humbaba could be a reference to the planet Mercury or possibly Jupiter. Mercury has an erratic orbit that changes regularly. It winds around and can be likened to intestines twisted around in the abdominal cavity.

When the heroes Gilgamesh and Enkidu reach the forest of cedars, which extends for "ten thousand double-hours" (seventy thousand miles), they cut off the head of Humbaba after felling the largest cedars entrusted to his guard. But they have help; the powerful Shamash (Helios, or sun) sends a great storm to blind the monster and put him at their mercy.

Upon returning to Uruk, Gilgamesh washes his hair and garbs himself in festive attire. As he puts on his tiara (crown), Ishtar, the goddess of love (Sumerian Inanna), enthralled by his good looks, asks him to marry her. Gilgamesh declines and reminds her in scornful words of the fate of her previous mates, including the unfortunate Tammuz (Adonis). Only two celestial personalities are possible candidates for the role of Ishtar: the planet Venus; and Sirius, the dog star (Sothis). Both are associated with the qualities of a harlot.

Scorned, Ishtar goes up to heaven in a rage and persuades Anu to send down the Bull of Heaven to avenge her. The Bull descends, awesome to behold, and kills a hundred warriors with his first snort. The two heroes tackle him. Enkidu holds him by the tail so that Gilgamesh can strike between his horns for the kill. Ishtar appears on the walls of Uruk and curses the two heroes who shamed her. Enkidu then tears out the right thigh of the Bull of Heaven and flings it in her face amid brutal taunts. Celebration follows, but the gods decide that Enkidu must die, and he is warned by a somber dream.[5]

There is no need to continue the tale, for it is clear that the characters of the story, much like in Greek mythology, are symbolic of the movements of heavenly bodies. Later, in the ninth tablet of the *Epic of Gilgamesh*, the Gilgamesh author tells the story of Enki's direct intervention in advising the construction of an ark to survive the Great Flood (the forerunner and source of the biblical story of Noah). This ark, the ark of Ziusudra, has nothing to do with a literal flood, but rather corresponds to Enki's constellation of Argo and a heavenly "flood." This, of course, has obvious and far-reaching implications: the great flood described in Genesis was perhaps not a literal flood but instead a description of celestial events.

According to de Santillana and von Dechend, "floods refer to an old astronomical image, based on an abstract geometry."[6] Simply put, the plane of the celestial equator (an imaginary great circle in the sky drawn concentric to the Earth's equator) divides the series of constellations into halves. The northern half of the constellations, those between the spring and autumn equinoxes, represent dry land. The southern half, those between the autumn and spring equinoxes, including the winter solstice, represent the waters below. The four points on the zodiac (the two equinoxes and the two solstices) define the conceptual plane of the flat Earth. A constellation that ceases to mark the autumn equinox, thereby falling below the equator, sinks into the depths of the "water." It is in this abstract way that a celestial "flood" occurs. This makes it easier to understand the Gilgamesh flood. It also makes it easier to grasp the ideas from similar myths, such as the Greek story of Deucalion, in which devastating waves are ordered back by Triton's blowing of the conch.

The works of the twentieth-century psychologists Carl Jung *(Man and His Symbols)* and Erich Neumann *(The History and Origins of Consciousness)* lend support to this theory in their assertions that ancient thought relied more on natural symbolism than on the kind of specific scientific language modern society uses today. The symbolism in myth is understood as a way of describing nature and as a vehicle for introspection concerning humanity's evolution and consciousness.

To the various ancient cultures that recounted the story, the tale of

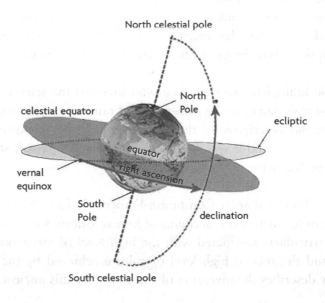

Fig. 5.1. The celestial poles and the equator
(based on an illustration from the Office of Naval Research)

Gilgamesh must have represented some grand celestial occurrence. In ancient literature, as well as in modern reasoning, it represents a dividing line for time. For the Sumerians who first told the story, it divided their history into events of "before" and "after." We have followed their lead and refer to a post- and antediluvian world—the separation of two ages.

Mythology as Ancient Science

Contemporary thought refuses to accept that ancient civilizations could mark time past the simple seasonal observations that define a year. But throughout history there have been astronomers, mathematicians, and historians who measured time in sophisticated ways.

The historian John G. Jackson (1907–1993), in his study of ancient Greek folklore and tradition, has shed invaluable light on the relationship between ancient myths and ancient observation of the stars. In Greek mythology, we read of the great mythical Ethiopian king Cepheus, whose fame was so great that he and his family were immortalized in the stars. He and his wife, Queen Cassiopeia, and his daughter, Princess Andromeda, all became stars in the celestial sphere. While this personal connection to the stars may seem strange to us, Jackson observes that for the ancient Ethiopians, it was not uncommon. Jackson notes that Lucian, the ancient Greek writer and historian (180–120 B.C.E.), described the early Ethiopians' careful observation of the stars.

> The Ethiopians were the first who invented the science of stars, and gave names to the planets, not at random and without meaning, but descriptive of the qualities which they conceived them to possess; and it was from them that this art passed, still in an imperfect state, to the Egyptians.[7]

The French scholar Constantin-François Volney (1757–1820), who is known for meticulous accounts of his explorations in northern Africa, was particularly fascinated with the high level of astronomical knowledge and the related high level of culture achieved by the Ethiopians. Volney describes the invention of the zodiac by this ancient civilizaton:

> It was, then, on the borders of the upper Nile, among a black race of men, that was organized the complicated system of the worship

of the stars, considered in relation to the productions of the earth and the labors of agriculture. . . . Thus the Ethiopian of Thebes named stars of inundation, or Aquarius, those stars under which the Nile began to overflow; stars of the ox or bull, those under which they began to plow; stars of the lion, those under which that animal, driven from the desert by thirst, appeared on the banks of the Nile; stars of the sheaf, or of the harvest virgin, those of the reaping season; stars of the lamb, stars of the two kids, those under which these precious animals were brought forth . . .

Thus the same Ethiopian, having observed that the return of the inundation always corresponded with the rising of a beautiful star which appeared towards the source of the Nile, and seemed to warn the husbandman against the coming waters, he compared this action to that of the animal who, by his barking, gives notice of danger, and he called this star the dog, the barker (Sirius). In the same manner he named the stars of the crab, those where the sun, having arrived at the tropic, retreated by a slow retrograde motion like the crab of Cancer. He named stars of the wild goat, or Capricorn, those where the sun, having reached the highest point in his annuary tract . . . imitates the goat, who delights to climb to the summit of the rocks. He named stars of the balance, or Libra, those where the days and nights being equal, seemed in equilibrium, like that instrument; and stars of the scorpion, those where certain periodical winds bring vapors, burning like the venom of the scorpion.[8]

Volney determined that the date of the origin of the zodiac had to be 15,194 B.C.E.:

Now estimating the precession at about seventy years and a half to a degree, that is, 2,115 years to each sign; and observing that Aries was in its fifteenth degree, 1,447 years before Christ, it follows that the first degree of Libra could not have coincided with the vernal equinox more lately than 15,194 years before Christ; now, if you add 1790 years since Christ, it appears that 16,984 years have elapsed since the origin of the Zodiac.[9]

Charles-François Dupuis (1742–1809), professor of rhetoric at Lisieux, France, believed that there was a common origin for the astronomical and religious opinions of the Greeks, Egyptians, Chinese, Persians, and Arabians. In his books *The Origin of All Religious Worship, The Origin of Constellations,* and *The Chronological Zodiac,* Dupuis correlates the myths of ancient times to the observation of a series of celestial events, and sets forth the logical progression from sun worship to Son worship. Now out of print, these books were the source of Giorgio de Santillana's inspiration as he began to study early Egyptian mythology and astrology.

> The title was enough to make one distrustful—one of those "enthusiastic" titles which abounded in the eighteenth century and promised far too much. How could it explain the Egyptian system, I thought, since hieroglyphics had not yet been deciphered? . . . I had dropped the forbidding tome, only jotting down a sentence: "Le mythe est né de la science; la science seule l'expliquera" [Myth is born of science; science alone will explain it]. I had the answer there, but I was not ready to understand.[10]

Later de Santillana and von Dechend would look again at Dupuis's ideas and find them to be enormously insightful.

De Santillana and von Dechend's book *Hamlet's Mill* explores the theme that many ancient myths can be interpreted as metaphorical means of communicating the astronomical knowledge of the precession of the equinoxes. They argue that ancient mythology was an exact science that was later suppressesd and then forgotten by the emerging Greco-Roman worldview. De Santillana and von Dechend explore the Sumerian cuneiform "tablets of the Era-Epos"[11] and examine an important myth in which Era (Mars) is sternly reprimanded by Marduk (Jupiter) for sending weapons to destroy what remained after the Flood. Era prophesies and Marduk replies:

> *Era (Mars):* Open the way, I will take the road,
> The days are ended, the fixed time has past.
> *Marduk (Jupiter):* When I stood up from my seat and let the flood
>   break in,
> then the judgment of Earth and Heaven went out of joint . . .
> The gods, which trembled, the stars of heaven—
> their position changed, and I did not bring them back.[12]

For de Santillana and von Dechend, this is the "clearest statement ever uttered by men or gods concerning the precession [of the equinoxes]." The tablet text specifically says that the stars are actually the "gods of heaven" and that they have changed their position, precisely what happens in the precession of the equinoxes when observed over time. The constellations seen at night slowly move in reverse order of the zodiac. The Sumerians clearly knew that.[13]

In order to know that the precession of the equinoxes actually occurs, one must observe the nighttime sky over a very long period of time. At the summer solstice, the rising sun appears just below one of the twelve constellations assigned to the months of the year. Today, the sun rises into the constellation of Pisces on June 21, but as time moves forward, in a hundred years the constellations will have shifted enough that the sun will rise into the constellation of Aquarius. Since the Sumerians ceased to exist as a culture around 2000 B.C.E., knowledge of precession requires that they had been observing the night sky for perhaps two thousand years, the time it takes for the zodiac to rotate from one constellation to the next. This means they likely had been astronomers since at least 4000 B.C.E.

Arthur Harding, a professor of mathematics and astronomy at the University of Arkansas, argues that the zodiac must have been conceived in prehistoric times. Agreeing with Jackson, Volney, Dupuis, and de Santillana and von Dechend, he writes, in *Astronomy: The Splendor of the Heavens Brought Down to Earth,* that "[t]he signs of the constellations of the Zodiac coincided about 300 B.C.E. and also about 26,000 B.C.E. We know that they were in use before 300 B.C.E. They must, therefore, have been invented not later than 26,000 B.C.E."[14]

Scholastic opinion over the origins of astronomy, particularly advanced knowledge such as understanding the precession of the equinoxes, has always favored a relatively late date, during the latter part of the first millennium B.C.E. Most believe that it is not possible for prehistoric, "primitive" cultures to have such sophisticated knowledge. However, with the discovery of the astronomically aligned megaliths at Nabta Playa and the detailed information they represent, the scholars who have argued for an older origin are now vindicated. There is convincing evidence that the science of the stars, including precession, was born in Africa long before the formation of Egypt's first dynasty (2920–2770 B.C.E.). More than six thousand years ago, ancient astronomers already knew what the genius of Einstein mathematically proved—that the heavens above, *space,* perform the eternal function of keeping time.

The early knowledge of astronomy demonstrated at Nabta Playa, Sumer, and Ethiopia predates the birth of Egyptian civilization. Opponents of John West and Robert Schoch's redating of the Sphinx, which requires a redating of Egyptian civilization or at least a reassignment as to what culture carved the Sphinx, claim that there is no cultural context of a previous civilization. This prehistoric knowledge of astronomy, so well documented in ancient texts, adds to the evidence that there was such a culture, of which pharaonic Egypt was a legacy. As we will soon discover, the pyramids of the Giza plateau attest to a sophisticated technology indicative of a far more advanced culture than has been commonly believed to exist during or before dynastic Egypt.

PYRAMID TECHNOLOGY
The Evidence Speaks for Itself

Anyone will tell you that the pyramids of Egypt were grand tombs for the pharaohs, the ultimate mausoleum. Elementary through collegiate textbooks have reinforced this claim, generation after generation. And for all we know, they *may* have been tombs. It is as valid a theory as any other. It is also the generally accepted theory. Yet there is no physical proof that they were, in fact, tombs. Although a small amount of skeletal remnants were found in the Red Pyramid, built by Snefru (2575–2551 B.C.) at Dahshur, no mummies, grave goods, or inscriptions have ever been found inside a pyramid. However, these items have been found in tombs of later dynasties—for example, in Tutankhamun's royal tomb in the Valley of the Kings. In spite of the absence of evidence, the simplest explanation and assumption has been that the pyramids are tombs. As the theory goes, they are empty as a result of grave robbers who plundered their wealth.

The traditional theory is that the pyramids sprung from egotistical pharaohs who wanted a bigger and better mastaba—a low, rectangular, mud-brick tomb structure—for their burial. In this respect, the archaeological evidence is clear that kings and nobles were buried in mastabas during the Old Kingdom. The deceased was placed in a wooden chest, which was placed inside a stone sarcophagus. Four containers, called

111

canopic jars, sat next to the sarcophagus and held his stomach, intestines, lungs, and liver. His burial chamber was filled with funerary texts and inscriptions, an important rite for the king or noble to find his way during the afterlife. However, as I have already stated, no such articles have ever been found in a pyramid. In this chapter, we will explore the possibility that the pyramids were built not as tombs, but for a far more intriguing purpose.

Egypt's Ten Pyramids

By geometric definition, a pyramid is a solid object having a polygonal, usually square, base whose four sides form the bases of triangular surfaces meeting at a common vertex. There are really only ten true pyramids.* Built during the third and fourth dynasties (between 2650 and 2467 B.C.E.), they are all within fifty miles of each other near the base of the Nile Delta. Later pyramids were built of rubble and sand, sandwiched between stone walls, most of which are now in ruins. Once the stone casing of this type of construction is damaged or removed, the structure deteriorates rapidly.

Excluding the first pyramid, built by Djoser, the following nine have a combined total of fourteen undecorated rooms containing three empty, unmarked stone chests that are assumed to be sarcophagi. Yet they contain no religious inscriptions, offering rooms, or other funerary features found in earlier and later tombs. Even more interesting, Snefru, the first king of the fourth dynasty, built three pyramids, two at Dahshur and one at Meidum. No one knows why he ordered this. Why would he order three tombs?

Djoser's pyramid began as a mastaba with two vertical shafts. One shaft leads to a storage room and the other to a burial chamber. But later a small step pyramid was added, and later expanded even further, achieving the first genuine Egyptian pyramid.

Sekhemket's pyramid, which is now rubble, contained a descending passage, a vertical shaft, and one underground room. The evidence suggests that this structure was conceived as a pyramid during the planning stage. A stone chest, carved from alabaster with a sliding lid and sealed

---

*Although later pyramid-shaped structures were constructed for various reasons, they were not true pyramids in the early dynastic sense—a true pyramid is literally a solid structure, although one or more chambers typically exist within.

TABLE 6.1 PYRAMIDS AND THEIR ASSIGNED BUILDERS

Ruler	Reign (B.C.E.)	Location	Pyramid Name/Type
		3RD DYNASTY	
Djoser	2630–2611	Sakkara	step
Sekhemket	2611–2603	Sakkara	step
Kha-ba	2603–2599	Zawyet el Aryan	layer
		4TH DYNASTY	
Snefru	2575–2551	Meidum	collapsed
Snefru	2575–2551	Dahshur	Bent
Snefru	2575–2551	Dahshur	Red
Khufu	2551–2528	Giza	Great
Djedfre	2528–2520	Abu-Rawash	unfinished
Khafre	2520–2494	Giza	Giza #2
Menkaure	2494–2472	Giza	Giza #3

with cement, was found in its underground room. In 1954, the chest was opened and found to be empty. No inscriptions were ever found in the chamber or any of the passages.[1]

Kha-ba's pyramid, also now rubble, was constructed with a vertical shaft that connected two horizontal passageways ending in a single underground room. As was the second pyramid, it was originally designed as a true pyramid, solid with inner chambers. It was also found empty, with no inscriptions in the underground room or in its shafts.[2]

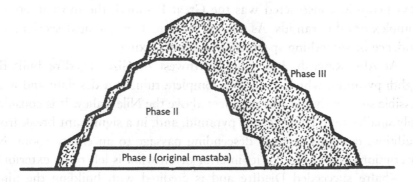

Fig. 6.1. Djoser's step pyramid. Illustration by Kevin Siembieda,
© 1983 Palladium Books, Inc.

Snefru's Meidum pyramid is in a collapsed state with its core standing as a tower above the ruins. It contains a descending passage, which becomes horizontal near the pyramid's center. A vertical shaft, measuring 3.8 by 2.8 feet, connects it to an empty, corbeled room. It is composed of seven steps, identical in design to the Great Pyramid's grand gallery. Originally it was a step pyramid, but it was later converted into a true pyramid with smooth sides. It was also found empty and uninscribed.[3]

Snefru's second pyramid, known as the Bent Pyramid, has a double-angled profile with two separate sets of rooms. One entrance is on the customary north side and a second one is on the west. The descending passage from the northern entrance is three feet, seven inches high, too small for a person to stand up in. It leads to two internal rooms with corbeled roofs. Both were found empty. A second passage, measuring three feet, seven inches high, connects the upper room with an opening high in the pyramid's western face.[4]

Snefru's third pyramid, popularly known as the Red Pyramid because of its core stones' reddish tint, is in good condition. It still retains large areas of its original casing stones and is the earliest complete monument that is in pyramid form. Again, there are no inscriptions within its interior or exterior.

The inclination of this pyramid's face is identical to the upper section of the Bent Pyramid. The entryway, a diagonal of a 1:2 rectangle, leads down a long, sloping, four-foot high corridor to the bedrock; then it leads to two adjoining and identical rooms with corbeled roofs. A short passage leads upward to a third, larger room. The corbeled roof of this third room rises to a height of fifty feet.[5]

During Khufu's reign, attention turned to the Giza plateau, and the next pyramid constructed was the Great Pyramid, the most internally complex of all pyramids. As we will investigate in the next section, it is evidence of something spectacular, but perplexing.

At Abu Rawash, five miles northwest of Giza, Djedfre built the eighth pyramid, which is now in complete ruin, at a desolate and inaccessible site nearly five hundred feet above the Nile Valley. It is considerably smaller than Djoser's step pyramid, and, in a significant break from tradition, contains a single descending passage to an empty room. No inscriptions were found in its interior or on what is left of its exterior.[6]

Khafre succeeded Djedfre and is credited with building the ninth pyramid, the second one built on the Giza plateau. It is the best-preserved of the Giza pyramid group and stands next to Khufu's pyramid. In size, it is almost its twin, but looks larger because it was built on higher ground and has an intact summit. (Khufu's pyramid has lost its top thirty-three feet.) Its internal structure is simple when compared to Khufu's pyramid. There are two entrances, one directly above the other. The upper entrance is fifty feet above ground and opens into a narrow passage lined with red granite. It descends into the bedrock, where it levels off, then continues horizontally to a large limestone room (46.5 by 16.5 by 22.5 feet) hewn out of rock. The room is roofed with gabled limestone slabs placed at the same angle as the pyramid's face.[7]

At the western end of this room is an empty, unmarked, polished-granite box 8.5 by 3.5 feet wide and 3.3 feet deep. It is set into the floor at the level of the lid, which is broken in two pieces and lies nearby. In 1818, the Italian adventurer Giambattista Belzoni discovered it in this condition.

The second entrance is carved into the bedrock. At the bottom of this passageway exists a large, uninscribed, and empty subterranean chamber.

The third pyramid of Giza is attributed to Menkaure and, like the other nine pyramids, it is void of any inscriptions or markings. Only the account of Herodotus, and references to his name in the surrounding mastabas, makes him the likely builder. It is much smaller than the other two Giza pyramids—7 percent the size of Khufu's pyramid. The lower half of casing blocks is made of rough granite. Its northern face, around the entrance, and an area on the eastern face are built with fine granite. The top half of the pyramid was fully dressed with fine-grained limestone.[8]

The main underground room is cut out of the bedrock, lined with red granite, and void of any inscriptions. Its ceiling appears to be vaulted, but on closer examination is actually formed of large, tightly fitted granite slabs laid in facing gables. Their undersides have been carved to form a false vault. A basalt chest was found in the chamber, but was removed in the early twentieth century by British adventurers. Unfortunately, it was lost at sea off the coast of Spain.

The Great Pyramid

With three chambers, eight passageways, and a grand gallery, Khufu's Great Pyramid is the most internally complex of all Egyptian pyramids. The original entrance opens to a narrow passage (3 feet, 11 inches high by 3 feet, 6 inches wide), which descends 345 feet into the bedrock and ends in a subterranean room. Although large (46 by 27 by 11 feet), this room is crude and void of any inscriptions. With its purpose unknown, some theorize it was intended to house the king's sarcophagus but the builders changed their minds, abandoned it, and built what is referred to as the queen's chamber. Others theorize that the plan was again changed to include another chamber higher in the pyramid that would finally be the king's chamber.

According to the Greek historian Herodotus, the body of Khufu was placed in a room deep below the pyramid so water from a Nile-fed canal would turn the room into an underground island. No one knows if the subterranean chamber is the room Herodotus referred to, but if it is, it would have to be a hundred feet lower to exist at the level of the Nile.[9] Herodotus, who lived two thousand years after the Great Pyramid was built, was probably recalling a legend. No evidence suggests that his story is true.

An ascending passage junctures with the descending passage near the ground level. It is very narrow (3 feet, 11 inches high by 3 feet, 6 inches wide) and rises at an angle of 26.5 degrees for 129 feet. It then levels off into another very small corridor that leads to the queen's chamber.[10] Since the original floor was slippery, handrails and wooden

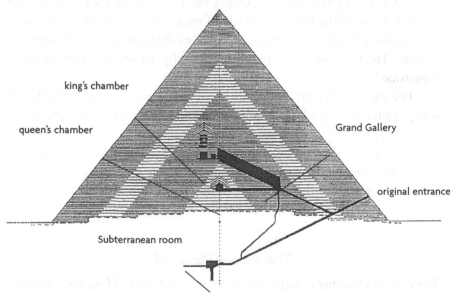

Fig. 6.2. Cross section of the Great Pyramid
(from W. M. Flinders Petrie's The Pyramids and Temples of Gizeh*)*

ramps with metal footings were installed during the 1940s to make the passage less difficult to maneuver through. Just before the queen's chamber, the passage floor drops a foot and a half.

The queen's chamber is empty, with walls of limestone sealed with plaster. Its floor was left rough. What is strange about this room is that there are two eight-inch-square shafts, believed at first to be airshafts, that extend into the upper reaches of the pyramid. In 1993, Rudolf Gantenbrink and his engineering team found that these shafts are sealed at the ends with a block of limestone. With this discovery, it is clear they were part of the original design and added to the core masonry, level by level, as the pyramid went up. The southern shaft extends more than sixty feet higher than the floor of the king's chamber and runs for eighty-two feet.

At the junction of the ascending and horizontal passages is the Grand Gallery—157 feet long, 29 feet high, and 62 feet wide at the bottom with a corbeled ceiling. Interestingly, there are seven layers of stone leading to the corbeled ceiling, just like Snefru's Meidum pyramid.[11] The gallery, oddly large when compared with the rest of the passages, rises to another corridor that leads to the king's chamber.

From the Grand Gallery, a small passageway lined with granite provides access to the king's chamber. Only by crawling can one fit through this tunnel. This chamber is by far the most puzzling, constructed entirely of smooth slabs of granite. Its walls are fitted with five courses of stone consisting of one hundred granite blocks. Each slab weighs thirty tons. No mortar was used to join them, since each piece was perfectly carved to match the adjoining pieces. Nine slabs of granite, some weighing more than fifty tons, form the ceiling.[12]

Above the ceiling, a series of rough-cut granite blocks are stacked together, one on top of the other. Spacers between the slabs create five compartments, referred to as Davison's Room, after its discoverer, Nathaniel Davison.[13] Some believe this room was designed in this manner to reduce the pressure from the colossal weight of the stone above. However, the queen's chamber below, which is subject to even greater stress, lacks a ceiling like this. Although the pyramid is void of any inscriptions, on one of the upper slabs there exists the name Khufu, believed to be a quarry mark from an ancient worker.

At the west end of the king's chamber there is an empty, open box carved from granite and polished smooth. The passageway into the room is too narrow for the box, so it was likely placed there when the pyramid was under construction. If a lid to the box ever existed, it has been removed from the room without a trace. Not even portions of a lid, chunks or fragments, have ever been found in any of the passages or chambers.

On the northern and southern walls, airshafts lead to the pyramid's exterior. They are identical in angle and size to those of the queen's chamber. The Great Pyramid is unique in this manner. No other pyramids exhibit such channels.

Lack of Evidence Supporting the Tomb Theory

According to the independent Egyptian Egyptologist Moustafa Gadalla, the lack of funerary items alone invalidates the theory that the pyramids functioned as tombs. Remnants, scraps, or fibers from the mummy and its wrappings surely would remain in the burial chamber, or somewhere else in the pyramid, if it was a place of rest for the deceased. Furthermore, the pyramids' passageways are too low—almost all are less than four feet high—and too narrow to provide for the movement of sarcophagi. In general, all of Egypt's genuine pyramids, those that were built as a solid structure, simply lacked adequate accommodations for people and ceremony, which was essential for the deceased's journey into the afterlife.

Finally, human remains have never been found inside a genuine pyramid. Thieves steal treasure, grave goods of monetary value, but would avoid a corpse. Valuables within the wrappings would have been removed and the corpse left next to its sarcophagus. If the idea was accepted that tomb raiders smashed the lids of the sarcophagi to gain access to the pharaoh's personal treasure, why would they go to the trouble of taking the sarcophagi with them? Not to mention the brute force required to "make off" with such an item. Fragments of these hypothetical broken sarcophagi, or their lids, have never been found anywhere in the pyramids' passages or chambers.

The observable evidence suggests that the pyramids were never intended to house human beings, dead or alive. Since passageways and chambers were designed and built into the pyramids, the time and trouble it took to build them logically requires utility in their purpose. The inner structure of the Great Pyramid, the most internally complex of all the pyramids, appears as an unfathomable series of ascending and descending passages with a single grand, ascending passage. Of course, this raises the question: If the pyramids were not tombs, then what were they?

The Science of Reverse Engineering

There is no shortage of theories about what purposes the pyramids served. With its unusual internal design, the Great Pyramid, along with the others on the Giza plateau, has been the focus of numerous speculations. Arguments exist for the pyramids having been tombs, monuments to commemorate the beginning of Egyptian civilization, harmonic temples, and objects to attract spiritual energy. As interesting as these theories may be, none of them fully explains the visible evidence within the Great Pyramid.

It is logical to assume that if so much time, effort, and materials were sunk into such a massive project as the building of the pyramids, there was likely some benefit gained, at least for the pharaoh and possibly for the entire civilization. During wartime, it is typical for a technical department of military intelligence to take apart, analyze, and put back together captured equipment to understand how the item was made and what its function was, and to determine the technical capabilities of the enemy. This is referred to as "reverse engineering," and its role is to determine how things work. Although it is not possible to dismantle the Great Pyramid, over the years a number of researchers have contributed to the mass of accumulating information about the pyramid's construction and to our understanding of what it could mean. Reverse-engineering research on the Great Pyramid involves comprehensive knowledge of mechanical engineering.

The Great Pyramid is a giant puzzle, although a maze would seem a more appropriate term. Fortunately, almost all of the pieces are still there. All it would take is for a mechanically inclined sleuth, skilled in the crafts of manufacturing, machining, and design, to have a long look at the pyramid's passages, chambers, construction techniques, materials, and any residual evidence to determine what its purpose was. Only by explaining the bizarre mix of passages and chambers as a whole, in a comprehensive way, would such an analysis be successful. Christopher Dunn, the expert machinist discussed in chapter 4, is such a sleuth. Over the course of twenty years, Dunn has visited Egypt several times and applied his knowledge of precision machining and manufacturing techniques to a mechanical analysis of the Great Pyramid. But his conclusions are not for the closed-minded.

The reaction of the casual bookstore browser to the title of Dunn's book, *The Giza Power Plant,* typically is "this sounds nuts"—an effect that is clearly a consequence of a traditional education. However, his analysis and theory are, by far, the most comprehensive ever performed within the confines of the Great Pyramid. Inspired by Peter Tompkin's *Secrets of the Great Pyramid* during the 1970s, Dunn spent the next twenty years visiting Egypt whenever he could and applying his mechanical expertise to answering the question of what the pyramid could have been used for. For Dunn, the arrangement of the chambers and passageways hinted at something mechanical, and examination of the evidence confirmed what he suspected. According to Dunn, the totality of evidence suggests that the pyramid was a structure whose purpose was to absorb the Earth's tectonic vibrations (a form of energy) and transform them into electrical energy.

A Geomechanical Power Plant

The Earth's crust consists of a number of moving pieces, nine large tectonic plates and twelve smaller ones, that are always colliding or pulling apart. Pressure builds up in fault zones, and eventually is released. We recognize this release as a massive vibration, an earthquake. The mechanical properties of the rocks that seismic waves travel through quickly organize these waves into two types. Compression waves, also known as primary or "P" waves, travel fastest, at speeds between 1.5 and 8 kilometers per second in the Earth's crust. Shear waves, also known as secondary or "S" waves, travel more slowly, usually at 60 to 70 percent of the speed of P waves. P waves shake the ground in the direction they are propagating, while S waves shake perpendicularly or transverse to the direction of propagation. Although the actual frequencies of seismic waves are below the range of human hearing, it is possible to hear them by speeding up a recorded seismogram. Typically, high-frequency P waves are followed by the rushing sound of the drawn-out, lower-frequency S waves.

As a consequence of the constant colliding of Earth's plates, very small earthquakes continually occur. We notice only the larger ones. What this means is that the earth vibrates all the time and has its own fundamental frequency. One could draw out these vibrations if one had an object that would respond sympathetically with earth's fundamental frequency.

If a device was designed in such a way that its own resonant frequency was the same as, or a harmonic of, the earth's, it would have the potential to become what is called a coupled oscillator—an object that is in harmonic resonance with another, usually larger, vibrating object. When set into motion, the coupled oscillator would draw energy from the earth and vibrate in sympathy, as long as the earth continues to vibrate at this frequency. In this way, energy could be efficiently transferred from the earth.

What Dunn discovered is that the Great Pyramid, which covers a large area of land, is in harmonic resonance with the vibrations of the earth and acts as an acoustical horn for collecting and channeling the earth's vibrations. After analyzing its internal structure, he also concluded that its passages and chambers were designed to maximize the throughput of sound.

By creating alternating pulses at the top of the pyramid and in the subterranean chamber—a feature that all Egyptian pyramids have—the structure would be set into motion. Once the vibration of the pyramid is coupled to that of the earth, the transfer of energy from the earth would continue until the process is reversed. Chris Dunn explains precisely how this was achieved through the internal structure of the pyramid. All that would then be needed is a system that could make use of the energy.[14]

An Electricity Generator (the King's Chamber)

Quartz crystal has a peculiar reaction when subjected to vibration. Known as the piezoelectric effect, vibration alternately compresses the crystal, producing electrical output. (Microphones, for example, work on this principle.) Quartz crystal does not create energy; it only converts it from one kind of energy into another. In effect, it serves as a transducer. Interestingly, the king's chamber is built from Aswan granite, which contains 55 percent or more silicon-quartz crystal. So the king's chamber, in one respect, is a transducer.

The evidence for this is very compelling. Above the king's chamber are five rows of granite beams, forty-three of them, each weighing up to seventy tons. Each layer of granite is cut square and parallel on three sides, rough on top, and separated by spaces large enough for a person to crawl into. The result is that each granite beam could vibrate if subject to a suitable amount of energy. If tuned to the same frequency, the other beams would also vibrate at the same, or harmonic, frequency as the first beam. Furthermore, if the source frequency, the sound input, matched the beam's natural frequency, then the transfer of energy would be maximized and so would the vibration of the beams.

To enhance the ability of the forty-three granite beams to resonate with the forcing frequency, the natural frequency of the beams would need to be at the same frequency as, or in harmony with, the forcing frequency. To accomplish this, the beams would have to be shaped by cutting away some of the stone until the desired frequency was met. The principle at work here is the same as that of a tuning fork. Large tuning forks resonate at low frequencies and smaller ones, higher frequencies. Making the granite beams resonate at the same frequency would require them all to be generally the same shape and weight. This is precisely what the observable evidence indicates. The chamber's builders worked the rough sides of the beams before installing them, removing chunks and gouging holes. In effect, they were "tuned." Acoustical tests confirm that the granite beams do resonate at a fundamental frequency. In fact, the chamber itself reinforces this frequency by producing dominant frequencies. The chamber creates an F-sharp chord, which is believed to be in harmony with the natural vibration of the earth.

Acoustical tests inside the king's chamber also reveal that the entire room is freestanding from the surrounding limestone masonry. The granite floor sits on "corrugated" limestone; the walls are supported from the outside and sunk five inches below the floor. The end result is that the entire room is free to vibrate at peak efficiency and ready to convert vibrations from the earth into electricity. The vibrating crystal within the granite creates an electrical field, but harvesting the energy requires a medium of transfer, which was provided by the result of chemical processes in the queen's chamber, utilizing hydrogen gas. In the presence of an electrical field, the hydrogen gas becomes excited—atomically speaking, its electrons widen their orbit around the nucleus. By forcing the hydrogen electrons back to their resting (original) state, the energy they held would be released, and with the appropriate equipment to collect and focus the energy, it could be used by some device. (Current research has been investigating this type of electricity production to power laptop computers and prosthetic devices, although other mediums besides hydrogen are more efficient in today's miniature devices.)

Interestingly, the coffer itself inside the king's chamber resonates at 438 hertz—in synch with the room. What is needed is sufficient energy to drive the beams and activate their piezoelectric properties.[15]

The Resonator Hall (the Grand Gallery)

The key to making the king's chamber vibrate is a structure or device that focuses vibrations received through the pyramid—precisely the purpose of the Grand Gallery. The Grand Gallery is an enclosed area with resonators installed in slots along its length. A resonator is an object with specific dimensions chosen to permit internal resonant oscillation of acoustical waves of specific frequencies. Vibration resonates within the object's cavity to produce airborne sound at a certain frequency, which is based on the size of the cavity. Wooden frames were constructed to house the resonators of the Grand Gallery and were mounted onto the floor and ceiling, the ends of the frames fitting into rectangular slots carved into the limestone. When the resonators were actually in place it likely would not have been possible to walk through the gallery because of the equipment and its rigging. The role of the resonators was to convert and concentrate vibrations into airborne sound.

According to Dunn, the design of the gallery, its angles and surfaces, reflects sound and directs it into the king's chamber. When sound is channeled into the granite resonating cavity, forcing the granite ceiling beams to oscillate, the beams above them, in turn, begin to resonate in harmonic sympathy. As a result, the maximization of resonance is achieved and the entire granite complex becomes a vibrating mass of energy. The specific design of the Grand Gallery was to transfer energy captured by the large area of the pyramid into the resonant king's chamber.

Although an acoustical engineer's confirmation is needed to corroborate that the Grand Gallery reflected sound in the manner proposed, Dunn was able to extrapolate other information concerning acoustical devices that are no longer in place. He theorizes that the Grand Gallery housed resonators that converted the coupled earth and pyramid vibrations into airborne sound. Twenty-seven pairs of slots in the side ramps of the gallery could have contained a resonator assembly. This would do much to explain the existence of the slots, which have always been a mystery. If their function was to respond to the earth's vibration, then they might be similar to a Helmholtz resonator (see fig. 6.3), a contemporary device that has a similar function.

A Helmholtz resonator responds to vibrations and maximizes the transfer of energy from a vibration's source. It is a hollow sphere with a round opening between one tenth and one fifth of its diameter, normally made out of metal but it can be made from other materials. The size of the sphere determines the frequency at which it resonates. If the frequency of the resonator is in harmony with its source, it will draw energy from the source and resonate at greater amplitude.

Dunn theorizes that each resonator assembly in the Grand Gallery was equipped with several Helmholtz-type resonators that were tuned to different harmonic frequencies. Each resonator in the series responded at a higher frequency than the previous one, and raised the frequency of the vibrations coming from the earth. To accomplish this, the ancient scientists would have to make the dimensions smaller for each succeeding resonator and reduce the distance between the two walls. In fact, the walls of the Grand Gallery step inward seven times from the floor to the ceiling. At their base, the resonators were anchored in the ramp slots. Along the length of the second layer of the corbeled wall there is a groove cut into the stone, suggesting that the resonators were held in place and positioned by first being installed into the ramp slots. "Shot" pins, in the groove, held them in place. Vertical supports for the resonators were likely made of wood, since it is one of the most efficient responders to vibration.

The Cairo Museum holds some of the most remarkable stone artifacts of Egyptian civilization. According to Dunn, given the shape and dimensions of some of these vessels, they are likely the Helmholtz-style resonators used in the Great Pyramid. One such item, a bowl, has a horn attached to it. Another bowl does not have handles normally seen on a domestic vase, but rather trunnion-like appendages machined on each side of it. These trunnions would be needed to hold the bowl securely in a resonator. A little-publicized fact concerning these artifacts is that there were thirty thousand of them found in chambers underneath Djoser's step pyramid.[16]

An Acoustic Filter (the King's Antechamber)

The antechamber to the king's chamber has been the subject of much concern and discussion. Despite its small size, nine feet long by nine feet high and three and a half feet wide, it is one of the most unusual chambers in the pyramid. In comparison with the rest of the pyramid's construction, it is rough—the surface of the stone blocks was not polished to an even smoothness. On the south wall above the entrance to the king's chamber are four grooves running vertically from the entrance to the top of the chamber. Along the east and west walls are two granite

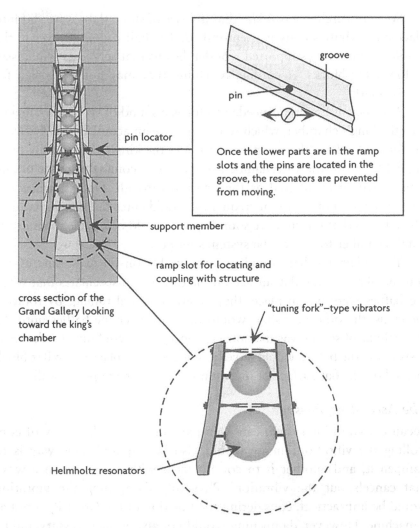

pin locator

groove

pin

Once the lower parts are in the ramp slots and the pins are located in the groove, the resonators are prevented from moving.

support member

ramp slot for locating and coupling with structure

cross section of the Grand Gallery looking toward the king's chamber

"tuning fork"–type vibrators

Helmholtz resonators

Fig. 6.3. Diagram of resonator apparatus (from Christopher Dunn's The Giza Power Plant*)*

wainscots (linings) of different heights. The east side is eight and a half feet high; the west side is a little over nine feet. Three grooves are carved into the granite wainscots of the west wall beginning at the south end of the chamber, measuring approximately one and a half feet in width. At the top of each groove is a semicircular notch, as though intended for a pole to be placed across the chamber. However, since no notches are cut into the grooves on the east side, any hypothetical beams would have to rest on the top.

Some researchers postulate that a series of stone slabs were slid into place after Khufu's body was entombed. The half-round grooves in the granite wainscoting supported wooden beams that served as windlasses to lower the blocks. According to Dunn, they may not have been far off the mark.

The ancient Egyptians needed to focus a sound of specific frequency into the king's chamber, which would require an acoustic filter between the Grand Gallery (the resonator hall) and the king's chamber. By placing baffles inside the antechamber, sound waves coming from the Grand Gallery would be filtered as they passed through. Only a single frequency, or harmonic of that frequency, would enter the king's chamber. The effect is that interference sound waves would be unable to enter the king's chamber to reduce the system's output.

To explain the half-round grooves visible on the west side of the antechamber and the flat surface on the east, Dunn speculates that when the baffles were put in place, they received a final tuning. By rotating the cams, the off-center shaft would raise or lower the baffles until the throughput of sound was maximized. Once they were "tuned," the shaft suspending the baffles would have been locked into place in a pillar block located on the flat surface of the wainscoting on the opposite wall.[17]

The Ascending Passage

Because a vibrating system can eventually destroy itself, a way of controlling the vibration energy would also be required. One way is to dampen it, and another is to counteract it with an interference wave that cancels out the vibration. Physically dampening the vibration would be impractical, considering the function of the Great Pyramid as a machine. However, dampening would not always be necessary, unlike the dampening needs of a bridge, for example. It would reduce the efficiency of the machine, and likely involve moving parts, like dampers in a piano.

Canceling out excess vibrations by using an out-of-phase interference sound wave would have been a logical choice. The ascending passage is the only feature inside the Great Pyramid that contains devices (granite plugs) that are directly accessible from the outside. Dunn refers to them as devices for the same reason he calls the granite beams above the king's chamber devices. They are overdesigned and over-crafted for their supposed use. Limestone would have been sufficient to keep out robbers. So why use granite?

Dunn studied them and realized they may have performed two critical roles. First, they would provide feedback to the plant operators by responding to the sound that was generated inside the Grand Gallery, and traveling through the ascending passage. Second, they may have been able to respond to vibrations from equipment in the descending passage and transmit out-of-phase interference sound waves to prevent vibrations from reaching destructive levels. Of course, the operators would be using vibration sensors attached to the bottom granite plug in order to monitor the energy level inside. This explains not only the builders' logic for selecting granite, but also the means by which the ancient Egyptians controlled the level of energy in the system. Dunn also speculates that by directing a signal of the correct frequency up the ascending passage, the operators would have been able to prime the system. According to Sir Flinders Petrie, the adjoining faces of the blocks had a wavy finish (± .3 inch). Some granite was still cemented to the floor, indisputable proof that the granite plugs were positioned as the Great Pyramid was being built.[18]

The Granite Box in the King's Chamber

After transducing the mechanical energy into electrical energy, there needs to be a medium through which electricity can flow and be utilized. Most likely, when the plant was in operation, the king's chamber was filled not with air but rather with a gaseous medium that would resonate with the entire system, thereby maximizing the output. Hydrogen, the atom responsible for the emission of microwave radiation in the universe, as well as the simplest of all elements, would fit these needs. Its atoms, with a single electron, would most efficiently absorb the energy. The stepped-up frequencies entering the king's chamber from the Grand Gallery would excite the hydrogen gas to higher energy levels. In other words, it would efficiently absorb this energy as each atom responded in resonance to its input.

The vibration of the granite beams converts the sound energy, through the piezoelectric effect of the silicon-quartz crystals, into high-frequency radio waves, which would be absorbed by the hydrogen atoms. How this works is that the single electron in the hydrogen atom is induced to increase its distance from the proton, which is an unnatural state. In time, the electron will return to its normal state and, in doing so, release a packet of energy. It can also be stimulated to return to its normal state through the action of an input signal, which is another packet of energy of the same frequency. What results is that the input signal continues its path, after stimulating emission from the hydrogen atom, and carries away the released energy.

In the Great Pyramid, the northern shaft served as a waveguide for the input microwave signal. It was constructed to pass through the masonry from the north face of the pyramid into the king's chamber. This microwave signal could have been collected off the outer surface of the pyramid and directed into the waveguide. The original surface of the pyramid's outer casing stones, which was smooth and slightly concave, may have been treated to collect radio waves from the microwave region that is constantly bombarding the earth from space. According to Dunn, the waveguide leading to the chamber has dimensions that closely approximate the wavelength of microwave energy, which is 1,420,405,751.786 hertz. It is the frequency of energy emitted by atomic hydrogen in the universe. This certainly helps explain the gold-plated iron that was discovered embedded in the limestone near the southern shaft. Lining the shafts with gold-plated iron would make it a very efficient conduit for the input signal and the power output.

The granite box inside the king's chamber is an important component to the system. Dunn believes that it occupied a position between the waveguides in the north and the south walls. Here, it served as an amplifier of the microwave signal that entered the chamber. It is densely opaque to us, but would allow electromagnetic radiation (invisible to us) to pass through. The evidence suggests that the granite box could refract electromagnetic radiation as it passed through the box's north and south walls.

Although accurate measurements for the optical characteristics have not been made, the nineteenth-century British explorer Piazzi Smyth's measurements show that the box's surface is concave. So, when the granite box was positioned in the path of the incoming signal from the northern shaft, and with oscillating crystals adding energy to the microwave beam, it may have served to spread the signal inside the box as it passed through the first wall. Inside the granite box, the spreading beam would then interact and stimulate the emission of energy from the energized hydrogen atoms.

Across the king's chamber, at the opening for the southern shaft, there is a feature in the granite wall that closely resembles a horn antenna, much like a microwave receiver. The radiation picked up more energy as it passed through the opposite wall of the box, then was once more refracted and focused into this horn antenna. The mouth of this opening is severely damaged. However, because of its curved geometry, someone in the distant past likely found it necessary to remove some of the granite to retrieve the gold or gold-plated lining. According to Dunn, what is left unmistakably identifies this as the receiver of microwave energy that entered the chamber from the north wall's waveguide.[19]

The Hydrogen Generator (the Queen's Chamber)

The queen's chamber is situated in the center of the pyramid with two ascending shafts that terminate five inches from the inside of the chamber wall. The nineteenth-century British explorer Wayman Dixon discovered these shafts in 1872 when he thrust a rod through the wall. He also noted that the area of limestone at the shaft was particularly soft. In 1993, research conducted by German robotics engineer Rudolf Gantenbrink revealed, as previously mentioned, that the ends of the shafts, high in the pyramid, were sealed by limestone blocks. Obviously, they were never intended to be airshafts.

In the late nineteenth century, Piazzi Smyth deemed it noteworthy to record that there were white flakes of mortar exuding from joints inside the shaft. Later, it was determined that the flakes were plaster of Paris, also known as gypsum. He also noted that the chamber contained a foul odor that hastened visitors' exit from the room. According to Dunn, the odor was not likely the result of unclean conditions, but instead the residual elements of the chemical processes that once occurred there.[20]

Another seemingly unexplainable fact is that salt was encrusted on the walls, and also in the horizontal passage in the lower portion of the Grand Gallery, in some places up to a half-inch thick. Ironically, salt is a natural by-product of the chemical reaction designed to produce hydrogen. It probably formed when hot, hydrogen-bearing gas reacted with the calcium in the limestone walls. In 1978, Dr. Patrick Flanagan, a physician and researcher, took a sample of this salt to the Arizona Bureau of Geology and Mineral Technology for analysis. They discovered that it was a mixture of calcium carbonate, sodium chloride, and calcium sulfate, which is limestone, salt, and gypsum (plaster of Paris)—precisely the minerals that would be produced if a hydrogen-bearing reaction occurred in the queen's chamber.[21]

The corbeled niche with a small tunnel cut to a depth of thirty-eight feet, which ends in a bulb-shaped cavern, is another interesting feature in the queen's chamber. Its flat, level floor and almost perfect right-angled left side surely mean it was part of the original construction. It likely had a mechanical purpose. The hydraulic engineer Edward Kunkle proposed that it was part of a large ram pump, which also involved other features located inside the Great Pyramid.[22]

Dunn believes that the termination of the shafts, five inches from the chamber, was part of the original design. Each shaft originally contained a small hole that ran through to the chamber, which would be a way to control a specific amount of fluid entering the chamber. Since the northern shaft exhibits a dark staining, the Egyptians may have been using the shafts to introduce two different chemicals into the queen's chamber.

The corbeled niche inside the chamber would have provided an anchor for an evaporation tower, and may have also contained a catalyst. The chemicals pooled on the floor of the chamber and wicked through the catalyst material.

Dunn sought out a chemical engineer, Joseph Drejewski. Drejewski agreed that two chemical solutions could be introduced into this chamber to create hydrogen or ammonia under ambient conditions of 80 degrees Fahrenheit, plus or minus twenty degrees. He also agreed that the niche in the wall of the chamber could have been used to house a cooling or evaporation tower. According to Drejewski, zinc is the most commonly chosen metal used to create hydrogen. When treated with dilute hydrochloric acid, it produces a reasonably pure hydrogen gas at a relatively fast rate.[23]

Additional support for Dunn's chemical theory came in 1993 when Rudolf Gantenbrink guided a robot, Upuaut II, up the southern shaft and discovered at its end a "door" with copper fittings. The filming of this shaft by Gantenbrink's robot revealed erosion in the lower portion of the shaft. Its walls and floor were extremely rough, and the erosion displayed horizontal striations. There were also signs of gypsum leaching from the limestone walls. Gantenbrink's robot came to a dead end at the upper part of the southern shaft, encountering a block of limestone with two mysterious copper fittings protruding from it.

It was publicized that a hidden door had been found inside the Great Pyramid. What was not told is that the shaft itself is only about nine inches square. Thus, it really wasn't a "door." The copper fittings were theorized as stops to prevent the limestone block from being raised. However, for Dunn, this explanation does not fit. Why would the pyramid builders want to include a sliding block in an inaccessible area? And even if they did, how was it activated?

According to Dunn, the copper fittings looked like electrodes, which could deliver an accurate measure of hydrochloric acid solution to the chamber. They would serve as a switch to signal the need for more chemicals. Early explorers discovered, in the shafts leading to the queen's chamber, a small bronze grapnel hook, a piece of wood, and a stone ball. For a while they were misplaced. But in 1993, they turned up in the British Museum in a cigar box at the Department of Egyptian Antiquities. According to Dunn, these items probably composed the necessary switching mechanism to alert that more chemicals were needed.[24] In the shafts where the chemicals were stored, floating on the fluid's surface would have been the piece of cedarlike wood joined together with the bronze grapnel hook. It would rise and fall with the fluid level in the shaft. When the shaft was full, the copper prongs would make contact with the electrodes, closing the circuit. As the fluid dropped, the prongs moved away from the electrodes, opening the circuit, thereby sending a signal to pump more chemical solution. Once the hook made contact with the electrodes, the pumping would stop.

Gantenbrink offered to go through the small gap at the bottom of the door with another robot but was denied the opportunity. Later, the American engineer Tom Danley tested the southern shaft using an acoustic device and discovered that another thirty feet existed beyond the limestone blocks. Although there is no tangible evidence of what lies behind Gantenbrink's "door," what has been discovered fits extremely well into the power plant theory.[25]

In 1992, French engineer Jean Leherou Kerisel conducted ground-penetrating radar and microgravimetry tests in the short horizontal passage that leads from the descending passage to the subterranean pit. His team detected a structure underneath the floor of the passageway. It could possibly be a corridor oriented south-southeast/north-northwest with a ceiling at the same depth of the descending passage. A "mass defect," as Kerisel calls it, was also detected on the western side of the passageway eighteen feet before the chamber entrance.[26] This anomaly corresponds to a vertical shaft at least fifteen feet deep with a section very close to the western wall of the passageway. Kerisel believed he identified, off the subterranean chamber's entrance corridor, something that looks like a completely separate passageway system that terminates in a vertical shaft. Although it may be traces of a large volume of dissolved limestone, he strongly suspects it is a man-made feature.

What Kerisel's findings indicate is that the supply shafts leading to the queen's chamber may have been supplied with chemicals through a vertical shaft connected to an underground chamber. Kerisel detected the vertical anomaly on the west side of the passageway, which is the same orientation as the shafts leading to the queen's chamber. According to Dunn, it would not be out of order to postulate that when Gantenbrink's "door" is penetrated, a vertical shaft leading to a bedrock chamber will be found. Dunn would not be surprised if copper cables or wires, which were attached to the copper fittings, are found beyond Gantenbrink's "door."

The Horizontal Passage, Well Shaft, and Subterranean Pit

The long horizontal passage that connects the queen's chamber with the Grand Gallery was also constructed from limestone. Its purpose would have been to remove residual moisture and impurities from the hydrogen gas as it flowed toward the Grand Gallery. At the juncture where the horizontal passage meets the ascending passage, there exists a five-inch lip. There was likely a slab resting against the lip that bridged the ascending passage and the floor of the Grand Gallery, where another, similar lip is found. The lip, and a bridging slab, would have prevented the fluid from flowing down the ascending passage. Slots in the side wall indicate there may have been supports for this slab. Holes would have to be drilled into it to allow the gas to rise into the Grand Gallery.

At this juncture, and to the west, a hole leads to the well shaft. Spent chemical solution from the queen's chamber would flow along the horizontal passage, down the well shaft, and into the grotto or subterranean pit if the shaft was connected to the lower descending passage.[27]

The Giza Power Plant

Here's how the Giza power plant probably worked. The massive structure of the pyramid collected, and funneled, tectonic vibrations from the earth below. The Grand Gallery further collected these vibrations, and through its resonators converted it into airborne sound. The sound traveled past an acoustic filter, which baffled all but a certain frequency just before entering the king's chamber. In the king's chamber, the filtered sound vibrated the massive granite walls, ceiling, and granite stack above, converting mechanical energy into electrical energy.

Since the king's chamber was filled with hydrogen gas produced from the queen's chamber, the hydrogen absorbed the electricity, pumping its atoms into an excited state. Microwave signals were collected off the outer surface of the pyramid and directed into the northern shaft leading to the king's chamber. There, the granite box refracted electromagnetic radiation, and, with oscillating crystals adding energy to the microwave beam, served to spread the signal inside the box as it passed through its first wall. Inside the granite box, the spreading beam would then interact and stimulate the emission of energy from the energized hydrogen atoms. Passing through the other side of the box, the microwave energy was then focused into an antenna device, and exited the pyramid through the southern shaft where it could be utilized.

Unfortunately, any external equipment that utilized the electricity produced by the power plant was removed long ago. After the fourth dynasty, for reasons unknown, the Giza necropolis was abandoned, only to be rediscovered nearly a thousand years later by the pharaoh Thutmoses IV of the eighteenth dynasty. Nonetheless, it boggles the mind to think that all the precision-crafted artifacts and objects discussed in chapter 4, made from the hardest stone available, were handcrafted. And what about the pyramids? They too are built of materials

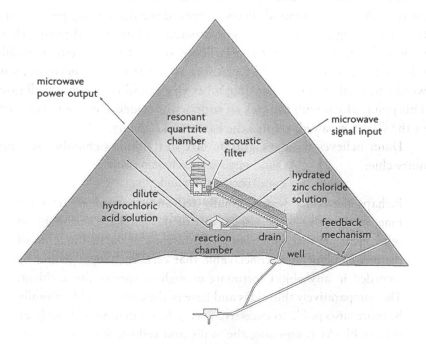

Fig. 6.4. Mechanical analysis of the Great Pyramid
(from Christopher Dunn's The Giza Power Plant)

crafted with exceptional precision. It seems reasonable to speculate that specialized machines and equipment would have had to be designed and manufactured in order to produce such precision-made objects and building materials, as well as to place the enormously heavy blocks of stone. Dunn's research and theories about the utility of the Great Pyramid are objective and it remains to be seen whether the Great Pyramid can be re-created (on a much smaller scale) to demonstrate that it was indeed a power plant.

What Happened to the Plant?

One of the questions that is always posed to Chris Dunn is: What happened to the power plant and all its internal equipment? His answer is that he thinks there was a tremendous explosion inside the pyramid, likely the result of an earthquake-induced power surge. In *Pyramids and Temples of Gizeh,* Petrie notes that the king's chamber had been subject to a powerful force that pushed out the walls over an inch. For Dunn, cracks in the ceiling beams do not seem to be explained very well by settling, and the historical explanation that this damage was from an earthquake does not add up. There is no similar damage in the lower parts of the Great Pyramid. Petrie surveyed the descending passage and found amazing accuracy in its constructed and excavated parts. There is no indication, then, that the building shook to the extent it would take to move a chamber 175 feet above the bedrock. Furthermore, why would an earthquake cause a chamber to expand rather than collapse? This point, along with the lack of supportive evidence in the lower parts of the Great Pyramid, refutes the earthquake theory.

Dunn believes the dark granite box in the king's chamber is a primary clue:

> Perhaps the coffer was originally red and quarried at the same time, in the same place, as the rest of the granite. Depending on other elements that were present at the time of the malfunction of the power plant, it is conceivable that certain changes would be recorded in any object fortunate enough to survive the accident. The comparatively thin sides and base of the coffer would naturally be more susceptible to excessive energy levels than would the huge granite blocks comprising the walls and ceiling. It could be suggested, therefore, that the coffer, without the ability to conduct the

heat to which it was subjected, simply over-cooked, with a change in color being the result.[28]

In 1999, Dunn returned to Egypt and found that the Great Pyramid had been thoroughly cleaned. Originally believed to be limestone, Dunn discovered that the Grand Gallery was made of smooth, highly polished granite, logical for the builders to use since it would be more resistant to heat. However, the most interesting evidence was that there were scorch marks on the walls of the Grand Gallery. There was heavy heat damage underneath each of the corbeled layers for a distance of about twelve inches. It seemed as though the damage was concentrated in the center of the burn marks. If a straight line was measured from the center of each scorch mark and projected down toward the gallery ramp, the line extended down in alignment with the slot in the ramp![29]

For Dunn, the pattern was unmistakable and pronounced. The scorch marks on the ceiling approximate the design and location he hypothesized in his book. Furthermore, there are pairs of scorch marks where the resonator support structure would have been placed.

The Spirit of Science

The Giza power plant is a radical theory, but only from the perspective of tradition. In the true spirit of scientific investigation, Christopher Dunn explains every aspect of the Great Pyramid's complex internal passages and chambers. He also insists that such a precise construction could not have been accomplished without the proper tools, not only to cut and shape but also to measure precisely. In his model, he even predicted that it endured a serious explosion. The scorch marks in the Grand Gallery testify to his theory's accuracy.

In the spirit of true science, Dunn throws out a challenge to all Egyptology to critically and skeptically examine the tomb theory and provide evidence to support their conclusions. In the past, they have not been able to, nor will they ever be able to. There is much evidence that Khufu's pyramid was indeed a station constructed to transform mechanical, vibration energy into electrical energy. This places an exclamation point after the question that has been chased by amateurs and professionals alike for over a hundred years: Who were the first Egyptians?

WHO WERE THE
FIRST EGYPTIANS?
A Century of Theories

Evidence from various scientific disciplines paints a complex picture of what may have occurred during Egypt's predynastic times. Archaeologists have discovered the existence of a number of ancient cultures, some of which survived and became part of dynastic Eypt and some that did not. There is also evidence that the impetus of dynastic Egyptian culture may have come from the regions of Mesopotamia. The question of who the first Egyptians were has been a matter of debate over the last hundred years as new evidence has come to light and new ideas have been put forth.

As is the case with Egypt's pyramids, theories abound regarding how Egyptian civilization began and where the first Egyptians came from. A prevailing theory is that early Egyptian settlers were indigenous to Africa, former herdsmen who roamed the lands following the rains but were forced to seek a continuous supply of water in the Nile Valley when the Sahara returned to extremely arid conditions.

During the 1950s, an Italian team of archaeologists led by professor Mario Liverani, from the University of Rome, explored the Libyan Sahara and, by chance, discovered the mummified remains of a young boy at the Uan Muhuggiag rock shelter a hundred miles west of the

Nile Valley, which dated to 3500 B.C. Although no other mummies have been found in this area, it is proof that the tradition of mummification is far older than originally believed. This Libyan mummy is a thousand years older than the first Egyptian mummy and the oldest ever found in Africa.

In preparing the boy for burial, he was eviscerated and embalmed with an organic preservative, then wrapped in skins and insulated with leaves. The sophistication with which he was mummified suggests he was not the first, but rather the result of a long-standing tradition.

According to current research in the Libyan Desert, now under the direction of Dr. Savino di Lernia, there was once a central Saharan society that spanned the width of North Africa. During the late 1990s, environmental studies performed by Dr. Kevin White, of Reading University in Great Britain, provided proof that the area was once teaming with rivers, a requirement to support such a population. NASA scientists examined images of the Western Desert while testing radar instruments. They scanned the desert using radar, then compared those images with more conventional satellite images. What they discovered was a series of buried river networks underneath what is now a sand sheet. The radar penetrated the surface and revealed an ancient river system that once fed into vast lakes. According to White, the area is dense with an interconnected network of river channels, invisible in an optical image.

Rock art dating to 5000 B.C.E. corroborates what the radar equipment revealed. In Libya, Egypt, and Mali, petroglyphs depict not only grazing animals, but also aquatic life such as crocodiles. This indicates that the desert was inhabited during a time prior to 4000 B.C.E. and as far back as 8000 B.C.E., when the climate was wet. There are also scenes of hunting and rituals involving men wearing animal masks. Some believe that these people were responsible for an extraordinary array of innovations such as mummification, which was later adopted by the Egyptians.

According to di Lernia, ten thousand years ago Humas, a black race of people, came from the south following the monsoon belt and occupied the center range of the Sahara near the Acacus Mountains. However, they were not the only ones. Around seven thousand years ago, people from Mesopotamia and Palestine also arrived, introducing cattle and goats. Di Lernia points out that the rock art in the area, by the profile of the face and the style, depicts white people. According to the theory, it was this mixed-race culture, the blending of these two populations, that mummified the boy at Uan Muhuggiag.

Other theories, today as well as during the past, suggest the possibility of Iberian or Mesopotamian migrations. Some theorists think in terms of conquest; others describe more peaceful motivations for migration. The difficulty in deducing precisely who the Egyptians were stems from a lack of evidence. Mesopotamia certainly shows a background of development, whereas Egypt does not.[1]

There are similarities between cultures of the Euphrates and those of the Nile, such as their architectural conception of the paneled façade. Important buildings and tombs in Egypt were decorated with paneled "palace-façade" architecture, essentially the same as the ornamental buttressing on Sumerian temples and palaces. But in comparing structures of this type, dated from the same period, it is apparent that Egypt's design and construction were superior, which casts doubt on the theory that this knowledge was imported from Mesopotamia. Of course, there is also the Eyptians' highly skilled use of stone to consider, which is unparalleled in history by any other culture.

Whoever the people were in northeast Africa during the fourth millennium B.C.E., there is general consensus that they migrated into the Nile Valley. However, there is a problem in understanding the relationship between human activity and climatic changes. In the crucial area of the Nile Delta, continuous silting has buried Stone Age sites beyond recovery. The closest source of information are the archaeological remains of the Neolithic (New Stone Age) settlement of Merimde beni-Salame, in the western regions of the Nile Delta, where settled villagers kept cattle, sheep, and pigs.[2] Furthermore, over the course of many thousands of years, the Nile has changed its course. The boundaries of the Sahara Desert have changed too. This perpetual shifting of geography continues today.

In the Sudan, the encroaching desert is destroying a way of life that is centuries old. According to local farmers, the sand movement is exhausting their effort to sustain life. It has buried their agricultural land and is now encroaching upon their homes. Thousands of communities, along a narrow strip of arable land that borders the Nile River, have watched the sand move closer every day. They have stood by helplessly as the riverbanks erode, the river changes course, and their only source of water thickens with silt and other debris.

Early History of Egypt and the Nile Valley and Its Inhabitants

Although scientists find it difficult to date African sediments in absolute terms, what information does exist suggests that Egypt underwent a period of aridity at the beginning of the Pleistocene, two million years ago. At that time, the Nile River ceased to exist and a long period of aridity ensued, lasting for a million years. It was interrupted by two short periods of frequent rains, and the Nile became a vital but fleeting river unconnected with any other tributaries of sub-Saharan Africa. Some scientists claim a human presence existed during these less arid periods, but the evidence is not conclusive. Outside of Ethiopia, a likely place for the earliest Africans to live would have been along the Nile. However, the narrow valley has been swept many times by the river, leaving little in the way of sedimentary deposits that could preserve human remains.[3]

Toward the middle of the Pleistocene, around five hundred thousand years ago, formation of the Nile developed from water flowing from the Ethiopian plateau. It created a waterway between East Africa and the Mediterranean coast and a route through the Sahara. Below these pre-Nile deposits, human artifacts have been found, but their characteristics are not distinctive enough to classify them as belonging to the north or south. In Nubia, numerous undated artifacts with typical African characteristics have been found outside of Nile Valley deposits.[4]

The picture that emerges in the Egyptian Middle Paleolithic, between one hundred thousand and forty thousand years ago, is complex. For archaeologists, evidence for the first humans whose cultures could eventually have led to Egyptian civilization lies in late Acheulean technology. Tools of this time include hand axes and bifacial, leaf-shaped stone blades that were created through a typical Nubian knapping method of striking a rock to chip off a flake that would later be used as a tool. In Egypt, artifacts from this era are found scattered all over the desert, but no well-preserved sites have been found. However, the large number of artifacts suggests a relatively high population density.[5]

After 40,000 B.C.E., occupation sites increased throughout Lower Egypt. Archaeologists describe two groups, based on their toolmaking techniques—Nubian and Denticulate. Tools from both of these cultures are Mousterian, meaning that they are simplistic (hand axes, scrapers, etc.), typically associated with Neanderthal man. In Bîr Tarfawi and Bîr Sahara (two basins in the Western Desert), numerous settlements from the Nubian tradition exist. Sites in this area were habitable only during wet climates, which were little more than brief episodes during a period of aridity.[6]

From 19,000 to 10,000 B.C.E., Stone Age settlements became concentrated in Upper Egypt close to the Nile River, but dispersed to the west around 8000 B.C.E. as the rains moved into the Sahara. Stone Age sites prior to 7500 B.C.E. were typically found in regions where the climate was wet. Carved rock images from early cultures depicting animals are found on the cliffs along the Gilf Kebir, Gebel Uwein'at, Wadi Hussein, and the Libyan plateau near Dahkla, as well as the route through Abu Ballas. A diversity of animal life is represented that includes giraffe, lion, rhinoceros, crocodile, hippopotamus, elephant, horned oryx, sheep, ibex, and antelope. Although the rock art has not been dated, it may be quite old. According to regional archaeo-zoological records, the animals depicted were not widely present after 10,000 B.C.E., and existed primarily in areas of a humid microclimate. Besides animals, rock art depicts humans as pastoralists, with herds of cattle. Requirements of the animals depicted in the art, as well as the needs of humans, suggest that the rainfall averaged somewhere between eight and thirty-two inches.[7]

Prehistoric Pastoralism

Evidence for prehistoric pastoralism exists in the southern area of the Great Sand Sea, which likely supported grasslands during wetter conditions. Numerous clusters of large stones, with a notched portion or groove around the middle of each stone, exist within the dune corridors. They were likely anchors designed to hobble cattle and control them during times of good grazing. Although the exact timing and nature of these activities are unknown, the widespread distribution of these stones across southern Egypt suggests that herders were transferring their livestock from one grazing area to another.

Humid conditions arrived at Nabta Playa after 6100 B.C.E., with New Stone Age (Neolithic) settlements appearing a few hundred years later. The Neolithic began around 10,000 B.C.E. and was characterized by the development of agriculture and the advancement of stone tools. Archaeologists discovered that early Khartoum-style pottery exists immediately above the latest Paleolithic (Old Stone Age) artifacts. The Old Stone Age is characterized by the earliest chipped-stone tools and lasted from 750,000 to 12,000 years ago. The Neolithic sites may have been continuously occupied, and became more sophisticated, with stone houses arranged in rows. In the Kiseiba region of southern Egypt, the Neolithic Two Hills Playa settlement experienced moderately rainy conditions from 7100 to 5900 B.C.E. In the nearby playa at El Ghorab, housing structures were found to contain extensive underground storage areas. Many of the settlements in the Kiseiba-Nabta region have wells, some of which appear to have sunken access ramps.[8]

Plant fossils, dated between 6600 and 5400 B.C.E., found at Nabta and Kiseiba are dominated by perennial, dry-soil species of grasses, legumes, and sedges. The most common are edible plants, including seeds, nuts, fruits, tubers, wild sorghum, and millet. The remains of edible plants have been discovered in storage pits, stone-built structures, and granaries, and around cooking holes at many sites across the Sahara, such as the El-Kortein and El Ghorab playas. The evidence is clear that Saharan people exploited local food cereals as early as the eighth millennium B.C.E.

Animal remains discovered include hare, gazelle, mongoose, wildcat, hedgehog, and domesticated cattle. Ceremonial burials of cows dated to 4500 B.C.E. Fred Wendorf interprets the concentrations of cattle bones as ritualistic slaughter practices. Various herding camps, located in the sand sheets near Nabta and Kiseiba, were likely used until 4000 B.C.E.

Beyond the Nabta and Kiseiba region, wet conditions persisted at many localities in southern Egypt, such as Black Hill and Bîr Tirfawi. Playa lakes also developed at the Dahkla Oasis and attracted relatively sedentary groups of the Masara (a Neolithic culture that settled in the area of Memphis), as did the playa at the Siwa Oasis. Similar playas were developed in the Khârga basin and along the Libyan plateau. One cultural group, the Sheikh Muftah, occupied the Dahkla lowlands until Old Kingdom times (2650–2152 B.C.E.).[9]

Settlements in the Nile Valley

Before 5500 B.C.E., cultures of the Nile Valley were undergoing a transition from hunter-gatherers to village-dwelling agriculturists. Most of the information during this period comes from El Kab, a site between the east bank of the Nile and the Red Sea Hills. Three major groups of peoples have been discovered, with the oldest dating to 6400 B.C.E. The Belgian archaeologist Dr. Pierre M. Vermeersch classified over four thousand artifacts, most of which were artfully detailed microblades, burins, and scrapers, as well as beads made of ostrich shell. In the northern Sudan, two prominent cultures were discovered near Wadi

Hal-fa—the Arkinian and the Sharmarkian. Arkinian artifacts have been found at only a single site and date to 7440 B.C.E. Like many of the settlements near the Nile, it was likely a seasonal camp. Arkinians made use of very small, skillfully crafted stone tools, but also used large blades and developed the double-platform core, a method for extracting more material from a stone. The Sharmarkian culture covers a longer time period, from 5750 B.C.E. to 3270 B.C.E. However, its tool-crafting abilities appear to be at a lower level of skill. Over time, the Sharmarkians' seasonal camps grew into small villages.

Around 5500 B.C.E., the archaeological evidence indicates that a population explosion occurred, possibly because of attempts at agriculture. Permanent agricultural activity began at about 4800 B.C.E., although for the next fifteen hundred years, agricultural methods were relatively primitive. Unfortunately, it is unknown precisely when agriculture developed, or by what method, or who introduced it in Egypt. A thousand-year gap in the archaeological record exists between river settlements and the true farming villages of predynastic Egypt.

Predynastic Times (5500–3100 B.C.E.)

During the fourteen-hundred-year transition from the predynastic to the early dynastic period, nearly all the typical characteristics of early Egyptian civilization appear. In permanent settlements, it is clear that hunting was no longer a major means of providing sustenance. Domesticated cattle, sheep, pigs, and goats, as well as cereal grains (wheat and barley) played a much greater role in the diet. Items crafted from stone and metal, basketry, pottery, weaving, and the tanning of animal hides became part of daily life. Burial customs also changed. Before, most burials were performed where it was convenient, often in a central cemetery near or inside the settlement. Now they were placed farther away from the village and field, usually on the edge of the village's territory. Children, previously buried under the floor, were now laid to rest in cemeteries.

A belief system began to take shape. The deceased were buried with provisions (pottery, jewelry, and other artifacts) for the journey into the afterlife. Offerings of cereals, dried meat, and fruit were included, as well as implements for hunting and farming. Interestingly, the dead were buried in the fetal position, facing west, and surrounded by their kinsmen's offerings.

Predynastic societies soon began to form in the north as well as the south. Southern cultures, particularly the Badarian, were almost completely agrarian, but their northern counterparts, such as El Faiyûm, who were oasis dwellers, still relied on hunting and fishing. Stoneworking, principally the making of blades and points, reached greater levels of skill. Furniture also became a focus of the craftsmen. The aesthetic value of goods became important. Pottery was painted and decorated, particularly the black-topped clay pots and vases typical of this culture. Bone and ivory combs, figurines, tableware, and jewelry of all types and materials have also been found in great numbers dating between 3300 and 3000 B.C.E.

Sometime around 4500 B.C.E., predynastic Egypt began with the Amratian period, also known as Naqada I, as most of the sites from this period date to the same time as the occupation of Naqada. A change in pottery decoration in this period reflects a developing, artistically advancing culture. Earlier ceramics were decorated with simple bands of paint, but the new designs show skillful geometric shapes and the figures of animals, either painted on or carved into a vessel. For practical reasons, as well as aesthetic, vessel shapes became more varied. Decorative items were also popular, chiefly the "dancer" figurines, small painted figures of women with upraised arms.

However, the most important innovation of this period was the development of architecture. Several clay models of homes, discovered in graves, resemble the rectangular clay-brick houses of the Old Kingdom. It seems the idea of individual dwellings, towns, and perhaps urban planning started around 4500 B.C.E.

Around 4000 B.C.E., city-states may have developed at Naqada, Hierakonopolis, Gebelein, and Abydos. Archaeologists label this period Gerzean or Naqada II. This period is vastly different from the Amratian, and is characterized by the growing influence of northern peoples on those of the south as seen in cultural artifacts, particularly ceramics. In time, these city-states resulted in the mixed people and culture of the late predynastic era known as Naqada III.

The greatest difference between the Amratian and Gerzean peoples is their ceramics. Amratian pottery, although decorative, was clearly functional. Gerzean pottery, on the other hand, was crafted more along decorative lines and adorned with geometric motifs and realistic depictions of animals and people. Animals, such as ostriches and ibexes, uncommon near the Nile, provide a clue that the Gerzeans may have hunted in the sub-desert. They are also accredited with the first representations of gods, typically shown riding in boats and carrying standards, items that resemble the later standards representing the various provinces of Egypt. It may also be the case that these depictions were simply of historical records, but since they were almost always painted on symbolic artifacts buried with the dead, sacredness is a reasonable explanation.

With furnished underground rooms, replicas of the homes that the deceased occupied in life, Gerzean tombs foreshadowed what was to come. Amulets and other ceremonial items, many depicting early gods in animal form, were common grave goods. Some scholars believe that the Gerzean view of the afterlife eventually grew into the Cult of Osiris and the magnificent burials of Egypt's dynastic civilization.

At one time, it was thought that the transition from predynastic to dynastic culture was the result of revolution and warfare brought on by the discovery of metals, the development of metallurgy, and new social structures of the city, individual dwellings, and writing. More recent views suggest the slow process of technological evolution. It is also believed that writing developed during this time. Pottery motifs distinctly evolved over a period of time into a standard set of images that resemble traditional hieroglyphics. They show a combination of pictograms and phonograms (a picture that stands for a sound), the fundamental principle of hieroglyphic writing. Systems of writing like this still exist today, such as Japanese.

A general exodus of people from the desert areas of southern Egypt, around 3000 B.C.E., created new and significant settlements in the Nile Valley. The final act during predynastic times was the unification of Upper and Lower Egypt—although there are still more questions than answers regarding the establishment of Egyptian civilization. Exactly who conquered whom is still largely unknown. A number of sources point to a victory of the south (the Naqada culture) over the north (the Maadi culture), yet the resulting social system resembles the north more than the south. However, this could be explained by a blended theory. Egypt was first unified under the north, but its power structure collapsed and was picked up by the southern kings, who kept the original form of government set up by the north. Another theory is that the south conquered the north but adopted northern culture. Such a scenario exists in the government of Ptolemy. The Ptolemies were the Greek rulers of Egypt after Alexander the Great, yet absorbed Egyptian culture, called themselves pharaohs, and were buried according to Egyptian custom.

It is difficult to say who the first king of a unified Egypt was, or when this occurred. The Narmer Palette, a triangular piece of black basalt depicting a king named Nar-Mer in hieroglyphs, is the most conclusive piece of available evidence. On its face, the king is shown wearing the white crown of the south and holding a mace ready to crush the head of his northern enemy. The same figure is also depicted wearing the red crown of the north while a bull (a symbol of the pharaoh's power) rages below, smashing the walls of a city and trampling yet another foe.

The "Scorpion" mace-head, another artifact, depicts a similar figure, but this time his name is revealed by the pictogram of a scorpion. In various documents, this king figure is alternately referred to as Narmer or Aha, and could be the legendary king Menes. Whether King Scorpion is the same person as Narmer is debatable, but the two are generally accepted as the same. If these artifacts, as well as others from the same period, do depict this as the first king of unified Egypt, then the date for the unification is somewhere between 3150 and 3110 B.C.E.

Egyptology and the Origins of Egyptian Civilization

At a young age, William Matthew Flinders Petrie (1853–1942), whose work we have discussed previously, taught himself trigonometry and geometry and developed an interest in archaeology, particularly in the area of ancient weights and measures. At the age of thirteen, he read Charles Piazzi Smyth's *Our Inheritance in the Great Pyramids* (1864) and convinced himself to go to Egypt to see the pyramids. In 1880, at the age of twenty-four, he published his first book, *Stonehenge: Plans, Description, and Theories*. That same year, he started a forty-year career of the exploration of Egypt and the Middle East. From 1880 to 1883, he meticulously excavated and studied Giza's Great Pyramid, scrutinizing every layer of earth and every shovelful of soil. Because of his thoroughness, he became known as a great innovator of scientific methods in excavation. In 1883, his book *Pyramids and Temples of Gizeh* was published. It told of the skill and precision of Egypt's ancient builders.

Over the years, Petrie wrote over a hundred books and nearly nine hundred articles and reviews. One of his most significant works was published in 1904, *Methods and Aims of Archaeology,* defining both the methodology and the goals of archaeology.

Invaders from the East

As Egyptology grew into a specialized discipline during the late nineteenth century, early investigators sought evidence to explain the initial stages of Egyptian civilization. Excavations conducted by Petrie revealed evidence of a much older culture predating Egypt's first dynasty (2920–2770 B.C.E.). He was struck by the marked differences between this new predynastic culture and the better-known material from the Old Kingdom (2650–2152 B.C.E.). Petrie found artifacts unknown and unfamiliar to early researchers, which he believed must have been left by a new race of people who had migrated to the Nile Valley.

At Naqada, Petrie unearthed nearly twenty-one hundred graves containing clay pots, palettes, and various amulets made of stone, bone, and ivory. He dated the newest graves to 3100 B.C.E. and the oldest to the predynastic period (5500–3100 B.C.E.). The predynastic objects were common to three major periods: the Amratian (3800–3500 B.C.E.), the Gerzean (3500–3200 B.C.E.), and the proto-dynastic (3200–3100 B.C.E.) periods. In the 1920s, a fourth period was added, the Badarian (before 4000 to 3800 B.C.E.). Using what evidence they had, Petrie and other archaeologists concluded that life before the pharaohs was primitive, and that it was just prior to dynastic times that Egyptian culture evolved.

Early-twentieth-century Egyptology concluded that a "dynastic race" of invaders brought classic Egyptian civilization to the Nile Valley. According to the theory, these invaders were culturally and politically superior to the native, primitive Egyptians. As a consequence, they quickly established themselves as rulers of the country. During that time, the science of cranial metrology—the use of skull measurements to determine race—was popular and used to support the dynastic race theory. Those skeletons that were attributed to this dynastic race were typically more robust and exhibited a dolichocephalic skull shape, oblong from front to back—unusual by today's standards.

Egypt's ruling class was believed to have come from the East, reflecting the then common view that the Orient was the source of early culture. Royal art of the first dynasty was believed to be similar to that found in Mesopotamia. During the 1930s, Hans Winkler, a German explorer, advanced the theory, stemming from his discovery of ancient rock art in the Eastern Desert, that Egyptian civilization was the result of migration from Mesopotamia. Between the Nile Valley and the Red Sea, he found numerous images of boats, very similar to watercraft seen in early Mesopotamian art. He argued that Mesopotamian invaders used the Red Sea to gain access to Egypt, and as they made their way to the Nile River, they left traces on the rocks. Ironically, the petroglyphs of "Mesopotamian boats" that Winkler found in Egypt actually predate Mesopotamian depictions of boats by many centuries.

In the early part of the twentieth century, Africa was known in the West as the "dark continent" and was thought to be incapable of internally producing an advanced culture. So, with growing worldwide fascism, the invasion theory was a product of its time. Diffusionist theories, involving superior cultures bringing civilization to indigenous peoples, were also popular among many of the colonial powers of western Europe.

The mystery of Egypt's predynastic period and the dynastic race solution was entertained for a long time before any real evidence would be exposed. In 1969, archaeologists from the American Museum of Natural History discovered a structure dating to the proto-dynastic period (4000–3000 B.C.E.), close to the place where James Quibell had discovered the town of Nekhen. Excavations outside Hierakonopolis led to the discovery of an entire Amratian village along an ancient dried-up creek bed, the Wadi Abul Suffian. This discovery finally helped archaeologists to reconstruct what daily life might have been like. According to archaeologists, the village population was composed of farmers and craftsmen. It appeared that the village leaders managed the manufacture and trade of the goods. During this period, it was also evident that the villagers began to build simple irrigation systems. The first signs of a written language also appeared. Tombs grew larger and more sophisticated, and by the end of the Gerzean period (3500–3200 B.C.E.), the tombs were similar to those of the early pharaohs.

For most Egyptologists, the excavations at Hierakonopolis proved that a "dynastic race" did not invade the Nile Valley during the late fourth millennium B.C.E. Although invasion theories persisted among a minority of Egyptologists (even into the 1990s), most scholars began to look instead for indigenous development and the roots of dynastic Egypt within the Nile Valley itself.

Current research about Egypt's predynastic era and its linguistic background points to mixed origins that include influences from northern Africa; the Middle East, particularly Mesopotamia; and sub-Saharan Africa. Most scholars believe the ancient Egyptians likely resembled their modern descendants and were ethnically diverse.

Explanation: Hypothetical

Although excavations and the publishing of archaeological findings have continued to this day, scholars still cannot specify how a centralized Egyptian state emerged at the beginning of the third millennium B.C.E. Explanations for the origin of the early Egyptian state remain hypothetical.[10] In Upper Egypt (southern Egypt), the problem is a lack of sufficient data about settlements to make theoretical generalizations. However, cultural evidence from both simple and complex societies has been found in Upper Egypt at large settlement centers, such as Naqada, in predynastic cemeteries. During the fourth millennium B.C.E., two agriculturally based cultures, the Naqada in the south and the Maadi in the north, were evolving. Maadi settlement sites are better preserved. However, Naqada sites, primarily cemeteries, show greater evidence of the evolution of social hierarchies, suggesting that the early state had its cultural origins in the south. What is missing is predynastic evidence for changing settlement patterns over time.

Egypt, particularly the Nile Valley, has always been a densely populated country, and has been aggressively cultivated for the past five thousand years.[11] Furthermore, the Nile has shifted its course to the east. These factors, along with modern real estate development, have limited the excavation of early sites. Relatively little data exists on subsistence during the predynastic period, except for recent fieldwork, and it is unknown when, why, and where agricultural intensification and irrigation first occurred. Hierakonopolis has been important in revealing predynastic production and distribution of crafted goods, but most technical evidence comes from graves. There is little archaeological evidence that demonstrates the rise of political elites, regional integration, and the formation of the earliest state, as well as the process of unification that led to the first dynasty, often referred to as "dynasty 0."[12]

In the Naqada II ritual area at Hierakonopolis, basalt and diorite vases and drill bits for bead making were crafted. Pottery kilns were found in the low desert where straw-tempered wares and "plum red ware" pottery were fired. Vats found at two different sites hint strongly at the brewing of a wheat-based beer. Later, nine more cemeteries in the Hierakonopolis region were discovered covering all three phases of Naqada culture (3800–3000 B.C.E.). A number of animals were buried in the western part of the cemetery and include elephants, hippopotamuses, crocodiles, baboons, cattle, sheep, goats, and dogs.

A large tomb contained bead fragments made of carnelian, garnet, turquoise, faience, gold, and silver. Artifacts carved in lapis lazuli and ivory, obsidian and crystal blades, early pottery, and a wooden bed with carved bull's feet were also found. Postholes hint that structures once covered some of the large tombs and were surrounded by fences. According to archaeologists, this is possibly the earliest elite tomb with a superstructure that symbolized the deceased king's shrine. From 1978 until his untimely death in1990, the codirector of the Hierakonopolis expedition and the head of the predynastic research team at Hierakonopolis, Michael Hoffman, believed that the tombs of the area belonged to the proto-dynastic rulers of Hierakonopolis (3500–3000 B.C.E.) and that the largest tomb was King Scorpion's.[13]

Two points of difficulty prevent a proper fact-based conclusion. The most important cemeteries in Upper Egypt represent the acquired wealth of a higher social class, but the economic sources cannot be adequately determined. On the other hand, settlements in Lower Egypt permit a broader reconstruction of their predynastic economy, but they do not suggest great social and economic complexity.

Some argue for a Naqada colonization of Nubia. Trade goods of the Naqada culture have been discovered at most sites in Nubia, between Kubania in the north and Saras in the south: jars for beer or wine, pottery, copper tools, stone vessels and palettes, linen, and beads of stone and faience. According to this theory, an "A-Group" of Nubians was in contact with Upper Egypt and was influenced by their culture.[14] A-Group burials are similar to those of the Naqada culture. Others believe that this A-Group consisted of commercial middlemen. Luxury materials, such as ivory, ebony, incense, and exotic animal skins, came from farther south and passed through Nubia.

Another theory, based on evidence at a royal cemetery discovered at Qustal, proposes that Nubian rulers were responsible for the unification of Egypt and the founding of the early Egyptian state. For some, this best explains the archaeological data—that the A-Group in Nubia was a separate culture from the predynastic culture of Upper Egypt. However, there is conflicting evidence. Materials from the Naqada culture with no Nubian elements were later found in northern Egypt, which argues against the idea of a Nubian origin for Egypt's early dynastic state.

In contrast to the other political entities of the time, such as Nubia, Mesopotamia, and Palestine, the rule of the Egyptian state extended over a large geographic area. The formation of the ancient Egyptian government was unique. It seems there is consensus that the emerging state had its roots in Upper Egypt, in the Naqada culture. Grave types, pottery, and artifacts show a growth from the predynastic form to the first dynasty, which cannot be demonstrated from the culture of Lower Egypt. Eventually, the Nubian culture was displaced by the culture originating in Upper Egypt. Most scholars agree on some aspects of the unification, such as the time it took, based on the earliest writings in Egypt and, later, the king's list. However, the Naqada culture expanded north into the Faiyûm region and then into Cairo and the delta area, suggesting that the unification actually began much earlier than the period immediately before the first dynasty. It has also been suggested that unification of southern city-states, such as Naqada, Hierakonopolis, and Abydos, occurred earlier through a succession of alliances. Some historians postulate that the northward expansion of the Naqada culture was a result of refugees leaving the developing states in the south; others argue that it was a result of Naqada traders engaged in commerce with southwest Asia.

There is little evidence that the unification of Egypt was wrought through armed conflict and warfare. According to excavations at Minshat Abu Omar, one hundred miles northeast of Cairo, performed by the archaeologist and director of Berlin's Egyptian Museum Dietrich Wildung, there is no indication of conflict in the Nile Delta of Lower Egypt. The site was occupied between 3300 and 2900 b.c.e., and shows continuous cultural evolution from south to north.[15] Wildung suggests that there never was a military conquest of the delta by the kings of Upper Egypt, as some believe to be represented on the Narmer Palette, a flat plate of schist of about sixty-four centimeters in height found in Hierakonopolis in Upper Egypt. Other recently excavated sites in the delta, such as Tell Ibrahim Awad, Tell el Fara'in, and Tell el'Iswid, corroborate Wildung's conclusions.[16] There is no evidence of destruction in their layers. Furthermore, ceramics at Tell el-Fara'in suggest Upper and Lower Egypt grew together through amicable means: trade and an increasing cultural exchange. In general, the evidence suggests the Egyptian state system that developed and its expansion into northern areas were too complex to be explained solely by military conquest.

However, the abandonment of Maadi lands in the north must be taken into account. Gold and various types of rock used for stone vessels and beads, highly desired materials in long-distance commerce, were resources of Upper Egypt. One motivating factor for Naqada culture to expand northward would be to control trade routes that led to the Mediterranean. The logic is that large boats were crucial to controlling the Nile and for engaging in large-scale exchange of goods. Since the timber needed for boat construction did not grow in Egypt but came from the area of Palestine, establishing outposts first and later settlements in the north would be a logical move. Perhaps the flow of southerners moving into more northern areas required a formal military presence. This could account for why the Maadi abandoned their lands in the north.

Whatever the case may be, by the first dynasty, the north was more densely inhabited than the south. One result of the annexing of the north would have been an enhanced administration of the state. By the beginning of the first dynasty, then, writing would be required to provide proper management, official seals, and tags for state goods.

As with most cultures, Egypt was not immune to foreign influence. Contact with cultures in southwest Asia during the fourth millennium B.C.E. is undeniable. Palestinian-style artifacts have been found at Maadi and later at Abydos. Naqada pottery and stone vessels were also crafted in such a way as to resemble Palestinian styles. Furthermore, Egyptian cylinder seals unquestionably originate in Mesopotamia, and have been found in a few late-predynastic graves. However, what effect, if any, this had on establishing the Egyptian state is unknown. Even so, the social, political, and material culture, as well as the belief system of the Egyptians, is very different from that of its Bronze Age neighbors. Although it is clear that Egypt's predynastic culture was receptive to ideas from neighboring lands, Egyptian culture emerged as a civilization with a unique character. With evidence from various local cultures and other evidence suggesting that migrations from neighboring lands occurred, it is difficult to claim that one single culture emerged as the "Egyptians." Perhaps it was the diversity of peoples uniting under a common goal that provided the impetus for dynastic Egypt.

Who Were the First Egyptians?

If a time machine were available, we could simply travel back to 4000 B.C.E., spend a few months learning early Egyptian language, then ask all our questions. Needless to say, the evidence provided by a century of research will have to do. Although it has become politically incorrect to suggest that Egyptian settlers came from somewhere else, the evidence does not prove they were eternally, and exclusively, indigenous to the

Nile Valley or North Africa. Human beings have always been explorers, and geneticists tell us that humans migrated from their original homeland in Africa to every corner of the world in the past one hundred thousand years. There can be no doubt that native Africans played a role in the prehistory of Egypt. But given the evidence of at least some foreign influence, the situation becomes more complex.

Some researchers propose that herdsmen who lived a nomadic life banded together in the Nile Valley simply to secure a ready source of water, thereby producing Egyptian civilization. For those who espouse this theory, often referred to as the isolation view, how can they explain the agriculture, magnificent stonework, statues, temples, and other super-structures that rival today's best engineering efforts? Perhaps if the Sphinx, the astronomically aligned megaliths of Nabta Playa, the granite and diorite bowls, vases, and plates in the Cairo Museum, and the expert evidence that the pyramids were constructed to produce electricity did not exist, the theoretical struggles over ancient Egyptian history would not either. But they do, and the anachronisms that have been verified by qualified scientists and researchers, which occurred very early on in Egyptian history, must be explained in some other way.

The writing, the monumental architecture, and the arts and crafts, which developed to an astonishing degree, point to the existence of a well-organized, even luxurious, civilization. All this was achieved within a comparatively short period, with little or no background (except for pastoralism) for these truly fantastic achievements. This is a problem, and can be explained at this point only by saying that "something is missing." The developmental precedents that explain the evidence have been either overlooked or underestimated.

The North African Dark Age

Excavations in the Nile Valley have revealed campsites that date from 16,000 B.C.E. to around 9000 B.C.E., but these sites reflect a society subsisting on rigorous hunting and fishing. Known as the Sebilian culture, these sites clearly show a decrease in the size of tools. Although knowledgeable about animal domestication near the end of the period, the Sebilians were nothing more than the traditional hunter-gatherers of the Old Stone Age.[17] From 9000 to 6000 B.C.E., there exists a "dark age" in North African history, from which little information is available. During this time, the Sebilians were living in the valley. Afterward, New Stone Age communities began to dot the landscape with a new concept of living centered on agriculture, yet the Sebilians held fast to their traditional ways of hunting and fishing. Some believe that agriculture was introduced from outside to these hunter-gatherers, who were not eager to become farmers.

Mediterranean-style woodlands, such as those of the Mesopotamian Fertile Crescent, were the most favorable environment for the domestication of wheat and barley, sheep and cattle. The archaeology bears this out. Between 10,000 and 8000 B.C.E., the earliest known culture, developing a life based on the gathering of wild cereals and then on cultivation, was in the modern-day countries of Israel, Jordan, and Lebanon. These early farmers were known as Natufians, from the site where they were first identified, the Wadi en-Natuf just north of Jerusalem. They were a people with a slight build and a long head (dolichocephalic), and were, no doubt, *Homo sapiens.* They wore skins and headgear made from shells, and lived in permanent settlements in caves or on hilltops close to springs. According to James Mellaart, in *The Neolithic of the Near East,* Natufians were descendants of Europe's Cro-Magnon. They were of rugged Euro-African descent from the Mediterranean area, "linear basic white," he calls them, with dolichocephalic skulls.

It can be argued that the spread of such major societal changes is through the passing on of ideas from one culture, or region, to another. In the case of agriculture, its source is generally believed to be the Levant—countries on the eastern shores of the Mediterranean, specifically Lebanon, Syria, and Israel—during the eighth millennium B.C.E. However, in Egypt there are difficulties with this theory. New Stone Age sites occur in Egypt three thousand years later, and much evidence indicates that the source from which Egyptians gained their knowledge of agriculture must be sought in the south and west rather than the northeast. Yet how could the strong agricultural societies of the Levant, only 160 kilometers away, not have played a role in Egypt's development of farming?[18]

In defense of the dynastic race theory, carvings on an ivory knife handle from the town of Gebel-el-Arak (near Denderah, 250 miles south of Cairo) and paintings on the walls of a late-predynastic tomb dated to 3500 B.C.E. at Hierakonopolis suggest invasion of the Nile Valley by a seafaring people. Some believe the style of the ornamentation on the knife handle to be Mesopotamian or possibly Syrian. The scene possibly represents a sea battle against invaders; this is also depicted in the Hierakonopolis tomb. Both of these show Egypt's native ships and strange vessels with a high prow and stem, unmistakably Mesopotamian in origin. There is also the discovery of late-predynastic graves in the northern part of Upper Egypt, where the skulls unearthed were of greater size and the bodies were larger than those of the natives. According to Walter Emery, the difference is so distinct that any suggestion that these people derived from the earlier stock is impossible.[19]

During this "dark age" of Africa's prehistory (9000–6000 B.C.E.), from which little is known about human events, early southwest Asian Natufian farmers were responsible for the citylike settlements of Jericho and Çatalhöyük in modern-day Turkey, and were also responsible for the domestication of the dog. The earliest domesticated dog discovered so far is from the Belt Cave in Persia, dated to 9500 B.C.E. The next earliest is one found in the Natufian layers near Jericho, which date to 8940 B.C.E.

Because of a lack of archaeological evidence, it is difficult to determine precisely what occurred in northern Egypt between 9000 and 6000 B.C. There is evidence that suggests agriculture was introduced from cultures from Mesopotamia. However, there is also evidence to suggest that farming spread to the north from the south and west. Could it be the case that both are correct and what occurred was a mixing of cultures?

Teeth as Evidence

Other evidence of who the first Egyptians were comes from the discipline of dentistry. Studies of late-Pleistocene and recent human teeth from the Nile Valley, compared with those of other Africans, the British, Spaniards, and Israelis, strongly suggest that genetic isolation of North Africa from Eurasia did not exist. A series of studies that examined dental morphology in the Nile Valley in late-Pleistocene and Holocene times found that an extraordinary amount of change had occurred in the shape of human teeth from these earlier eras to modern times. So much change in tooth shape had occurred that adaptation (natural selection) clearly was not a sufficient explanation. According to Christy G. Turner II, professor of anthropology at Arizona State University, large amounts of rapid diachronic dental morphological changes are found only in populations that had received large numbers of migrants over short periods of time. These comparative dental studies of North Africa show that there was genetic discontinuity between the Pleistocene (prior to 9000 B.C.E.) and the Holocene (after 9000 B.C.E.). Continuity is the case for most of the Holocene.

Lower Egyptian Nubians, during the late Pleistocene and Mesolithic (a period from approximately 11,000 to 5000 B.C.E.), were dentally very similar to West Africans and other Africans south of the Sahara. However, the more recent Nubians were more like southwestern Eurasians. The latest of these North African dental studies involved archaeologically derived materials from Israel, specifically Natufians, and more recent samples. Analyses showed that Natufian dentition was similar to that of more recent southwest Asians, as well as to Holocene (later-era) Nubians. This study, by Christy Turner, concluded that the only way to explain these similarities and differences was to propose significant gene flow and/or actual migration from southwest Asia to the Nile Valley at the end of the Pleistocene. The immigrants may have included Natufians along with their trading partners, the Mushabians, a New Stone Age culture located in the steppe and arid zones of the Negev and Sinai Deserts between 12,500 and 10,500 B.C.E.[20]

According to Turner, there is an archaeological and physical anthropological reason to believe that the Natufians were related to modern Semitic-speaking peoples of the Levant. He suggests that some, if not all, of the Afro-Asiatics originated north of Africa proper. He also believes that the "isolation view" of the origins of Egyptian culture has been propagated for many years as a paradigmatic reaction against the use of migration to explain cultural change in North Africa. According to Turner, some scholars have gone so far as to label anyone a racist who proposes a Eurasian influence on the cultural evolution that occurred near the Nile Valley.

Archaeologists give names to cultures usually after the site where their style of living was first identified. From the perspective of the researcher, then, numerous cultures throughout history emerge that, in appearance, seem to be unrelated to any other culture. However, in reality, almost every culture, past and present, has been influenced by other cultures. Other evidence supports Turner's conclusion that people from the Iberian Peninsula may be linked to the progenitors of Egyptian civilization. But there is a more mysterious connection—with the Mayan culture of prehistoric South America. We will explore this in the next chapter.

TOXIC EVIDENCE FOR
AN OLD THEORY
Ancient Contraband: Trick or Trade?

In 1976, the mummified remains of the Egyptian pharaoh Ramses the Great were displayed at the Museum of Mankind in Paris. It was a unique opportunity for scholars across Europe. The bandages wrapped around the mummy needed replacing, so botanists were given pieces of the fabric to analyze its content.

Dr. Michele Lescott, from the Museum of Natural History in Paris, was fortunate enough to receive a small sample of the royal burial cloth for study. Upon close inspection, she discovered what looked like specks clinging to the fibers of the fragment. Under a microscope, they appeared to be specks of the tobacco plant. She tried several different views, but always found the same result. She was advised that the cloth sample had probably been contaminated by a pipe-toting worker. However, tobacco wasn't introduced into Egypt until modern times.

More than a century ago, the king of Bavaria brought the ornate sarcophagus of Henut Taui, mummy included, to a museum in Munich. In 1992, researchers began a project to investigate its contents. For chemical analysis, they relied on Dr. Svetla Balabanova, of the Institute of Forensic Medicine in Ulm. From her tests, she obtained very baffling results. The body of Henut Taui contained large quantities of cocaine and nicotine, but during ancient times, tobacco grew only in the Americas and coca only in the Bolivian Andes.

The first five positive results were shocking, so she sent samples to three other labs. They were also positive, so she published her results. The academic reaction was fierce, Balabanova says:

> I got a pile of letters that were almost threatening, insulting letters saying it was nonsense, that I was fantasizing, that it was impossible, because it was proven that before Columbus these plants were not found anywhere in the world outside of the Americas.[1]

Yet, the tests Balabanova performed on hair shafts are a well-accepted method for determining drug use. They have been for the last twenty-five years. There is no chance for contamination. Drugs, and other substances consumed by humans, get into the hair proteins, where they stay for months and remain even after death. In fact, they can stay there forever.

To be sure no external contamination is present, the hair sample is washed in alcohol and then the washing solution itself is tested. If the testing solution is clear but the hair tests positive, then the drug must be inside the hair shaft, which means the person consumed the drug at some time during his or her lifetime. Toxicologists consider hair analysis a way to disprove contamination after death. Balabanova stands by her methods and results:

> There's no way there can be a mistake in this test. This method is widely accepted and has been used thousands of times. If the results are not genuine, then the explanation must lie elsewhere, and not in my tests, because I'm one hundred percent certain about the results.[2]

The lotus flower could explain these baffling results. It contains powerful nicotine and was actually used, as inscriptions on the grand temple at Karnak depict. The inscriptions show Egyptians dropping the lotus flower into a cup. Its contents, possibly wine, would react with the plant, thereby releasing the nicotine. But there is a problem with this solution. The levels of nicotine found in the mummies were lethal. Balabanova believed that tobacco had to be used in the mummification process. High doses of nicotine are antibacterial, and would help in the preservation process. Was this part of the well-kept secret of mummification? Another explanation could be that a species of tobacco existed that is now extinct. Botanists assure us, however, that if another ancient species of tobacco had existed, they would have known about it.

Finding cocaine in these ancient remains is a completely different matter. According to Dr. Sandy Knapp, of the Natural History Museum in London, finding cocaine in Egyptian mummies is almost impossible.[3] Tests were performed on the mummies to ensure that they were authentic. They were. Balabanova says it is a mystery, but admits it is conceivable that the coca plant was imported into Egypt before Columbian times, the only alternative to explain the facts. Could there really have been an ancient international drug trade with links extending all the way to the Americas? Egyptologists, such as John Baines of Oxford University, believe this idea is ludicrous:

> The idea that the Egyptians were traveling to America is, overall, absurd. I don't know of anyone who is professionally employed as an Egyptologist, anthropologist, or archaeologist who seriously believes in any of these possibilities, and I also don't know anyone who spends time doing research into these areas because they're perceived to be areas without any real meaning for the subjects.[4]

But in fact there are people doing this research, such as Alice Kehoe of Marquette University, and Martin Bernal of Cornell University, as well as Robert Schoch, who set forth his theory in *Voyages of the Pyramid Builders*. Kehoe believes there is evidence of both transatlantic and transpacific contact between the eastern and western hemispheres, but admits some archaeologists avoid discussing the issue. The sweet potato, she claims, proves it, and there are sculptures of eastern Indian goddesses holding an ear of corn. Peanuts, found in western China, add more credence. Bernal, professor emeritus of ancient Eastern Mediterranean history, agrees, in theory, and calls these voyages to the Americas "overwhelmingly likely."[5]

These beliefs are backed, in part, by Roman jars found in 1975 in a Brazilian harbor called the Bay of Jars. Some scholars suggest that a sunken Roman galley could be the source, but this interpretation is vigorously disputed. However, in Brazil there is also an inscription that appears to be that of an ancient Mediterranean language. And in Mexico, there are three-thousand-year-old figurines with beards, a feature unknown in Native Americans, plus colossal statues that are said to look African. These items were pointed out by the best-selling author Graham Hancock in *Fingerprints of the Gods*.

The problem that faces those who espouse such theories of transoceanic travel is the lack of artifacts to back them. Physical evidence, in Africa or America, is hard to come by. It may be that the Egyptians were not a seafaring people, but it could be the case that others were. The question, then, becomes: Who were the transoceanic travelers? Opinions are divided. Some fully believe that exploring peoples crossed the oceans. Others believe the idea is absurd. However, science has a history of labeling theories absurd only to find out, one day, that they are true.

Augustus Le Plongeon's Legacy of Mayan Voyages

Some of today's scientists believe that ancient cultures, as explorers or traders, crossed the oceans seeking new lands. They are not the first to believe this. Augustus Le Plongeon did so over a hundred years ago. His story is as fascinating as it is shocking.

During the twilight years of his career, Augustus Henry Julius Le Plongeon (1826–1908) was labeled "absurd" by the scientific community of his day. This judgment was regarding not the difficult, and sometimes dangerous, fieldwork he performed, but rather the conclusions and theories he set forth from the data he collected. Despite the stamp of illegitimacy, Le Plongeon was a brilliant man whose career moved from gold mining to photography to medicine to archaeology. He spoke French, English, Spanish, and Yucatecan Mayan, which he learned by living and working in the Yucatán for twelve years at various Mayan ruins. He and his wife, Alice, never gave up on their convictions. Amid vigorous opposition, they died promoting their work and their theories.

Arriving in the Yucatán

In 1873, the Le Plongeons arrived in the Yucatán Peninsula, a land that was divided between the Mexican government and Mayan rebels. There they planned to document the Mayan ruins by the new photographic method Augustus had helped to perfect—the wet collodion glass-plate negative process. Le Plongeon brought with him years of experience in surveying and photography (recently in Peru), and a hunch he planned to test by systematic observation. He believed that a culture from South America was the founder of the civilized world, a speculation that he first postulated while surveying the ancient ruins at Tiahuanaco. The facts they were going to uncover would either prove or disprove his hypothesis. He wanted to judge for himself rather than rely on the theories of other scholars.[6]

A week after they arrived in Merida, Yucatán's capital, Alice was struck with yellow fever. After her recovery, they moved from their hotel to better accommodations and began investigating the local area. They studied nearby ruins, noting architectural features, inscriptions, and carvings that they hoped could point the way to further research. They also spent considerable time learning to speak the Mayan language and searching the Merida historical archives. Le Plongeon viewed understanding the Mayan language, and the ability to communicate with the living Mayans, as an important step to interpreting the past.

The Le Plongeons first visited the ancient city of Uxmal during the 1873–74 dry season, one of the more accessible and larger ruins in the Yucatán. Controlled by the Mexican government, it was beyond the reach of Mayan rebels. It was also an opportunity to attend a number of festivals and to observe the customs of the people. As a result of their increasing involvement with the natives, it was their conviction that the Yucatán people were the direct descendants of the ancient Mayans who had built the once magnificent cities and temples. Uxmal provided some evidence in support of his theory, but the primary proof would have to come from Chichén Itzá, the largest of the pre-Columbian archaeological sites. However, it lay in land controlled by the rebels. Getting there proved to be an adventure in itself.

Upon arrival in Chichén Itzá, Le Plongeon's first goal was to find the Akab Dzib (the house of dark writing) in order to examine the hieroglyphic text that Mariano Chable, a very old man from Merida, had described. Chable had said that this text contained an inscription that was a prophecy, and that one day the inhabitants of Saci (Valladolid, a town in the Yucatán) would converse with those of Ho (Merida, the capital) by means of a cord that would be stretched by people foreign to the country. Le Plongeon discovered the building overgrown by brush and behind a rotunda-styled observatory known as the Caracol. The glyphs he sought were found on a stone lintel atop a door in an interior room, the portrait of a Mayan priest or ruler beneath it. As soon as it was cleared, he began deciphering. According to Le Plongeon, some of the glyphs did represent lightning or electricity. It also included a reference to the cord the old man spoke of. The find was so important that

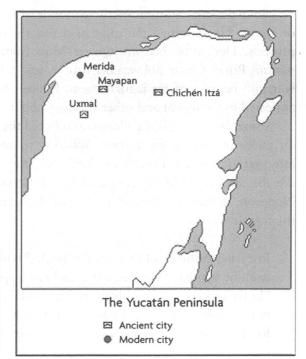

Fig. 8.1. The Yucatán Peninsula, showing sites of Le Plongeon's research

he set up his photographic equipment and embarked on a thorough documentation.

Le Plongeon wrote of his discovery to the president of Mexico and to the American Antiquarian Society, noting that the text was "said to be a prophecy." The American Antiquarian Society published it in 1877, and thereafter, those who opposed his views claimed that he believed the Maya used the telegraph for communications. It was the beginning of the end of his formerly reputable career.

Excavating the Story of Queen Moo

In Chichén Itzá, from the Upper Temple of the Jaguars, the Le Plongeons copied the remnants of murals depicting scenes of village life, religious events, warfare, and rulers. After studying these scenes, Le Plongeon concluded that they told the story of a single generation of rulers and that it offered the answer to the question of Mayan diffusion. For Le Plongeon, it was evidence of history as opposed to myth, as well as the origin of other civilizations and their mythology.

Animal representations on these murals were symbols of their totems, or spirits. He identified the eagle as a macaw, the symbol of a Mayan princess. Her name became Queen Moo from the Mayan word for *macaw*. Prince Chaacmol was her brother and referred to as a "powerful warrior" because of his jaguar totem. Prince Chaacmol's spotted shield appeared in the mural and other carvings about the temple.

Using these murals, Le Plongeon selected the spot where he believed an important statue lay buried. Whether it was because of a correct interpretation of the murals or sheer luck, the spot where he chose to dig did, in fact, hold the statue of Prince Chaacmol. According to Le Plongeon, it was the same character as the warrior image depicted on the temple walls:

> In tracing the figure of Chaacmol in battle, I remarked that the shield worn by him had painted on it round green spots, and was exactly like the ornaments placed between tiger and tiger on the entablature of the same monument. I naturally concluded that the monument had been raised to the memory of the warrior bearing the shield.[7]

He immediately sent word of his discovery north to his colleagues. The stateside editor of Le Plongeon's field reports, Stephen Salisbury, changed the spelling of "Chaacmol" to "Chacmool," a Mayan word for puma. Unknown to Salisbury, Le Plongeon had specifically used *chaac* and *mol,* the Mayan words for "powerful warrior." However, "Chacmool" became the accepted spelling, although Le Plongeon reasserted his authority and later changed the name in his own writings to Coh, a more common Mayan word with the same meaning.

The Chaacmol

Deep in the mound where Le Plongeon ordered the dig, they found a large stone sculpture of a reclining jaguar with the same round dots inscribed on the murals of the temple walls. Le Plongeon identified it as the Mayan prince Chaacmol, the youngest brother and consort of Queen Moo. Along with the statue, they uncovered a number of artifacts. Eighteen flint projectile points were found at the base of the statue. Seven were chipped from green stone; two were flat ceramic plates. There was also a ceramic pot. Le Plongeon had a jade tube mounted in a gold brooch as a gift for his wife, which symbolized her spiritual connection with the ancient Mayan queen. It became Alice's talisman.

On the chest of the figure was a bowl containing a broken flint blade, a jade bead, and organic remains that Le Plongeon believed to be the cremated remains of Prince Chaacmol's heart. Le Plongeon verified the material through Charles Thompson, a professor of chemistry at the Worcester Free Institute. Thompson's analysis declared that it was "once part of a human body which has been burned with some fuel."[8]

With this discovery, Le Plongeon believed that he had correctly deciphered the murals. It gave him the interpretative perspective to further construct Mayan history.

In light of their findings, the Le Plongeons returned to Uxmal to inspect figures carved there, and to obtain a broader view of Mayan iconography. The brief visit was long enough to convince Augustus and Alice that Queen Moo and other Mayan figures were historic, since they were at both sites, Chichén Itzá and Uxmal. They believed Queen Moo's profile was included in the façade of the Governor' Palace, although the image was unclear and not visible from all angles. Nevertheless, according to Le Plongeon's Mayan history, it was carved under the direction of Queen Moo's other brother, Prince Aac.

In documenting their work at Uxmal, Le Plongeon photographed the façade and highlighted some of the details to help clarify Queen Moo's profile. It fostered another charge from his antagonists, one of great damage. He was accused of intentionally falsifying his pictures in order to promote his theory of Mayan cultural diffusion.

Prince Cay

During their final field season at Uxmal, they discovered an inscription Le Plongeon believed to be a reference to Chaacmol's elder brother, Prince Cay (the Mayan word for fish). With a hunch that the effigy of Prince Cay was hidden in a lower section of the Adivino pyramid at Uxmal, he tunneled into a wall and found the splendid sculpture of a royal man, head adorned with a fish, his totem.

Excited about his find, Le Plongeon showed two Americans from Merida the sculpture of Prince Cay and asked them to keep it under wraps. They did not, and leaked it to a Merida newspaper. Hearing the news, a nearby plantation administrator embarked on a mission to discover where Le Plongeon found the sculpture, not only for its historic value, but also for the limestone blocks that would naturally be part of the site. He wanted them for their resale value. To prevent this, Le Plongeon devised a plan that would frighten him and any other scavengers considering a raid. He published a false notice in the *Eco de Comercio*, a local newspaper, explaining that he had rigged the site with dynamite for demolition. Although the structures were never really rigged to explode, it brought Le Plongeon harsh criticism. His already tainted reputation, in the eyes of American scholars and archaeologists, grew worse.

In 1883, the Le Plongeons returned to Chichén Itzá to record the murals in the Upper Temple of the Jaguars (referred to as the Memorial Hall) and excavate what they hoped was the mausoleum of Prince Cay. On the exposed portion of the Venus Platform was the carving of a fish. This, of course, led Le Plongeon to believe it was his tomb. The similarity of the mound adjacent to the Venus Platform to the one next to the Platform of the Eagles (where he found the Chaacmol) suggested it was a good place to start digging. They planned to be meticulous in recording this excavation so that their work, and subsequent interpretation, would allow no room for criticism.

Work began with a trench in the northwest corner of the platform, where a few facing stones remained. Core stones, now rubble with a little mortar still between them, were soon found. After eight days, workmen finally uncovered a sculpture four feet north of the platform at ground level. Alice reported the results of this excavation in *Scientific American:* "The figure was thickly coated with loose mortar. One leg was broken off below the knee, but we found it under the figure, and afterward adjusted it in place to make a picture."[9]

The statue rested on small conical pillars placed on their sides. It was part of a design that included 182 cones covering twenty-four square feet. Two thirds were painted blue; the other third, red. All were varying in height from three to four feet. Twelve serpent heads, oriented in various directions, were on a level with the pillars. Their decorations and colors had survived undisturbed, although they had been broken before their burial. Here is a description from *A Dream of Maya,* Desmond and Messenger's biography of the Le Plongeons (text in quotations are Le Plongeon's own words):

> "From the top of each head rises a kind of plume or perhaps flame, and on each side of the front of the head perpendicular ornaments like horns." The heads were painted green and had feathers incised on the upper part. Their undersides were covered with serpent scales. The edges of the jaws were also yellow, while the forked

tongue and the gums were red. The teeth were white. Around the eyes and "over the brow" was blue and the eyes were filled with a white "shell." The horns or nose plugs projecting from the snout were green, and tipped in red as was the "feather" on the top.[10]

Also found in the area of the stone cones was an urn set into the floor that contained a flat trapezoidal object, two half-beads of jadeite, a jade tube, a small spherical crystal ball, and the remains of a mosaic.

Digging continued through three earlier floor levels, where they uncovered more artifacts, including an obsidian projectile point, shards of pottery, and the bones of a small animal. After reaching the final floor, found at bedrock and painted red, Le Plongeon directed work toward the southwest. There, they uncovered several flat stones carved in low relief. Farther to the south, they discovered a stone with a fish engraved on it and enclosed by the folds of a serpent's body. At that point, Le Plongeon was convinced that they had found the burial chamber of Prince Cay. All he needed to do was publish his work and his theories.

Developing Mayan History, Le Plongeon–Style

Using murals, sculptures, and engravings from Uxmal and Chichén Itzá, Le Plongeon re-created and narrated a history of several key Mayan rulers and their link to other cultures. The story, according to Le Plongeon, occurred 11,500 years ago. His history appeared fully developed in his book *Sacred Mysteries Among the Maya and Quiches,* and told of the love between Queen Moo and Prince Coh, and of his death by the hand of his jealous brother Aac. According to Le Plongeon's interpretation, during a period of civil unrest after the death of Prince Coh, Queen Moo was forced to flee to Egypt and on her arrival was recognized as a long-lost sister. The story was substantiated, Le Plongeon felt, not only by the wealth of artifacts recovered during excavations from Uxmal and Chichén Itzá, but also by what he interpreted as the cremated remains of Prince Coh's heart. Le Plongeon tells us it was the story that was graphically illustrated on the walls of the Upper Temple of the Jaguars and in the story of the Troano Manuscript.

However, some believe he had other motives for developing the connection between Egypt and Maya. He wanted to find the origin of Masonry, a secret fraternal order, which some wanted to trace to Egypt. As a Mason himself, he was familiar with its symbolism and believed he had discovered ample evidence of it at Uxmal. Le Plongeon decided that the Maya were direct antecedents of the founders of Masonry, which implies that its origins were more ancient than if it had begun in Egypt.

The skull and crossbones carved on the Adivino Pyramid and a sculptured torso with an inverted hand on an apron, both Masonic symbols, were convincing. He showed the torso to two friends in Merida, but the scupture later disappeared without a trace. Without this piece of evidence to support the Masonry connection, a more cautious person might have dropped that line of reasoning, knowing it would be controversial. But Le Plongeon persisted and even used certain architectural features, including corbeled arches, as further evidence of the connection. It was another strike against him.

Developing the Mayan Alphabet

In November 1880, when the Le Plongeons were at the ancient capital of Mayapan, they searched for the key to deciphering the Mayan hieroglyphics. It was a reaction to scholars who apparently dismissed the existence of a Mayan alphabet. This alleged alphabet was recorded in the sixteenth century after the Spanish conquest, and was believed to be an invention of the bishop of Yucatán, Diego de Landa. Le Plongeon hoped to prove the alphabet authentic. By studying the ancient monuments, and through his detailed knowledge of Mayan life and language, he hoped to be able to reconstruct the alphabet. With his experience and knowledge of their language and culture, could there be anyone better suited for the job? Le Plongeon thought not:

> My knowledge of them must, of necessity, be greater than that of
> gentlemen who write from behind their desks, ignorant of the true
> facts.[11]

Le Plongeon arranged Mayan phonetics into an alphabet and linked it not only with Egypt, but also with the Greek and Akkadian cultures of ancient Mesopotamia.

According to Le Plongeon, many of the key syllables of these languages had identical or near-identical meaning. For example, the Mayan character *ma*, ⌀, is composed of two different symbols, ⌐ and ⊙. The symbol ⌐ represents an outline of their country, the Yucatán Peninsula (see figure 8.2). The two *imix* symbols, ⊙, represent the bodies of water on each side of the peninsula—the Gulf of Mexico and the Caribbean Sea. The ⊙ symbol represents a woman's breast, with nipples and areola, meaning bosom. But bosom can mean more than a woman's breasts. It is also an enclosed place, such as "the bosom of the deep." Thus, Le Plongeon believed the symbol for *ma*, ᵥ✧, the angled chimney between two *imix*, signified their "earth" or "place"—an area of land between two bodies of water. Akkadians used this same syllable, *ma*, to express the idea of physical locality.[12]

The Egyptians also had a similar symbol for their letter *M*, ⊏⊐, which also means place or site. The Greek word τοπος (place or site) of the Greek text inscribed on the Rosetta Stone (a granite slab inscribed in hieroglyphics, demotics, and Greek with identical texts of a decree by a council of priests) is expressed in the hieroglyphic part of the tablet by an owl for *M* and the extended arm for the *A*, which gives the Coptic word μα (ma)—"site" or "place." Le Plongeon comments:

> No one has ever told us why the learned hierogrammatists of Egypt gave to the sign ⊏⊐ the value of *ma*. No one can, because nobody knows the origin of the Egyptians, of their civilization, nor their country where it grew from infancy to maturity.[13]

Le Plongeon offers other coincidences, such as the name for water. In Mayan it is *ha*, in Egyptian and Chaldean *a*.[14] The Egyptians called their land the "place of the crocodiles," since it was, naturally, swarming with crocodiles. *Ain* was the word they used on monuments and in the hieroglyphs. It depicted the tail of the animal that it stood for. It is also the Mayan word for crocodile. Its tail serves as rudder to the animal, so it symbolized a boat as well as a crocodile.[15]

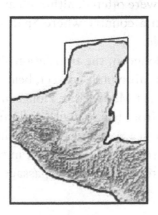

Fig. 8.2. Yucatán Peninsula and its Mayan symbol

Egypt has always been a relatively treeless land. During the inundations, trees were uprooted, carried away by the waters, and deposited all over the land. The farmer, in order to plow the soil, had to clear the land of debris. Assyrians gave the names Misur and Muzur to this land. Coincidentally, *miz* in Mayan means "to clear away rubbish of trees" and *muuzul* "to uproot trees."[16]

According to the scholars of Le Plongeon's day, the Greek word *thalassa,* for "sea," is of unknown origin. Had Greek scholars been acquainted with the Mayan language, Le Plongeon believes, they would have easily found it in the word *thallac,* which means a "thing unstable." The Greek verb *tarasso* or *thrasso* means "to agitate."[17]

In 403 B.C.E., during the archonship of Euclid, Greek grammarians arranged the Athenian alphabet to its present form. For the names of their letters, they adopted words formed by the combination of the various sounds composing each line of Le Plongeon's Mayan epic. In this most interesting philological and historical fact, as Le Plongeon refers to it, he found the reason why certain letters having the same value were placed apart, instead of juxtaposed, as they naturally should be. What else would have provoked Euclid and his collaborators to separate the Epsilon from the Eta, the Theta from the Tau, to place the Omikron in the middle and the Omega at the end of the alphabet?[18]

In August 1882, Le Plongeon published, in the *Revista de Merida,* a daily paper of Merida, a Spanish translation of the Mayan epic formed by the names of the letters of the Greek alphabet. He invited Mayan scholars to review and correct it, in case any word had been used incorrectly. He was also eager to present his discovery to the scientific world. No corrections were offered, although at the time it attracted the attention of students in a country where Spanish and Mayan were the vernacular of the people.

According to Le Plongeon, the translation shown in table 8.1 (page 170) may be regarded as absolutely correct, being an English rendering of that published in Spanish at Merida.[19] Le Plongeon believed that the Mayan alphabet, sounded out from beginning to end, told the story of Atlantis, or Mu, sinking into the sea. Le Plongeon's rendition of the story, which he describes as "freely translated," is shown in table 8.2 (page 171).[20]

This corresponds to a descriptive passage in Plato's dialogue of *Timaeaus:*

Afterwards there occurred violent earthquakes and floods; and in a single day and night of misfortune all your warlike men in a body sank into the earth, and the island of Atlantis in like manner disappeared in the depths of the sea. For which reason the sea in those parts is impassable and impenetrable, because there is a shoal of mud in the way; and this was caused by the subsidence of the island.[21]

Le Plongeon's language coincidences did not end there, but extended into ancient cosmology. According to Bishop Eusebius of Caesarea during the second century, in the Chaldean legend of the creation, at the beginning of time a woman ruled over all the monstrous beasts that inhabited the waters. Her name was Thalaatth. The Greeks translated it Thalassa, and applied it to the sea itself. Modern philologists believe the etymology of that word has been lost. Le Plongeon, again, finds the answer in the Mayan language. Thallac denotes "a thing without steadiness," like the sea.[22] He adds that the names Tiamat and Bel-Marduk add corroborating evidence to confirm this theory, since no language except Mayan offers such a natural etymon and simple explanation of their meaning. Tiamat, "the depths," is a Mayan word composed of the four primitives, *ti, ha, ma, ti* (that is, *ti*—"there"; *ha*—"water"; *ma*—"without"; *ti*—"land"). *Tiamat* thus means "everywhere water, nowhere land," or the "deep."[23]

The same evidence turns up in Hebrew studies. In an article published by *Century Magazine* in January 1894, Morris Jastrow Jr. explains that the word *tehom* occurs both in the cuneiform tablets and in Genesis with the meaning "the deep," which is precisely its import in the Mayan language. [24]

Mayan Migrations

With this linguistic evidence, Le Plongeon mapped out the prehistoric migrations of the earliest Maya. They journeyed from their homes in the "lands of the west," across the Pacific, along the shores of the Indian Ocean, to the head of the Persian Gulf, then up the Euphrates—on the banks of which they formed settlements. Le Plongeon does not claim that the Maya were the sole force that built Mesopotamian cities and societies. Local populations obviously played a role, as did the mixing of cultural ideas and traditions, but it was the Mayan explorers, he argues, who provided the impetus to civil growth. Sumerian mythology lends support to such an idea in the tale of the seven sages, where fishlike creatures, under the command of Enki (Akkadian Ea), arrived from the sea, full

TABLE 8.1. GREEK ALPHABET AND MAYAN VOCABULARY
(with their English meanings)

alpha	al (heavy) paa (break) ha (water)
beta	be (walk) ta (place)
gamma	kam (receive) ma (earth)
delta	tel (depth; bottom) ta (where)
epsilon	ep (obstruct) zil (make edges) on-om (whirlpool; to whirl)
zeta	ae (strike) ta (place; ground)
eta	et (with) ha (water)
theta	thetheah (extend) ha (water)
iota	io (all that lives and moves) ta (earth)
kappa	ka (sediment) paa (break; open)
lambda	lam (submerge) be (go; walk) ta (where; place)
mu	mu (mu)
ni [nu]	ni (point; summit)
xi	si (rise over; appear over)
omikron	om (whirlpool; whirl) ik (wind) le (place) on (circular)
pi	pi (to place by little and little)
rho	la (until) ho (come)
sigma	zi (cold) ik (wind) ma (before)
tau	ta (where) u (basin; valley)
upsilon	u (abyss) pa (tank) zi (cold; frozen) le (place) on (circular)
phi	pe (come; form) hi (clay)
chi	dhi (mouth; aperture)
psi	pe (come out) zi (vapor)
omega	o (there) mee (whirl) ka (sediments)

TABLE 8.2. LEPLONGEON'S TRANSLATION OF SINKING OF ATLANTIS
(italics are Le Plongeon's)

alpha	Heavily break—*the*—water
beta	extending—*over the*—plains.
gamma	*They—cover—the*—land
delta	*in* low places where
epsilon	*there are*—obstructions, shores form the whirlpools
zeta	strike—*the*—earth
eta	with water.
theta	*The*—water spreads
iota	*on* all that lives and moves.
kappa	Sediments give way.
lambda	Submerged is—*the*—land
mu	*of* Mu.
ni	The peaks—*only*
xi	appear above—*the water*.
omikron	Whirlwinds blow around
pi	by little and little,
rho	until comes
sigma	cold air. Before
tau	where—*existed*—valleys,
upsilon	*now*, abysses, frozen tanks. In circular places
phi	clay—formed.
chi	*A*—mouth
psi	opens; vapors
omega	come forth—and *volcanic* sediments.

of wisdom, to serve as counselors for the kings. They were responsible for the invention and the building of the cities.[25]

Some of these Mayan-speaking peoples, following the exploratory and migratory instincts inherited from their ancestors, left the Mesopotamian plain and made their way across Syria toward the setting sun in search of new lands. They reached the Isthmus of Suez, and continued until they entered the fertile valley of the Nile. Following the banks of the river, they selected an area of Nubia, where they settled. They named it Maiu, in remembrance of their cultural birthplace in western lands. There they established their worship and ways in a new country.[26]

Mayan History or Le Plongeon Heresy

Le Plongeon asserts that, according to their own history and legend, during prehistoric times, the Mayans entered the Yucatán from the west led by Itzamná, their earliest mentioned leader and hero. Along a pathway mysteriously opened through the waters, they came from the Far East beyond the ocean. A second migration occurred sometime later, during the second century C.E., led by Kukulcan, a miraculous priest and teacher who became the founder of the Mayan kingdom and civilization.[27]

During the fifth century C.E. invaders from the south, the Nahuatl, destroyed the principal Mayan cities, including the carvings of heroes, rulers, and celebrated women that adorned the public buildings. Philosophers and priests carefully hid the books containing the record of the ancient traditions and history, texts that reach back to the settlement of the peninsula by their ancestors. Le Plongeon asserts that these books have remained hidden to this day.[28]

According to Le Plongeon, the Itzaes (a local culture of the lowland-dwelling Maya), who preferred isolation to submission, abandoned their homes and colleges, preferring to wander in the desert.[29] The arts and sciences soon declined, as did their civilization. Political strife and religious dissension led to civil war. Before long, the kingdom was disassembled, and the capital, Mayapan, destroyed. During this horrific time, the old traditions and lore were forgotten. Mixed with the traditions, superstitions, and fables of the Nahuatls, their traditions and history assumed the form of myths. The great men and women of the primitive ages were transformed into gods of the elements and of the phenomena of nature. With their ancient libraries gone, new books had to be written to contain those myths, of which the Troano and Dresden Manuscripts seem to belong. The Troano and Dresden Manuscripts are pre-Columbian Mayan hieroglyphic texts held by Museo de América in Madrid and the Sächsische Landesbibliothek in Dresden. The Dresden codex is a calendar showing which gods are responsible for which days of the year, and explains the details of the Mayan calendar and number system. The Troano (or Madrid) codex deals with horoscopes and astrological tables and is believed to be authored by eight scribes.

With the disappearance of the old priesthood went the knowledge of their sacred mode of writing. Le Plongeon explains that the legends graven on the façades of temples and palaces, written in those characters, were no longer understood, except perhaps by a few who were sworn to secrecy. The names of the builders, their history, and the phenomena of nature they witnessed were as much a mystery to these people as they have been to others up to the present day.

Land of the Scorpion

Of special interest to Le Plongeon was a story contained in the Troano Manuscript that told of a dreadful natural cataclysm, most likely an earthquake. According to his research, four authors left descriptions of this same event in the Mayan language. One is found in the Codex Cortesianus, now considered part of the Troano Manuscript; another appears on an engraving above a doorway in the Temple of the Jaguars at Chichén Itzá; and the fourth account is part of an epic poem found in Athens. However, Le Plongeon offered no glyph-by-glyph translation of the Chichén Itzá engraving.

The discovery of a partial mural, painted on an edifice at Kabah (a city just south of Uxmal), enticed Le Plongeon to devote many months to the study of the Troano Manuscript. Several pages at the beginning of the second part were dedicated to recounting the "awful phenomena" that occurred during the cataclysm that submerged ten countries. Among them was the large island call the "land of Mu," situated among the strangely crooked line of islands historically known as the West Indies. To the Maya, it was the "land of the scorpion." Le Plongeon was astonished and gratified to find an account of the events written during the lives of the characters he found in the ruins. Their history, described in the mural paintings, was also told in the legends and sculptures still adorning the walls of their palaces and temples. He was also pleased to learn that these ancient celebrities had already been converted, at the time of the Troano Manuscript, into gods of the elements. To the new Maya, these beings became the agents who produced the terrible earthquakes that violently shook the "lands of the west," as told in the narrative of the Akab-cib, and laid the island to rest beneath the waves of the Atlantic Ocean.[30]

Queen Moo's Voyage

With the deciphering of the Troano Manuscript, the story of Queen Moo continued. Sailing out from the Yucatán, she sought refuge in the land of the scorpion (the West Indies), but discovered that Mu, the heart of the land, had vanished. With no alternatives, she continued her voyage eastward and succeeded in reaching Egypt. Le Plongeon substantiates this by implying that she is mentioned on Egyptian monuments and in papyri, always referred to as Queen Mau (Moo). To the Egyptians, she is better known as the goddess Isis, wearing vestments of various colors that imitate feather work, similar to the plumage of the macaw, after which she was named in the Mayan language.[31] According to Le Plongeon, Isis was a term of endearment applied to her by followers and new subjects, a corruption or possibly a dialectical pronunciation of the Mayan word *icin* (pronounced *idzin*), which means "little sister."

Before leaving the Yucatán Peninsula, Queen Moo ordered the erection of a memorial hall, the Temple of the Jaguars, which was dedicated to the memory of Prince Coh. She had the principal events of their life depicted in bright colors on the walls of the funeral chamber. Not satisfied with this, she also raised over his remains a mausoleum equivalent to the marble splendor of modern structures of similar purpose.

All four sides of the monument were decorated with sculptured panels in *mezzo relievo*. One frieze represents a dying warrior on his back, his knees drawn up, the soles of his feet planted firmly on the ground. His head, thrown backward, is covered with a helmet. From his parted lips, the breath of life escapes in the shape of a slender flame. His posture is the same as that given by the Maya, during those times, to all the statues of their great heroes, a position that represented the contour of the Mayan empire as nearly as the human body could be made to assume it.[32]

The upper part of the body, instead of being erect, is pictured lying down, and, with his head thrown back, is emblematic of the nation's chief being dead. In his right hand, which is placed upon his breast, he holds a broken scepter composed of three spears, the weapons that inflicted his mortal wounds. One wound is under the left shoulder blade, aimed at the heart from behind, indicating that the victim was treacherously murdered. Two others are in the lower back. His left arm is placed across his breast with the left hand resting on the right shoulder as a token of respect among the living. Le Plongeon interprets this as an attitude of humility in which the souls of the departed must appear before the judgment seat of Yum-cimil, the "god of death." Le Plongeon speculated that it was these same customs that were displayed in Egyptian inscriptions and papyri, where the souls, when standing before the throne of Osiris in Amenti, are waiting to receive their sentence.

"The Egyptians," says the pioneering Egyptologist Sir John Gardner Wilkinson, "placed the arms of the mummies extended along the side, the palms inward and resting on their thighs, or brought forward over the groin, sometimes even across the breast; and occasionally one arm in the former, the other in the latter position."[33] The French librarian and paleographer Champollion Figeac (1788–1867), commenting on Prince Coh's monument, observes that the upper end of the scepter he is depicted with is ornamented with an open dipetalous flower, with a half-opened bud in the center of the corolla.[34] This may represent the fact that the dead warrior was killed in the flower of life, before reaching maturity. The lower portion of the scepter is carved to represent a leopard's paw and intended for the name of the dead hero, Coh, or Chaacmol, "leopard."

> The etymon of the last word is Chaac, "thunder," "tempest," hence, "irresistible power;" and mol, "the paw of any carnivorous animal." The leopard being the largest and fiercest of the beasts of prey inhabiting the forests of Yucatán and Central America the Mayas, who, as we have said, named all things by *onomatopoeia*, called their most famous warrior Chaacmol; that is, "the paw swift like thunder," "the paw with irresistible power like the tempest."[35]

On the panels adorning the architrave were carved two figures. One is a leopard and the other a macaw in the act of licking (or eating) hearts. According to Le Plongeon, the first is the totem of the warrior to whose memory the mausoleum was erected. The other is that of his wife, Queen Moo, being portrayed in the act of licking the hearts of her enemies defeated in battle, so as to inherit their valor.

At the foot of the balustrades, large serpent heads with open mouths and protruding tongues adorn the staircase leading to the top of the mausoleum. These serpent heads, totems of the Cans (the ruling family), were used in all edifices erected by them to announce that they were built by their order. The tongue protruding from the mouth was the symbol of wisdom among the Maya, and was often used in the portraits of priests and kings, who were endowed with great wisdom.

The Mayan Sphinx

A very interesting statue crowned Prince Coh's mausoleum, a dying leopard with a human head. To Le Plongeon, it was a "veritable sphinx," and possibly the prototype of the mysterious Egyptian Sphinx. This Mayan sphinx, like the leopard in the sculptures, has three deep holes in its back, symbolic of the wounds inflicted by his brother Aac.

This brave Mayan warrior, whose enemies could not kill in a fair fight, was treacherously slain by his cowardly brother, just as Osiris, in Egypt, was murdered by his brother Seth, and for the same motive—jealousy. In Egyptian history, Osiris comes to us as a myth. However, according to Le Plongeon, Prince Coh, the beloved Ozil, was a tangible reality—the remains of his charred heart were found, as well as the weapons that caused his death.

Since its discovery, the Egyptian Sphinx has been a riddle of culture and antiquity that has remained unsolved to our day. It is still, in the words of Baron Christian Karl Josias Bunsen, author of *Egypt's Place in Universal History* (1848), "the enigma of history."[36] Bunsen observes that the name most conspicuous on the stela (an ancient upright stone slab bearing text or markings) in the temple between the

Fig. 8.3. Prince Coh's mausoleum
(from Augustus Le Plongeon's Queen Moo and the Egyptian Sphinx)

paws of the Sphinx is that of Armais, who was pharaoh between 1298 and 1394 B.C.E. according to a list of kings compiled by the Greek priest and historian Manethos. According to William Osburn, author of *The Monumental History of Egypt, as Recorded on the Ruins of Her Temples, Palaces, and Tombs* (1854), the Sphinx was the work of Khafre; but Osburn is still in doubt, for he adds:

> On the other hand, the great enigma of the bearded giant Sphinx still remains unsolved. When and by whom was the colossal statue erected, and what was its signification? . . . We are accustomed to regard the Sphinx in Egypt as a portrait of the king, and generally, indeed, as that of a particular king whose features it is said to represent. [37]

In the hieroglyphic written character, the sphinx is called Neb, "the lord."[38] Richard Lepsius (1810–1884), considered to be the founder of modern Egyptology, remarks:

> King Khafra was named in the inscription [on the stela between the Sphinx's paws], but it does not seem reasonable thence to conclude that Khafra first caused the lion to be executed, as another inscription teaches us King Khafra had already seen the monster, or, in other words, says that before him the statue already existed, the work of another Pharaoh. The names of Thutmose IV, of Ramses II, as well as that of Khafra, are inscribed on the base.[39]

Plinius, the first author to ever mention the Sphinx, refers to it as the Tomb of Amasis.[40] As discussed in chapter 1, the age of the Sphinx cannot be determined with certainty. Jacques de Rougé (1842–1923), in his *Six Premiere Dynasties*, supposes the Sphinx to be as old as the fourth dynasty (2575–2467 B.C.E.), but it is probably of equal age with, if not older than, the pyramids. As to its significance, Clement of Alexandria simply tells us that the Sphinx was the emblem of the "union of force with prudence or wisdom"[41]—that is, of physical and intellectual power, supposed attributes of Egyptian kings.

Le Plongeon points out certain analogies that exist between the Egyptian Sphinx and the leopard with the human head that crouches atop Prince Coh's mausoleum. In order to better understand these analogies, it is necessary to consider not only the meaning of the names of the Sphinx, but also its position relative to the horizon and to the edifices that surround it.

The Egyptian Sphinx faces east and is in front of the second (Khafre's) pyramid, overlooking the Nile. It represents a resting or crouching lion (possibly a leopard) with a human head. Piazzi Smyth tells us that "about the head and face, though nowhere else, there is much original statuary surface still, occasionally, painted dull red."[42]

The mausoleum of Prince Coh, at Chichén Itzá, stands in front and to the east of the Memorial Hall. The statue on top was that of a leopard with a human head. The sacred color of the Maya was red-brown, judging from the fresco paintings in the funeral chamber, and, according to the bishop of Yucatán, Diego de Landa, even during the time of the Spanish conquest the natives were in the habit of covering their face and body with red pigment.[43]

Concerning the Egyptian Sphinx, Henry Brugsch-Bey, the Egyptologist and author of *A History of Egypt under the Pharaoh*s (1881), writes:

> To the north of this huge form lay the temple of the goddess Isis; another, dedicated to the god Osiris, had its place on the southern side; a third temple was dedicated to the Sphinx. The inscription on the stone speaks as follows of these temples: He, the living Hor, king of the upper and lower country, Khufu, he, the dispenser of life, founded a temple to the goddess Isis, the queen of the pyramid; beside the god's house of the Sphinx, northwest from the god's house and the town of Osiris, the lord of the place of the dead.[44]

The Sphinx, placed between temples, dedicated to Isis and to Osiris by their son, Hor, seems to indicate that the person represented by it was closely allied to both these deities.

Another inscription shows that it was especially consecrated to the god Ra-Atum, or the "Sun in the West," thereby connecting it with the "lands toward the setting sun," with "the place of the dead," and with the country of their ancestors' origin. There the ancient Egyptians believed they returned after death and appeared in the presence of Osiris, who was seated on his throne in the midst of the waters. He would then judge them for their actions while they were on earth.

Samuel Birch, noting the work of Sir Gardner Wilkinson, *Manners and Customs of the Ancient Egyptians,* says that "the Sphinx was called

Ha or Akar."[45] In the Mayan language, these words mean "water" and "pond" or "swamp." In these names, Le Plongeon suggests, there is a hint that the king, represented by the Sphinx, dwelt in countries surrounded by water.

> Its position, again, with the head turned toward the east, its back to the west, may not be without significance. Might it not mean that the people who sculptured it traveled from the West toward the East? From the Western Continent where Isis was queen, when she abandoned the land of her birth and sailed forth, with her followers, in search of a new home? May not that lion or leopard with a human head be the totem of some famous personage in the mother country, closely related to Queen Moo, highly venerated by her and her people, whose memory she wished to perpetuate in the land of her adoption and among coming generations?[46]

Fig. 8.4. Osiris glyph
(from Le Plongeon's Queen Moo and the Egyptian Sphinx*)*

Le Plongeon asks, "Was the Sphinx the totem of Prince Coh?" In the Mayan language, on the entablature of the Memorial Hall, and in the sculptures that adorned Prince Coh's mausoleum, Prince Coh was represented as a leopard. In Egypt, Osiris, as king of the Amenti (king of the West), was likewise portrayed as a leopard, according to Le Plongeon (fig. 8.4). His priests always wore a leopard skin over their ceremonial dress, and a leopard skin always hung near his images or statues.[47]

In seeking to explain the meaning of the names inscribed at the base of the Sphinx, Le Plongeon make uses of the Mayan language and its phonetic coincidences with ancient Egypt. He cites Henry Brugsch-Bey's *History of Egypt*:

> The Sphinx is called in the text *Hu,* a word which designates the man-headed lion, while the real name of the god represented by the Sphinx was *Hor-makhu,* that is to say, "Horus on the horizon." It

was also called Khepra, Horus in his resting place on the horizon where the sun goes to rest.[48]

Herodotus tells us that Horus was the last of the gods who governed Egypt before the reign of Menes, the first of their terrestrial kings.[49] Horus, the youngest son of Isis and Osiris, came into the world soon after the death of his father. He stood forth as his avenger, combating Seth and defending his mother against him.

In the Mayan language, Hormakhu is a word composed of three primitives: *hool,* "head," or "leader"; *ma,* "country" (or radical of Mayach, which becomes syncopated by losing the inflection *yach* forming the compound name); and *ku,* "god." Hormakhu would then mean "the God chief in Mayach." It is noteworthy to add that Mayan inscriptions and other writings were read from right to left, as were Egyptian writings. Le Plongeon asserts that *ma* stands for Mayach in this instance since the sign ⊓, which is the shape of the peninsula of Yucatán, forms part of the Egyptian hieroglyph representing the name of the Sphinx.[50]

He deduces that if this was not intentional, the hierogrammatists would have made use of some other of the various signs to represent the Latin letter *M.* Le Plongeon reminds us that hieroglyphic writings were mostly pictorial. He further states that the Egyptian sign ☙, the "sun resting on the western horizon," makes it evident that the hieroglyph ⊓ was intended to represent a country, with a similar geography contour, situated in the regions to the west. The Maya made use of the same sign to designate regions situated toward the setting sun. (The sign forms part of the word Alau in the Troano Manuscript, in part 1, Le Plongeon's plate numbers 2 and 3.[51]) In Mayan, Khepra would read Keb-la—*keb* means "incline," *la* is the eternal "truth"—the god, in other words, the sun. So Kebia or Khepra is the sun inclined on the horizon. As for the name Hu, used in the texts to designate the Sphinx, it may be a contraction of the Mayan *hul,* which means "arrow," "spear."

As symbols of their attributes, the Greeks often placed offensive weapons in the hands of their gods. So did the Egyptians. They represented Neith, Sati, or Khem holding a bow and arrows. They gave Horus a spear, hul, with which he slew Seth, his father's murderer. Sometimes he was represented standing in a boat, piercing the head of Seth, who was swimming in the water.[52] Was this to indicate that the tragedy took place in a country surrounded by water, reached only by means of boats? They also depicted Horus on land, stabbing the head of a serpent with a spear.

Le Plongeon asks rhetorically, Was the serpent in Egypt one of the totems of Seth, Osiris's murderer, as a spearhead was a totem of the Mayan prince Aac, Prince Coh's slayer? Le Plongeon believed the answer is yes.

At the celebration of Osiris's feast, worshippers were accustomed to throwing a rope into their assembly and hacking it to pieces, as if they were avenging the death of their god. The rope represented the serpent, the emblem of his murderer. Le Plongeon asks again, "Was this reminiscent of the tragedy that occurred in the mother country, where one member of the Can (serpent) family slew his brother?"

From the portraits of his children carved on the doorway of Prince Coh's funeral chamber, we know that his youngest son was named Hul. Hul's totem was a spearhead, carved above his head. "Are not Hul, Hu, Hor, and Hol cognate words?" Le Plongeon asks.

In *Sacred Mysteries Among the Maya and Quiches,* Le Plongeon endeavors to show, from the identity of their history and from that of their names and totems, that the Egyptians worshipped Seb, Nut, and their children (Osiris, Seth, Aroeris, Isis, and Nike) as gods. Le Plongeon argues that these were the same personages as the Royal Mayan family: King Canchi; his wife, Zoc; and their five children, Cay, Aac, Coh, Moo, and Nike.

Not finding the land of Mu, Queen Moo went to Egypt, where she became the goddess Isis and was worshipped throughout the land. She knew that centuries before, Mayan colonists, coming from India and from the banks of the Euphrates, had already established themselves in the valley of the Nile. She sought refuge among them, and they received her with open arms, accepting her as their queen. They called her Icin, "the little sister," an endearing word that in time was changed into Isis. As time went on, her cult became superior even to that of Osiris.[53] The poet and philosopher Lucius Apuleius (123–170 c.e.), in his "Metamorphosis" (also known as "The Golden Ass"), writes that Isis says: "But the sun-illumined Ethiopians and the Egyptians, renowned ancient lore, worshipping me with due ceremonies, call me by my real name Isis."[54]

The Greek historian Diodorus Siculus (c. 90–21 b.c.e.) in *Bibliotheca historia* depicts her saying:

> I Isis, queen of the country, educated by Thoth, Mercury. What I have decreed, no one can annul. I am the eldest daughter of Saturn (Seb), the youngest of the gods. I am the sister and a wife of King

Osiris. I am the first who taught men the use of corn. I am the mother of Horus.[55]

In the *Book of the Dead* (The Papyrus of Ani from 1240 B.C.E., translated by Wallis Budge), Isis says: "I am the queen of these regions; I was the first to reveal to mortals the mysteries of wheat and corn. I am she who is risen in the constellation of the dog."[56]

Was it Queen Moo, to perpetuate the memory of her husband in the land of her adoption, who built the Egyptian Sphinx in honor of her departed husband in Chichén Itzá—similar to Prince Coh's mausoleum? There, she represented him as a dying leopard with a human head, his back pierced three times by a spear. In Egypt, she figured him also as a leopard with a human head, but she immortalized him as a proud and glorified soul watching over the country that had ensured her safety.

According to Le Plongeon, after her death Queen Moo was deified, worshipped, and referred to as the "good mother of the gods and of men." The Greeks called her Maia, the Hindus called her Maya, and the Mexicans, Mayaoel. Did she entrust to her son Hul the supervision of the carving of this lasting wonder of the world? Could this be the reason the various Egyptian texts refer to the Sphinx as Hu? Augustus Le Plongeon believed it is.

Reign of the Scorpion

The ancient Egyptians themselves remembered their history only in a vague, mythical manner. For thousands of years, King Menes was believed to be the first king of Egypt. He is clearly identified as such by ancient Egyptian records, but that was before the discovery of King Scorpion's tomb in Abydos and an elaborate proto-dynastic tablet called the Scorpion Tableau. The story of this man, whose symbol was the scorpion, has gone from mythical to historical during the past 110 years.

In 1898, at Hierakonopolis, the ancient predynastic Egyptian capital, a cache of sacred objects was unearthed relating to an unknown king. One of those objects was the famous Narmer (or Menes) Palette, a ceremonial cosmetic palette. Another was the ritual mace head of the Scorpion King. At first this king was relegated to the world of myth with other predynastic gods. But a hundred years later, the German archaeologist Gunter Dreyer discovered the evidence required to turn the myth of King Scorpion into factual history. Dreyer found his tomb, and among the artifacts was his ivory scepter. Dreyer went on to discover, within the tomb, small, stamp-sized tags of ivory and bone. Each tag was carved with simple pictures; possibly hieroglyph-like writing that predates the accepted birth of writing by more than two hundred years.[57]

More surprising is the discovery by John and Deborah Darnell of a predynastic tablet known as the Scorpion Tableau. Although obscured by five thousand years of erosion, much of its inscription is still visible. It depicts the familiar falcon (Horus) symbol over the scorpion, which identifies the subject as King Scorpion. The Darnells believe it was carved by order of King Scorpion to commemorate his victory over Naqada-A, a city that worshipped Seth, the god of chaos.[58]

These recent discoveries have shed some light on Egyptian prehistory. However, shrouded in a mythical time, the prehistory of Egypt is still as mysterious as the Sphinx. We know comparatively very little of those archaic years when the Sahara was green and the rainfall abundant. The Sphinx's diadem appears to be the work of fourth-dynasty carvers, but the signs of weathering in and around the Sphinx's enclosure suggest an earlier date of origin, during a mythical time long ago.

The Antilles of the Caribbean were known to the Maya as the "Land of the Scorpion," Zinaan, and were represented in Mayan hieroglyphs by the figure of the arachnid, or in cursive style by the symbol. Le Plongeon

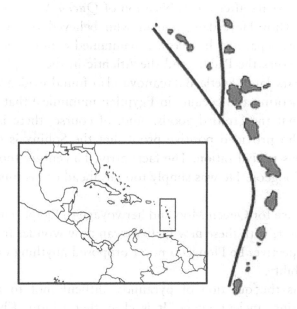

Fig. 8.5. Caribbean Antilles

believes this is evidence that the Maya were well acquainted with the general outline of the archipelago. Queen Moo found that the Mayan Land of the Scorpion had vanished under the waves of the Atlantic. What we see today, she found as the remnants. In honor of her island countrymen, did she or her descendants carry on the name in ancient Egypt with the Scorpion King? Le Plongeon believed it is so.

Schoching and Toxic Evidence for an Old Theory

The work Augustus and Alice Le Plongeon accomplished, and the record they created in the Yucatán, was as good as that of their contemporaries, but there was no one else working in the region to compare results. Augustus was a dedicated scholar and a resourceful, brilliant man, but without corroborating evidence, his theories and ideas were nothing more than a debunking exercise for his scholastic adversaries who had already accepted a late date for American civilizations. If Le Plongeon could have refrained from theorizing, his work would have likely been hailed as a great archaeological achievement. Instead, with the story of Queen Moo and the Mayan dissemination of civilization, his work was shoved aside and forgotten. Rarely is Le Plongeon's name mentioned in contemporary texts of Mayan studies.

More than fifty years after the publication of *Queen Moo and the Egyptian Sphinx,* Thor Heyerdahl, a man who believed firmly that ancient civilizations, separated by oceans, maintained contact, proved it was possible to cross the Pacific and the Atlantic in the simplest of seacrafts. Forty years later, Svetla Balabanova also found evidence (in her discovery of nicotine and cocaine in Egyptian mummies) that East knew West, and that they traded goods. And, of course, there is Dr. Robert Schoch, who provided positive proof that the Sphinx is older than Egyptian dynastic civilization. The facts arrived a century too late for Augustus Le Plongeon. He was simply too far ahead of his time for his own good.

Although the case for Queen Moo and her voyage to Egypt remains circumstantial at best, with these new facts we can now wonder from a very different perspective. Le Plongeon never proposed anything out of the realm of possibility.

Finally there is the question of pyramids, difficult not to mention when addressing ancient Egypt. It is clear that Khufu, Khafre, Menkaure, and others of those early dynasties built pyramids. It is also evident that anywhere during ancient times, if someone wanted to build big, it had to be a pyramid—it was a matter of physics. Yet while pyramids of various types and styles have been found all over the world, it is a common fallacy that the land of the Nile contains more pyramids than any other country. The cultures of ancient Mexico and central America hold that honor. They built more pyramids than anyone else. With its base a half-mile wide on each side and six times larger than Egypt's Great Pyramid, the Danta Pyramid in Guatemala is the largest pyramid ever built by mankind. The Maya built it.[59]

Is the Mayan–Egyptian connection suggested by Le Plongeon far-fetched? Maybe not. As we will see later, there is evidence from indigenous Egyptian traditions that supports the idea that the Maya, in some way, had contact with Egypt.

9

EGYPT'S PREHISTORIC ROOTS

The Legacy of Cro-Magnon

History, defined as the period of time that humankind has engaged in writing, is a very small percentage of the actual time humans are known to have existed in their modern anatomical form (bipedal, with upright posture and a high vertical forehead with a rounded cranial vault). A consensus of paleoanthropologists and archaeologists says that we humans *(Homo sapiens sapiens)* have been around for nearly two hundred thousand years. Furthermore, according to mitochondrial DNA studies, all of us modern humans are the descendants of a single woman who lived in Africa. Logically, then, all civilizations that developed and made the leap from prehistoric to historic have an ancestry that reaches back to Africa.

Although there is no written history describing how prehistoric cultures lived, paleo-science has discovered a considerable amount of evidence as to where and how they lived and when they migrated into new lands. The first-known culture to be anatomically modern, Cro-Magnon, dates back to forty thousand years ago and and thrived in western Europe for thirty thousand years. Yet there is strong evidence suggesting that they originated not there, but in Africa.

Today, among the populations of the world, the physical traits that characterized Cro-Magnon have nearly disappeared. What happened to them, and why they seem to have vanished from the archaeological record, has been a matter of contention for anthropologists for some time. However, there can be little doubt that we are their descendants.

Like all peoples everywhere, the ancient Egyptians who formed the first dynasty in 2920 B.C.E. also had ancestors. In chapter 7 we discovered they were the Badarian, Naqada, Amratian, Gerzean, Maadi, and Nubians who lived in various regions of North Africa near the Nile Valley. In this chapter we will investigate who may have been the ancestors of these predynastic cultures. The evidence suggests the cultures that led up to civilization and the birth of dynastic Egypt in the distant past began with Cro-Magnon.

Cro-Magnon of the Canary Islands

It may seem an unlikely place to look for clues to the past inhabitants of Egypt, but the pieces of this puzzle are scattered far and wide. The Museum of the Canaries on the island of Gran Canarie boasts the largest collection of Cro-Magnon skulls in the world. Also of interest are agricultural terraces built from rounded boulders, of unknown origin, found throughout the islands. On the island of Tenerife lies a pyramid complex made of black volcanic stone. The architectural and engineering techniques used to build its six "step"-style pyramids are similar to those found in Mexico, Peru, and ancient Mesopotamia.

Skeptics believed the pyramids were a random pile of stones, but archaeologists from the University of La Laguna and Dr. Thor Heyerdahl (of *Ra* expedition fame) proved the structures to be of human construction. Excavation revealed that they were built systematically with blocks of stone, gravel, and earth. Carefully erected stairways on the west side of each pyramid lead up to the summit, a perfectly flat platform covered with gravel. The main pyramid complex, including its plazas, was found to be astronomically oriented to sunset at the summer solstice in the same way the pyramids of Egypt were oriented to cardinal points.

Who built them is a mystery, and no theory is forced upon the visitors to the town of Guimar and its pyramids. A sign with a simple question mark labels the exhibit. The earliest-known inhabitants of Tenerife are the Guanches (now extinct as a distinct culture), who could not say when the pyramids were built or by whom. However, as we will see, the Guanches proved to be a cultural link between ancient and modern societies.

When the first modern Europeans arrived in the Canary Islands during the early fourteenth century, they were surprised by the physical characteristics of its Guanche inhabitants, which were not too different from those of white populations in the southern regions of the Mediterranean. Investigators of the nineteenth century were further surprised by the similarity between the forty-thousand-year-old skeleton of Cro-Magnon man found in Dordogne, France, and remains of the Guanches. Some researchers believe the similarities were not only physical, but also cultural, as evidenced by the Guanche cave paintings at Gáldar, Belmaco, Parque Cultural La Zarza, and Los Letreros caves, for example. As did Cro-Magnon cultures, the Guanche painted caves with zigzags, squares, and spiral symbols using red and black paint. The Guanche continued the practice of cave painting until the fourteenth century.

According to the German anthropologist Ilse Schwidetzky, the Canary Islands offer an extraordinary field for anthropological investigations. The prehistoric population living there buried its dead in caves, which has provided exceptionally abundant skeletal material. Despite the fact that the Guanches no longer exist as a culture, groups of pre-Hispanic people have survived to the present, even after the process of Christianization and acculturation. Numerous scholars have addressed their identification in the eighteenth, nineteenth, and twentieth centuries.

In a 1984 study, the University of Provence professor Gabriel Camps was very explicit on the matter of correctly identifying the Canary Islanders and their predecessors. In his research, he focused on the old Cro-Magnon population of North Africa, which he specifically referred to as Iberomaurusians. These Iberomaurusians were a sixteen-thousand-year-old culture in northwestern Africa who inhabited the coastal plain and interior of modern Tunisia and Morocco. They lived by hunting wild cattle, gazelle, hartebeest, and Barbary sheep, and by collecting marine mollusks. Nowadays, Cro-Magnon physical characteristics are rare in North African populations. The general characteristics of North Africans belong to the different varieties of Mediterranean types of people. At the most, the Cro-Magnon-like group represents 3 percent of the present population of the Maghreb (Morocco, Algeria, and Tunisia). But they are much more numerous in the Canary Islands.[1]

The term "Iberomaurusian" refers to a late-ice-age tool industry characterized by smaller stone tools and weapons compared to tools of previous cultures, and featuring tiny, obtuse-ended blades with one end dulled so they could be held opposite the cutting edge. Makers of these tools were present in numerous northwest African Maghreb sites, such as Afalou-Bou-Rhummel, La Mouillah, Taza Cave I, and Taforalt, between 20,000 and 10,000 years ago. Most sites are clustered along the Maghreb littoral in caves and rock shelters. Several contain human burials. In the past, Iberomaurusians have been called Mechta-Afalou, Mechta el-Arbi, and/or Mechtoid types. They were a skeletally robust people that resembled European Cro-Magnon, although they were more rugged and varied in additional ways. The origins of the North African Cro-Magnon are unknown. Scholars have postulated that they came from Europe, West Asia, or somewhere else in Africa, or developed indigenously in North Africa. They were relatively tall (5 feet 8.5 inches for the men and 5 feet 4 inches for the women), and had a wide and strong, distinctive face with an extended and narrow cranium. A skull shape that is extended and narrow is referred to as dolichocephalic.

According to a 1996 study by Dotour and Petit-Maire, the prehistoric Saharan Atlantic coast population can be classified into three groups.[2] One group has a certain number of specific characteristics and is referred to as Mechta. They are a Cro-Magnon type from Tunisia. Their uniqueness is not seen in the present population. A second group displays proto-Mediterranean characteristics (described in the next paragraph) and is seen in present-day Algerians. The third group displays attenuated characteristics and particularities similar to the first group. According to Dotour, this third group is poorly defined and of great variability. Although there are three groups, since the third is poorly defined and similar to the first, we will refer to two general groups based on skeletal type: Cro-Magnon and Mediterranean.

In contrast to Cro-Magnon skeletal characteristics, Mediterranean types usually had a high and delicate face with a short and wide cranium. From deposits in Gafsa, Tunisia, proto-Mediterranean remains date to about ten thousand years ago. Some researchers believe that these two human groups, Cro-Magnon types and Mediterranean types, represented a regional adaptation and, as a result, exist as a species of great anthropological variability. The study of grave mounds on the coast from Rabat, Morocco, south to Mauritania supports the evidence for two different human groups. One corresponds to tombs located between 20° and 23° north. Dotour characterizes skeletons found there to be of the Cro-Magnon (Mechta) type. The other group corresponds to an area north of the thirty-third parallel, near Rabat. Since their skeletal structure is graceful, they are attributed to the Mediterranean type.

The Cro-Magnon (robust and archaic) population has been always related to the Iberomaurusian culture and is likely indigenous. The more graceful is attributed to the Neolithic Capsian (Algerian) culture, and is not thought to be indigenous. It is believed they came from the east and, little by little, moved into the Cro-Magnon (Mechta) population, primarily along the Mediterranean coast.

Other studies confirm that the Cro-Magnon (Mechta) population had been living in North Africa for a very long time. According to recent genetic research published in 2004, part of the modern population displays a genetic marker that is characteristic of a transition from Cro-Magnon (Mechta) type to the Mediterranean type, and is restricted to North Africa. This suggests that an expansion of the Mediterranean group took place in North Africa around 10,500 years ago and spread to neighboring populations.

What anthropological studies of prehistoric peoples demonstrate is that the Cro-Magnon (Mechta)–type people were the sole inhabitants of the Mediterranean and North Africa regions, including the Canary Islands, prior to 10,500 years ago. Afterward, a different type of human (the Mediterranean type) began to occupy these regions, moving from the northeast to the southwest. Other studies also indicate that a migration and mixing of Cro-Magnon and Mediterranean types occurred over a long period. Strategically positioned in the northeastern-most part of Africa, the Nile Valley would have been an area of refuge as well as of convergence for both types of people.

Historical Population Patterns in North Africa

The first evidence of human populations in Africa are classified as *Homo erectus* 200,000 years ago. During the early part of the ice age, between 200,000 and 100,000 years ago, *Homo sapiens* first appeared as Neanderthal in Europe. Modern man appeared in Europe much later, around 40,000 years ago. In North Africa, modern man *(Homo sapiens sapiens)* appeared as Iberomaurusians (an African Cro-Magnon variation) between 19,000 and 10,000 years ago. Proto-Mediterraneans later appeared as the Capsian culture between 10,000 and 5,000 years ago, apparently coming from the east. These two groups constitute the human types that were the origin of the Berbers, who genetically are a minority, as well as the non-Berber segment of today's North African population.

Anthropologists associate prehistoric North Africans with the European Cro-Magnon type. Among other physical characteristics, they were of great stature (5 feet 7 inches for the average man), had a wide face and a dolichocephalic (oblong) skull, and great cranial capacity (1,650 cubic centimeters). The North African Cro-Magnon was the dominant human type in North Africa until the arrival of proto-Mediterranean (Capsian) cultures.

According to Francisco García Talavera, around 5000 B.C.E. the Cro-Magnon type began to diminish demographically and retreated to the west into the mountains of the Mediterranean, the Atlantic coast, and the Canary Islands, as well as the Saharan southwest and the Sudan. Yet they didn't truly disappear in the Maghreb. It is believed that 8 percent of that area's population were Cro-Magnon types during the third century B.C.E., and that percentage has steadily dwindled.

The proto-Mediterranean type, similar to the present Mediterranean populations, made its appearance in the eastern part of the Maghreb nine thousand years ago. This new type was composed of two varieties, one that was robust and of great stature (5 feet 8 inches for men) and the other more slender looking, who lived in the mountains. According to all indications, the slender type comes from the Near East, and are also the predecessors of older North African populations such as the Natufians,[3] who were native to the eastern shores of the Mediterranean.

According to Camps, these proto-Mediterraneans could very well be called proto-Berbers for their culture and propensity to use geometrical motifs in their decor; their body adornment and ceramics are also very similar to Berber traditions. At the beginning of historical times along the North African coast, tumuli (grave mounds) and megalithic monuments begin to appear, along with the geographic expansion of Mediterranean types. However, this megalithic culture seems to have come from the European countries of the western Mediterranean and is more likely from Cro-Magnon cultures. What is clear is that Cro-Magnon influence in the physical anthropology of the region is much smaller than the genetics contributed by eastern Mediterranean populations.[4]

The North African population and culture were also influenced, from the east, by the Phoenicians, who established colonies in the ninth and tenth centuries B.C.E., and by the Muslim conquerors of the seventh and eleventh centuries C.E. One would think that these invasions would somehow alter the North African genetics, especially the last one—a contingent of one hundred thousand people contributed to a fast

Arabization of the region. Other invasions and conquests on the part of Europeans of the eastern Mediterranean include the Romans (146 B.C.E. to 439 A.D.), the Vandals (439 to 533), the Byzantines (533 to 647), and later Ottoman, Turkish, Portuguese, Spanish, French, and Italian invasions. Ironically, the invading peoples have contributed very little in demographics and genetics to present-day North Africans. The vast majority of North Africans are descended from the proto-Mediterraneans (Capsians).

The Canary Islands have the same prehistoric components as does North Africa: the Cro-Magnon type and the Proto-Mediterranean. The first and more primitive human type arrived on the islands, according to some authors, between 2500 B.C.E. and 1000 C.E. However, because of the numerical proportion of Cro-Magnon type (Tenerife, 34 percent; Great Canary, 33 percent; and Gomera, 45 percent), an early arrival to the Canary Islands from the continent is more likely when Cro-Magnon types dominated North Africa prior to 10,500 years ago.[5]

Simultaneously, or possibly later, proto-Mediterraneans arrived. However, in the Canary Islands, only the robust Mediterranean type is found. They were also of great stature, with an extended and narrow face that is of a pentagonal or quadrangular contour. This type is associated, at least in Great Canary, with the "culture of the tumulus," since they buried their dead in funeral monuments, whereas the Cro-Magnon types did so in caves. Lately, it has been suggested that a clear racial separation between the two did not exist, as it seemed to the first anthropologists. Despite their peculiar insulation, the language and the culture of the Canary natives appear to be early Berber, as archaeology, the toponymy, and the anthropology testify. Except for sporadic contacts with Phoenicians, Carthaginians, and Romans (generally with commercial aims) and more recently with European Arabs, the population of the Canary Islands remained isolated until the Spanish conquest during the fifteenth century.

There are two long-standing questions concerning these people. First, what was the genetic connection between Iberomaurusians (twelve thousand years ago) and northwest Africans of historical times—the Capsians, Berbers, and Guanches? Second, were the skeletally robust Iberomaurusians and northeast African Nubians variants of the same population? Dental studies help answer these questions.

Dental Studies

Joel D. Irish, an anthropologist from the University of Alaska at Fairbanks, has been investigating the question of genetic continuity in North Africa through the analysis of dental traits. In 1993 and 1998, he compared North African to European teeth, using samples from different time periods. In his results, he describes how thirteen post–ice age North African dental samples show a resemblance to those of Europeans. Traits from these people show simplification and mass reduction in dentition. The homogeneity of this pattern, termed the "North African dental trait complex," was found despite vast expanses of time and geography, from eight-thousand-year-old Capsians to recent Berbers, and from the Canary Islands to Egypt and Nubia (southern Egypt and northern Sudan). Irish also found that any North African deviations from this simple dental pattern are in the direction of sub-Saharan traits, which suggests that there was some mixture between these peoples. Furthermore, his findings agree with genetic-based studies that link North Africans to Europeans and west Asians, but also show genetic influence from sub-Saharan peoples. He also noted that the frequency of Iberomaurusian dental traits suggests that the time scale for this North African evolutionary pattern may be older than previously believed.[6] In a more recent study (2001), he compared Iberomaurusian, Capsian, Berber (Shawia and Kabyle), Canary Island Guanche, Nubian, Egyptian, Carthaginian, and Bedouin Arab teeth.

What Irish found is that Cro-Magnon types, Iberomaurusians of twelve thousand years ago, are related to North Africans who lived later in history, during Egypt's dynastic times. However, despite purported similarities in culture and robust cranial characteristics, Iberomaurusians are wholly unlike Nubians from twelve thousand years ago or more. The Iberomaurusian samples show resemblance to all later North Africans, as suggested by the features found in the North African dental trait complex. Extreme divergence between ice age Iberomaurusians and Nubians suggests they are not closely related. Nubians exhibit a mass-additive dental pattern, like that found in sub-Saharan peoples. The latter possess a suite of eleven traits that Irish calls the "sub-Saharan African dental complex."

Irish also contends that Natufians (a culture native to the eastern shores of the Mediterranean originating around 8000 B.C.E.) are significantly different from Iberomaurusians and other North Africans. They lack resemblance to Capsians and are contrary to a proposed ancestor/descendant relationship.

The dental evidence supports the theory that the older of the two general types of people were the North African Cro-Magnon, which existed throughout North Africa and the Iberian Peninsula. However, for some unknown reason, they appear to almost vanish in North Africa, allowing Mediterranean types to become more prominent.

Cro-Magnon

Cro-Magnon is the name given to all anatomically modern humans who lived in Europe and the Middle East during the ice age between forty thousand and ten thousand years ago. In contrast to the earlier Neanderthals, who are believed to be more primitive, Cro-Magnon is classified as *Homo sapiens sapiens,* which means that they are our ancestors. Although some of their physical characteristics are displayed in humans today, they are considered extinct as a distinct type.

Since the invention of the motion picture camera, Hollywood films and television have dramatically influenced the general perception of Cro-Magnon man, often known as "caveman." He was portrayed as muscular and large, a brute wearing animal skins, dragging his mate around by the hair. "Ugh," he would say to his fellow cavemen as he held a hunk of meat to his face. In childlike fashion, he painted the walls of his cave. This has been the general perception, but it could not be further from the truth.

If you happened to meet a Cro-Magnon today, dressed in jeans and a sweatshirt, you would be unable to distinguish him or her from anyone else. Although it is believed that Cro-Magnons built no cities and wrote no literature, they were as behaviorally modern as anyone today, with the same affinity for symbolism, technology, art, and family.

Cro-Magnon man was tall, with an erect posture, well-defined chin, small brow, prominent nose, and domed head that was curiously elongated. During his time, he wore garments made of softened leather that were sewn with needles of bone and thread from the dried gut of an animal. He adorned himself with necklaces, bracelets, and amulets created from shells, flowers, teeth, and bones. He also built permanent settlements that were designed to withstand the cold winters.

He lived in pit huts, similar to the tepees of the Great Plains Indians. A hollow served as a floor, with poles erected as a frame for which a quilt of animal skins served as an insulating shell, and rocks placed along its bottom edge provided stability. During the summer months, he lived in portable, lightweight tents while following animal herds, and dug shallow pits in the permafrost to serve as natural refrigerators. Lamps and hearths were used for lighting and baking. Campsites were typically complex and displayed forethought of construction. They were typically facing east to catch the warmth of the morning sun.

The Discovery

Since the dawn of modern civilization, and what we call history, no one knew this type of human ever existed. The forces of nature buried the evidence of their life deep in the ground. Our history, as far as we knew, began some time around 4000 B.C.E. However, discoveries in France and Spain during the nineteenth century changed everything.

In March 1868, workmen laying a railway line near Les Eyzies, in the Valley of Cro-Magnon, dug into deposits of an ancient rock shelter and exposed its layers. The archaeologists Edward Lartet and Henry Christy soon discovered that the strata contained the skeletal remains of five individuals: three adult males, an adult female, and a child. Buried with them were stone tools, carved reindeer antlers, ivory pendants, and marine shells. An unknown people, they were obviously very old and the first human remains of their kind that had been discovered. Since then, all skeletal remains of this kind are assigned the name Cro-Magnon, and there were many more to follow. As years of work continued and many more sites were uncovered, it became clear that forty thousand years ago, these people settled in the western regions of Europe in the modern-day countries of Spain and France.

Cultures of the Ice Age

Cro-Magnon has often been the source of study for the theoretical progenitor of modern man, not only because of his anatomy, but also for his great ability in artistic expression. In their encampments and caverns, art was expressed in almost everything they did. Archaeologists have separated Cro-Magnon into five cultures existing at different times during the ice age and based upon the craftsmanship of their tools: Aurignacian, Gravettian, Solutrean, Magdalenian, and Azilian. All of these groups are subgroups of Cro-Magnon, but each had its own distinctive culture based on the type of tools it made and what material it used to craft them, and the epoch in which it lived. The North African Iberomaurusians (Cro-Magnon types) were likely relatives of the Magdalenian and Azilian cultures that thrived during the same period.

Named from the site of Aurignac, in the Pyrenees, where it was first discovered, the earliest society of Cro-Magnon is known as Aurignacian. Their culture lasted from forty thousand to twenty-eight thousand years ago and was a geographically widespread phenomenon. It spanned lands from Spain (the Santander region) to South Wales, with concentrations in the High Danube region of Germany and Austria, and the Moravian region of Slovakia. In France, they occupied small valleys in the Dordogne around Les Eyzies-de-Tayac and in the piedmonts of the Pyrenees.

Tools and tool types of the Aurignacian culture displayed standardization. Over time, they included end scrapers for preparing animal skins and burins for engraving. Flint tools were made from blades of stone rather than flakes. Projectile points (for hunting) were made from antler, bone, and ivory. Among their significant innovations was the development of body ornamentation, including pierced shells, animal teeth, carved bone pendants, bracelets, and ivory beads. The sudden explosion of exquisite art found at the Chauvet-Pont-d'Arc cave was certainly among their most striking achievements.

Named after the cave at La Gravette in the Dordogne, in southwest France, the Gravettian culture existed between twenty-eight thousand and twenty-two thousand years ago. Like their predecessors, their culture was widespread. Settlements ranged from southwest France to Wales and eastern Europe. Artifacts have also been found in mammoth hunters' campsites in Russia. Although regional differences exist, Gravettian lifestyles are remarkably similar wherever artifacts have been found. Speculatively, communication between settlements may account for such similarities.

When Gravettian culture appeared, a significant behavioral shift emerged. Large, organized settlements, comprising mostly simple tent structures, were founded in open lands. Animal remains suggest that some settlements were occupied for most of the year. Other settlements were quite elaborate, such as Dolni Vestonice, in modern-day Czechoslovakia. There, huts were made from mammoth bones and included storage pits for food preservation.

Excavation analyses also suggest function may have varied among huts. One hut, set apart from the main settlement, was likely used to produce small figurines of clay, then "fired" in a nearby hearth. The well-known small female figurines called Venuses, usually emphasizing breasts and buttocks, were of Gravettian origin.

To live in such cooperative style, it is likely that a social hierarchy existed, one that included behavioral rules. Weapons technology and hunting methods became more complex. Small, pointed stone blades, with one blunt edge, became their standard. Remarkably, uniform stone and bone projectile tips have been found, suggesting that they were highly skilled craftsmen.

Their burial practices mark a revolution in thinking and the beginnings of a belief system. Certain individuals, possibly the hunt leaders, were covered with red ocher (thought to be symbolic of a return to the womb) and buried in caves with the remains of large herbivores. The "Red Lady of Paviland" in Wales (actually a young adult male who died twenty-seven thousand years ago) was covered with a mammoth skull. A triple burial at Dolni Vestonice contained a female flanked by two males; the hand of one was extended over her pelvic area. Two adolescents at Sungir in Russia were buried head-to-head wearing thousands of ivory beads made from mammoth tusks and a headdress comprised of arctic fox canines.

Solutrean culture, named after the site of Solutré and known for a unique style of toolmaking, flourished roughly seventeen thousand to twenty-one thousand years ago in southwestern France. They were known primarily for beautifully made symmetrical, bifacial flakes of a laurel-leaf design with shouldered points. The origins of their industry are somewhat disputed, but there is evidence to suggest that it was an invention indigenous to the Dordogne. Others assign its sudden appearance to the arrival of a new people.

The laurel-leaf and willow-leaf styles of point and blade construction, highly regarded because of detail and fine workmanship, distinguished the Solutrean as a great toolmaking culture. These techniques would be used for thousands of years to come, and marked the transition from unifacial points (points flaked on only one side) to bifacial (two-sided flaking). Unifacial points were common early in the Solutrean period. Laurel-leaf blades and bifacial points gradually replaced them.

Solutrean technology also marked the first use of the edge-to-edge percussion flaking technique called outre passé. Some items that were made this way were used for adornment. They were so fine in their craftsmanship that they preclude use as tools (suggesting purposes of luxury alone). Bone needles have also been found, pointing to the use of fitted clothing, quite useful in a near glacial climate. Although bracelets, bead necklaces, pendants, bone pins, and colored pigments are evident for personal adornment, examples of Solutrean art are rare. They consist of sculpture in low relief and incised stone slabs.

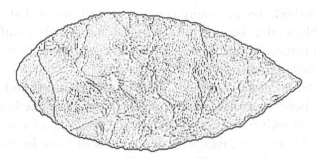

Fig. 9.1. Laurel-leaf point
(from a photograph by Bruce Bradley)

The Magdalenian culture, named after the rock shelter in Le Madeleine, France, existed between seventeen thousand and thirteen thousand years ago. It is perhaps the most impressive culture of the Old Stone Age. During this time, the bone industry reached its highest level. Elaborate harpoon points, tridents, and even needles were common. Bone tools were often engraved with animal images, and included adzes, hammers, spearheads, harpoons, and needles. Magdalenian stone tools included blades, burins (chisel-like implements with a beveled point), scrapers, borers, and projectile points. Some tools, which ranged from microliths to instruments of great length, display an advanced technique of fabrication. Weapons were highly refined and varied, and the atlatl (spear-thrower) first came into use during this time. Along the southern edge of the ice sheet, small boats and harpoons were developed, which reflected a society of fishermen and hunters.

The most extraordinary achievement of Magdalenian culture was its spectacular cave paintings, which reached a zenith in the latter part of its period. Early cave art is characterized by coarse black drawings. Later, however, it included beautifully made figures in various colors. The famous artwork in the caves of Altamira and Lascaux belongs to this period, the most intriguing stage of human development ever (or at least in the Franco-Cantabrian area). After visiting Lascaux, Picasso himself declared that "nothing of its quality has been painted since."

First recognized at Le Mas d'Azil (a cave in Arige, France), the Azilian culture was a declining remnant of scattered Magdalenian communities. It lasted from 11,500 to 11,000 years ago. Centered in the Pyrenees region, it spread to Switzerland, Belgium, and Scotland, and was one of the earliest representatives of Mesolithic (Middle Stone Age) culture in Europe. Bone and flint items were less refined, with a focus on small, geometric-shaped tools commonly used in composite tools called microliths. Bone work was limited to crude, flat, barbed points. Schematically painted pebbles have also been found at several Azilian sites. Some think these were the beginnings of a simple alphabet. The Azilian, the last ice age people, were followed by the Tardenoisian culture, which covered much of Europe after the ice age.

Art and Expression

From cave paintings to figurines, Cro-Magnon man expressed himself creatively, especially his interest in hunting and the essence of womanhood. Some cave paintings, thought to be a later endeavor of the Magdalenian period, are now proved to be thirty thousand years old. A newly discovered (1994) cave in Chauvet displays three hundred or more animal images on its walls. "Venus" figurines (small, fire-hardened clay idols of women), although predominant in Gravettian culture, have been found in all periods of Cro-Magnon culture all across Europe.

Art was also used as an expression of respect for the deceased. Carved pendants, bracelets, and other grave goods accompany most skeletal remains. In a twenty-eight-thousand-year-old burial site in Russia, two youths and a sixty-year-old man were entombed and adorned with pendants, bracelets, and necklaces. Their burial clothes contained more than three thousand ivory beads, each bead of which took an hour to craft. Perfectly straight mammoth tusks were lying next to the juveniles, their natural curves straightened by boiling in water. However, not all the deceased were buried in such a lavish way. Some bodies were disposed of modestly, indicating a class structure and social hierarchy. Regardless of the scale, burial ceremony was a regular part of their culture.

Spectacular items of artistic merit suggest a depth of culture and multifarious thought. Bone and stone plaques have been found with complex markings. One, in particular, is thought to be a lunar calendar. Other plaques have been interpreted as tally marks of hunting expeditions. One of the lesser-known, but more impressive, discoveries was that Cro-Magnon played music. Bone flutes, percussion instruments, and even xylophones have been found in some of the oldest Aurignacian sites, and have been dated up to thirty thousand years old.

Clearly, any intellect that displays such art, especially when found in all facets of life, can by no means be primitive, and indeed must be regarded as highly intelligent. Artistic expression and intelligence go together; perhaps the former is a result of the latter. Whatever the reasons for their art, it was as much of an important part of their society as it is in ours.

Today, possession of great works of art is a symbol of accomplishment and wealth. Although not everyone is an artist, we all have the capacity. Art is part of us. Finger painting is often one of the first acts of self-expression we teach our children. Some continue this tradition of expression throughout adolescence and into adulthood; others never stop. It is this concept of self-expression, the relationship of art and intellect, that is found so majestically painted in the ice age caves of Cro-Magnon.

Venus figurines have been of great interest to researchers, possibly providing insight into Cro-Magnon religious beliefs. Several theories have been offered over the years to explain the widespread occurrence of these figurines. The most recent theory is that they represented the "Mother Goddess" from which all life comes, her swollen belly depicting pregnancy. Others believe the figurines symbolize fertility. But it is unclear why these hunter-gatherers would need aid in fertility, unless they were already domesticating animals and growing crops. Some believe the figurines were cult-based; others disagree. According to scholars, there simply isn't enough evidence concerning ice age societies to develop a solid theory.

Ice-Age Fashion

University of Illinois professor Olga Soffer, a fashion expert turned anthropologist, has taken a new approach in studying Venus figurines. After discovering impressions of woven fibers in clay fragments from central Europe, she believed one might find evidence of textile accessories. Soffer and her team completed and published a study of two hundred Venus figurines from the Gravettian age. Although her interpretations of the significance of figurines are debated among her peers, the body of evidence she amassed was groundbreaking. It is noteworthy to mention that Soffer and her team studied the originals—an important approach, as some of the more intricate designs on the surface of the figurines are too shallow to project a similar cast image.

She discovered that caps, belts, bandeaux, and skirts (originally made of woven fiber) were found carved intricately into the figurines. Some of the items bear realistic depictions of fiber-based construction. Others consist of horizontal lines encircling the body, as in the Venus of Dolni Vestonice.[7]

 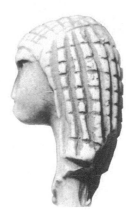

*Fig. 9.2. The Venus of Willendorf, left, and the Lady of Brassempouy
(courtesy of Olga Soffer)*

Previously thought to be a Paleolithic hairstyle, the patterns about the head of some figurines portray a net or snood, such as the twenty-two-thousand-year-old carving called the Lady of Brassempouy. According to Soffer, the Venus of Willendorf is the best example of headgear that portrays a fiber-based cap or hat. A close examination shows a spiral, hand-woven item that may begin with a knotted center, in the style of some types of coiled baskets.[8] Although far removed from ice age Europe, netted headgear has been found on female bodies in Danish bogs.

Soffer also discovered regional differences among western, central, and eastern European figurines. Bandeaux are present in almost all the eastern European figurines wearing headgear. Bracelets and necklaces are found in eastern and central European Venuses but are nonexistent in western Europe. String skirts are portrayed in western Europe, with an occasional attached belt. Basket hats are often found with a woven bandeau, belt, necklaces, and bracelets in central and eastern Europe.

All this points to differences in cultures, and complements the Soviet archaeologist Maria Gvozdover's earlier analysis of the figurines. Gvozdover's figurine study concluded that western Europeans favored accenting the hips and thighs while easterners chose breasts and bellies, with a mixture of both in central areas.

One of the more intriguing pieces of evidence is that male figurines are rare and only female statuettes of the Upper Paleolithic depict garments. Soffer believes that each figurine had its own role in the

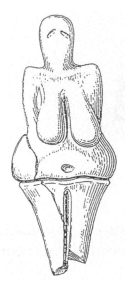

Fig. 9.3. The Venus of Dolni Vestonice
(courtesy of Olga Soffer)

society based on body type. In conjunction with two previous studies (Gvozdover 1989 and Kloma 1991), Soffer believes that women of the Upper Paleolithic engaged in fashion. Her set of data (and that from Leisure in 1997) suggests that between the eighteenth and twenty-eighth millennium B.C.E., Upper Paleolithic women in Europe were talking about what was important to them: woven and plaited clothing, headwear, and other accessories made from plant material.[9]

Evidence of the clothing they actually wore, however, is found only in burials. It is sparse, for biodegradable material does not survive the corrosive forces of nature over time. Three complete burials in Sungir (near Vladimir, 150 kilometers east of Moscow), from twenty-five thousand years ago, clearly contain a placement of beads on the individuals. The unique placements of these beads and deformations of the strands are evidence of hooded shirts, pants with attached footwear, and hats, caps, and capes. The three individuals buried are an elderly male, an adolescent female, and a boy between seven and nine years old. They wear many bracelets, amulets, necklaces, and rings.[10]

In conclusion, Soffer suggests that female labors, in producing woven baskets and textile goods, were symbols of achievement and part of a highly regarded economy in Paleolithic societies. Therefore, they wore woven garments to depict the female of the time correctly and woven accessories were carved into the figurines. Some of her colleagues suggest that her approach may be too female-centric, but it must be remembered that differences between the sexes, throughout history, have always been depicted in opposing social roles.

Her research hints that a highly sophisticated and social culture existed more than twenty-thousand years ago, and possibly as long ago as forty thousand years. It also suggests a very different culture from what developed later in historical times, one that was centered on the woman and her role in life.

Cro-Magnon and the Mother Goddess of Old Europe

Growing up in Lithuania, Marija Gimbutas was familiar with the traditions of the Goddess Laima, the "spinner," or the weaver of life. She remembers how the women would offer gifts of towels and woven articles to her. At night, the Goddess would often check on her believers by peering through a window.

Although Lithuania was Christianized during the fourteenth century, it remained predominantly pagan for the next several hundred years because of the missionaries' lack of language skills. The Goddess remained a part of eastern European culture in some areas as late as the nineteenth and twentieth centuries. Fascinated by the culture she grew up with, Gimbutas focused her early studies on linguistics, ethnology, and folklore.

In 1942, Gimbutas received her master's degree from the University of Vilnius in German-occupied Lithuania; four years later, she earned her Ph.D. from the University of Tubingen in Germany. Both degrees were in archaeology. Her dissertation focused on ancient and pagan religions, symbolism, burial rites, and beliefs in the afterlife. It was published in Germany in 1946.

Born during a time when Lithuania was as much pagan as it was Christian, Gimbutas had a unique perspective on Europe and its history. For years, she worked in excavations in southeastern Europe and the Mediterranean, and began to develop a theory of a culture that was once, long ago, prevalent in the land. Thus, when the excavation team she worked with began to unearth small sculptures of women, found throughout Europe, she had an easy time grasping their significance. Gimbutas alone unearthed at least five hundred sculptures; as the work continued in Yugoslavia, Greece, and Italy, the evidence mounted, as did her confidence in the theory she was considering.

In 1955, she was named Research Fellow of Harvard's Peabody Museum. A year later, in Philadelphia, she presented her theory to the world for the first time. In 1956 she published the first of many books, *The Prehistory of Eastern Europe,* and in 1958, *Ancient Symbolism of Lithuanian Folk Art.* In 1963, she accepted a position at UCLA and continued to direct excavation at various European sites. In 1974, with the evidence she needed, she published *Gods and Goddesses.* The original title was *Goddesses and Gods of Old Europe,* but the publisher (most likely for marketing reasons) ordered it to be changed. Eight years later it was published in a second edition under her original title. In 1991, she published her final book, *Civilization of the Goddess,* the culmination of her life's work. She passed away on February 2, 1994, at her home near Los Angeles.

Her story of prehistoric European peoples is also a tale about a clash of cultures and, specifically, the once prominent culture of the Mother Goddess. Today Europe is composed of many different ethnic groups with an assortment of languages. It is a widely held theory, however, that all these ethnic groups were once a single group called Indo-Europeans, with a single language. Gimbutas's research provides evidence that before these Indo-Europeans dominated the lands, a completely different culture existed, a culture she refers to as the "Great Goddess" or "Mother Goddess" culture. It was a culture that was egalitarian, yet focused on the maternal as a foundation for its cosmology. According to Dr. Gimbutas:

> The earliest civilizations of the world were all matristic. The Goddess worship was there. In China, in the Near East, in Europe, in Americas, so we can say that this is a universal Goddess in the very beginning. And perhaps I should add that the sovereignty of motherhood has decided the earliest development of social structures and religion.[11]

Gimbutas refers to this culture as "matristic" or "matrifocal," and not "matriarchal" (because the latter implies dominance). It was a balanced society. Women were not so powerful that they usurped the male role. Men had their own power and position, and performed their own duties for the benefit of the family and clan. According to Gimbutas, it was a communal society and communistic in the best sense of the word. Goddesses were actually creators, and in fact were creating from themselves, whether it was items for the household or a child.[12] She refers to the deity they worshipped as the "Great Mother Goddess."

During the 1960s, new dating methods gave her a better perspective on just how long-lasting this culture really was. Symbols and sculptures suggest that it was in existence as long ago as thirty-five thousand years, and existed until 3000 B.C.E. Parts of the female body, specifically the creative or life-giving parts, are typical in ice age art.

Gimbutas believed they had a completely different worldview and that their natural artistic expression had nothing to do with pornography. For example, the vulva was one of the earliest symbols to be engraved. It was symbolic in that it relates to growth and the seed. In some art, next to the image of a vulva is an image of a branch or other plant design, or within it a seed or plant. This style of symbolism was very long-lasting and continued for twenty thousand years or more.[13]

European cultures of the ice age carved what archaeologists call Venus figurines. Gimbutas believed the term "Venus," used to describe these figurines, is a poor choice of words. Venus evokes the idea of beauty. They were not beauties and typically lacked facial features. She believes these figurines were the epitome of the Mother Goddess and depict birth, regeneration, and death.

Many types of goddess figurines appeared in the ice age, but they did not form a pantheon. In essence, they represented different functions of the same Goddess. The deity was nature itself: the nature that is life giving, life taking, and life regenerating. These were the three important functions of the Goddess, and they compose the natural cycle of life. Perhaps it is the origin of the common term we use for naturally occurring phenomena, "Mother Nature."

Post–ice age figurines with accented breasts were typically carved with a bird's head. Ice-age figurines also have large breasts with bird heads. From this, it was clear to Gimbutas that they were the same type and that their culture continued until historical times. The vulture, owl, crow, and raven were also common. They, however, were symbols of death, as were the "white goddess" figurines, which portray postmortem stiffness. Some "death" figurines were carved as if wearing a mask, and were associated with the vulture.

Over the course of history, in these Goddess-based societies there were stunning cultural developments from the simple to the really sophisticated, especially in architecture and the construction of temples. Some buildings were two stories tall with painted walls. Nearly 140 wall paintings adorned the eight-thousand-year-old dwellings at Çatalhöyük in modern-day Turkey. They were finally published in 1989, twenty-five years after excavation. At first, archaeologists disbelieved the settlement's sophistication.[14] The paintings depict otherwise.

For Gimbutas, the vast amount of beautiful pottery and sculptures discovered during years of excavation was overwhelming. Surprised by the complex design of Goddess-culture settlements, she was convinced the older civilization was more advanced than the more recent culture. As her work continued, she began to recognize patterns of repetition in their iconography, especially in the bird and snake goddess. Their religion became clear.

Religion has always played an important role within a culture, modern as well as ancient. The goddess culture was no different. Its cosmology was based on the "water bird" and the "cosmic egg." In the beginning, the world began when the water bird brought the egg. The egg split, and one part became earth and the other part became the sky.

For the Mother Goddess culture, the temple was the focus of religious life. Beautiful artifacts were produced for its shrines and the goddess. Evidence suggests that these people were grateful for the sustenance the earth provided, and gave to the Goddess in thanks. The high priestess and queen were the same person within a hierarchy of priestesses. Women were more honored because new life came from them and, as a result, women had more influence in the religious life. They ran the temple and performed rituals at births, deaths, and the change of seasons.[15]

Gimbutas also believed that the Goddess culture incorporated the use of mushrooms or other hallucinogenic plants in its rituals. According to her research, this knowledge still existed in rituals like those of Eleusis in Greece, where the cult of the goddess Demeter clearly used psychedelics when members performed the "Eleusinian mysteries" in her honor. From the Goddess culture's portrayal of mushrooms, it can be assumed that they were sacred. In Minoan engravings on seals, for example, poppies were often displayed. Poppy seeds have also been found in Neolithic settlements. It seems, then, they were aware of what they were collecting and using. Possibly, they were growing poppies as they grew other domesticated plants.

Some scholars believe the Goddess religion was a simple fertility rite. Gimbutas thought this idea was silly. She believed that people who say so are usually not knowledgeable and have never studied the subject. There is no question that fertility was important to the continuity of life on earth, but the religion was about life, death, and regeneration. Although they existed in a primitive environment, they were not a primitive people.[16]

There can be no doubt that the birth of a child is a true miracle of life, and those who were able to give birth were very special. This mystery of giving birth, and the woman herself, may be the origin of the shaman and Goddess cosmology. Geoffrey Ashe, a British scholar of shamanism, believes the oldest form of the word *shaman* referred to a female. The female group, he believes, practiced ancient shamanism.[17]

Dr. Gimbutas's findings, based on the physical remains and what can be deduced from their mythology (mythology reflects their social structure), suggest that political life was regulated by an avuncular system (derived from a word meaning "uncle"). The rulers of the community were the queen, who was also the high priestess, and her brother or uncle. The man (either the brother or uncle) shared in her authority. Its existence was expressed in classical mythology where sister-brother couples of goddesses and gods were often encountered.

It is presumptuous to suggest that this was just a woman's culture and that there were no male gods. In their art, the male is less represented, but male gods did exist. In all mythologies—for instance, the Germanic, Celtic, and Baltic—the earth mother (or earth Goddess) exists with her male companion next to her.

There are other "god couples," like the Greek goddess of nature (Artemis, the regenerator, who appears in springtime and gives life to all animals and plants) and her counterpart, the Master of the Animals. According to Gimbutas, these representations appeared in Çatalhöyük eight thousand years ago and throughout prehistory. In their culture and religion, there was a balance between the sexes.

This Goddess culture of Old Europe was not without a written form of communication. This peaceful, agrarian civilization developed a near uniform language of symbols that reached from Ireland to Turkey. Elements of a "sacred script" have been discovered in eastern and central Europe. Attempts have been made to decipher it, but sentence structure and phrases have not yet been ascertainable. During the Bronze Age, in Cyprus and Crete, the script persisted, and was similar to what existed in the fifth millennium B.C.E. Some of it has been preserved, but there are no clear links. Gimbutas believed it could have been a syllable-based script and would have developed into something more structured if it were not for the culture's destruction. Today, scholars continue to research this script with hopes that it will someday be deciphered.[18]

The difficulty is that this pre-Indo-European language is studied very little. Substrates of the languages are studied in Greece and Italy, but the only words that can be reconstructed are place-names like Knossos, which is, in fact, an Old European name. *Apple,* for example, is also pre-Indo-European. Little by little, linguists discover what words are not Indo-European. Names for seeds, various trees, plants, and animals are easily deciphered. There also exist several pre-Indo-European names for the same thing, such as the pig, and both names were used. Some languages use pre-Indo-European names, others use Indo-European names, or both.[19]

Prehistoric Roots of the Egyptians

Some researchers speculate that the Guanches of the Canary Islands descended from Europe's Cro-Magnon and were influential in founding the first civilizations in the region of predynastic Lower Egypt around 4000 B.C.E. The Guanche homeland, the Canary Islands, was known as the Elysium and the Garden of Hesperides by the classical Greeks, and was considered a mysterious place. According to the Guanches' own traditions, their land was submerged off the coast of northwest Africa and they migrated east. Some theorists argue that it is no coincidence that the predynastic Egyptians also maintained the tradition of near-submergence and migration from a far-off land to the west (the Land of Amenti). According to this theory, proto-Guanches, descendants of Cro-Magnon people, migrated to the Canary Islands from northwest Africa sometime prior to 10,000 B.C.E. In *A History of Iberian Civilization,* Portuguese historian Oliveira Martins theorizes that the descendants of the Cro-Magnon people in northwest Africa call themselves by names with the suffix *tani,* such as Lusitani, Aquitani, and Mauritani.

Frédéric Falkenburger compiled and analyzed skull measurements from 1,787 ancient Egyptian male skulls and divided them into four main groups, giving the following results: 36 percent Negroid; 33 percent Mediterranean; 11 percent Cro-Magnoid; and 20 percent not falling in any of these groups, but related to either Cro-Magnoid or Negroid.[20]

A British anthropologist, George M. Morant, produced a comprehensive study of Egyptian skulls from common and royal graves from all areas of Egypt and from all times. He concluded that the majority of Lower Egypt's population were members of a now nearly extinct Mediterranean type. In Upper Egypt, this population pattern was repeated, except they showed a certain percent of Negroid mixture, probably due to neighboring Nubian settlements to the south. Morant found that with the passage of time, the differentiation in skull types between Upper (southern) and Lower (northern) Egypt became less distinct, and eventually the types were indistinguishable.[21]

Those who espouse the Guanches as the progenitors of dynastic Egypt believe that a very high percentage of Egyptian pharaohs, from predynastic through New Kingdom times, share the Guanche genes. According to the theory, a migration of Guanches came from the west, led by the mythical Thoth, during predynastic times, and they brought their religion to Lower Egypt. To support their claims, these theorists cite the Guanche practice of mummifying the dead, which sometimes included the removal of internal organs; the taming of dogs for hunting; and the similarity of their myths and religion to those of predynastic and early-dynastic Egypt.

Although an interesting idea, it is more likely that the Cro-Magnon element in the ancient Egyptians is a result of an indigenous population that also inhabited the Canaries. This question has confounded researchers for a hundred years.

Africa: A Wider Focus for the Culture of Cro-Magnon

Where Cro-Magnon arrived from is unknown but, according to some scholars, they were not indigenous to Europe.[22] Sudden changes in Cro-Magnon culture, most noticeable in their tool kits, suggest they were migrating over a long period of time and appearing as sequential waves over a thirty-thousand-year period. Based on the presence of innovative tools in eastern Europe, the orthodox belief is that Cro-Magnon originated in eastern Europe and western Asia, following the general theory that man originated in Africa, moved north and east, and then later west. However, recent finds from the Aurignacian age in the Spanish peninsula predate the earliest eastern sites, suggesting that an eastern origin may not be the case.[23] L'Arbreda, El Castillo, and Abric Romani all date between thirty-seven thousand and forty-one thousand years ago. Obviously a northern origin is not possible due to the Scandinavian ice sheet, which made northern Europe virtually uninhabitable. This leaves only the south or west as a possible source.

Cro-Magnon settlements existed in Africa, and clearly tool technology existed there well before 40,000 years ago. Blade tool technology is obvious up to 80,000 years ago. Barbed bone points found in Zaire have been dated from 60,000 to 80,000 years old. There is also evidence in Africa of long-distance exchange of raw materials 140,000 years ago, as well as surface mining 100,000 years ago.

Modern African cranial structure, more similar to Cro-Magnon than to later Europeans, also suggests the prehistoric Cro-Magnon population originated in the south and migrated north. However, supporting archaeological evidence of an advanced culture in Africa before 3000 B.C.E. is sparse. African Cro-Magnon sites contain little of the symbolic and behavioral evidence so distinctive in European sites, which is a requirement for being the host culture for such a massive migration.[24] If such a culturally well-defined people were to migrate from a particular geographic area, one would expect to find substantial roots of their culture, both technological and behavioral, in that area. Yet in Africa, this does not seem to be the case.

Professor emeritus of cognitive archaeology at the University of Witwatersrand, South Africa, David Lewis-Williams disagrees. He argues that although there was a comparatively sudden burst of symbolic activity, the explosion of art in Europe during the ice age was not universal, nor was it an indivisible "package deal." The idea that all the different kinds of art, and fully developed symbolic behavior, suddenly appeared there, he believes, is an illusion. He insists that events need to be placed in a wider perspective. If the modern mind and modern behavior evolved sporadically in Africa, it follows that the potential for all the symbolic activity that we see in Upper Paleolithic western Europe was in existence before *Homo sapiens* communities reached France and the Iberian Peninsula.[25] He believes in a wider focus in addressing the origins of the distinctive and artistic cultures of Cro-Magnon.

Western Europe is a well-documented region of prehistoric human activity. Hundreds of caves in France and Spain display thousands of truly magnificent images. Some forty-five thousand years ago, anatomically modern humans arrived on the Iberian Peninsula and brought with them complex social structures, sophisticated planning, hunting, diverse symbolic behavior, and—what they are most recognized for— art. The speed with which they replaced the Neanderthal way of life, and the suddenness with which they appeared, is remarkable. From our perspective, unable to know the details of how the Cro-Magnon arrived and from where, it is no wonder that contemporary authors write of a "creative explosion" or "human revolution." Although it is understandable that they describe this period in these terms, they should not ignore the evidence of cultural precursors from Africa and the Middle East.

The overall picture looks much less explosive, and it is in the regions of Africa and the Middle East where the seeds of the "creative explosion" exist. According to Lewis-Williams, Africa contains the earliest evidence for the human revolution. Some scholars argue that modern human behavior *was* a package deal, which appeared everywhere forty thousand to fifty thousand years ago, and ascribe its apparent sudden change to species-wide neurological changes. Lewis-Williams believes this view results from focusing too narrowly on evidence from western Europe.

In order to achieve a less biased account of the human transition in western Europe, Lewis-Williams distinguishes between what we may see as an anatomically modern feature of the human body and behaviorally modern features of human life.[26]

The first concept, anatomical modernity, is easy to define. There is general agreement about which features distinguish modern human skeletons from older specimens. However, the second concept, behavioral modernity, is not as easy to define. Archaeologists have derived their notion of modern human behavior from evidence in western Europe. As a result, they compile lists to characterize modern human behavior, such as:

Abstract thinking—the ability to act with reference to abstract concepts not limited in time or space.

Planning depth—the ability to formulate strategies based on past experience and to act upon them in a group context.

Behavioral—economic and technological innovation.

Symbolic behavior—the ability to represent objects, people, and abstract concepts with arbitrary symbols, vocal or visual, and to reify such symbols in cultural practice.[27]

According to Lewis-Williams, this list is reasonable enough, but it is unfair to expect all early modern populations to express these characteristics in precisely the same way. For example, all early, anatomically modern humans did not make bone tools, eat fish, or use paint to make images in caves. When African evidence for the emergence of modern humans and their behavior is considered, the importance of this point is clear.

Today, researchers generally accept the "out of Africa" theory for the origins of humankind. The fossil evidence shows conclusively that the precursors of anatomically modern human populations developed in

Africa and left the continent in two waves of migration. It explains why archaic humans, Neanderthals, occupied western Europe for thousands of years before *Homo sapiens* made their way into Europe. Some believe that the second wave leaving Africa were modern populations that did not have fully modern behavior, and acquired it at a time between forty thousand to fifty thousand years ago.

The African evidence challenges this point. According to Lewis-Williams, the shift to modern behavior started in Africa as long ago as 250,000 to 300,000 years, and possibly even earlier. He also contends that we should refer to humans as having "modern behaviors," plural, as opposed to "modern behavior." Furthermore, modern behavior did not suddenly appear as a complete package. There was no "revolution" in behavior.

The four characteristics of modern behavior he lists manifested themselves in various ways and appeared at different times and in widely separated places on the African continent. The making of blades and the processing of pigments, using grindstones, is 250,000 years old. Long-distance trade and shell fishing started 140,000 years ago. Bone tools and mining are about 100,000 years old. Ostrich eggshell bead making started between 40,000 and 50,000 years ago. Yet the art that we call representational imagery dates back to only 30,000 and 40,000 years ago.

However, recently found geometric-style engravings have been dated to seventy-seven thousand years ago. In a cave called Blombos, near the southernmost tip of South Africa, Chris Henshilwood and his colleagues discovered a piece of ocher carefully engraved with crosses, with a central and a containing line. Although not a representational image, at seventy-seven thousand years old it is the oldest dated "art" in the world. For Lewis-Williams, it shows indisputable modern human behavior at a very early date.[28] Although the details of all this evidence are debatable, for Lewis-Williams it is clear that modern human behavior was appearing piecemeal in Africa long before the transition in western Europe.

Without any other evidence, Lewis-Williams is limited to saying that changes in the behavior of the earliest Africans were episodic, and contact between scattered groups was likely intermittent. The explosion of art within the cultures of Cro-Magnon, indeed, was important, but it should be placed in a wider perspective, one that opens up new lines of explanation.[29]

According to Lewis-Williams, if the modern mind and behavior evolved sporadically in Africa, it follows that the potential for all the symbolic activities that we see in western Europe forty thousand years ago was in existence *before Homo sapiens* reached the Iberian Peninsula. This preexisting potential means that a neural-based event such as the triggering mechanism for the western European "creative explosion" should not be sought.[30] But are there other possibilities we should consider?

Various scholars in the past have likened the Cro-Magnon cultures appearing in western Europe to "waves of invasion." The reason for this is that the tools and art of these cultures don't show stages of development; they simply appear, full-fledged. This is highly suggestive that a host culture, somewhere else, was already in existence. But where is the evidence? Africa has suffered greatly since 4000 B.C.E. with an increasingly arid and hostile environment. The blowing winds and sands scour and bury what evidence may have existed.

In a study of ancient teeth, Joel Irish found that sub-Saharan Africans express characteristics, similar in form, to those of other modern populations (see page 193). To him it is evident that intrapopulation heterogeneity, and a worldwide gradual dental change, originated from the African subcontinent. His research provides evidence consistent with an African origin model. Genetic and fossil evidence points to Africa as the source of human culture, but there is a lack of evidence of continuous cultural development. Some hypothesize that this evidence does exist, but that it has been misidentified and/or misdated.

Despite Arabization and a fundamental change in religion during the sixth century, Egypt has never lost its ancient heritage. There are those who have passed it down from generation to generation over a score of millennia. Cumulative evidence—genetic as well as archaeological—suggests that Africa's ancient Egypt is the host of modern man's original culture. The Guanches did not spur Egyptian civilization, nor did anyone else. From Africa spawned all other cultures, including those responsible for the creative explosion in western Europe forty thousand years ago. As we have seen with the Sphinx, Nabta Playa, and the Great Pyramid, the evidence has always been there. The host culture that produced the magnificent and artistic cultures of Cro-Magnon can be in no other place but Africa. The Cro-Magnon traditions not only support the "out of Africa" model, but also bring a whole new understanding of mankind's history.

10

THE SYMBOLIST'S EGYPT

A Legacy of Knowledge

Although physical facts are an important element in establishing when, where, and for whom ancient cities and tombs were built, history is more than a paradigm built from the trowel of archaeology. The evidence of history is also found in culture and beliefs; art, philosophy, religion, and science provide a view into the nature and mind of peoples of the past—what they believed and how they viewed the world. For Egypt, in this matter of culture there seem to exist two different histories. There is the archaeologically based version we learn through our educational institutions, with which most everyone is familiar. However, there also exists another, subtler version based not on forensics, but on the sacred writings of the ancient Egyptians themselves. From the hieroglyphs inscribed on temples and monuments, it is evident that in the mind of the Egyptian there existed a level of knowledge just as sophisticated as our own modern thinking. Using science and theology, the ancient Egyptians endeavored to explain the physical universe, just as we endeavor to do today.

According to Egyptologists, more than two thousand gods were worshipped over the course of Egypt's three-thousand-year history. This super-sized pantheon of deities typically has been explained as animal worship, and a primitive's way of relating to the animating forces of nature. Referred to as *animism*, derived from the Latin word *anima*, meaning breath or soul, it is believed to be mankind's oldest belief system, with ice age origins. In animistic beliefs, a soul or spirit exists in every object, living as well as inanimate. Yet in a future state, an object's soul will exist as part of an immaterial soul, and is thought to be universal.

Primitive peoples believed that human life emanated from the soul. They pictured these souls as vapors or shadows going from one body to another, passing among human beings, plants, animals, and inanimate objects. During the nineteenth and early twentieth centuries, scholars reasoned that primitive man arrived at his animistic beliefs to help him explain the causes of sleep, dreams, and death. Other scholars were convinced that early religion was more emotional and intuitional in origin. According to this theory, early man recognized some inanimate objects because they had some particular characteristic or behaved in some unusual way that mysteriously made them seem alive.

This primitive view of the world fits well with today's evolutionary model of mankind, but there have been and continue to be scholars who believe this view is too simplistic and that the philosophical doctrines of the ancient Egyptians had nothing to do with animism. According to these scholars, known as *symbolists*, ancient Egyptian science, art, and philosophy were not separate, but rather part of a holistic system of thought. Their science, which encompassed religion as well as philosophy, and which was expressed through temple art and architecture, was established not only for civil benefit, but also to answer the ages-old question of mankind's nature. It was a sacred science. John Anthony West explores this in his documentary series *Magical Egypt:*

> The sacred science that fueled or underpinned these temples involved mathematics, philosophy, religion, art, and in fact, ancient Egypt, perhaps the greatest of these ancient civilizations, or in any event the ancient civilization to which we have most access, left us the greatest legacy of sacred art and architecture. This was a profound doctrine that fused art, religion, philosophy, and science into an extricable whole, whereas, in our society art, religion, philosophy, and science are separate disciplines with little or no relationship to each other.

In ancient Egypt they were extricably entwined, so there was no art that wasn't religious, no religion that wasn't philosophical, no philosophy that wasn't scientific, no science that wasn't art. When we are in the presence of one of these Egyptian temples, we are, whether voluntarily or involuntarily, put into the presence of the divinity, or the principle to which that temple was consecrated, and whether we like it or not we often respond with awe and wonder. This awe is not, let us say, an artifact of our susceptible imagination or romanticism on our part. It is an example of the high science of the ancients' sacred science.[1]

In the symbolist school of thought, ancient Egyptian theology and philosophy were pure and complete, and attest to a long-standing civilization with sophisticated knowledge of the physical world. Even at the beginning of Egyptian civilization, more than five thousand years ago, their ideas of God and man were highly sophisticated. For those who endeavor to understand the sacred life of the Egyptian, it is inconceivable that a society fresh out of the Stone Age could develop such an erudite worldview, complete with language and symbolism, so quickly.

Egyptian Monotheism

One of the early Egyptologists to delve into the religious and philosophical worldview of the ancient Egyptians was Ernest Alfred Thompson Wallis Budge (1857–1934). Budge was the curator of Egyptian and Assyrian antiquities at the British Museum from 1894 to 1924, as well as a scholar at Christ's College, the University of Cambridge, and Tyrwhitt. His interests were broad, and he collected a large number of Coptic, Greek, Arabic, Syriac, Ethiopian, and Egyptian papyrus manuscripts. He was also involved with archaeological research in Egypt, Mesopotamia, and the Sudan. But what he is most famous for is the translation of the *Papyrus of Ani,* more commonly known as *The Egyptian Book of The Dead.* Budge's written works were the first books geared toward students and consisted of translated texts and a complete dictionary of hieroglyphs. He was also very interested in Egyptian culture, religion, mythology, and magical practices.

In his *Egyptian Ideas of the Future Life,* published in 1901, based on a study of ancient Egyptian texts, Budge concluded that the Egyptians "believed in One God, who was self-existent, immortal, invisible, eternal, omniscient, almighty, and inscrutable; the maker of the heavens, earth, and underworld; the creator of the sky and the sea, men and women, animals and birds, fish and creeping-things, trees and plants, and the incorporeal beings who were the messengers that fulfilled his wish and word."[2] However, it is also true that during certain periods of Egyptian history, they developed beliefs that could be perceived as polytheistic, especially by outsiders and neighboring nations. According to Budge, this transcendent idea was never lost and was reproduced in their religious literature during all periods.

It may seem to be contradictory, or at the least confusing, that the Egyptians believed in one God, yet accepted the idea of multiple gods. However, with a better understanding of their language, it is possible to determine how this might be. The word that scholars translated as "god" is *neter,* and according to the twentieth-century Egyptologist and independent researcher René Schwaller de Lubicz (1887–1961), whom we discussed previously, *neter* is a principle or an attribute of divinity. Other researchers agree.

According to the Egyptologist Moustafa Gadalla, ancient Egyptians believed in a single God who was self-produced, self-existent, immortal, invisible, eternal, omniscient, and almighty, and was represented through the functions and attributes of "his" domain. These attributes were referred to as *neteru* (masculine singular: *neter;* feminine singular: *netert*). In his opinion, scholars' use of the terms *gods* and *goddesses* is a misrepresentation of the word *neteru.*

The Egyptians did not define God as a person—by questioning "who" God is. Instead, they questioned "what" God is, in terms of his multitude of attributes, qualities, powers, and actions. In light of today's science and philosophical understanding, this is indeed an appropriate line of reasoning. God, by definition the omnipotent source of the physical universe, can never really be described in human terms. God is neither male nor female, although often referred to as "he" because of patriarchal tradition. It is a concept beyond comprehension. Appropriately, the Egyptians never represented God, but rather described him through the functions and attributes of his domain.

Only by knowing the numerous qualities of God does one know God. So the more one learns of these qualities, or neteru, the closer one gets to man's divine origin. "Far from being a primitive, polytheistic" belief system, Gadalla asserts that "this is the highest expression of monotheistic mysticism."[3] Neter, therefore, is an aspect of God, but not the entire concept. Another way to describe a neter is that it comprises features of the natural environment as well as traits of the human being. In their sacred writings (hieroglyphics), the Egyptians represented neteru in highly symbolic ways, such as Thoth (Egyptian Tehuti), who was portrayed as a man with the head of an ibis, representing writing, wisdom, and time.

The ancient Egyptians used symbolism, typically animals and plants, to express their knowledge of the natural world. Through careful observation they were able to identify certain animals with specific qualities that symbolized certain divine functions and principles in a pure and striking fashion. In other words, an animal symbolized a particular aspect of divinity. It is an effective mode of expression, and consistent with all cultures. Examples such as "quiet as a mouse" and "sly as a fox" illustrate this principle in a modern way. It is the heart of the expression "a picture is worth a thousand words." According to symbolist John Anthony West, "The symbol is a brilliant and sophisticated means for transmitting very complex meanings. Symbolism allows the mind to intuitively see what is not directly visible in the material world around us. The symbol, at once, contains not only a specific object or concept, but also a bundle of invisible qualities and tendencies that it embodies."[4]

Symbols engage a different part of the brain than does ordinary writing or language. It addresses the intuitive, nonverbal, visually based right hemisphere of the brain, which deals with spatial and abstract relationships, intuition, and the subconscious. It is the part of the brain that is not bound by rational and linear thought, and perhaps the area of the mind that is host to our higher self, that which instinctively seeks out divinity. The language of symbolism serves as a bridge between the two types of intelligence humans are endowed with, rational and intuitive. As such, the symbol goes beyond language, promoting cooperation between and the unification of the brain's two hemispheres.[5]

With this symbolic view of Egyptian beliefs, one can understand how the animal and animal-headed neteru expressed a deep spiritual understanding. The whole animal represented a particular function or attribute in its purest form. When a man was depicted with an animal head, it conveyed that particular function or attribute in the human being.[6]

For example, Anbu (Anubis) represents the right sense of direction— in other words, "the divine guide." He is often shown as a jackal, or as a man with the head of a jackal. The jackal is famous for its reliable homing instinct and is useful in searches. As such, it is an apt choice for guiding the soul of the deceased through the regions of the Duat, the place where humans live after they die.

The metaphysical role of the jackal is reflected in his diet; the jackal feasts on decaying flesh, turning it into nourishment. So Anbu represents the capacity to turn waste into useful food for the body and soul. He also represents absolute loyalty, and as such is depicted at the scene of the weighing of the heart, overseeing the correctness of the procedure. In human terms, Anbu represents the right sense of direction in whatever we do, absolute loyalty, and the capacity to turn lead (carrion) into gold (worthiness). [7]

Another example of the Egyptians' symbolic use of animals is the depiction of soul, known as the *ba*, represented by a human-headed bird—the opposite of the normal depiction of neteru (animal-headed humans). This represents the divine aspect of the terrestrial. The ba was depicted as a stork, which was known for its migrating and homing instinct, as well as being the bird that delivers newborn babies. Consistently returning to its own nest, this migratory bird is the perfect choice to represent the soul.[8]

At the core of Egyptian symbolism and philosophy was the idea that in man lies the ultimate representation of the created universe. Accordingly, their symbolism and measures were simultaneously scaled to man, earth, and the universe. Schwaller referred to this philosophy as the *anthropocosm,* or the "man cosmos." What this refers to is the idea that the universe was created for man to perceive, and for God as absolute, pure consciousness to experience through man (consciousness being the awareness or perception of experiencing, and the essence of identity that is not bound by time). The anthropocosm is likely the source of the Hebrew/Christian belief that man was created in the image of God.

Pythagorean Number Mysticism

During the mid-twentieth century, the pioneering scholar René Schwaller de Lubicz embraced the challenge to understand why the Egyptians used symbols in their sacred writings. Although originally published in French, all of his works are now available in English. In his books such as *Esotericism and Symbol, Symbol and the Symbolic, The Egyptian Miracle,* and the monumental work *The Temple of Man,* he argues that the Egyptians were highly sophisticated in their thought, understood certain natural geometric principles, and viewed numbers and language as sacred.

Schwaller, as the father of the symbolist view, saw the Egyptian language not just as a means of communication, but also as a connecting point between man and the divine. The use of harmonic proportions in their art and architecture, as well as the numerical basis underlying Egyptian myth, moved him to consider Pythagorean number mysticism in reconstructing their system of thought. Based on years of research, he believed their worldview was a combined philosophical and theological approach wherein there existed relationships among number, sound, and form. It was his conclusion that the Greek philosopher Pythagoras did not invent number mysticism, but merely advanced an existing knowledge that had been an integral part of Egyptian civilization for thousands of years. In a sense, "number mysticism" may be viewed as mankind's earliest attempt to explain the physical world through the use of numbers.

Pythagoras (560–480 B.C.E.) was born on the island of Samos, off the coast of Asia Minor. According to some accounts, at the age of twenty he visited Thales in Miletus, who encouraged his interests in mathematics and astronomy, and was advised to travel to Egypt in order to learn more. Although some scholars believe such visits are stereotypical features in the biographies of Greek wise men, expressing legend rather than fact, Egyptian civilization, then already two thousand years old, was a well-known center for learning during ancient times. Whatever the case may be, Pythagoras was responsible for important developments in mathematics, astronomy, and music theory. Later, he moved to Croton and founded a philosophical school that attracted numerous followers.

Pythagoras knew—as did the Egyptians before him (suggestive that he did visit and study in Egypt)—that any triangle with side lengths in the ratio 3:4:5 was a right-angled triangle. One of his more important discoveries was that the diagonal of a square is not a rational multiple of its side length (a number that can be expressed as the ratio of two whole numbers)—suggesting the existence of irrational numbers. At the time, this was a revolutionary idea for mathematicians.

At the heart of Pythagorean number philosophy is the belief that all relationships can be reduced to number relations, and that all things are numbers. Its approach was that the world could be understood through mathematics, which was extremely important to the development of the sciences. In the Pythagorean world of numbers, each digit expresses a metaphysical concept that is neither an abstraction nor an entity in itself. The numbers are names applied to the functions and principles upon which the universe is created and maintained. As the numbers progress from one to another, each number not only symbolizes and defines the specific function ascribed to it, but also incorporates all combinations of functions leading to it.

One

The number one is the Absolute and the unity of all things. This absolute principle can be seen as omnipotence or God, or, in a scientific way, as the pure energy from which the entire physical universe manifests. It is the "All."[9] Viewing the number one in this fashion brings added meaning to Hebrew scripture, where it is announced in Deuteronomy 6:4, "Hear, O Israel! The Lord is our God, the Lord is one!" In other words, God is absolute, as opposed to the more modern interpretation that "one" refers to a single god.

Two

With the Absolute becoming conscious of itself, duality, or polarity, is created, and as a result, the number two exists. This expresses the opposition that is fundamental to all natural phenomena. Schwaller refers to this separation as the "primordial scission." Two is not the sum of one and one, but a state of primordial tension. It is the metaphysical concept of forever unreconciled opposites. A world of two, and nothing else, is static, so nothing would ever happen. By nature it is divisive, and if unchecked, it is chaos. Two is "the fall of man," representing spiritual tension; it is not a fall from a perfect to a sinful state, but the creation of human consciousness from the divine, or supreme consciousness.[10]

Unity is eternal, undifferentiated consciousness. When it becomes conscious and creates differentiation, then there exists polarity. Polarity, or duality, therefore, is a dual expression of unity.

Three

When the Absolute created duality, the number three was simultaneously created, providing a reconciling principle between opposing forces. Three, therefore, is the principle of relationship. Volumes have been written by theologians in attempts to explain this third principle as the triune God, the trinity. Yet even today this concept is a mystery. However, in a more down-to-earth manner, the principle is easy to understand. For example, male/female in itself is not a relationship, but one can exist through the intangible (the spiritual). In human affairs love, desire, or friendship is the third force between two people. Here, one may speculate that the duality of existence is God and man, and that the third force, a relationship, provides the reconciling force that completes the triune god—Father (God), Son (man), and Holy Spirit (relationship). [11]

Our society has been increasingly built around the logic and reason of science. Yet it cannot account for the most important facet of everyday experience. Whether sexual, friendly, or parental, human relationship through the bonds of love is what drives the human experience. The reconciling principle of three, then, is a spiritual relationship.

Four

The idea of substance cannot be accounted for in two terms or in three. In the example of love there is 1) the lover; 2) the beloved; and 3) desire. Only through the number four is there substance to the example, which in our case would likely be, at first, an affair, and if everything went well, later a household. So substance or matter is a principle beyond duality and relationship. In a sense, when four is reached, a new unity exists as an analog of absolute unity. [12]

We see the concept of four born out in the "elements" of the ancient world: earth, water, air, and fire. However, these are not physical elements themselves, as seen in the periodic chart, but principles in which the physical universe operates. Ancient philosophers used these four common, natural phenomena to describe the functional roles of the principle of substance. Earth, fire, air, and water represented the abstract principles of reception, activation, mediation, and composition. Earth is the receptive and formative principle. Fire is the active, coagulating principle. Air is the subtle, mediating principle; and water, the material, or composite principle.

Everything that physically exists operates by at least one of these principles, and most involve a combination. For example, without exception everything in the physical universe is active, in motion. Our planet spins, moves in orbit around the sun. So does our solar system, as well as the galaxy. It is also true at the quantum level. In fact, action defines existence. An atom, the most basic unit of matter, is nothing more than vibrating energy with a particular charge. For example, a uranium atom is made of 92 electrons orbiting a nucleus of 146 neutrons and 92 protons. (Breaking apart this atom releases a tremendous amount of energy.) On a slightly larger scale, everything physical, except air, is also formative. In other words, everything we see has been formed from some process. Air, the mediating aspect, separates all physical objects.

Physical objects are also a composition of various elements and require the formative, active, and mediating principles to exist. Water is the only substance that can serve as the combined representative of these three principles. It serves as a mediating factor in the same way air does; yet it is also formative (it combines into a form) and active (it flows).

This fourth principle is the idea of matter or the methods that define how matter will be formed, as opposed to matter itself. It is insubstantial, yet contains the four elements that describe physical reality. Manifest, these principles form the number five, which is life.

Five

The number five can also be derived from the union of the first female number (two) and the first male number (three) to represents life (or love). Remember that two represents polarity, a state of tension, and three, relationship, the act of reconciliation. In combining two and three, there is the manifested physical universe in five. All naturally occurring phenomena are polar by nature and treble in principle. Being the principle of life, five accounts for the act of creation.[13]

The female numbers, those that are even, represent a state that is acted upon. Male numbers, those that are odd, represent functions that are initiative, active, creative, positive, aggressive, and rational. Female numbers are correspondingly receptive, passive, created, sensitive, and nurturing. The Pythagorean concept of male/female refers not to the social roles of the man and woman, but to the states and actions of the natural world. Furthermore, according to Pythagoreans, the number one (the Absolute) is neither even nor odd, nor a number properly speaking, but the source of both the even and odd numbers. Two is the first even number and three the first odd.

From two, three, and five, all harmonic proportions and relationships are derived, and with the exchange of commands form matter and all processes of growth. Remember that four accounts for the idea of matter but not the creation thereof. Five, the union of male and female principles, is its creation. We see examples of this in everyday life. The husband and wife, male/female, is a polarity yet joined by desire in a relationship where a household results. Both the man and woman play active, masculine, initiating, passive, feminine, and receptive roles simultaneously. Both lovers are active toward the other and receptive to desire. Interestingly enough, in this example the couple usually winds up creating physical matter in the form of a baby.

Six

The first five numbers still do not describe the structure in which all natural events take place—the framework of time and space. The principles of the numbers one through five are the intangible (metaphysical or spiritual) aspects of the natural world we are confined to. The number six creates time and space and is the number of the world. We live in the product of six, the world that is defined by sensory interpretation of time and space, what we define as, and call, reality. Although some interpret time and space as creation, in essence, time and space are the effects of creation, and a measure of motion. We experience and thereby view time as a flow, while space is that which contains.[14]

Seven

The number seven accounts for the phenomenon of growth, which is an all-encompassing principle in the observable, physical world. It is an inbuilt aspect of creation. However, seven cannot be related directly to experience. In other words, we cannot, ourselves, initiate growth. The fundamental cause of growth—from sperm and egg into fetus, then baby, then adult human, for example—is a mystery. As such, seven signifies the union of spirit (three) and matter (four).[15]

In the physical world, there are numerous examples in which seven manifests itself in growing or active systems, such as the seven tones of the harmonic scale. Between the original note and its octave there are seven intervals that, despite their inequality, the ear interprets as harmonious.

In biological systems, growth is built in, most likely at the level of DNA, although this is still somewhat of a mystery. Growth, however, is not a continuous process. Everything has a cycle. We are born, grow up, and then die. This is not just a natural phenomenon of the earth; everything in the physical universe exists in a cycle. Our sun, for example, will last another four billion years, then expand, turning our planet into a cinder, and shrink into a white dwarf star. Our galaxy, the Milky Way, will someday, far in the future, collide with our nearest neighboring galaxy, Andromeda, and cease to exist. Yet the synthesis of the two galaxies will combine and continue as a new galaxy.

The number seven is a combination of four and three, which is the union of matter and spirit. But it is also a combination of five and two, the duality united by the action, and six and one, the fundamental note, *do,* actualized by six. In other words, our physical reality of time and space produces an octave tone, which is in itself a new unity.

Eight

The number eight is a new unity analogous to the first unity. It is renewal or self-replication and the physical world as we experience it. It is Thoth (Greek Hermes, Roman Mercury), who is "master of the city of eight" and the messenger of the gods. He is the neter of writing, language, knowledge, and magic, and allows man access to the mysteries of the world, which is symbolized by eight.[16]

As for the number nine, we will discuss that later in this chapter. It is a special case.

Egyptian Mythology as Number Mysticism

According to Schwaller de Lubicz, the ancient Egyptians deliberately used harmonic proportion in their art and architecture, based on the previously described numerical system of thought. It was an all-encompassing worldview that included philosophy, mathematics, mysticism, and theology. John Anthony West, a contemporary symbolist in the tradition of Schwaller de Lubicz, believes that what is today called Pythagorean number mysticism is really Egyptian in origin, and even predates ancient Egypt.

When number symbolism is applied to Egyptian myth, it becomes clear that Egyptian stories and myths are based upon an understanding of number and not upon animism. It is a philosophy, but not in our sense of the term. There exists no explanatory text. Nevertheless, it is systematic, self-consistent, and organized on principles that can be expressed in a philosophical way.

For example, in Egyptian mythology, Atum (or Tum) represents the transcendent cause, the absolute or all, the One, the first true God and Creator who made the world and everything in it. Within him was the potential for all life. The name Atum comes from a word meaning "completeness" or "totality." In regarding himself, he created Shu (male, the neter of air) and Tefnut (female, the neter of water). Aware of his loneliness, he masturbated, fertilized himself with his own semen, and gave birth to the twins Shu and Tefnut. Atum was often shown in human form holding or sucking his erect penis, symbolizing the act of creation. Although disgusting to some, Atum's self-gratifying act is an apt way of communicating the concept of creation from one's self.

The ancient Egyptians believed that life itself manifested great cycles of existence. At the beginning and end of each cycle, Atum took form in the primeval waters as a snake or an eel. Some Egyptologists have interpreted Atum and the Apophis serpent as the positive and negative forces within chaos—the disordered state of unformed matter and infinite consciousness that existed before the ordered universe.

In later myths, Ra-Atum and his warrior daughter fought a great battle against the forces of chaos in order to slaughter the serpent Apophis under the *ished* tree, which was a sacred tree in Heliopolis linked to the destiny of all beings. It was believed that the names of the kings were written on this tree at their coronation to assure them that their lives would be perpetuated. During the war against the forces of chaos, Ra-Atum often took the form of a cat, mongoose, or other predator of snakes.

The fundamental opposition, duality or polarity of life, is depicted in the myth relating the conflict between Seth and Horus, summarized below. This allegory illustrates the conflict-prone nature of man, and also symbolizes the Egyptian philosophical concept of the number two.

Osiris, the god of the earth, taught mankind how to farm, which in the eyes of the people made him the greatest of all gods. As a result, he ruled the world. Enraged with jealousy over his popularity Osiris's brother Seth murdered him and threw his body into the Nile River. Osiris's wife, Isis, then recovered his body with the intent to give him a proper burial. Infuriated, Seth stole the body, cut it into pieces, and scattered it over the land. However, Isis found all of Osiris's remains and with the aid of the god Anubis brought him back to life. Afterward, Osiris and Isis gave birth to a son named Horus, who was destined to succeed Osiris as ruler.

In order to prevent his enemies from killing his son, Osiris hid him in a marsh where he was suckled by a cow, who was the goddess Hathor. After he grew into a man, Horus left the marsh to take his rightful place as ruler. However, the god of the sun and leader of the council of gods favored Seth for that role. Arguments erupted within the council and the appointment of a ruler was delayed. Finally, Osiris sent a letter to the arguing gods that Horus should be the ruler. This proved to be the decisive factor in deciding who would be the new king.

It would be Horus. However, Seth refused to accept the decision and challenged Horus.

In the ensuing battle between Seth and Horus, both were severely wounded. Horus lost an eye and Seth his testicles. The god of wisdom, Thoth, found Horus's eye and restored it, and later Horus presented it to Osiris. Seth also recovered his missing parts, and their battles continued. But they also aided each other as other myths portray.

The mythical story of Horus and Seth characterizes the rhythmic structures of duality. From the smallest bits of reality—the proton and electron—to organic life and us humans, male and female—there is a constant rhythm of duality in natural life. It is how the physical world functions, animate as well as inanimate. The proton attracts the electron to create a physical reality. The male and female of all animal life are attracted to each other to ensure the continuance of life. Duality is contained within the absolute unity. Herein is the meaning of the number two. Every human experiences this duality just as the natural world projects it with the male and the female division of all organic life. Yet this division must find reconciliation, as did Horus and Seth. This reconciliation is described in the number three.

The number three represents the relationship and reconciliation between the absolute cause (one) and the duality (two) it created from itself. It exists purely on a spiritual plane. With that philosophical decree, there exists an indelible association between cause and duality. We can understand it as what we might call "effect." We try very hard to affect people and events, many of us through prayer or positive thinking when direct actions are not or cannot be successful. Some wear medals such as the cross of Saint Christopher to gain what they believe to be protection or safety during their travels. The ancient Egyptians behaved in the same way. Instead of calling it prayer or positive thinking, they called it magic. Instead of wearing medals, they wore amulets in order to make themselves complete or for protection. They also cast spells or recited incantations in order to help the deceased make his or her way in the afterlife. Ancient Egyptian magic relied on this relationship and reconciliation between our cause and our duality.

The number four, representing the idea of the material world, was recurrent in Egyptian symbolism—the four regions of the sky, the four sons of Horus, the four children of Geb, the four canopic jars in which organs of the deceased were placed at burial. According to one Egyptian myth, Geb married his sister Nut, the sky goddess, without the permission of the powerful sun god, Re. Re was so angry at Nut and Geb that he forced their father, Shu, the neter of air, to separate them: this is why the earth is divided from the sky. Re further prevented Nut from having children in any month of the year. Fortunately, Thoth, the divine scribe, decided to help and induced the moon to play a game of checkers, where the prize was the moon's light. Thoth won so much light that the moon had to add five new days to the official calendar. And Nut and Geb had four children:

Osiris: god of the dead, also known as the underworld

Seth: a god of chaos, confusion, storms, wind, the desert, and foreign lands

Isis: loving wife and mother, who was also a great magician

Nephthys or Nebt-het: "mistress of the house," where "house" refers to the portion of the sky that was the abode of the Sun god

The Egyptian understanding of the number five, or life, is seen in the concept of the realized man, connected with the Absolute and achieving unity with Cause (God). He was to become a star, and "become one in the company of Re."[17] In hieroglyphs, the symbol for a star was drawn with five points. Viewed as sacred in numerous cultures, the pentagram and pentagon also reflect the mystical value of five.

Schwaller de Lubicz found that the proportions of the inner sanctuary of the Temple Amun-Mut-Khonsu (originally built by Amenhotep III of the eighteenth dynasty) were derived from the square root of five. He also found that the proportions of certain chambers were ordered by a hexagon produced from a pentagon.

The Egyptians chose to symbolize temporal and spatial phenomena with the number six, the number of the material world, time, and space. Six represents the basic temporal divisions, such as the twenty-four hours in a day, the thirty days in the month, and the twelve months in the year, all of which are multiples of six. Six is also seen in the Egyptian cube, the symbol for volume, with its six directions of extension (up, down, backwards, forwards, left, and right). The pharaoh sits squarely upon his throne, which is a cube, where man is placed unmistakably in material existence. According to Schwaller, the dimensions of certain halls in the Temple of Luxor were determined by the geometric generation of the hexagon from the pentagon, a symbolic expression of the materialization of matter from the spiritual creative act.

The number seven, signifying the union of spirit and matter, is expressed in the pyramid, which is a combination of the square base—symbolizing the four elements—and the triangular sides—symbolizing the three modes of spirit. It is not only symbolic, but also mathematically practical. The mystical importance of seven is also prevalent in other cultures of the ancient East.

The shaman of central Asia believed that the "cosmic tree" had seven branches and that there were also seven planetary heavens. It was a concept where the shaman, in his ritualistic quest, would ascend to the sky along the axis of the world. According to Mircea Eliade's *Shamanism: Archaic Techniques of Ecstasy,* the cosmic tree is an archaic, universal idea. The myth of the rainbow, with its seven colors as the road of the gods and the bridge between sky and earth, existed in the religious beliefs of Mesopotamia as well as in Japanese tradition. The seven colors of the rainbow have also been incorporated into the idea and symbolism of the seven heavens. Traditions like this are found in India and Mesopotamia, and in Judaism as well. The symbolism of the rainbow surrounding the throne of the supreme being persisted well into the Renaissance, in the art of the Christian era.

During the Middle Kingdom, the number eight was portrayed in the Ogdoad—eight entities that form another variation of Egyptian creation mythology. Although these beings were worshipped primarily in Heliopolis, aspects of the creation were combined with existing myths. Each entity or aspect is a member of a masculine/feminine (or husband/wife) pair, and each pair represents an aspect of the primordial chaos from which the physical world was created.

Nun and Naunet represent the primordial waters; Kuk and Kauket, the infinite darkness; Hu and Hauhet, empty space; and Amun and Amaunet, the secret powers of creation. The gods were usually depicted as men with the heads of snakes, and the goddesses as women with the heads of frogs. They built an island in a vast emptiness where the "cosmic" egg was placed. From this egg came Atum, the sun god, who began the process of creating the world. This corresponds to the physical world as mankind experiences it.

At times the Ogdoad were depicted as baboons heralding the first sunrise, showing seven of the Ogdoad and Horus, the falcon representing the sun god Ra-Harakhty. The place referred to as the "island of flame" saw the birth of the sun god and was also called Khemenu, or Eight Town. The Greeks referred to it as Hermopolis.

"Becoming" and the Number Nine

For the ancient Egyptians, the biggest mystery of all was the "becoming" of the Creator from the Unseen into the Seen, the One who manifests as many. This becoming was revealed through four successive stages: Atum (or Re) at Heliopolis, Ptah at Memphis, Thoth at Hermopolis, and Amun at Thebes. According to the Leyden Papyrus of Qenna, written during the twenty-eighth dynasty:

> All the gods are three: Amun, Re, and Ptah, who have no equals. He whose nature [literally, "whose name"] is mysterious, being Amun; Ra is the head, Ptah the body. Their cities on earth, established forever are: Thebes, Heliopolis, and Memphis [stable] for eternity. When a message comes from heaven, it is heard at Heliopolis, it is repeated at Memphis to Ptah, and it is made into a letter written in the letters of Thoth [at Hermopolis] for the city of Amun [Thebes].[18]

This idea of a message represents the progress of "the becoming" from Heaven to Earth. Because Heliopolis was considered to be "the ear of the heart," it is there that the message was heard.[19] In esoteric texts, the sun was deemed to be the heart of the solar system, so Heliopolis was the heart of Egypt, the city of the Sun. The name Heliopolis, as it is used in the funerary texts, also means "the absolute origin of things,"[20] not to be strictly confined to the physical city of that name. When it is stated in Egyptian texts: "I have come from Heliopolis" or "I am going to Heliopolis," the meaning is that "I have existed from the beginning" or "I am returning to the Source."

According to the teachings at Heliopolis, the One who began the "becoming" is Atum, whose name means "all" and "nothing" and represents the unmanifest potential of creation. Atum is "one" with Nun, which is the indefinable, cosmic ocean. Atum's first act was to distinguish himself from Nun, which is described in Egyptian mythology. As Atum (the All or Absolute) realizes himself, he emerges from Nun as the primordial hill and creates Shu, the principle of space and air, and Tefnut, the principle of fire, which, according to the Sakkara Pyramid Texts, he spits into existence. (The Sakkara Pyramid Texts are a set of hieroglyphics, dating to the Old Kingdom's fifth and sixth dynasties, approximately 2350 to 2175 B.C.E., that were inscribed on the walls

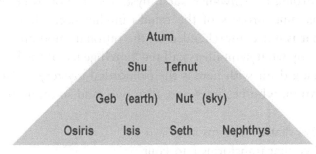

Fig. 10.1. The Great Ennead

of the pyramids, although they are believed to have actually been composed much earlier, around 3000 B.C.E.)

In another version, mentioned previously, Atum gave birth to himself by masturbating and created Shu and Tefnut. In a third version, he creates himself by projecting his heart,[21] bringing forth the eight primary principles known as the Great Ennead of Heliopolis. The Great Ennead was comprised of the nine great Osirian gods: Atum, Shu, Tefnut, Geb, Nut, Osiris, Isis, Seth, and Nephthys. The term is also used to describe the great council of the gods as well as a collective term for all the gods. Osiris, Isis, Seth, and Nephthys represent the cyclical nature of life, death, and rebirth, none of which is apart from Atum, according to the Pyramid Texts.

Atum represents the unknowable "Cause." It can be thought of as the modern Western concept of God. From him everything is created. He is at the top of the Ennead. From him all other principles of the universe emanate. From Atum is born Shu (air/wind) and Tefnut (water/moisture), the most important elements for life, representing the establishment of social order. Shu puts forth the principle of Life and Tefnut, the principle of order. From Shu and Tefnut, Geb and Nut, the earth and sky, were created. From Geb the sun is born. When Nut and Geb meet Tefnut, darkness occurs. Nut and Geb give birth to Osiris, Isis, Seth, and Nephthys.

In applying the four principles (unity, duality, reconciliation, and the concept of matter), Osiris represents the incarnation and reincarnation, life and death, which is renewal. Isis is the feminine aspect of Osiris. Seth is the principle of opposition, or antagonism, and Nephthys, the feminine aspect of Seth.

These creation events are taking place outside of the limits of terrestrial time, beyond the realm of temporal. They occur in heaven, not on earth. According to Schwaller, such mysteries are not to be understood by the reasoning process of the mind's intelligence.[22] It is an esoteric mystery that is not comprehended by the rational mind and can be perceived only by what symbolists call the "intelligence of the heart." What is really being dealt with here is the primordial mystery of God and his creation, Atum, who becomes one, then two, and so on up to eight.

> I am One that transforms into Two
> I am Two that transforms into Four
> I am Four that transforms into Eight
> After this I am One
>   —coffin of Petamon, Cairo Museum, [artifact] no. 1160[23]

This manifestion or proliferation of one into many, which occurred at Heliopolis, is the abstract principle of creation. At Memphis, Ptah further carries this abstraction and brings down fire from heaven. At Hermopolis, the divine fire begins to interact within the terrestrial world. At Thebes, a reiteration of these three processes is combined into one, represented by the triad of Amun.

According to John Anthony West, in *Serpent in the Sky*, the Great Ennead emanates from the Absolute, or "central fire." The nine neteru (principles) are bounded by the One (the Absolute), which becomes both one and ten, and is the symbolic likeness of the original unity. The Great Ennead is repetition and a return to the source, which is seen in Egyptian mythology as Horus, the divine son who avenges the murder and dismemberment of his father, Osiris.

The Egyptians espoused a natural, holistic philosophy that described the creation of man not as being thrust into a dangerous and violent world, but as the incarnation of the divine in a spiritual sense. Man *was* the Cosmos and the role of the individual was to realize this in order to achieve eternity. Pythagoras understood their philosophy and described it quite coherently in his writings and teachings. The Egyptians spoke it as myth that held an esoteric truth.

Ten and the Sacred Tetractys

For Pythagoreans, the most important number of all is the number ten, made from the sum of one, two, three, and four. It is expressed geometrically as a triangle referred to as the "sacred tetractys." The tetractys,

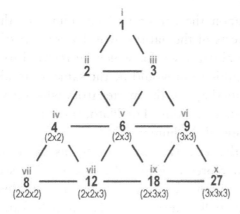

Fig. 10.2. Tetractys
(courtesy of John Opsopaus)

also known as the *decad,* is a triangular figure consisting of ten points arranged in four rows: one, two, three, and four points in each row.

Pythagoreans believe the tetractys's marvelous properties are the source and root of eternal nature. In essence, it is an expression of metaphysical reality and the "ideal world" of Plato. The Pythagoreans' oath includes a reference to the tetractys; they swear by "him that gave our family the Tectractys, which contains the Fount and Root of ever-flowing Nature."[24] According to West, the Greek tetractys may be viewed as the demythologized, manifested Egyptian Great Ennead. Although not necessarily an improvement over the Egyptian concept of the Ennead, the Greek tetractys is a way to approach understanding the many meanings behind the Ennead.

The triangular form of the tetractys represents the arithmetic progression of creation from the abstract and absolute to the concrete and discrete. The left side of the triangle (1, 2, 4, and 8) symbolizes the movement of life out of absolute unity. The right side (27, 9, 3, and 1) represents the rise of consciousness and a return to absolute unity. In essence, it is the description of everything (the universe) coming from nothing. Before anything existed there was one, a geometric point, a nondimensional existence. When the point moved, a line was created and the nondimensional became the one-dimensional. When the line moved, a plane (or surface) emerged and then there existed two dimensions. When the surface moved, a solid emerged along with three-dimensional reality. Therefore, depicted in the tetractys are four planes of existence, from the nondimensional to the three-dimensional.

Plato built upon the earlier understandings of the tetractys. He believed that objects of the natural world were part of a larger reality that included an abstract world, which he referred to as "Form." (In modern thought, this form would be the same as an idea.) An object's essence was not its shape or the matter from which it was constructed, but its essence—its true Form. For Plato, these forms were knowledge that existed outside of the human mind.

Interpreting the tetractys according to his theory of Form, planes two through four represent levels of existence. The second plane represents absolute existence of forms where ideas are divine and eternal, where "being" actually takes place. The fourth plane represents the physical manifestation of forms, where a form becomes a thing, and it was referred to as the "realm of becoming." The third plane is an intermediary or "between state" for planes two and four. Plane three is where the soul exists, thereby mixing states of abstraction with the concrete world. However, plane one, the source of everything, is indescribable. This level of reality is the basis for progression from the abstract to the concrete.

Although the Sacred Tetractys is clearly an elucidation of Pythagoras, it is not solely a Pythagorean concept. As the wisest of ancient sages, Pythagoras, according to various histories, traveled the world in search of wisdom. After learning all there was from the Greek sages, he went to Egypt, sometime around 535 B.C.E., with a letter of introduction from Polycrates, the ruler of Samos. According to the second-century Neoplatonist Porphyry, he was continually refused admission into the "Mysteries of Isis," the curriculum of higher learning for priests and nobles. However, at Thebes the priesthood finally accepted Pythagoras after he completed the necessary rites.

Recently, there has been considerable historical research into the relationship between the Greeks and the Egyptians during the first millennium B.C.E. In his monumental work *Black Athena*, vol. 1 (1987), Martin Bernal sets forth the history of how Western academics during the nineteenth and twentieth centuries fabricated the role of ancient Greece as the progenitor of civilization. In volume 2, he describes the archaeological and documentary evidence showing that the true source of knowledge and civilization is ancient Egypt. Although not all scholars agree with his thesis, it is clear that a relationship did exist and that the ancient Egyptians were influential during the budding Greek state.

Symbolism of the Serpent

Egyptian philosophy and mythology explained the physical and spiritual worlds through a system of numbers and mathematics. Their teaching was esoteric, reserved for nobility and the educated, yet it was made available to the commoner in the guise of mythology. A symbolist interpretation of Egyptian mythology explains its sophisticated philosophical concepts in a convincing way. Even today, certain symbols have survived and remain as icons of religious expression, particularly the serpent and the dove (or bird)—Christian symbols for the forces of good and evil.

Interestingly, more than two thousand years before Christianity, the pharaoh's diadem expressed these two symbols. His crown boasted a cobra, poised to strike, and a vulture. It was the ultimate symbol of power in ancient Egypt. One of the pharaoh's titles was "lord of the diadem of the vulture and of the serpent." It symbolized the divine man, which consisted of the serpent (the function of divine intelligence) and the vulture (the function of reconciliation). According to John Anthony West, parallel thinking directs the union of cobra and vulture on the royal diadem worn by the pharaoh, which stands for the union of Upper and Lower Egypt. At the same time, it symbolizes the triumphal union of the faculties of discernment and assimilation, which is the mark of the perfected or royal man.

The serpent represents intellect, the faculty by which man can break down the whole into its constituent parts, just like a serpent that swallows its prey whole and then digests it by breaking it down into more-manageable parts. The divine man must be able both to distinguish and to reconcile. Since these dual powers reside in the human brain, the form of the serpent's body in the diadem follows the physiology of the brain. This dual function of the brain is vivid in its two sides. The part of the diadem located in the middle of the forehead represents the "third eye" and its intellectual faculties.[25]

The Egyptians chose the snake as this representation of authority because that power is itself dual in expression. The serpent, what seems to be a unity, is actually dual in expression. It is verbal and sexual, dual and divisive by nature. It is simultaneously creative and destructive in the sense that multiplicity is created out of unity, and that creation represents the destruction of the perfection of the Absolute. Since the serpent bears both a forked tongue and a double penis, the intelligence of the choice is a logical one. Neheb Kau, meaning the provider of forms and attributes, was the name given to the snake representing the primordial serpent. Neheb Kau is depicted as a two-headed serpent, indicative of the dual spiral nature of the universe.

However, duality and intellect are not only a human function but also a cosmic one. There exists a higher intellect and a lower one. The serpent represents the lower as well as the higher intellect. The higher intellect allows man to know God, and is represented by the heavenly serpent, the "serpent in the sky"—often depicted by the Egyptians as a man riding the back of a serpent to the stars. The winged serpent was also a common symbol to many early civilizations.

However, duality unchecked is chaos, and is nothing more than destruction. To gain knowledge without going further to produce something new is, as West puts it, to parody God. In this way the serpent represented the chaotic, destructive forces inherent in the cosmos. In general, a single name was provided for each animal except the serpent, with its role of "separator" or obstructer of the works of Ra, or the Absolute. In Egyptian mythology, the serpent was vilified under various names, possibly to qualify a specific kind of obstruction or negation. This original concept of "duality unchecked," or "chaos," an aspect of the universe, later, through the Christian tradition, came to be known simply as evil—referring to a person who is not reconciled to God. It is why the serpent is seen as the personification of evil.

According to West, the symbol of the serpent has another, more scientific meaning. Energy, the substance of which all matter is formed, is really another name for "despiritualized consciousness." Consciousness is the creative impetus for energy, and therefore all matter, to exist. Thus, through energy, the spiritual is made physical.[26]

Energy is vibration, or the movement between negative and positive poles, and is exemplified by the sine wave. The sine wave is unique in that it represents energy entirely concentrated at a single frequency (the number of complete cycles per second), and is a waveform produced by simple harmonic motion. A sine wave can be mechanically constructed by moving a point around a circle. At the left side of the circle a radius is drawn from the center to a point on the circle. Move the point up the circle some distance, and draw another radius to it. The height of the second point above the original radius is the sine of the angle formed by both radii. If the circle is spinning at a constant rate, a graph of the height of the point versus time results in a sine wave, and is expressed as a fraction of the radius, and must fall between 1 and −1.

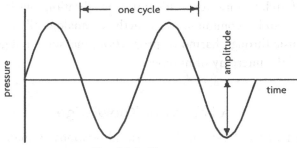

Fig. 10.3. Sine wave

The sine wave also applies to AC electricity, because it is constantly moving from negative to positive and back to negative again, causing an analog wave of the rising and collapsing voltage. Yet sound and light waves are also created simply by vibration. Ironically, this simple movement between opposing poles is the basis for our physical reality at the quantum level.

According to West, ancient civilizations portrayed vibration (energy) as a snake, which moves along the ground or in water. Its movement, as we all know, produces an "S"—a sine wave on its end. The snake, then, is the perfect and universal symbol to represent the act of unity becoming duality, which is the cosmological basis for all valid philosophical systems. Furthermore, these vibrations are the means whereby the arts are transmitted to us through our emotional faculties. It is obvious in case of music, with which we are familiar—sound waves orchestrated through volume, intensity, and key. Depending on the piece of music, sound produces an emotional effect.

Architecture has a similar effect, which by some is referred to as "frozen music." There are many ways in which the arts of music and architecture are similar. Both contain the ideas of proportions, time signatures, rhythms, and the creativity to arrange notes or structural ideas, aspects that can be seen in the same perspective.

West believes this is not just poetic, or metaphoric, but actually true.

A great temple, or for that matter a shopping mall, communicates its meaning or lack of meaning, as the case may be, entirely through vibration. We tend not to think of it that way because it's visual vibration; obviously color transmits itself to us as visual vibration. This we are accustomed to and recognize, but we don't think of architectural form. It's static, as vibration, but it is indeed vibration and it communicates exactly, or analogically anyway, as does music through harmony, proportion, measure, and geometry, which is the interplay of numbers.[27]

A Legacy of Knowledge

At the heart of the Egyptians' holistic philosophy is man's role in the universe, his origins, and the nature of consciousness—a sophisticated and complex subject even by today's standards, and still the greatest mystery of all. The generally accepted theory for the formation of the physical universe holds that all matter was the result of a cosmic "big bang." Unequivocally, it is a paradox, where something was created out of nothing. All physicists understand that matter is nothing more than configured or "shaped" energy, yet energy remains undefined. It is simply movement, but the movement of "what" cannot be answered—and may never be answered.

The ancient Egyptians seemingly understood the implications of this conundrum and viewed mankind's role at a level of sophistication rivaling a modern blend of the best science, philosophy, and theology. They viewed mankind as well as all of nature as the ultimate act of a supreme consciousness, its manifestation from the metaphysical into the physical. While modern physicists endeavor to explain the physical universe through mathematics, the ancient Egyptians blended numbers into philosophy to do the same. According to John Anthony West, "It is possible to say that Egypt regarded the entire universe as a gigantic act of magic, the transformation of consciousness into the material world."[28] Even today, notable scientists, such as the Apollo astronaut and physicist Edgar Mitchell, physician Stuart Hameroff, and evolutionary biologist Bruce Lipton, toil to unravel the mysteries of human consciousness.

More than five thousand years ago, Egypt's mythical Tehuti (Thoth) is said to have invented writing, and revealed to the people all knowledge of astronomy, architecture, geometry, medicine, and religion.[29] He was venerated as the god of wisdom and the divine messenger who had written down the nature of the physical universe. Although never canonized by the Egyptians, the writings accredited to him became an integral part of the Egyptian esoteric tradition that was described by temple art and architecture and taught by the temple priests to initiates.

Later, as Greece began to emerge as a world power, this knowledge was accepted by the Greek intelligentsia as ancient wisdom, and its legendary author took on the name Hermes Trismegistus (thrice-great Hermes). By the third century, within the Greco-Egyptian civilization of Alexandria, a group of Greek treatises was assembled to make up what is known as the *Corpus Hermeticum,* or simply, the Hermetica. Although scholars debate its Egyptian origin, the Greek historian Herodotus (484–432 B.C.E.) is clear on the antiquity and originality of its Egyptian spiritual ideas:

> The Egyptians are religious to excess, beyond any other nation in the world . . . [T]hey are meticulous in everything which concerns their religion . . . It was only, if I may put it so, the day before yesterday that the Greeks came to know the origin and form of the various gods . . . The names of all the gods have been known in Egypt from the beginning of time.[30]

The Greeks, whom the Western world credit as the source of modern society, derived their word *nature* from the Egyptian *neter,* acknowledging the ancient Egyptian teaching that there is no separation between nature and the divine.

In 1952, the renowned Egyptologist and professor of Semitic languages Samuel Mercer (1879–1969) composed the first complete translation of the Sakkara Pyramid Texts. Although difficulties exist dating the inscriptions themselves, they have aroused much speculation concerning their origin. They appear to have emerged as a fully fledged collection of mortuary texts without any precedent in the archaeological record. Since the texts are composed of distinct utterances, with no strict narrative sequence to link them, scholars believe they were not composed specifically for the purpose of pyramid inscription but may have had earlier uses. What is clear is that these forty-three-hundred-year-old hieroglyphics contain doctrines identical to those put forth in the Hermetica, the essence of which is that consciousness is the true nature of man.[31]

According to Hermetic teachings, the physical world is temporal, and each person, through his or her consciousness, has the ability to achieve immortality through knowledge of the divine. The teachings' underlying theme is the belief that what is above parallels what is below. In other words, what first exists in the spiritual is later manifest in the physical. Thus, the spiritual and the material are interwoven and must be pursued together. It is a philosophy that is pure and simple, unencumbered by dogmatic thought or ritual.

In Michael Maier's *Symbola aureae mensae duodecim nationum* (The Symbols of the Golden Table of the Twelve Nations), published in Frankfurt, Germany, in 1617, Hermes is depicted in what was believed to be the robes of an Egyptian priest (see fig. 10.4). He holds up a globe of the earth in his right hand while gesturing with his left to the sun and moon united in a fire, alluding to the Emerald Tablet. One of the key documents of alchemy (an ancient sacred science and philosophy, the forerunner to chemistry), the Emerald Tablet was highly regarded by the father of modern physics, Sir Isaac Newton. A rediscovery of the Hermetica during the fifteenth century helped to inspire the Renaissance and the push toward modern science. Those who have acknowledged a debt of gratitude to it reads like a list of "who's who" among Western civilization's greatest minds, including Leonardo da Vinci, Nicolaus Copernicus, Roger Bacon, and Sir Walter Raleigh.

Despite the incredible technology and wealth of knowledge we have amassed in the twenty-first century, we can do no better in explaining why we are here than the lessons taught in the Hermetica and Egypt's ancient mystery schools. Although controversial, modern scientific investigations into the nature of the physical universe, particularly quantum physics, suggest these ancient ideas have merit despite the natural aversion of the scientific intelligentsia to metaphysical matters. It also appears that the Egyptian "Man Cosmos" is likely the source of religious and philosophical teachings familiar to the modern world.

A particularly interesting teaching of this ancient esoteric tradition is that human history is cyclical. Civilization, consciousness, understanding, and technical ability rose to remarkable heights in the past and then fell back into barbarism again and again. According to this ancient view of history, a vast accumulation of knowledge and ability was handed down from previous epochs. The Egyptians inherited a legacy of wisdom and technology that was the source of powerful and unexplained ancient accomplishments, such as the pyramids of Giza. Even by today's standards, they appear to be something of a construction miracle.

Symbolists recognize that Egyptian culture appears to have started out at its height and then gradually declined over the course of their three-thousand-year history. Clearly, Egypt, with its longevity as well as its technical skill, was a civilization unparalleled by any nation since, and has left us with more questions than answers. How could Egyptian culture appear seemingly complete at the beginning of civilization? Where did their knowledge come from? Where did they learn their science?

Although it is conceivable that the Egyptians developed their construction techniques over a long period of time leading up to the first dynasty, according to legend, the "followers of Horus" ruled Egypt before the first dynasty, and before them there were kings who were referred to simply as "the gods." Traditionally, these predynastic kings have been viewed as mythological, but not all scholars and researchers think so. Evidence exists supporting the theory that Mesopotamians migrated into Egypt, or perhaps invaded, prior to the third millennium B.C.E. In Egypt's Eastern

Fig. 10.4. *Hermes, depicted as an Egyptian priest*
(from Michael Maier's Symbola aureæ mensæ duodecim nationum*)*

Desert, petroglyphs tell of a people who entered the region in high-prow boats, different from the papyrus vessels used by predynastic communities that lived along the Nile. Besides these rock carvings, figurines of the "Mother Goddess" have been found, as well as a falcon, the symbol of Horus, one of the most famous Egyptian gods.

By modern standards, the description of Egypt's earliest kings as gods certainly indicates the role of myth in their history. However, in the context of ancient Egypt's beliefs, there exists a plausible explanation. According to the Hermetic view, men could be considered gods. When the Hermetic tradition referred to men as gods, it was not referring to egotistical rulers who believed themselves to be on equal footing with God the absolute, or to God incarnate in a single individual. Instead, this tradition would refer to someone as a "god" who was spiritually enlightened and who worked for the cause of good.

Those who espoused this view believed that wherever life is, there is also soul—the animating and vital principle of life, credited with the faculties of thought, action, and emotion. In unreasoning animals, the soul is devoid of a higher consciousness. Animals live from instinct, feeding their corporal hunger and desires. Human souls that have not attained a higher consciousness (spirituality) as a guide to life are affected by desires in the same way as are the souls of animals. They exist irrationally driven by their appetites and longings, which leads to unreason. And like animals without reason, they never cease their anger and longing, and never have enough of evil (the instinctive pleasures of their bodily functions).

Higher consciousness comes from the essence of God, and in humans this state of being can be considered God's manifestation through spiritual reconciliation. To describe a person in this state of being is to call him or her a god. So among humans, those who attain such spirituality are gods, and their humanity is near to divinity. Therefore, it can be said that gods are immortal humans, and that humans are mortal gods.[32]

Proponents of modern, mainstream religions tend to view such statements as blasphemous, but this is not the intent. What a human god is being described as is someone who has been "born again" or "born of spirit"—to borrow phrases from the Christian tradition—or who has "become enlightened," "attained transcendence," "awakened," or "become one with the all"—to use more Eastern and mystical terms. In Schwaller's terms, the idea of the human as god refers to those individuals who have realized that within themselves, within their consciousness, there exists the cosmos, and that they, along with all others who have realized this, are the physical expression of the absolute God himself sharing His Consciousness.

In light of this rediscovered, ancient spirituality and the symbolist view of Egyptian culture, it is difficult to accept that a tribal and pastoral culture grew into a nation of such sophistication and splendor in so short a time. Did enlightened rulers reign in prehistoric Egypt? The answer may lie in the oral traditions of the Egyptians themselves.

11

BU WIZZER
Land of the Neteru

Oral traditions exist for almost every culture, ancient and modern. The study of oral traditions is not a media-oriented, high-profile area; however, it is an up-and-coming academic discipline, particularly in the classical and literary fields. The Center for Studies in Oral Tradition at the University of Missouri, Columbia, has been publishing a journal entitled *Oral Tradition* since 1986. Its articles cover folklore, biblical studies, and ancient Greek, English, Irish, Spanish, Portuguese, Yugoslav, Chinese, French, German, African, African American, Persian, Norse, Italian, Welsh, Romanian, Mayan, (Asian) Indian, Arabic, Hungarian, Finnish, Japanese, Tibetan, central Asian (Kirgiz), and South Pacific traditions. Other, special issues include topics on Native America, the epics of the Euro-Asian Silk Road, and South Asian women's traditions.

Before the advent of writing, history was an oral art, and in some respect it still is. Consider, for example, the story of a G.I. who survived campaigns in North Africa, Italy, and France during the Second World War. He never wrote about it and told no one of his struggles except his wife and children, who, years later, told their children. If the story bears significance in some way, it will likely continue to be passed through successive generations. Maybe someday a great-grandson or great-granddaughter, thrilled by the part their great-grandfather played in the war, will write it down.

Storytelling is part of the human experience, and distinguishes us from all other forms of life. We share memory with our descendants so they may know where they came from and why. Eventually, someone will deem it important enough to record those memories in a written form. For the Egyptians, during the reign of Ramses the Great (1314–1224 B.C.E.), an unknown scribe created a list of all the kings of Egypt, as far as memory would serve. The list was written on eleven sheets of papyrus discovered at Deir el-Medina in ancient Thebes by Bernardino Drovetti sometime prior to 1824. The first sheet contained ten rulers who lived before dynastic Egypt, a time for which there is no history. These rulers were considered very special, and were referred to as Horus God Kings.

Over the years, fragments of the Palermo Stone (a large inscribed stone, dated to approximately 2500 B.C.E., that details many Egyptian cultural practices and is considered the world's oldest history book) were brought together, revealing another list of prehistoric kings. Although the first two kings listed on the Turin Papyrus were not incised on the Palermo Stone, the remaining eight were.

TABLE 11.1. ANCIENT EGYPTIAN KINGS
from the Palermo Stone and the Turin Kings list

Palermo Stone	Turin papyrus
—	Ptah
—	Ra
Shu	Su
Keb	Seb
Ausar	Osiris
Sht	Seth
Hwr	Horus
Djehuti	Thoth
Mch	Ma
Hwr	Horus

According to Egyptologists, the Palermo Stone is believed to be a historical document because the names are in their correct chronology. Whoever inscribed the stone likely had access to the other historical, state documents that were handed down from the first dynasty.

These records hint at an oral tradition that was maintained since 3000 B.C.E. and at least until the twelfth century B.C.E. Since there is no other ancient civilization as grand as Egypt spanning three thousand years, one would suspect that its oral traditions would not be lost to history.

According to the independent Egyptologist Stephen Mehler, this is indeed the case. In his book *The Land of Osiris,* Mehler outlines the ancient Egyptian oral tradition as it was explained to him by an Egyptian "master" and wisdom keeper named Abdel'El Hakim Awyan. According to Mehler, besides his traditional training, Hakim received a formal education and holds degrees in archaeology and Egyptology from Cairo University. Although Hakim's oral tradition of Egyptian history is an entirely subjective matter from an academic standpoint and surely has its opponents, it is a thought-provoking account of Egyptian prehistory.

Mehler describes Egyptian oral history as "Khemitology," a term that refers to the ancient name of Egypt. The ancient Egyptian symbols for the name of their country correspond with the consonants KMT, which have been written as Kemet, Kemit, Khemet, Khemit, Khem, and Al Khem. It literally means "the black land," in reference to the rich black soil deposited by the Nile River. The indigenous tradition of Egypt explains that its civilization was Khemit (pronounced Khemph), and their language was known as Souf. According to Hakim, the Nubian people, particularly the Matokke tribe, speak a language similar to ancient Khemitian.[1] The ancient Egyptian population consisted of forty-two tribes who together made up the Sesh, which means "the people."

Al Khem, the term early Egyptians used for Egypt, is also believed to be the origin of the word *alchemy,* indicating that those who later created the word *alchemy,* the Arabs, were aware of the ancient Egyptian tradition of alchemy. How the word *alchemy* was derived from ancient Egypt is not clear. According to *theosophists* (those who believe in the oneness of life and an independent spiritual search), another definition exists: *Al* means "mighty sun" and *chemi,* fire. However, the most likely origin of the word *al-chemi* is from Arab culture of the eighth century. Although the meaning of *klmya* (the orignal Arab word for chemi) is debatable, it likely comes from ancient Greece. The Greek *kemia* may mean two things: either "the black land" (according to Plutarch), in which case alchemy would be "the science of Egypt"; or simply "the black," a reference to the alchemic First Matter, which is black and serves as the basis for transmutation into the various elements of the physical world. *Klmya* may also be derived from the Greek *khymeia,* which means fusion. In any case, it seems that alchemy, a process of altering matter for mankind's use, has its origins in ancient Egypt.

Abdel'El Hakim Awyan, Stephen Mehler's Egyptian teacher, lives in Egypt and is a wisdom keeper for an indigenous tradition of long-standing oral teaching that goes back thousands of years, before the introduction of writing. It is esoteric, meaning that it is meant only for the privileged. According to this ancient tradition, Khemitian civilization is nearly seventy thousand years old, and was based upon a matri-archal way of life centered on an ancient river system eight miles to the west of the Nile Valley, called the Ur Nil.

Abdel'El Hakim Awyan reports that the Sphinx was built fifty thousand years ago, and is a she, not a he.[2] His oral tradition also insists that the pyramids, genuine ones (meaning those that are solid with chambers carved within), were not tombs but rather structures to generate, transform, and transmit energy—a tradition that supports Christopher Dunn's theory of the Giza power plant. The pyramids were built more than ten thousand years ago, and not in the order believed by modern Egyptology.[3]

So why is the history purported by Herodotus, of which modern Egyptology was initially based, so different? Herodotus was considered part of an invading patriarchal culture, and as an interloper was not told the truth about Egyptian history and culture. The Greek priest Manetho, serving under Ptolemaic patriarchal rule of Egypt, wrote Egyptian history based upon dynastic male kingship. He did so as if this was the genuine epitome of Egyptian social structure and history. He was led to believe this because the Egyptians regarded the Greeks as barbarians. As such, the Greeks had no real sense of their own history. It is interesting to note that the Greeks saw Egypt as the fount of all knowledge. The word *philosophy* is derived from *philo,* which is related to the Egyptian term meaning "son of the Egyptian culture."

The Sphinx

According to ancient tradition, as noted above, the Sphinx is about fifty thousand years old. She was carved first above ground before any of the per-neters or per-bas (pyramids or temples) were built, and represents the feminine expression of a leonine-human combination. The Sphinx represents Tefnut, Sekhmet Men-Het, and Nut, who were later expressed by Egyptologists as lioness goddesses. Particularly, the Sphinx is identified with Tefnut, which translates as "she of moisture." Tefnut was generally shown as a woman with a lion's head or as a full lioness. The netert Nut (a goddess) represented the sky, the feminine consciousness of space that existed before the creation of the physical world. Tefnut literally means "the spittle of Nut" and represents the first physical manifestation. As Nut spat on the Earth, Tefnut came forth, and so the Sphinx was carved—the first structure ever built at Giza.

Although the Sphinx was associated with Hathor (a goddess embodied as the celestial cow) in early dynastic times, it still held a feminine association. It was much later, during the eighteenth dynasty of the New Kingdom, that a patriarchal interpretation was placed upon the Sphinx, identifying it with the male principle Hor-em-akhet, or "Horus in the horizon." Accordingly, some scholars believe that a beard was not original to the Sphinx, but later attached to represent a male pharaoh. Ancient tradition teaches that the structures in front of the Sphinx were not temples, but were constructed as part of the Sphinx complex. A king, possibly, built these structures as a monument to his descent by honoring his mother.[4]

The Pyramids

Mainstream Egyptology asserts that the term for pyramid was MR. However, ancient traditional sources claim that Mer (MR) meant "beloved," and had nothing to do with the pyramids. The word *pyramid* is derived from the Greek words *pyramis* and *pyramidos*. Although *pyramis* is an obscure word and may refer to the pyramid shape, *pyramidos* has been translated as "fire in the middle,"[5] a meaning eerily reflective of Dunn's power-plant theory. According to Abdel 'El Hakim Awyan, the ancient Khemitians unambiguously used the word *per-neter* to mean pyramid.

Per simply means "house," and *neter,* as we have discussed, means "principle or attribute of divinity," what we call nature. So in the light of the indigenous tradition, *per-neter* means "house of nature" or "house of energy." A temple was referred to as a per-ba, which means "house of the soul"; and a tomb was referred to as per-ka, which means "house of the physical projection." With this translation in mind, it is easy to see why no burial remains have been found in the pyramids. They were not built for that purpose. Mehler states this emphatically, and asserts that their primary purpose was to generate, transform, and transmit energy. According to Hakim, this is supported by the indigenous wisdom keepers of Egypt.

Sakkara

As discussed earlier, the step pyramid at Sakkara is believed to be the first pyramid built by the ancient Egyptians. It began as a mastaba (a rectangular tomb with a flat roof), then was rehabilitated twice and converted into a pyramid shape. However, according to the ancient Khemitian tradition, it was originally a per-ka, a tomb that was stepped and enlarged to resemble a per-neter. Hakim says that it is actually younger, not older, than the true pyramids, or per-neters. Tradition also holds that it is at least six thousand years old, thirteen hundred years older than its official Old Kingdom date. However, its surrounding enclosure, according to tradition, was built more than twelve thousand years ago.[6]

Mehler examined an elaborate tunnel system at Sakkara, which had been exposed by previous excavations. Egyptologists have little or no comment on these tunnels. Mark Lehner refers to underground chambers or passages under the step pyramid as part of Djoser's funerary cult, but makes no mention of the myriad tunnels elsewhere.[7]

Mehler's observations at Sakkara appear to confirm the ancient tradition that the tunnels were carved as channels for flowing water:

> It appeared to us that the water was channeled from the west, the direction of the ancient Ur Nil, not the current river about eight to ten miles to the east of Sakkara. The downward sloping of the ground was from west to east, and the tunnels seemed to be coming from the west also. The tunnels and channels we observed were in different layers of bedrock under the surface, cut in rectangular, smooth-sided, serpentine passages going, apparently, for miles under and through the limestone bedrock. These passages all seemed man-made, not natural formations.[8]

The only way these tunnels could have been carved is with machine tools, not with copper chisels and "stone pounders."

Mehler relates the story of Hakim's boyhood, when he first investigated the tunnels at Sakkara. For hours he wandered through the tunnels, practically lost. When he finally found his way out, he was at the Giza plateau, some eight miles away. Interestingly, a concrete slab now covers the tunnel he had ventured into as a young man. Although this is likely a function of tourist safety, other tunnel entrances at Sakkara are guarded with simple fencing, and some with nothing at all. If the ancient Khemitians drilled these tunnels to draw water from the ancient Ur Nil in the west, then Sakkara must have been an active, living site, not a necropolis, more than ten thousand years ago.

Around the courtyard, fragments of carved stone lying in the desert sand are remnants of the original alabaster pavement. The ancient tradition holds that Sakkara was a site for healing. Accordingly, the great physician-priest Imhotep is said to have worked in this area, the last of the ancient masters who knew and taught medicine.

Abusir

An extension was made to Sakkara in the area called Abusir, two miles to the north. Its structures originally consisted of fourteen pyramids, but only four are still standing. Of the four, the first encountered is the pyramid of Neferefre as one arrives from the main Sakkara complex. It was never finished, and is in very poor condition.

At Abusir, Mehler again found evidence of water channels and the remnants of ancient lake beds. Abusir Lake still exists east of the site, and Egyptologists believe it was formed as a result of today's Nile River. Yet to the west of the lake there appears to be a number of extinct lake beds and ancient water channels. The present lake may be all that remains of a much more extensive system of lakes and canals, going west to east, from the ancient Ur Nil.

At the remains of a pyramid attributed to a king Sahura, limestone channels led to an ancient lake bed. The area in front of the pyramid had basalt floors with granite walls, and what appeared to be a series of docks for boats. Mehler also found remnants of aqueducts coming from the lake bed. The most revealing evidence is that the area slopes downward from west to east for the water to flow naturally. Since the present Nile River is eight to ten miles east, these aqueducts too appear to be built for a source in the Western Desert, such as the ancient Ur Nil. These channels seem to go under the pyramid, suggesting that the per-neter was constructed after the aqueducts and water channels were built.⁹ Mehler proposes that Abusir Lake is the remnant of a much larger lake system derived from the ancient Ur Nil, making the original structures more than ten thousand years old.

Giza

According to ancient tradition, the middle pyramid was built first on the Giza plateau, and not by the direction of a king. It was constructed on the highest point on the plateau, which would be a likely place to build the first per-neter. There is also evidence from mainstream Egyptologists that this is the case. According to John Baines and Jaromir Maiek, the middle pyramid was known in ancient times as "the great pyramid" and the current Great Pyramid by another title. Mehler believes that the middle pyramid was constructed on top of a mound in order to fuse with the earth and serve as a seismic tap, resonating with earth's vibration—a coupled oscillator, as Dunn's theory postulates.

In front of the middle pyramid is what Egyptologists call a mortuary temple, built for King Khafre. However, according to ancient tradition, it is a waterway from the pyramid to the Sphinx Lake. Large shoulders, constructed of massive limestone slabs, form a passageway in which the water flowed. It included docks for boats as they passed through to the pyramid. Huge pavement stones were laid in front of the pyramids, some weighing more than a hundred tons and extending as much as thirty feet. On the Great Pyramid's east side, basalt slabs cover the limestone pavement, possibly to increase resonance.

Abu Rawash

It is unknown whether the pyramid at Abu Rawash, five miles north of Giza, was left unfinished or quarried away for its stone during later times. Little remains of it. Estimates place its original base at nearly 380 feet. Its casing stones indicate an angle of 60 degrees. Since a cartouche was found with the title Djedefra, it is assumed King Djedefra ordered the pyramid's construction. When compared to the Great Pyramid, the pyramid at Abu Rawash appears quite small. Why would the son, after becoming king and having the same resources, material, and manpower available to him as his father (who built the Great Pyramid) did, have chosen to build such an inferior monument to himself?

According to ancient tradition, the pyramid at Abu Rawash was completed. The small mountain in which it sits was excavated to construct the pyramid's inside. There is evidence that the core stones are still fused to the hill's limestone bedrock. Since the core stones are still in place, it is likely that is was fully functional but later quarried for its outer stones. Mehler descended more than a hundred feet into the hill and observed the smooth walls of the hollowed hill, reminiscent of the tunnels he inspected at Giza and Sakkara. It is his belief that the same people who carved the tunnels at Giza and Sakkara cored out the hill at Abu Rawash and built the pyramid there. While visiting the site, Mehler found it was:

> virtually deserted, and there was no one else there to interfere with my and Hakim's investigations. We were able to locate the "socket" stones marking the pyramid's layout and to find the pavement stones. We also saw many remnants of granite blocks to indicate the ancient Bu Wizzer construction style of the Khemitians.[10]

Bu Wizzer

Bu Wizzer is what the ancient Khemitians originally called their land. *Bu* means land, and *wizzer* is the correct Khemitian title for "god," which the Greeks named Osiris, also called Osar or Ausar. Bu Wizzer also translates as "the land of Osiris." It was the land from Abu Rawash in the north to Dahshur in the south, bordered by the Libyan Desert to the west and Helwan to the east, and incorporated Giza, Sakkara, Dahshur, Zawiyet el Aryan, Abusir, and Abu Ghurab (site of an ancient ruined obelisk). Ancient oral tradition claims it was one of the earliest settled areas of Khemit, going back to 70,000 B.C.E.

There has been much speculation around the mythical figure of Osiris. However, according to ancient tradition, the Wizzer (Osiris) was considered to be one of Khemit's early leaders. Whether he was mythical or an actual man, he became the model for all later kings. He introduced agriculture, architecture in stonework, engineering, law, spirituality, science, ethics, and all the other elements of modern civilization to the people.

The civilization of Bu Wizzer is responsible for the anomalous evidence found in ancient Egypt, all the stoneware that experts say was made with precision machine tools, the thirty thousand artifacts found at Sakkara and Giza.

The civilization of Bu Wizzer built the Sphinx, its cyclopean temple, and the pyramids. Its civilization was based on an older river to the west, the Ur Nil, now buried in the desert sands.

Fig. 11.1. Geographic area of Bu Wizzer

The anthropologist Karl Butzer extensively studied soil deposits in order to trace the early geological history of northern Africa. According to the evidence, tools and sites of human occupation existed in the Western Desert, and date to more than seven hundred thousand years ago, during a rainy period. As discussed earlier, alternating periods of rainfall and drought have plagued North Africa throughout history. The current arid conditions in the Western Desert are no more than six thousand years old.

Although some Egyptologists and geologists believe the western Nile disappeared over one hundred thousand years ago, there is climatic basis to support that this western river has been active more recently, particularly during a time between twenty-five thousand and thirty-five thousand years ago. Today, it may still be the source of water for the oases Bahariya, Farafra, Dakhia, and Khârga in the Western Desert. An Egyptian agronomist told Mehler that during prehistoric times, a river flowed in this area and that the present groundwater was its remnants. The agronomist refers to the ancient area of the western river as the "old valley." According to the agronomist, the underground water table has been fairly abundant for thousands of years, and a major source of water for humans in this area.

Northeast of the Khârga Oasis, toward the city of Assut, there is a magnificent landscape of valleys and rock formations that extend for hundreds of miles. From a bird's-eye view, one can see how an ocean or sea, and later the Ur Nil River, has carved out valleys and other formations. For Mehler, there appears to be the outline of an ancient

Photo courtesy of NASA

Fig. 11.2. Nile Valley from orbit. Notice the ancient lake beds,
rivers, and tributaries, now filled with white sand,
that surround and lead into the Nile River.

riverbed, many miles wide and hundreds of miles long. NASA photographs corroborate Mehler's observations.

The Qattara Depression, a large desert basin in northwest Egypt, looks like a huge gouge in the earth that may have been a lake bed during ancient times. In researching the possibility of water in the Western Desert, Mehler uncovered a 1963 report from an international meeting of geologists.[11] The report stated that there was enough groundwater under Egypt's Western Desert to supply all of the Middle East with fresh water for years. This is an indication of how extensive scientists believed the water table was, which confirmed observations in the field.

Mehler believes the water table under the Western Desert is a flowing river, and not an aquifer. The water, flowing through natural underground passages, gave the ancient Khemitians the idea to create their own passages in order to link to the natural ones and bring the water to the sites farther east. When the climate changed during the latter part of the last ice age, and rainfall nearly disappeared, the Ur Nil dried up, allowing the formation of the Sahara and Libyan Deserts. Only the underground river remained. According to Hakim, the ancient Khemitians had "followed the water" from the west and channeled it to the east, all the way to the present Nile Valley. In an area that has suffered from drought for millennia, and knowing that water is the basis of all life, it would be logical for any civilization, at any time, to commit large expenditures in manpower and materials to ensure a source of water.

According to the ancient teachings, anhydrous zinc and dilute hydrochloric acid were not the original sources of the hydrogen used in the Great Pyramid's energy transformer; water was.[12] Mehler puts forth a hypothesis that the rushing water, amplified by the igneous rock and heated by solar energy, would enter into the Great Pyramid in the underground chamber called the pit. He argues that the water was broken down by electrolysis, or catalytic conversion, into its components, oxygen and hydrogen. As Dunn has stated, the hydrogen gas, energized by the Great Pyramid acting as a coupled oscillator, could be converted into a source of power for the ancient Khemitians, as well as producing radio and microwave energy. With this, Mehler creates a new paradigm for why the glyph *asgat nefer* appears so frequently at the Bu Wizzer sites. It refers to the "harmony of water" that provided a major source of energy utilized by the pyramids.

The Osireion

At Abydos, in the south of Egypt, there stands a temple built in honor of Osiris. Mainstream Egyptologists claim that Seti I built it around 1250 B.C.E. However, according to ancient traditions, there was never a single ruler named Seti; it was a title held by many kings. Mehler reports that the Osiris temple was built much earlier than 1250 B.C.E. Dedicated to Wizzer, it is a sacred per-ba (temple).

The Temple of Osiris is one of the best-preserved structures in all of Egypt. It contains reliefs with the original paint still visible. According to Hakim, different styles of reliefs attest to their age. With few exceptions,

Fig. 11.3. Osireion at Abydos

raised reliefs are older than incised reliefs (those that are chiseled into the stone).[13] Carvings at the Temple of Osiris at Abydos are beautiful examples of ancient, raised reliefs and are much older than the 1250 B.C.E. date attributed to them by orthodox Egyptologists.

Abydos was an ancient site dedicated to Wizzer, and the per-ba (temple)—the Osireion—was erected to the neter, not to any one king. According to Hakim, the Temple of Osiris is thousands of years older than the so-called Pyramid Texts found at Sakkara.

A short distance from the Temple of Osiris is an even older temple, known as the Osireion. It is composed of megalithic blocks of granite, a building unlike most others in Egypt. The architecture closely resembles that of another structure, the Valley Temple, in front of the Sphinx and near the Great Pyramid. Also dedicated to Wizzer, the Osireion, now in ruins, is fifty feet lower than the Temple of Osiris. Despite its obvious stratigraphic age, Egyptologists assign to it a date contemporary with early dynasties. Since there are no naturally raised hills or cliffs present, the lower structure must be from an earlier archaeological layer and, therefore, older than the Temple of Osiris. Furthermore, the dynastic Egyptians, whom Egyptologists claim built the temple, typically used

Fig. 11.4. The flower of life

softer stone, such as sandstone, to construct their temples, not granite, as did the ancient Khemitians.

Ancient tradition holds that the Osireion is more than fifty thousand years old, and that it was constructed during the same era as the Sphinx and her related structures. A few inscriptions exist at the Osireion, but they are incised and were likely carved later, during dynastic times. One of the more intriguing symbols in the Osireion is the "flower of life." It is a symbol that some believe to be a pattern of creation and the movement of our consciousness into the physical realm. No one really knows how old it is or who created its design.

However, represented in red paint, it is no doubt not original to the structure. Hakim believes the symbol was painted somewhere between 300 B.C.E. and 300 C.E. Mehler believes that followers of the great Greek mathematician Pythagoras may have made it. Pythagoras and his followers were initiated into the Egyptian teachings of sacred geometry.[14]

Zep Tepi

Zep tepi, meaning "the first time," is a creation myth, according to Egyptian tradition. The myth explains how the neteru were created and tells the story of a time when there was nothing but a powerful being called Nun. Nun was so powerful that a shining egg arose from her, which was Ra. Ra was thought to have been so mighty that he willed his children into being. The first was Shu, who was considered the god of the space and light between the sky and the earth. Next, Ra created Tefnut, who was the personification of moisture in the sky. Then the god of the earth, Geb, was created, and then Nut, the goddess of the daytime sky. The final god was Hapi, the ancient god of the Nile. After the gods were created, Ra created men and descended to earth in human form to rule Egypt as the first pharaoh.

In *The Orion Mystery,* Robert Bauval sees zep tepi related to a date around 10,000 B.C.E. However, according to Mehler, in Egypt's ancient traditions there was no "first time." They did not envision a beginning or an end of creation. Existence, they believed, was a series of cycles, with the current cycle beginning over sixty-five thousand years ago. Zep tepi was thought of as the period of Wizzer, as an ancient era, and nothing more.

In *The Mythological Origins of the Egyptian Temple,*[15] the British Egyptologist E. A. Reymond suggested a variation of the meaning of *zep tepi,* which he said came from the walls of the Temple of Horus at Edfu. According to Reymond, the full text of zep tepi is *ntr ntri hpr m sp tpy,* and is translated as "the Sanctified God who came into being at the First Occasion," where *zep tepi* refers to the "First Occasion." Reymond believes it must be understood in the context of creation mythology in which the neteru first manifested to humans.

The ancient oral tradition puts forth a meaning that generally agrees with Reymond's translation. Zep tepi corresponds to a time when the people (the Sesh) achieved a new level of consciousness. It began over sixty-five thousand years ago. Mehler believes this time refers to an era between twenty thousand and sixty thousand years ago, when the Khemitians attained a higher level of consciousness and knowledge. It allowed them to build their great structures and carve their tunnels. In essence, it allowed them to create their civilization. Later, all this formed the basis of their creation mythology.[16]

Some scholars believe that the texts referring to *seshu hor* on the walls of the Temple of Horus at Edfu, forty miles north of Aswan, refer to an advanced people who entered Khemit in prehistoric times and brought knowledge and civilization. R. A. Schwaller de Lubicz agrees with Wallis Budge in translating the term *seshu hor* to mean "followers of Horus" and he does interpret it as a record of prehistoric rulers. Everyone from Atlanteans to extraterrestrials have been believed to be the progenitors of the Egyptian civilization. However, the ancient tradition has a more down-to-earth interpretation. The people came into full consciousness by themselves, according to preordained cosmic cycles. Hor (or Horus) was the realized human male. Prior to the concept of kingship in Egypt, Hor was used as the term for the male who had achieved a flowering of the senses, a degree of enlightenment.[17] This "flowering" was significant at that time because the society was organized matrilineally, with the female choosing the male who would be her consort. It can be reasonably assumed that the realized male would have been the most desirable mate, and that this played a significant part in the advancement of the Egyptian civilization.

The Age of Myth precedes our current historical age. This is apparent for all cultures. According to Erich Neumann, in *The Origins and History of Consciousness,* what happened during the mythological age is that the human ego (the ability to view one's self apart from nature) began to develop. Mankind's mental processes started to separate from the purely instinctive ones. Originally, instinctively, the communication and dissemination of knowledge was symbolic and took the form of the myth. Within the myth lay absolute truths concerning the processes of the natural world. As the ego continued to develop, so did the conscious level of mankind, and with it came more and more sophistication in language as well as arts, philosophy, and science. What Mehler is claiming, I believe, is that zep tepi—the first time—relates to the initial development of the ego and a new way of viewing the world. There can be no doubt that civilization was the progeny of the Age of Myth; every world history text says as much. The reason ancient Greeks were so instrumental in the formation of Western civilization, and why they are viewed as its founders, is that their philosophers and sages were able to bridge the communicative gap between the language of myth and the new language of the ego.

Mehler believes that the Edfu texts' references to the zep tepi (first time) and seshu hor (follower of Horus) tell the story of when humans came into a high state of consciousness and began large-scale construction in stone to build the Bu Wizzer civilization. He suggests that the "prayers" in the texts are really funerary psalms, since the structure of the Edfu temple was not a true pyramid but rather a tomb. He believes the meaning of the Edfu texts later was deliberately distorted by the Egyptian priesthood, called the Hanuti, during dynastic times. These priests obscured the true Khemitian wisdom during the Old Kingdom in order to create a religion that allowed them to control information and knowledge of the inner mysteries. The priests identified the king with the wisdom of Wizzer—as Sahu, the symbol of the High Initiate and the Enlightened One—because the king was the one with the wealth to sustain the Hanuti in their greed and newfound power. Instead of revealing knowledge and consciousness to the people so they could reach enlightenment, the priests restricted access to this knowledge and hoarded it for themselves. The priests then became the spokesmen for the neteru, and only they and the royal families had access to them. The old knowledge, and its connection to Sa-Ptah (Sirius), was obfuscated. The rise of patriarchy, the "age of Amen," occurred between four thousand and six thousand years ago.[18] The male king became all-important, instead of the true per-aa, the matrilineal "high house." In this way, the Hanuti began keeping the Khemitian teachings hidden from the people and distorting this knowledge.

The Mayan Connection

A mile south of the Sakkara step pyramid the remains exist of a small, New Kingdom temple built during the eighteenth dynasty (1539–1295 B.C.E.), according to orthodox chronology. Scholars believe it was dedicated to an individual named Maya, but according to ancient traditions, *maya* was a title, not a name. Although the origin of the word is uncertain, Hakim suggests Maya was indeed a title, not the personal name of an individual who may have traveled to Egypt from Central America. *Maya* is one of the terms used today in Egypt for water. In Khemit, *maya* may refer to the phrase "from across the water." It may seem like pure speculation to suggest that ancient Egyptians had contact with people from the other side of a vast ocean; however, there exists some intriguing evidence.

On the ceiling of a small chapel enclosure of the purported Maya temple there are some unusual geometric glyphs that do not appear to be typically Khemitian in style. Mehler photographed the glyphs and sent them to Hunbatz Men, a Mayan shaman/astrologer (known as a daykeeper), in November 1997. Since Men specifically recognized two of the glyphs, as well as the overall style, patterns, and colors, it was Mehler's belief that they were of Mayan origin. In February of 1998, Mehler showed the photo to another Mayan elder, Flordemayo. Although she could not confirm that the glyphs were actually Mayan, her first impression was that the photograph was from Mexico or Central America. She showed the photograph to her teacher, Mayan elder Don Alejandro Cirilo Oxiaj Peres, a leader and wisdom keeper of the Guatemalan Quiche Mayan tradition. He confirmed that the glyphs were ancient Mayan. According to Mayan mythology, the ancient ancestors of the Maya came "from the stars" to four areas of the world. One of those areas was ancient Khemit, where they were called the Naga Maya. It is Hakim's belief that the word *naga* is from the ancient Khemitian word *ng* or *nag*, which means tribe. Naga Maya, therefore, possibly means "the tribe that came from across the water."

In addition to Mehler's physical evidence linking the Maya with the ancient Egyptians, evidence exists in the correlations between the philosophical beliefs of both cultures. Ancient Mayan cosmology, in principle, was similar to that of the ancient Egyptians. Nature, all of physical life, was a manifestation of an abstract consciousness, or will, as the Maya chose to call it.

According to Augustus Le Plongeon, the Maya believed their universe was infinite darkness in which dwelt the unknowable, the enigmatic Will, called uol. They also believed that in nature the circle is the ultimate source (divinity) from which all life extends, so they conceived that "Will, that Eternal One Being," as a circle, which they also called Uol, whose center was everywhere and circumference nowhere.[19]

This Will was believed to be androgynous, two in one and one in two, and in it, life unconsciously pulsated. At the awakening of consciousness, when the Infinite Sexless ceased to be sexless, the male principle, remaining distinct, fertilized the virgin womb of nature (the cosmic egg), pictured in the tableau of creation at Chichén Itzá.[20]

This new manifestation of the "Boundless One" was envisioned by the Maya as a circle with a vertical diameter, and they called it Lahun, the "all-pervading one." The name is derived from *Lah,* which means "he who is everywhere," and *hun,* or "one." It became the image of the universe growing from the boundless darkness.

From this vertical diameter (symbol of the male principle impregnating the virgin womb of nature) originated the idea of the phallus as the emblem of the Creator. The circle divided into four parts, vertically and horizontally, forming the *tetraktis,* the symbol of "the sacred four." The cross, enclosed in a circle, symbolized the universe under the jurisdiction of these four powerful intelligences or principles, similar to the Pythagorean principle of four—the absolute, duality, relationship, and the idea of matter. To these powers were entrusted the building of the physical world and the guardianship of the cardinal points (north, south, east, and west). To distinguish the powers, or natural energies,

Fig. 11.5. Winged circles from Guatemala (top) and Egypt.
(from Le Plongeon's Queen Moo and the Egyptian Sphinx*)*

which Le Plongeon defines as genii or guiding spirits, of the north and of the south, wings were added to the circle with its crossed diameters. This metaphysical concept of the winged circle is evident in the inscriptions that adorn the façade of the sanctuary at Uxmal and in the Troano and other Mayan manuscripts.

Both the Egyptians and the Maya chose a winged circle to symbolize the divine in man (fig. 11.5). In hieroglyphic inscriptions, on the royal cartouches, and on the entranceways of temples, the winged circle appears throughout Egyptian architecture. In Egypt it was originally a pair of falcon wings symbolizing the ethereal, but during the fifth dynasty two serpents and a sun disk were inserted between the wings, representing Horus of Behdet. Although the artistic depiction of the winged circle is slightly different for the ancient Maya and Egyptians, the underlying principles and meaning as well as its representation in art are nearly identical.

The Civilization That Once Was

One can easily suspect that the ancient civilization of Bu Wizzer, believed to have existed between sixty-five thousand and ten thousand years ago, is pure, unfounded speculation. It runs counter to established theories concerning mankind and civilization. So what could possibly lead one to believe that Egyptian civilization is far older than ever imagined? In a word: evidence. If eight feet of water erosion did not exist on the walls of the Sphinx enclosure, if the alignments of Nabta Playa did not exist, if thousands of pieces of precision-made stoneware had never been found within the Sakkara complex, and if the Great Pyramid could not be effectively explained as an energy-transforming machine, then one should accept the mainstream idea that Egyptian civilization began shortly before the third millennium B.C.E. But that is not the case.

In order for the described evidence to make sense, there must have been a civilization existing before the end of the ice age that reached a high state of knowledge and technology, just like the indigenous Egyptian tradition suggests. If this civilization did indeed exist, it would explain the gap in mankind's history between twelve thousand years ago and five thousand years ago. Very little is known about this period, referred to as the Mesolithic (Middle Stone Age), because of a lack of evidence. Many believe that mankind, during this period, was first beginning to organize and become "civilized." However, it can also be postulated that mankind was recovering from a far-reaching regional catastrophe.

As previously discussed, the cultures of Cro-Magnon appeared from nowhere on the Iberian Peninsula forty thousand years ago. By most scholarly accounts, they appeared as modern humans with an already defined culture. Lewis Spence, in his *History of Atlantis,* claims that the various Cro-Magnon cultures were waves of invasion from the mythical island country of Atlantis. Although it is an apt metaphor in describing the settlement of western Europe, there is a more realistic explanation that accounts for the evidence.

Professor David Lewis-Williams points out that the evidence for human cultures in Africa suggests that man was displaying modern behaviors a very long time ago. He maintains that the source of Cro-Magnon cultures in Europe was Africa, despite the missing "host culture" that would be required to sufficiently explain their appearance in Iberia. Researchers including David Hatcher Childress, Graham Hancock, and John Anthony West have pointed out that the oldest megalithic structures are the most magnificent, requiring very precise movement of giant stones, some of which weigh in excess of fifty tons. They question how these structures could have been built by "primitive" cultures, when mankind was just beginning to organize into civilization. It makes little sense that their technical know-how would deteriorate as civilization progressed. It makes more sense that these grand cyclopean structures are the ruins of a once intelligent, vibrant, and prosperous civilization that lived in and around the Mediterranean and North Africa—but who were decimated by some catastrophic event. It also makes sense that the remnants of this civilization reorganized and began to rebuild the society they once had.

I put forth the theory that the mysterious appearance of Cro-Magnon in western Europe was not a sudden burst of mankind coming into being. In fact, Cro-Magnon creativity is no mystery at all, but the natural expansion of an already existing culture in North Africa and the Mediterranean. Cro-Magnon remains (typified by a tall skeletal structure and a dolichocephalic skull) are the oldest-known evidence of anatomically modern humans. They are abundant in Europe, but are also common in Africa.

A civilization existing before the end of the ice age would find the Mediterranean a hospitable region. Europe near the glaciers would have been a harsh environment and most of North Africa would have been a desert, but the Mediterranean would provide a temperate, if not warm, climate most of the year. However, the Mediterranean would have not been the sea we see today. During the ice age, sea levels were nearly four hundred feet lower than current levels. Thus the Mediterranean would have been significantly smaller than it is now, exposing millions of square miles that are now under water. A likely scenario would be that four or five large lakes existed in the area, akin to today's Great Lakes of North America. And it is near these lakes and rivers, which extended from the continental highlands, that a civilization would build for a ready supply of water and food, as well as transportation.

As the ice age ended, vast glaciers in the northern hemisphere melted, feeding the now rising sea levels. At some point in time the natural dam at Gibraltar, which separated the Atlantic Ocean from the Mediterranean basin, gave way, allowing the ocean to spill forth into the valley. An ensuing wall of water charged to the east, destroying everything in its path. Sea levels continued to rise, and finally the new Mediterranean Sea broke forth into the Black Sea basin around 5600 B.C.E. The civilization that once existed was washed away in a violent surge, but there were those that survived. The Khemitians of the Nile Valley and the oases of the Western Desert avoided destruction because of their favorable position within the continent of Africa. They were alone to continue civilization, and they did. As time went on, refugees and explorers from eastern areas moved into Egypt and joined the struggling people of Bu Wizzer. The older, indigenous culture maintained leadership and continued life. The indigenous Egyptian tradition does speak of an ancient civilization that existed well before a major cataclysmic event that occurred more than ten thousand years ago.[21]

The dynastic-race theory has suffered harsh criticism during the past twenty years, but it is almost certain that a dynastic race existed. However, this race of robust people comprised Egypt's original inhabitants, not intruders. The dynastic people were the indigenous Africans, and the newcomers (those who have been identified as Mediterranean types) were foreigners who likely made up the common people in Egypt's early society. As time went on, the more numerous commoners mixed with the aboriginals. So did their culture, and by the onset of historical times, a patriarch-based culture replaced the matriarchal one of Bu Wizzer. Despite the dilution of their culture, their knowledge and technology continued, forming the great civilization of historical Egypt, although that too waned and eventually ended during the first millennium C.E.

1 2

BREAKING INTO
A NEW HISTORY
The Mediterranean Civilization

If such a catastrophe as we have described occurred in the Mediterranean, there would be very little evidence for succeeding generations to discover and investigate. The force of water is unmatched in nature, and can literally move mountains. Only those settlements and perhaps cities located on the highest ground in the Mediterranean basin would have survived. The twin islands of Malta are a case in point, with a number of megalithic temples built by an unknown prehistoric culture.

An officer of the Royal Engineers, Mr. J. C. Vance, first excavated the ruins of Malta in 1839. Within a few months, he presented his findings: statuettes, an engraved slab, two clay figurines, and a monstrous skull. Unfortunately, he made no detailed report, and discarded "rubbish" in heaps outside the ruins. More than likely, this was valuable material that would have provided insight into the culture that built the temple.

Another excavation began in 1906, which led to a better understanding of the prehistoric Maltese culture and its structures. *National Geographic* magazine reported the findings with a thirty-three-page article in May 1920. It described most of the structures' rooms as being half filled with earth, human bones, and broken pottery. Estimates claim that the ruins contained nearly thirty-three thousand individuals, most of whom were adults, although this number has been reduced to seven thousand in recent times. The skeletal remains were found in complete disarray, with no formal burial. With this evidence, there can be little doubt that the citizens of Malta met their fate in a disaster of monumental proportions. The author of the *National Geographic* article also commented that the great skill displayed in the making of Malta's prehistoric buildings showed that even in ancient times, humans had reached a high state of knowledge.

Prehistoric Malta

Egypt was not alone in its construction of megalithic temples during prehistory. The cyclopean style of architecture in early Egyptian structures, such as the Osireion, the Sphinx temple, and the Giza pyramids, also exists in Malta. In fact, Malta is well known for its megalithic structures and cyclopean architecture.

Thirty-five megalithic ruins exist on the islands of Malta and Gozo. Seven of the more impressive sites are on Gozo, the Ggantija complex, and, on Malta, the temples of Hagar Qim, Mnajdra, and Tarxien; the Ta' Hagrat and Skorba complexes; and the Hal Saflieni Hypogeum (an enormous dual-level, subterranean chamber under a surface shrine). The style of these temples is found nowhere else, yet their walls and

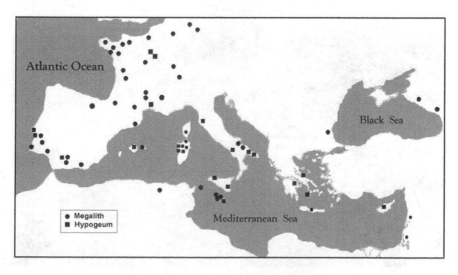

12.1. European and Mediterranean structures of the Neolithic

ceilings, decorated with spirals painted with red ocher, suggest a connection with the Cro-Magnon cultures of the Pyrenees.[1] Although similar structures exist in other parts of Europe, some scholars maintain that they have little or no relation to their Maltese counterparts.

In Malta's Hal Saflieni Hypogeum, estimated at twenty-two thousand tons of rock, there are long shafts carved from solid sandstone that descend thirty feet below the surface. The shafts lead to numerous odd rooms, including an altar, a long hallway, and a treasure vault.[2] The entire structure appears to have been illuminated with polished-stone mirrors arranged in periscope fashion in the shafts above. One chamber, found littered with bones from a previous age, exits to the outside through a long shaft where snakes and wild animals once fell to their death. There is also a reservoir, and a deep, tapering rain catcher. In another chamber a hollow exists in the wall where a priest may have spoken. His words could be heard in any room in the temple. Eerily, the entire structure seems to vibrate with sounds. Curiously, only low tones can be heard throughout the structure; high-pitched notes do not carry farther than the chamber itself.[3]

Cart Ruts

Throughout the island, where the bare rock is exposed, deep parallel lines, called cart ruts, wind their way, regardless of structures or land

Fig. 12.2. Cart ruts

Photo courtesy of Tony Ford

formations. Some lead into cliffs, others go under an arm of the sea, surfacing again on the opposite shore. Yet in other cases, the tracks are broken by a geological fault and continue at a different level. Many ruts are now covered by several feet of earth; fields having been formed on their sites.[4] These cart ruts are likely the oldest evidence of Malta's civilization. Although found in abundance on the islands of Malta, they also exist in Sicily, Sardinia, Italy, Greece, southern France, and Cyrenaica.

At the southeast end of the island of Malta, in the Bay of Marsa Scirocco, there are close to sixty round, bottlenecked pits, wells probably, carved into the rock. A number of these are now under the sea. Over the mouths of some of these wells run two deep cart ruts that lead into the sea and reappear on the opposite shore, about a quarter of a mile away.[5]

If all the tracks from cart ruts were traced and inserted on a map, the sites of the centers of habitation in prehistoric times would doubtless be revealed. One theory proposed by Birmingham University's Claudia Sagona explains that they are irrigation ditches from the Stone Age. She suggests that torrential rains washed away the topsoil, forcing ancient farmers to invent new ways of growing their crops. In the Aran Islands, off the west coast of Ireland, farmers created soil out of sand and seaweed, then protected it with stone walls. At Malta, Sagona believes that the inhabitants carved the channels to collect rainfall as well as to protect the soil from erosion. Although interesting, the theory does not explain why the ruts are parallel and vary in depth but maintain a consistent gauge between the tracks.

Another explanation is that heavy carts or sledges, moving tons of stone blocks across the land, wore the ruts. At Misrah Ghar il-Kbir (also known as Clapham Junction), the large number of ruts carved into solid limestone form a traffic jam through an open stretch of field. According to researchers Joseph Magro Conti and Paul Saliba, the cart ruts there outline an area where intensive quarrying was performed. Blocks were cut from the surface and carried to the road in different directions in a number of vehicles, then transported to areas where structures were being built. Two quarries that are interlinked by cart ruts are clear evidence that the quarries and the cart ruts were associated with one another. Like the Egyptians, the inhabitants of Malta used stone in astounding ways to construct the infrastructure of their society. The argument from traditional historians is that Malta and Egyptian civilizations developed this technology independently. I argue that the technology was previously in place in an older civilization common to both. The cataclysm that occurred destroyed much of what existed, so there is no obvious link, such as a line of cities running from Egypt to Malta.

The Ruins of Hagar Qim

For many years, Joseph S. Ellul's father was the caretaker of Malta's Hagar Qim, which means "standing or upright stones." In 1988, Ellul published his experiences and lifelong observations in *Malta's Prediluvian Culture*.[6] One of his most telling observations concerns the original state of the ruins at Hagar Qim. When first built, believed to be in 3200 B.C.E., a protecting wall encircled the temple complex. Today, a large portion still stands on the northwest, north, and east sides of the main ruins. However, the west wall has been not only toppled over, but also swept away. Huge blocks of the outer wall were lifted up and thrown inside the temple. Most of the big blocks were carried away, and what was not carried away was left exposed to the wind and rain.

In constructing the surrounding outside wall, huge stone slabs were fitted edge to edge. Hagar Qim boasts the highest stone wall in all the Malta ruins, seventeen feet high. Although appearing natural, at its base is a deliberately carved cavity. Cavities were cut while the shoring stone was still in the quarry so a wooden pole could be used as a lever to dislodge, move, and then position the stone at the base of the wall. Most of these carved cavities are not visible today, since the temple has been reconstructed. However, before the 1950s, one shoring block was still

Fig. 12.3. Ruins at Hagar Qim

three feet away from its proper position and, at that time, the cavity was clearly visible. The intriguing question is, how could this huge block have been moved such a distance away from the wall? Between the highest stone, where it meets the other blocks, and its nearest neighbor on the right, is a nine-inch space. The wall was evidently hit by something with such force that it dislodged the stone at its base and threw out its shoring block a distance of three feet.

Like the rest of the western wall, a chapel, referred to as Room H by Ellul, was discovered in ruins but was reconstructed during the 1950s. Large blocks that once formed the doorway to this chamber today are piled up on top of each other, nearly blocking the passage to the Main Chapel. These blocks, each weighing several tons, have been thrown into their present position by a force that apparently came from the west. According to Ellul, a close look at the stones allows one to see that some of them are now joined together with petrified mortar. For Ellul, this simple fact involves a number of related, essential truths. First, whoever built the temple had mortar and used it to cover up cracks or unwanted hollows in the walls. But more important, the mortar, which is now petrified, proves that after the cataclysm, the entire area was submerged for a period of time. Under dry conditions, the mortar would have crumbled to dust without ever solidifying again. There was so much mortar that some of it was deposited on the stones' sides before being petrified. In appearance, it formed an integral part of the stone's surface.

Outside this chapel, the outer wall, with its horizontal base of shoring blocks, is in a very advanced stage of erosion, the result of being exposed to the weather for a very long time. The positioning of these shoring blocks shows that at one time a wall was erected here. According to Ellul, blocks such as these are found around all the remaining walls of the temple.

What happened to this temple and to the people who inhabited it long ago? Some suggest that an earthquake destroyed Hagar Qim, but even the strongest quake could not have thrown large blocks of stone up to a distance of twenty feet. It had to have been the massive force of a tidal wave, a wall of water. The western wall bore the full force of the wave that came from the west. Only it was completely destroyed.

Ellul believes that an earthquake was responsible for the destruction of the natural dam at Gibraltar. According to deep-sea mapping of the Mediterranean, a valley of unusual depth runs very close to the Algerian coast of Africa in a straight line from Gibraltar to Sicily and then branches southeast to the south of Malta. He believes this is a rift valley that brought about the subsidence (lowering of a portion of the earth's crust) of the Mediterranean basin.

The Great Mediterranean Flood

Forty years ago, sonar studies of the Mediterranean Sea floor revealed a strange layer, possibly rock, between three hundred and six hundred feet below the bottom, along with unexpected layers of sediment. Buried salt domes were also detected. It prompted the Deep Sea Drilling Project (DSDP), an investigation that was carried out by the ship *Glomar Challenger* during the 1970s. Off the coast of Barcelona, the first core samples brought up gypsum, basalt, small fossil shells, and hardened ocean ooze. They expected to find sand, gravel, and mud. What came to the surface in the drill's hollow were fossils one would expect from a shallow, salty lagoon or a surface evaporation pond. More drilling in other areas showed that the Mediterranean's floor was underlaid with layers of "evaporites," a sedimentary deposit resulting from the evaporation of seawater. According to the associate director of the project, Kenneth Hsu, the fossils date to the end of the Miocene Epoch, five million years ago.[7]

The researchers concluded that the Mediterranean Sea had dried up and refilled a dozen times in a million years. Subsequent studies found that deep gorges in solid rock lay under the Nile and Rhone Rivers, suggesting that these rivers were once great torrents steeply dropping water into the empty Mediterranean basin.

A Russian scientist named I. S. Chumakov had been a member of a Soviet engineering team that built a dam across the Nile River near Aswan, Egypt. He was in charge of boring holes into the Nubian bedrock from bank to bank, in order to locate a secure foundation for the dam. In doing so, the team discovered a deep and narrow gorge from an ancient river. They also found deep-sea ooze in the bottom of the gorge between Nile mud and granite bedrock, nine hundred feet below the surface. Interestingly, the ooze was the same age as the sediment brought to the surface by the *Glomar Challenger*.[8] Chumakov concluded that the surface of the Mediterranean had dropped more than five thousand feet below its present level—evidence that at one time a severe earthquake lowered the region to its present position.

Chumakov realized that the ancient river beneath the Nile was a thin arm of the Mediterranean as it existed about five million years ago.

Yet the gorge was more than six hundred miles inland from the current coast. The ooze contained tiny shells of marine plankton, as well as shark teeth, so there was no doubt that it connected with the Mediterranean. To explain seawater so far inland, Chumakov postulated that while the Mediterranean was drying up, the Nile was digging a deep valley, continually adjusting to the depressed coastline. When flooding eventually refilled the Mediterranean, the gorge was drowned, causing it to become an offshoot of the sea that extended inland to meet the mouth of a river. It occurred so swiftly that the saltwater made its way into the interior of Africa, even the Nile unable to block its way. The seawater reached all the way to Aswan. It was confirmation to Chumakov that what is now the deep sea was once a desert that transformed back to a sea.

Later, the Phillips Petroleum Company, with Italian and Egyptian oil companies, was searching the Nile Delta in search of oil. Their attempts had been fruitless, but their searches did provide an explanation of the "reflecting" layer identified by the *Glomar Challenger*. The oil companies encountered a landscape of buried river valleys directly under Alexandria, on the Nile Delta, and extending inland well beyond the Giza plateau. The ancient Nile riverbed and its major tributaries were discernible. What this showed was that the entire edge of North Africa now submerged had once been exposed land that had become severely eroded. Rivers and streams washed away all the land formations that could have been reservoirs or traps for the hydrocarbons that are the precursors to petroleum.[9]

Most geologists will argue that the flooding of the Mediterranean

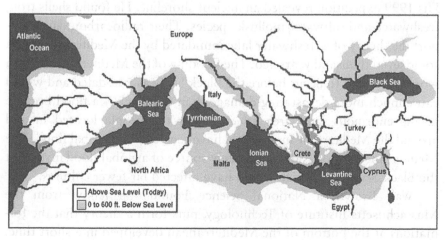

Fig. 12.4. Estimated pre-flood map of the Mediterranean

basin happened sometime over a million years ago, and since the basin is as much as sixteen thousand feet deep, the sea floor before the flooding must have been an unbelievably scorching desert for a very long period. However, not everyone believes that a catastrophe occurred. Although the various rock formations at the bottom of the Mediterranean may indeed be millions of years old, it is only guesswork that the Gibraltar dam also broke at that time. History, however, provides another kind of evidence—eyewitness testimony.

Tales of a great flood are prevalent in the myths of geographically and culturally diverse peoples: Greek, Arcadian, Samothracean, Scandinavian, Celtic, Welsh, Lithuanian, Transylvanian Gypsy, Turkish, Sumerian, Egyptian, Babylonian, Assyrian, Chaldean, Hebrew, Persian, Zoroastrian, Cameroonian, Masai (East Africa), Komililo Nandi, Kwaya (Lake Victoria), southwest Tanzanian, Pygmy, Ababua (northern Zaire), Kikuyu (Kenya), Bakongo (west Zaire), Bachokwe (southern Zaire), Lower Congolese, Basonge, Bena-Lulua (Congo River, southeast Zaire), Yoruba (southwest Nigeria), Efik-Ibibio (Nigeria), Ekoi (Nigeria), and Mandingo (Ivory Coast), as well as in the Bible. These epic flood stories likely have their source in a Mediterranean catastrophe.

In *Noah's Flood*, authors William Ryan and Walter Pitman suggest that the recent filling up of the Black Sea seven thousand years ago, confirmed by the explorer Robert Ballard, was the source for the biblical tale of Noah's flood. Ballard combed the floor of the Black Sea in search of the remains of ancient dwellings, which would bolster the theory that a cataclysmic flood struck the region some seven thousand years ago. His 1999 expedition revealed an ancient shoreline. He found shells from freshwater and saltwater mollusk species. Their radiocarbon dates support the theory of a freshwater lake inundated by the Mediterranean Sea some seven thousand years ago. The flooding of the Mediterranean basin would have had to occur before the Black Sea was inundated and would cause much more devastating damage than the Black Sea flood because of the enormous land area affected. For the people located in and around the Mediterranean, it would have seemed like a global flood. The Mediterranean flood is the more likely source of a global flood myth, not the Black Sea flood, which would have affected far fewer cultures.

Walt Brown, a National Science Foundation fellow from the Massachusetts Institute of Technology, puts forth a theory that the formations at the bottom of the Mediterranean developed in a short time. He proposes that the flood was the result of a very rapid rupturing of the earth's crust caused by an earthquake. As a result of the earthquake, superheated water from within the earth's crust erupted and merged with the cooler ocean water. This merging of hot and cold water may have precipitated the salt layers found under the Mediterranean. As a result, organisms living on the surface would have been suddenly killed and their bodies would have drifted to the sea floor, adding to the salt deposits being created.[10]

The Mediterranean basin is already known for its vigorous past volcanism. During the years the earth was recovering from the flood, it is possible that what we call "black smokers" (a type of hydrothermal vent found on the ocean floor) were present everywhere under the Mediterranean Sea. They could be responsible for the huge copper deposits under Cyprus and the vast salt layers under the Mediterranean Sea floor. Of course, rapid weather and climate changes were probably taking place during that same time as well.[11]

We have seen that the geological evidence indicates that at one time the Mediterranean Sea did not exist as we know it today. Sonar surveys also demonstrate that a different coastline around Egypt once existed, as well as a different river system that reached inland well beyond the Giza plateau. Assigning the catastrophic geographical changes to a more recent time period, as opposed to millions of years ago, supports the ancient multicultural tradition of a "global" flood. While it is not possible for a global flood to have ever occurred—that would require a volume of water five times that of the existing water in all the oceans— the infilling of the Mediterranean basin would have certainly appeared as one to the peoples of the time.

Malta's Mystery Culture

The Malta Skulls

In a chamber of Hagar Qim, between the largest stone and the south wall, a skull was found. It is now lost, but at one time it was on permanent display in the National Museum of Archaeology, in Valletta, Malta. The only image available is what the meticulous painter Schranz recorded at the time of the discovery.

The shape of the skull was unusual, and it appears to have been from a very peculiar, but human, race that lived during prehistoric times. It was dolichocephalic, or oblong, and resembled that of Cro-Magnon. According to Dr. Themistocles Zammit, in his report "Human Skulls at Hal Saflieni," the skull was not the same type as those found at the hypogeum. Nor is it like Denmark's Borreby Skull, which resembles the Neanderthal. Although the Negro skull is said to belong to the dolichocephalic type, it doesn't resemble the Hagar Qim skull either.

According to Ellul, this skull is very similar in its characteristics to the proto-Semitic, with its elongated cranium, slanting face, and the receding chin—possibly Natufian. No other bones from the rest of this skeleton were found, and no other skeletal remains of this type have been found except for a complete baby skeleton found inside a small cabin on a bed carved from stone at Mnajdra, a temple complex not far from Hagar Qim and dating to approximately the same time.[12]

Until 1985, a number of Cro-Magnon skulls that were found in the temples at Taxien, Ggantja, and Hal Saflieni were kept in the National Museum of Archaeology in Valletta. Most of the skulls were found in the Hal Saflieni hypogeum, along with a small statue of a sleeping goddess and a relic inscribed with the symbol of the snake. This hypogeum, next to a well dedicated to the Mother Goddess, was a sacred place. Recently, however, the skulls were removed from exhibition, never to be seen again by the public. Only the photographs taken by the Maltese researchers Dr. Anton Mifsud and Dr. Charles Savona Ventura are left to testify to the existence of the skulls.

The Italian researchers Vittorio Di Cesare and Adriano Forgione visited Malta in search of clues to Malta's ancient past. Books written by Mifsud and Ventura provided a lead for their search, particularly a collection of skulls with peculiar abnormalities. With the cooperation of the minister of tourism, Michael Refalo, Di Cesare and Forgione were allowed by the museum director to view the skulls. The museum's archaeologist, Mark Anthony Mifsud (Anton's brother), supervised the viewing in a private room. According to Di Cesare and Forgione, these Cro-Magnon skulls exhibited no medial cranial knitting lines (natural sutures, running front to back, where the skull grows together as a child ages), and had abnormally developed temporal partitions and drilled and swollen occiputs (the back part of the skull), possibly a result of trauma recovery. The skulls also displayed a very pronounced dolichocephalous (in other words, the posterior part of the head was unusually long). They were also larger than normal. (See fig. 12.5.)[13]

Medical experts consider this lack of medial cranial knitting impossible because there are no similar pathological cases in the international medical literature. It is noteworthy to add that these skull features are not typical results of bandaging or boarding, which some pre-Columbian civilizations practiced. Except for the lack of knitting, they appear to be natural.

Other skulls that displayed anomalies were also examined. Some were more normal but still presented a pronounced natural dolichocephalous typical of Cro-Magnon. Di Cesare and Forgione are confident that the unusual skull traits are characteristics of a distinct and different race of Cro-Magnon man native to Malta and Gozo, and older than other known Cro-Magnon types. Mark Anthony Mifsud and another Maltese archaeologist, Anthony Buonanno, agree that these skulls belong to a distinct Maltese race, although carbon-14 or DNA testing has not yet been performed.

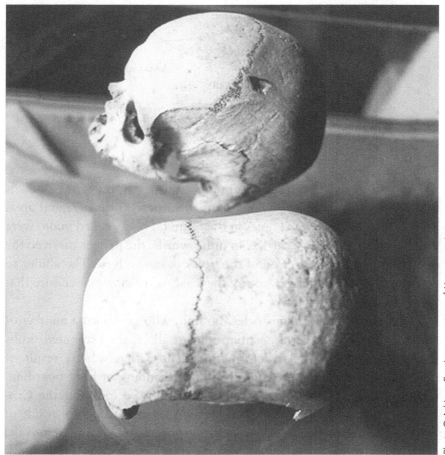

Photo © Adriano Forgione, courtesy of *Hera* magazine

Fig. 12.5. Dolichocephalic skulls found on Malta

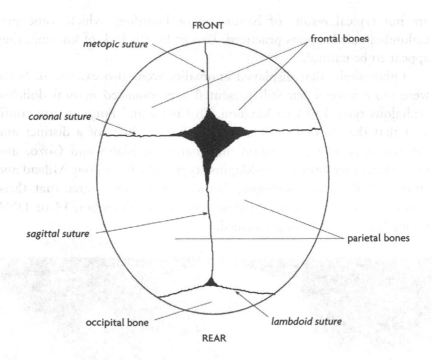

Fig. 12.6. Normal structure of the human infant skull.
Note medial sutures (metopic and sagittal).

From a medical perspective, another unusual aspect of the skulls is that a few of them show obvious signs of surgery in the occipital area. The outlines of three small holes in the occipital bone, called *inion*, were visible and had time to cicatrize. In other words, the patient survived the operation and the bone around the holes began to heal. The ability to perform such procedures is, to say the least, surprising in a culture that was believed to be primitive.

According to Dr. Themistocles Zammit, who examined a number of skeletons in 1921, a good portion, but not all, of the excavated skulls showed signs of artificial deformation. Those that were a result of artificial deformation were a result of head banding or head boarding, possibly Mediterranean-type peoples attempting to look like the Cro-Magnon type. Other skeletal deformations seemed to be the result of rituals or punishments: incisions, perforations, partial or total removals, cauterizations, abrasions, insertions of extraneous bodies in muscle tissue.[14] Di Cesare and Forgione speculate that one group of these modifications were for magical, medical, or cosmetic purposes, and were performed with the best of intentions for the community. But they wonder if later populations wanted to deform their infants' heads in order to make them similar to this older, perhaps ruling or priesthood race.

Malta and Egypt

The Cro-Magnon skulls Di Cesare and Forgione examined are unofficially dated to about 2500 B.C.E. but could be older. Malta's megalithic history ends at about this time, with no other evidence of human occupation until the arrival of the Phoenicians, which were a Mediterranean-type people, three hundred years later. In Malta, the Phoenicians also built temples to the Mother Goddess, calling her Astarte, the snake-faced goddess, who was associated with healing powers.

An intriguing aspect of the prehistoric inhabitants of Malta is that skulls with an unusual cranial form similar to Cro-Magnon have been found in Egypt and South America. *National Geographic* magazine reported in its May 1920 issue that the earliest inhabitants of Malta were long-headed and similar to the early people of Egypt who spread along the northern coast of Africa toward the west. Some of these people went to Malta and Sicily, others to Sardinia and Spain. According to the article, there appears little doubt that the early Maltese population belonged to the same type of people as the Iberians, the Basques of the Pyrenees, the Gauls of France, and the small dark men of Cornwall, south of Wales and Ireland—all of which are Cro-Magnon types.[15]

For some researchers, the dating of the skulls to 2500 B.C.E. may be a clue to understanding who these people were. As discussed previously, early Egyptologists referred to a "dynastic race" that was different from the typical Egyptian. Remains found in predynastic and early-dynastic Egyptian burials, dating from 3000 to 2500 B.C.E., were of the same, Cro-Magon type of human that was found in Malta. They displayed a dolichocephalous skull, and were larger than that of the local ethnic group. One skull, found in 1902 in a mastaba in Beith Khallaf, was from a third-dynasty ruler whose height was 6 feet, 2 inches. It may have been the remains of King Sanakht, whose name was found in the tomb.

In 1992, the keeper of the Egyptian oral tradition we met in chapter 11, Abdel'El Hakim Awyan, escorted the Egyptologist Stephen Mehler to a room in the Cairo Museum where a number of coffins were stored. What was unusual about these caskets is that they were between ten and fifteen feet tall. Clearly they were made for humans because their designers carved them in anthropoid style. "Do you think they are symbolic?" Mehler asked Hakim. They were not, according to Hakim. Mehler asked where the bodies were, but Hakim, who claims they were found with bodies inside, said that no one knows.[16]

According to Walter Emery, the dynastic race was not indigenous to Egypt, yet ruled as the elite, performing sacerdotal (priestly) and governmental roles and mixing only with the Egyptian aristocracy. Some scholars have associated the dynastic race with the Shemsu Hor, the "disciples of Horus," who were recognized as the dominant sacerdotal caste in predynastic Egypt until approximately 3000 B.C.E. The theory is supported by the discovery of individuals with larger skulls and robust frames, significantly greater than those of the native population. They are so different that they exclude any hypothetical common racial strain. A blending of the two races came about in the succeeding millennia, which began with the unification of Lower and Upper Egypt. During that critical time, just before the birth of dynastic Egyptian civilization, what occurred in Malta, it seems, also happened in Egypt. Peoples of the Mediterranean type permeated the population and began to replace (genetically) the older Cro-Magnon population.

I must point out here that I disagree with Emery. I believe the dynastic race was indigenous to Africa. I would argue that the individuals with larger skulls and robust frames were representative of a native, older culture since it is archaeological fact that that human type was dominant in North Africa and the Mediterranean prior to 10,000 B.C.E., and that the migrations of Mediterranean types did not occur until much later.

Cesare and Forgione put forth a theory that the Shemsu Hor (thought to be Egypt's dynastic race) were related to Malta's ancient culture, and that they both respected the solar religion. In Malta, the sun is still called Shem-shi. Shem, an Akkadian word, is derived from the Babylonian term for the sun, which is *shamash*. Cesare and Forgione believe this proves that the Shemsu Hor came from the Fertile Crescent of the Middle East (modern-day Iraq, Syria, Lebanon, and Israel). Still another correlation is that this priestly, long-headed race disappeared in Egypt, as well as Malta, in roughly the same period between 3000 and 2500 B.C.E.

Another interesting fact about Malta is that its language has no word for *mother*. The nearest word, *missier,* literally means instrument of generation, suggesting an origin at a time when descent was calculated through the maternal side.[17] According to the ancient oral traditions of Egypt, the original culture of the Nile Valley was also matristic, and in chapter 9 we learned that the archaeologist Marija Gimbutas came to the conclusion that the earliest societies of Cro-Magnon were matristic as well.

Through skeletal and dental comparisons, it is clear that the Cro-Magnon types were the dominant human group in North Africa and the Mediterranean prior to 10,000 B.C.E. Studies from both Egypt and Malta bear this out, and attest to the probability that Mediterranean type slowly mixed with the indigenous population. The Cro-Magnon types began to diminish around 5000 B.C. Eventually, the Mediterranean types became the dominant human type in the area. Since, as scholars such as Emery have noted, Cro-Magnon types were some of the earliest pharaohs, it is logical to conclude that they were members of the host culture that occupied the land in Egypt.

Mysterious Baalbek

In chapters 2 and 11 as well as this chapter, we saw that the architecture of early societies was characteristically cyclopean—megalithic (built of enormous stones) and void of inscription. The eastern Mediterranean has perhaps the most mysterious cyclopean ruins. At a place called Baalbek, forty miles east of Beirut, there is an ancient site whose builders are unknown. It boasts the world's largest quarried blocks. Three colossal foundation stones of red granite, together referred to as the Trilithon, weigh nearly eleven hundred tons each and make up an immense platform called the Grand Terrace. On top of this site the Greeks built a temple, and on top of the Greek site the Romans later built another three—one dedicated to Venus, the goddess of love; another to Bacchus, the god of fertility and wine; and the third to Jupiter.

The weight of these stones is so great that today there exists no modern machine that could move them. The largest block is sixty-five feet in length; fourteen feet, six inches in height; and twelve feet thick. The two others are the same height and thickness, but are slightly shorter, sixty-four feet, ten inches, and sixty-three feet, two inches. A fourth stone, called Hajar-el-Hibla, or "stone of the pregnant woman," was never moved from the quarry. It is the largest, weighing an estimated twelve hundred tons. Amazingly, they were quarried twelve hundred feet away

Photo courtesy of Middle East Documentation Center, University of Chicago

Fig. 12.7. Baalbek Trilithon (white arrows); for a sense of scale, notice the two people (black arrow)

from their final placement—in a valley, no less—and then moved into position. How this was accomplished is a mystery. The course of stone beneath the Trilithon consists of six megaliths, thirty to thirty-three feet in length, fourteen feet high, and ten feet deep, each weighing an estimated 450 tons.

Exacerbating the mystery is the technique used by the builders to position these stones, side by side, with such precision that not even a needle can be inserted between them. Who were the people behind this massive project? Unfortunately, they are nameless. Roman records do not mention anything about the architects and engineers for this structure. Nor do any contemporary Roman historians or scholars. However, the Beqa'a Valley's local inhabitants do preserve legends of Baalbek's origin. Baalbek derives its name from the Canaanite word meaning "Lord"; Baalbek means the "town of Baal."

According to oral tradition, the biblical Cain built Baalbek before the Great Flood. Tradition also holds that the citadel fell into ruins at the time of the deluge, and was later rebuilt by a race of giants under the command of the biblical Nimrod, the king of Shinar in the book of

Photo courtesy of Middle East Documentation Center, University of Chicago

Fig. 12.8. Hajar-el-Hibla, the fourth block, in the quarry at Baalbek

Genesis. The reason the locals tell this tale is perhaps because they are aware of no other plausible explanation, since the Romans did not have the capability to move such unbelievably heavy stones, nor did they need to. Roman architecture was sophisticated, but they always used smaller, more manageable stones. Without a logical explanation, biblical legend is relied upon. However, scholars maintain that the Romans did build the site, including the Grand Terrace. But would it have been possible for the Romans to do so?

The use of building stones of this size is unprecedented in construction projects of the classical age. There are no logical reasons why Roman architects, who were already experienced builders and planners, would have required the use of such huge blocks. Furthermore, the outer "podium" wall was left unfinished, suggesting that something went wrong, leading to the abandonment of the project, which is why the final twelve-hundred-ton block was left in the quarry. Also, according to Roman architectural standards during the first century B.C.E., the temple should have been placed at one end of a courtyard but remain within the courtyard. This is not the case. The courtyard ends at the temple façade.

Even if the "bury and excavate" method (continually placing soil or sand around the structure so that as stones are placed at higher levels, the workers will always remain at "ground level") were used to build this massive structure, how many men would it take to move a thousand-ton block? Although no one knows for sure, one scholar calculated that it would require forty thousand men to pull the sled that held the block. Logistically, it seems impossible for anyone, at any time, to coordinate such a feat.

Excavations near the courtyard of Jupiter reveal the existence of an Early Bronze Age occupational mound dating to 2900 and 2300 B.C.E. Later, a raised court was constructed around a vertical shaft, leading to a natural crevice fifty yards below the surface, where a small rock-cut altar was used for sacrificial rites. When the unfinished upper course of the Grand Terrace was cleared of rubble, workers found, carved into its surface, a drawing of the pediment, a triangular piece of architecture present in the Temple of Jupiter. So exact was this design that it seemed certain the architects and masons had positioned their blocks using this scale plan. It also means that the megalithic platform existed before the construction of the temple.

Although there have been attempts to rationalize a late construction for the lower portions of Baalbek, such as the Phoenician tradition of using three layers of stone for a podium or a Roman column supporting part of the podium, the quarrying and construction of the lowest level are beyond explanation. Its plain, precise, and squared architecture belong to a history that researchers know very little about. The theory that superhuman giants of some bygone age built the structures doesn't solve the mystery: if giants did build them, they would have had to be ten times bigger and stronger than we are. The best explanation for Baalbek's megalithic construction is that its culture was part of a technically advanced civilization, such as those that built similar structures in Malta and Egypt.

The Mediterranean Civilization as the Model for Atlantis

Based on a story his uncle Solon heard from the Egyptian priests at Sais, Plato wrote that the great island civilization of Atlantis sank into the sea after a great earthquake. The existence and the fate of the lost Atlantis have been a topic of debate for nearly four hundred years, and every new researcher hawks evidence that he or she has finally found it, albeit in vastly diverse places including Britain, Spain, the Mediterranean, and even the Americas.

What is clear, from the multitudes of researchers who have endeavored to find the fabled city, is that Atlantis is probably what Aristotle, in his treatise *On Meteorology,* said it was—a mythical place in a story.[18] Yet even the skeptical author of *Imagining Atlantis,* Richard Ellis, after studying those who quest for the sunken island, believes there is a kernel of truth somewhere in the myth.

Scholars suggest that the devastating volcanic eruption on the island of Thera (modern-day Santorini, in the Mediterranean near Crete) is the source for Plato's tale. Although destructive enough to indeed have destroyed a city, this volcanic event appears to have occurred too recently to serve as Plato's source. According to Plato, the event occurred nine thousand years before his time. Even if this number is only an estimate, it suggests that the cataclysmic event described in the story had to have occurred much earlier than the Thera eruption. Furthermore, other flood stories, particularly from Mesopotamia, predate the eruption on Thera.

The size of Plato's Atlantis is another problem. He claims that the landmass was as big as Africa and Asia Minor combined. Such a size would simply rule out all islands known to have existed in the Mediterranean and off the coast of Africa. However, there is some debate about the interpretation of this specific portion of text. Some scholars claim that the real meaning is "between Asia Minor and Africa" (referring to location, not size). And what lies between these two landmasses is the Mediterranean Sea.

At the Dingli Cliffs, which form the southern coast of Malta, steep reefs fall vertically to the sea, in stark contrast to the more sloping northern shore. It appears that as a result of an earthquake, the island's axis rotated around itself, submerging most of the coast that faces Sicily.

Some Maltese archaeologists, including Anton Mifsud and Charles Savona Ventura, consider this earthquake the source of the Atlantis legend's birth. As did Cro-Magnon man at the end of the ice age, the population that created extraordinary structures on Malta simply disappeared at some point in history. Later, the arrival of new populations spurred the now decimated Maltese culture.[19] The story appears the same in the Nile Valley.

According to the Leningrad (Egyptian) Papyrus, which was believed to be composed around 1450 B.C.E. or possibly 2000 B.C.E., a "star falling from the heavens" destroyed a serpentlike populace (perhaps described as such due to the appearance of their non-sutured, oblong skulls). Only one group of humans survived, on an island. It is a bizarre myth, but could this story represent the historical truth about "Atlantis" handed down by the ancients and subsequently recorded by scribes?

An Egyptian Tradition

Plato's story of Atlantis, found in the *Timaeus* and the *Critias,* can be interpreted as a parable of good triumphing over evil, ancient Athens over the invading Atlanteans. Plato was a writer and philosopher, and the story served a large philosophic purpose. The story of Atlantis depicted the evils of a once highly successful society gone bad through its own corruption. It is simply not possible to accept the story as historical fact without corroborating evidence. Yet there are elements of his tale that gave it a realistic tone during the fourth century B.C.E., just as it does today.

According to Herodotus and Aristotle, Solon—the Athenian lawmaker and one of the seven sages of Greece (c. 638–539 B.C.E.)—who originally told the story, really did visit Egypt, but later than when Plato says he did. Solon heard the story of Atlantis from Egyptian priests at Saïs who had obtained it from an engraved temple column. In addition, the Egyptians told a traditional tale of a land that was submerged under the sea. At the time of Solon's visit, the story was familiar to most Egyptians, as all of their mythologies contain a reference to the sunken city.

The Greek archaeologist Spyridon Nikolaou Marinatos, discoverer of an ancient Minoan port on the island of Thera, has contributed perhaps more than any other researcher to the search for Atlantis. In 1939, he published *The Volcanic Destruction of Minoan Crete,* which led to an association of the island of Crete to Atlantis. According to Marinatos,

> Plato's imagination could not possibly have conjured up an account
> so unique and so unusual to classical literature. . . . For this reason,
> the account is usually called a "tradition" by Plato. I should also
> like to add that if in some parts the account chances to bear the
> stamp of the fable, this must be attributed to the Egyptians and
> not to Plato.[20]

Marinatos further writes that the tale of this island that later vanished was clearly familiar to the Egyptians. The priests at Saïs confused it with other traditional accounts concerning Atlantis because of the similarities. Marinatos believes they invented the myth from their own, erroneous interpretation of the Thera explosion.[21]

What is noteworthy here is that the tale of Atlantis is not a Greek story but rather an Egyptian one. And if the Egyptians confused the Thera cataclysm with another, older story, then it must be the case that the original version was significant enough to be remembered throughout many generations—in the same way that the biblical flood story was handed down for thousands of years through oral tradition. Plato has received much attention for the tale, but given the circumstances, it is likely he wrapped a story around a very old tradition, as any good writer would do to get across a point. It is a common theme in the ancient Near East. The Sumerian *Epic of Gilgamesh,* the Hebrew Bible, and a passage in Sanskrit from the Mahabharata all tell the story of a great flood.

The Greater Mediterranean Culture

In June 2004, Rainer Kühne, of the University of Wuppertal, Germany claims to have found what could be the lost city of Atlantis in a saltmarsh region off Spain's southern coast. The study is based on satellite images depicting ancient ruins. They appear to match the descriptions given by Plato—rectangular structures surrounded by concentric circles. Even the sizes are correct.[22]

Regardless of whether or not any of these tales of Atlantis are historically accurate, the existence of an ancient civilization in the Mediterranean is supported by much evidence. Furthermore, its existence as well as its destruction go far in explaining why the Cro-Magnon cultures of western Europe seemed to appear from nowhere. These early humans migrated from southern Africa moving north and into regions of the Mediterranean and Europe. If the flooding of the Mediterranean had never occurred, there would be ample archaeological evidence to state confidently that Cro-Magnon moved into Europe from the south. However, since the flood did occur, all evidence of this migration has been washed away or buried at the bottom of the Mediterranean Sea.

The heart of the Mediterranean civilization was destroyed when its once bountiful valley turned into a sea. Those who lived in the Nile Valley were also orphaned from their kinsmen, yet they continued, in a majestic manner, as they had done for thousands of years. With the influx of a multitude of newcomers from other lands, their culture slowly developed into what we know as dynastic Egypt, a culture once matristic, replaced by the patriarch. It was not a unique development. Other areas, particularly in Mesopotamia, endured the same fate (as

*Fig. 12.9. Bench adorned with bull horns at Çatalhöyük, Turkey
(from James Mellaart's* The Neolithic of the Near East*)*

described in my previous book, *Sons of God—Daughters of Men*).

Most recently, in 2001, in Iran, a flash flood near the Halil River opened ancient graves packed with beautiful stone pottery. Local villagers began plundering, forcing police to confiscate hundreds of finely worked stone vessels carved with images of animals and decorated with semiprecious stones. Because the vessels were not scientifically recovered, their age and origin are open to debate. However, the Iranian archaeologist in charge of the site, Yousef Madjidzadeh, strongly believes most were made more than four thousand years ago, and that the society that made them predates ancient Mesopotamia.[23] This can be seen as another telltale sign of Bu Wizzer, the Land of Osiris, and the greater Mediterranean culture.

There are other indications of its existence in Turkey. In the eight-thousand-year-old settlement at Çatalhöyük, evidence indicates that the bull was worshipped and its skull built into shrines, a practice known to exist in Egypt. Bull worship was among the most important of animal

Fig. 12.10. Bench adorned with bull horns at Sakkara, Egypt
(from Walter Emery's Archaic Egypt*)*

cults, and appeared in Egyptian writings as early as the first dynasty. Slate palettes, dating back as far as 3100 B.C.E., even show kings as bulls. Unlike other aspects of the neteru, the bull spirit was never represented as a human with an animal's head. The Apis bull was closely linked with Ptah, and his cult center was Memphis. Primarily a deity of fertility, he was represented as a bull crowned with the solar disk and uraeus-serpent. The evidence indicates that the bull was venerated by a geographically wider culture (or cultures) during prehistoric times.

Is There a Bigger Picture?

The director of human origins at London's Natural History Museum, Chris Stringer, has said that he believes that most prehistoric humans were dolichocephalic, regardless of their origin.[24] He was referring to the thirteen-thousand-year-old skeleton of the Peñon woman found by Silvia Gonzalez near Mexico City, which had a dolicocephalic skull. Stringer, unlike other researchers, is not convinced that this skull shape proves her origins are European. His insights are likely to be correct, which deserves an explanation.

It is commonly accepted by anthropologists and archaeologists that the human race, *Homo sapiens sapiens,* first evolved in Africa between 100,000 and 150,000 years ago. Some claim it occurred as long ago as 200,000 years. Whatever the case may be, sometime around 100,000

Fig. 12.11. Early migration of Cro-Magnon

years ago, groups of humans moved north along Africa's Great Rift Valley and Nile Valley, then across the Sinai Peninsula into the Middle East. By sixty thousand years ago, they had made their way along the coastlines of India and southeastern Asia and then sailed to Australia. About forty thousand years ago, they migrated into Europe and from southeastern Asia into eastern Asia. Finally, sometime around ten thousand years ago—although Dr. James Adovasio, of Mercyhurst College, believes the date is closer to twenty thousand years ago—they made their way along a wide plain joining Siberia and Alaska and spread throughout North and South America.

Stringer maintains that all prehistoric peoples were dolichocephalic because human traits take a very long time to change in a population. For example, the accepted explanation for variations in skin color is that man first evolved in a tropical region. Since the sun is strong in equatorial latitudes, the skin needed protection from ultraviolet radiation, which is provided by melanin, our body's natural sunscreen. It is what makes the skin dark. When humans reached the northern hemisphere forty thousand years ago, the sun was not as strong during most of the year. Since the sun helps us to synthesize the vitamin D that we need for the proper growth of bones, we had to lose some of our pigmentation to allow enough sunlight through. According to geneticist Dr. Nina Jablonski, of the California Institute of Technology, it takes about twenty thousand years for dark-pigmented skin to become fair.

Some scientists also believe that a dolichocephalic, oblong skull is most effective in dissipating heat—the greater the surface area, the faster the cooling in a hot climate, which would be advantageous. In much the same way, a more compact, rounder head would conserve heat in cooler environments. Although this does not fully explain why some northerners in Europe have maintained dolichocephalic cranial shapes throughout the scores of millennia, it does help to explain why the earliest of humans had this specific skull formation. Their origin was Africa. As it is with skin color, so it is with skull shape. Any adaptations as a result of changes in climate would take a substantial amount of time.

One of the ways forensic experts determine the race of an individual is by the shape of the skull. According to the investigative author Andrew Muhammad, in his article "African Origins in the U.K.," even today the skulls of people of the Negroid race are generally described as dolichocephalic. With this evidence, he argues that the aboriginal peoples of western Europe were black. For example, in 1865, Samuel Laing discovered human remains near Kiess in the county of Caithness, Scotland, and wrote that these native Britons must have closely resembled the Australian Aborigines or Tasmanians. The remains were then sent to Professor Thomas Huxley (1825–1895), one of Charles Darwin's first adherents, who wrote, in his 1881 *Early History of Scotland,* that the first inhabitants of Britain had skulls like those of indigenous Africans or Australian Aborigines.

Skulls found in Great Britain's Neolithic (8000–5000 B.C.E.) *chamber mounds* (non-megalithic, rectangular stone burial mounds with human remains in small chambers called *cists*) were said to represent those of the earliest race in Britain, according to the anthropologist Sir Daniel Wilson (1816–1892). All of the skulls were generally dolicho-

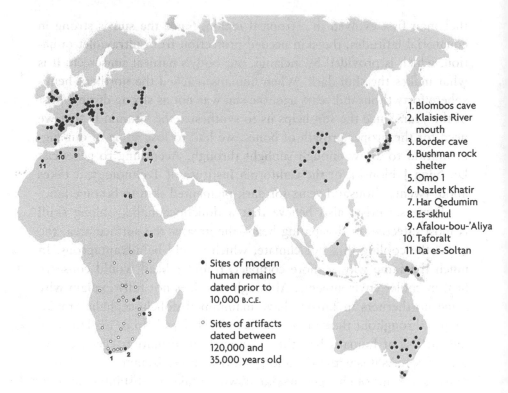

1. Blombos cave
2. Klaisies River mouth
3. Border cave
4. Bushman rock shelter
5. Omo 1
6. Nazlet Khatir
7. Har Qedumim
8. Es-skhul
9. Afalou-bou-'Aliya
10. Taforalt
11. Da es-Soltan

• Sites of modern human remains dated prior to 10,000 B.C.E.

○ Sites of artifacts dated between 120,000 and 35,000 years old

Fig. 12.12. Sites of Cro-Magnon graves and artifacts

cephalic, which proved to scientists that they belonged to the Negroid racial group. Another skull, found in a box-shaped burial chamber of stone found off Scotland's Uist Island, was said to belong to that of a Tasmanian.

According to Andrew Muhammad, while the Iberian people who once inhabited the modern-day countries of Spain, Portugal, and Italy were developing their civilization in Europe, the Buddha's "black nation" in India was spreading its Eastern philosophy. These nations were linked to their Khemitian mother culture through the "Mystery School" system, whose collegiate center was along the Nile River near Luxor. This Mystery School became famous in historical times through the Greek intellectual Pythagoras, who, as mentioned previously, studied in ancient Egypt. Muhammad believes that these original people—the Australian Aborigines, Iberians, Indians, and Egyptians—traveled to the corners of the earth and even to the shores of the United Kingdom.

Human cultures expand, explore, and move into new territories from a host culture or civilization. As we have seen in historical times, establishing colonies in other lands is a hardship and often requires aid and continuing contact from the "mother country." Since Africa is generally accepted as mankind's native land, from where all other cultures and civilizations sprang, it must have had the population and infrastructure to accommodate such an undertaking. People move to new lands for a reason. Usually they are looking for a better life. Those individuals who moved from North Africa and the Mediterranean into western Europe between forty thousand and twenty thousand years ago were such a people, looking for new lands. The genetic and archaeological evidence supports these waves of migration into the Iberian Peninsula. The host country of these immigrants must have existed somewhere. Although Abdel'El Hakim Awyan's oral tradition of Bu Wizzer is subjective, his claims regarding the age and sophistication of an ultra-ancient culture are well within the realm of reason. They also fit the evidence for an extensive civilization of the Mediterranean.

The Grecian Sphinx

The mountainous Greek island of Kea (Tzia) lies at the western end of the Cyclades, a group of islands in the Aegean Sea. Because of its proximity to the coast of Attica, the island's history is closely linked to Athens. At one time, it was called the Water Island (Ydroussa), and according to mythology, it was the home of the water nymphs. Since it was a handsome island, the story goes, the gods became jealous and sent a lion to ravage the land. The nymphs fled, which resulted in a drought. Those who lived on Kea asked Apollo's son Aristaeus for help, so he built a temple to Zeus. This pleased the powerful god, so he sent the rains and the nymphs returned.

According to archaeologists, Kea has been inhabited since around 4000 B.C.E., evident by the discoveries of Cycladic, Minoan, and Mycenaean pottery. The island has its share of ancient sites and statues. The best known is the Kouros (young man) of Keos, attributed to the seventh century B.C.E., now displayed at the National Museum of Athens. A more mysterious site lies on the side of a hill near the village of Chora. An unknown artist from an unknown period carved a lion out of the rock face, eighteen feet long and nine feet high. It resembles the Sphinx at Giza, but with the head of a cat. According to archaeologists, it was carved during the sixth century B.C.E., but they can establish no clear connection to any cultural context. However, the oldest local oral history, which goes back twenty-five hundred years, claims that the existence of the statue was inexplicable even to the island's first inhabitants.

Some researchers, such as the French professor of literature Jean Richer, believe the Kea lion may be linked to Greek sacred geography, which I further postulate may have Egyptian roots. Sacred geography is the practice of deliberately designing cities in such a manner as to make the land a living image of the heavens. Richer believes this may have played a role in the creation of the Delphi–Mount Olympus axis of monuments and temples to the northwest.

In *Sacred Geography of the Ancient Greeks,* first published in 1967, Richer correlated Plato's description of the ideal state to a pattern evident in the location of important structures in ancient Greece. In Plato's ideal state, explains Richer, the land was divided into twelve parts, each one named after and ruled by a zodiac "god" or constellation. From a bird's-eye view, the layout would appear as a wheel with twelve spokes, imitating the pattern of the heavens. Through the strategic placement of temples within this pattern, the constellations of the night sky would be transferred onto the earth. In other words, the arrangement of temples would mirror the night sky. The proper arrangement of temples was an act of honoring the twelve gods and harmonizing the movements of daily life into the grand order of the universe.

Interpreted in this way, the Lion of Kea can be precisely dated according to the solstice alignment. Lengthwise, the Kea lion is oriented almost northeast/southwest, so it is oriented to the summer solstice sunrise. But since its head is turned, it also gazes toward the sunrise at the winter solstice. According to Richer, the Lion of Kea symbolizes the constellation Leo. He attributes the monument to the era in which the summer solstice sun was in Leo, between 4400 and 2200 B.C.E. He also puts forth the theory that the Lion of Kea was part of a very old zodiacal wheel centered on Trachis and later transferred to Delphi. The wheel was a system that symbolically described the first known calendar, which was derived from Egypt. As far as Richer is concerned, it is no wonder that the lion gazes toward the land of the Nile.

What is so special about the structure's stellar alignments? As discussed in chapters 4 and 5, the nighttime sky played a crucial role in marking time in ancient Egypt. In *The Origin Map,* astrophysicist Thomas Brophy postulates that the arrangement of structures on the

Giza plateau marked the location of the galactic center, the dense ball of stars around which the Milky Way's spiral arms rotate, at its northern culmination circa 10,909 B.C.E.[25] In *Galactic Alignment*, John Major Jenkins also found it evident that other ancient cultures were aware of this special stellar event and made it a part of their traditions. Indeed, for the Maya, it signaled the beginning of a new calendar and the ending of an old one; it is why their calendar ends in 2012, during a period of galactic alignment (and not the end of the world). According to Jenkins, the constellation Leo is a critical marker for periods of galactic alignment. When it aligns with an equinox or solstice, either the axis of the solstice or equinox is aligned with the Milky Way and the galactic center.[26]

Despite its "official" sixth-century-B.C.E. date, some believe the Lion of Kea is a remnant of a vanished prehistoric civilization that at one time spanned the Mediterranean. Along with the astronomically aligned megaliths of Nabta Playa, the Lion of Kea indicates that during prehistoric, mythical times there may have existed a culture and a way of thinking that was based on meticulous observation of the natural world, particularly the night sky. According to the French archaeologist Georges Daressy, Ancient Egypt also employed such methods of geographical planning according to the celestial bodies. In his book *L'Egypte Céleste* (The Celestial Egypt), Daressy explains how certain Egyptian townships used emblems carved into the architecture of temples in order to depict a sequence of the zodiac. The large span of time it took to understand and map out the movements of the stars and plan cities and temples in accordance with these observed patterns supports the thesis that the cultures that gave birth to civilization arose in the very distant past.

The total years of Egyptian history according to its own documents reaches back 36,620 years. The Papyrus of Turin provides a complete list of kings who reigned in Upper and Lower Egypt from Menes to the New Kingdom in the first column and lists those who ruled before him in the second column. The last two lines are explicit:

. . . venerables Shemsu-Hor, 13,420 years
Reigns up to Shemsu-Hor, 23,200 years [27]

Emery agrees in principle. He believed that ancient Egypt's written language was beyond the use of pictorial symbols even during the earliest dynasties. According to his research, signs were also used to represent sounds only along with a numerical system. At the same time hieroglyphics had been stylized and used in architecture, a cursive script was already in common use. His conclusion was that "[a]ll this shows that the written language must have had a considerable period of development behind it, of which no trace has as yet been found in Egypt."[28] Given all the evidence, which has been discussed throughout this book, why should we not take the ancient Egyptians at their word? We should.

The African Origins of Dynastic Egypt

Nearly two hundred thousand years ago, a new creature, the human, appeared in Africa, and before the dawn of history had made its way into every habitable continent. These people who moved out of Africa into the rest of the world we call Cro-Magnon. They are our ancestors. After their migrations, geographic isolation caused certain groups of people to adapt to specific climates, which created "race." Distinct cultures developed, with their own identities and traditions. Although they lived in what we would call a primitive environment, they were not primitive.

Waves of migration always extend from an established base where the necessities of life are easily obtained. Migration begins at home. For the prehistoric Cro-Magnon cultures, home was Africa. In and around the Mediterranean, particularly northern Africa and the eastern areas that are now submerged, a civilization was built based on the perception of spiritual principles, what we call myth. For tens of thousands of years its people thrived, developing their own unique technologies and engaging in trade, only to be decimated by catastrophe around 8000 B.C.E.

Although precisely what the catastrophe was has been debated for years, there is no question that a cataclysm occurred resulting in the extinction of numerous species around the world, and a new topography for the face of the Earth. Whatever occurred, a comet or asteroid impact, perhaps, it proved to be disastrous for life on our planet.

Humans, of course, were among the species that suffered but managed to survive. Those who lived in Egypt and North Africa struggled to carry on, and with the Sahara Desert growing they found themselves migrating to the Nile Valley, where water was continuously available. As the inheritors and keepers of ancient knowledge and wisdom, whom twentieth-century Egyptologists refer to as the "dynastic race," they rebuilt their civilization as newcomers from the northeast migrated into the Nile Valley, providing an increasing level of manpower. Dynastic Egypt was, in a sense, the rebirth of this prehistoric civilization. But the steady influx of newcomers into Egypt from the Mediterranean eventually outnumbered this Cro-Magnon dynastic race, transforming what was a matriarchal-based culture into a patriarchal one.

Our modern civilization inherits its qualities from the patriarchal culture that began five thousand years ago in Egypt. However, the legacy of an earlier civilization imbued the history, myths, and stories of that Egyptian civilization and thus ultimately influenced our own. In Hebrew texts, history's precursors were referred to as "men of renown," "heroes of old," and "sons of God." Egyptian writings refer to them as "the followers of Horus," and before that simply "the gods." Even today we can trace our concept of the divine back to these predynastic roots.[29]

Scientific Revolution

Scientists often talk about the absence of evidence, and whether it does, or does not, mean the evidence of absence. In Egypt and the Mediterranean, neither condition is true. Evidence exists of an extraordinarily ancient civilization, and its extraordinary accomplishments, for all to see. The evidence is not scanty; it is substantial. When it rained in Egypt, more than twenty thousand years ago, the human race reached a new height in civilization, only to meet a cataclysmic fate. We may meet a cataclysmic fate ourselves one day. If history repeats itself, as it often does, will someone, ten thouand years from now, find our scattered ruins and connect the dots?

The renowned American philosopher and historian of science Thomas Samuel Kuhn (1922–1996) noted that major scientific breakthroughs have often come from outsiders or newcomers, precisely because these individuals didn't carry with them any of the biases or prejudices that prevented the veterans from seeing the obvious.[30] Researchers such as John Anthony West, Robert Schoch, Chris Dunn, Thomas Brophy, Vittorio Di Cesare, Adriano Forgione, and Stephen Mehler have endeavored to discover the truth in their respective fields, with true open-mindedness and willingess to question. In this journey to discover the roots of human civilization, we have, in the spirit of Kuhn's scientific revolutions, found ourselves breaking into a new history of mankind.

NOTES

Chapter 1: Rainy Days for the Egyptian Sphinx

1. Sir William Osler, *The Evolution of Modern Medicine* (New Haven: Yale University Press, 1921).
2. *Monumental Mysteries: Aging the Great Sphinx*. BBC/Discovery Channel, 1997, documentary.
3. *Mystery of the Sphinx*, Lavonia, MI: BC Video, 1993, documentary. (This documentary was based on the research of John Anthony West.)
4. Ibid.
5. Robert Schoch, "Redating the Great Sphinx of Giza," *KMT: A Modern Journal of Ancient Egypt*, vol. 3 no. 2, 1992.
6. Ibid.
7. Ibid.
8. Ibid.
9. *Mystery of the Sphinx*.
10. John Anthony West, *Serpent in the Sky* (Wheaton, IL: Quest Books, 1993), 229.
11. *Mystery of the Sphinx*.
12. Ibid.
13. *Monumental Mysteries: Aging the Great Sphinx*
14. Ibid.
15. Robert M. Schoch, "Response in Archaeology to Hawass and Lehner," letter to *KMT*, vol. 5, no. 2, Summer 1994; January/February 1995, online at: www.robertschoch.net/articles/Response_to_Hawass_Lehner. html (accessed 5/05/2004).
16. Ibid.
17. Schoch, "Redating the Great Sphinx of Giza."
18. K. Lal Gauri, "Geologic Study of the Sphinx," *American Research Center in Egypt Newsletter* no. 127 (1984): 24–43.
19. Robert M. Schoch, "Geological Evidence Pertaining to the Age of the Great Sphinx," in Emilio Spedicato and Adalberto Notarpietro, eds., *New Scenarios on the Evolution of the Solar System and Consequences on History of Earth and Man, Proceedings of the Conference, Milano and Bergamo, June 7–9th, 1999* (Milan: Università degli Studi di Bergamo,

Quaderni del Dipartmento di Matematica, Statistica, Informatica ed Applicazion, Serie Miscellanea, 2003), 171–203.

20. David Coxill, "Riddle of the Sphinx," *InScription—Journal of Ancient Egypt*, issue 2, Spring 1998.

Chapter 2: The Weight of Geologic Evidence

1. Colin Reader, "A Geomorphological Study of the Giza Necropolis, with Implications for the Development of the Site," *Archaeometry* 43, no. 1 (2001): 149–65.
2. Colin Reader, "Khufu Knew the Sphinx: A Reconciliation of the Geological and Archaeological Evidence for the Age of the Sphinx and a Revised Sequence of Development for the Giza Necropolis," 1999. www. ianlawton.com/as1.htm (accessed 5/1/2004).

Chapter 3: The Green Sahara

1. Andrew B. Smith, "Origins and Spread of Pastoralism in Africa," *Annual Review of Anthropology* 21 (1992): 125–41.
2. J. McKim Malville, Fred Wendorf, Ali A. Mazar, and Romauld Schild, "Megaliths and Neolithic Astronomy in Southern Egypt," *Nature* (April 1998): 488–91.
3. Ibid.
4. Ibid.
5. C. Vance Haynes Jr., "Geochronology and Climate Change of the Pleistocene–Holocene Transition in the Darb el Arba'in Desert, Eastern Sahara," *Geoarchaeology: An International Journal* 16, no. 1 (2001): 119–41.
6. Ibid.
7. Kathleen Nicoll, "Recent Environmental Change and Prehistoric Human Activity in Egypt and Northern Sudan," *Quaternary Science Reviews* 23, nos. 5–6 (March 2004): 561–80.
8. Haynes, "Geochronology and Climate Change."
9. Nicoll, "Recent Environmental Change and Prehistoric Human Activity."
10. Haynes, "Geochronology and Climate Change."
11. Ibid.
12. Ibid.
13. Ibid.
14. Ibid.
15. Ibid.
16. Ibid.
17. Ibid.
18. Ibid.
19. Nicoll, "Recent Environmental Change and Prehistoric Human Activity."
20. Ibid.

21. Ibid.
22. Ibid.
23. Ibid.
24. Robert J. Wenke, "Egypt: Origins of Complex Societies," *Annual Reviews Anthropology* 18 (1989): 129–55.
25. Schoch, "Geological Evidence Pertaining to the Age of the Great Sphinx."
26. P. Morel, F. von Blanckenburg, M. Schaller, M. Hinderer, and P. W. Kubik (PSI), "Quantification of the Effects of Lithology, Landscape Dissection, and Glaciation on Rock Weathering and Large-Scale Erosion as Determined by Cosmogenic Nuclides in River Sediments," *Annual Report: The Institute for Particle Physics*, ETH Zürich (Swiss Federal Institute of Technology), 2001.
27. John Stone and Paulo Vasconcelos, "Studies of Geomorphic Rates and Processes with Cosmogenic Isotopes Examples from Australia," *Cambridge Publications Goldschmidt 2000 Conference: An International Conference for Geochemistry*, Oxford, U.K., organized by the European Association for Geochemistry and the Geochemical Society.
28. A. Matmon, E. Zilberman, and Y. Enzel, "The Development of the Bet-Ha'Emeq Structure and the Tectonic Activity of Normal Faults in the Galilee," *Israel Journal of Earth Sciences* 49 (2000): 143–58.
29. Table data from sources cited in notes 25–28, and from the following: National Parks Service, U.S. Department of the Interior, www.nps.gov/miss/features/geology/geology.html, and www.factmonster.com/ce6/sci/A0817621.html, whose source is *The Columbia Electronic Encyclopedia*, 6th ed., copyright © 2005, Columbia University Press; National Park Service, U.S. Department of the Interior Geology Fieldnotes—Grand Canyon National Park at www.2nature. nps.gov/geology/parks/grca/; The Niagara Parks Commission Geology of the Falls at www.niagaraparks.com/nfgg/geology.php; and "Origins of Niagara—A Geologic History" at www.iaw.com/~falls/origins.html
30. Wenke, "Egypt: Origins of Complex Societies."

Chapter 4: What Culture, When?

1. Walter B. Emery, *Archaic Egypt* (New York: Penguin Books, 1961), 214.
2. William Matthew Flinders Petrie, *The Pyramids and Temples of Gizeh* (New York: Scribner and Welford, 1883), 175.
3. Ibid., 176.
4. Ibid., 174.
5. Ibid., 173.
6. Jay M. Enoch and Vasudevan Lakshminarayanan, "Duplication of Unique Optical Effects of Ancient Egyptian Lenses from the IV/V Dynasties: Lenses Fabricated ca. 2620–2400 B.C.E., or Roughly 4600 Years Ago," *Ophthalmic and Physiological Optics* 20, no. 2 (15 March 2000): 126–30.

7. Ibid.
8. Ibid.
9. Christopher Dunn, "Advanced Machining in Ancient Egypt," *Analog Magazine* (August 1984).
10. Ibid.
11. Ibid.
12. Christopher Dunn, "The Precision of the Ancient Egyptians" (March 2003). Online at www.gizapower.com/Precision.htm (accessed on 4/30/2004).
13. Ibid.
14. J. McKim Malville, Fred Wendorf, Ali A. Mazart, and Romauld Schild, "Megaliths and Neolithic Astronomy in Southern Egypt," *Nature* (April 1998): 488–91.
15. "Mysteries of the South Western Desert: The Megaliths of Nabta Playa," *Focus on Archeology ACADEMIA* 1, no. 1 (2004).
16. Ibid.
17. Ibid.
18. Malville, et al., "Megaliths and Neolithic Astronomy in Southern Egypt," 489.
19. University of Colorado Press Release, "Oldest Astronomical Megalith Alignment Discovered in Southern Egypt by Science Team," Boulder: University of Colorado Office of Public Relations, March 31, 1998.
20. Malville, et al., "Megaliths and Neolithic Astronomy in Southern Egypt."
21. Thomas G. Brophy, *The Origin Map: Discovery of a Prehistoric, Megalithic, Astrophysical Map and Sculpture of the Universe* (New York: Writers Club Press, 2002), 9.
22. Ibid., 14.
23. Ibid., 10.
24. Ibid., 14.
25. Ibid., 15.
26. J. M. Malville, F. Wendorf, A. A. Mazar and R. Schild, "Megaliths and Neolithic Astronomy in Southern Egypt," *Nature* (1998): 392, 488.
27. Brophy, *Origin Map*, 20.
28. Ibid., 18.
29. Ibid., 20.
30. Ibid., 21.
31. Ibid., 36.
32. Ibid., 40.
33. Ibid., 41.
34. Ibid., 45
35. Ibid., 48.
36. Ibid., 49.
37. Ibid., 51.
38. Ibid., 54.
39. Ibid., 53–54. Monthly Notices of the Royal Astronomical Society is a publication by the Royal Astronomical Society.

40. Ibid., 59.
41. Fred Wendorf and Romauld Schild, "Nabta Playa and its Role in Northeastern African Prehistory," *Journal of Anthropological Archeology* 17 (1998): 123.

Chapter 5: Keeping Time

1. John Fermor, "Timing the Sun in Egypt and Mesopotamia," *Vistas in Astronomy* 41, no. 1 (1991): 151–67.
2. For a more in depth-explanation, see Mary Weaver, "The Significance of the Beginning Date of the Julian Calendar," online at: www.lascruces.com/~jasm/julian.html. (Copyright Jasmine Tewa Business Trust, 2000.)
3. The actual date for the beginning of the Age of Pisces is a debatable matter. Some scholars believe it occurred close to the birth of Christ; others think it came a hundred or more years later.
4. Rupert Gleadow, *The Origin of the Zodiac* (New York: Castle Books, 1968), 177.
5. Giorgio de Santillana and Hertha von Dechend, *Hamlet's Mill: An Essay on Myth and the Frame of Time* (Boston: David R. Godine, 1977), 288–316.
6. Ibid., 57.
7. John G. Jackson, "Ethiopia and the Origin of Civilization: A Critical Review of the Evidence of Archaeology, Anthropology, History, and Comparative Religion According to the Most Reliable Sources and Authorities," 1939, online at: www.africawithin.com/jgjackson/jgjackson_ethiopia_and_the_origin.htm.
8. Constantin-Francois de Volney, *The Ruins, or, Meditation on the Revolutions of Empires and the Law of Nature* (New York: Twentieth Century Publishing Co., 1890). (See "Second System: Worship of Stars, or Sabeism" in chapter 22, "The Origin and Filiation of Religious Ideas.")
9. Ibid. (See "Third System: Worship of Symbols, or Idolatry" in Chapter 22, "The Origin and Filiation of Religious Ideas.")
10. de Santillana and von Dechend, *Hamlet's Mill,* x–xi.
11. P. F. Gössman, trans., *Das Era-Epos* (Würzburg, Germany: Augustinus-Verlaz, 1955).
12. de Santillana and von Dechend, *Hamlet's Mill,* 325.
13. Ibid., 326.
14. Arthur M. Harding, *Astronomy: The Splendor of the Heavens Brought Down to Earth* (Garden City, NY: Garden City Publishing Company, 1935), 252.

Chapter 6: Pyramid Technology

1. Moustafa Gadalla, *Pyramid Handbook* (Greensboro, NC: Tehuti Research Foundation, 2000), 80–81.
2. Ibid., 82–84.

3. Ibid., 90–91.
4. Ibid., 98.
5. Ibid., 100–101.
6. Ibid., 144.
7. Ibid., 148–49.
8. Ibid., 158–60.
9. Ibid., 121.
10. Ibid., 122.
11. Ibid., 130.
12. Ibid., 134.
13. Ibid.
14. Christopher Dunn, *The Giza Power Plant* (Rochester, VT: Bear & Company, 1998), 125–50.
15. Ibid., 151–59.
16. Ibid., 160–71.
17. Ibid., 172–75.
18. Ibid., 176–77.
19. Ibid., 182–90.
20. Ibid., 192.
21. Ibid., 198.
22. Ibid., 196.
23. Ibid., 197.
24. Ibid., 199.
25. Ibid., 201–204.
26. Ibid., 204.
27. Ibid., 205–208.
28. Ibid., 211.
29. Christopher Dunn, "Following the Evidence," March 16, 2004, online at: www.gizapower.com (accessed June 1, 2004).

Chapter 7: Who Were the First Egyptians?

1. Emery, *Archaic Egypt*, 31.
2. Smith, "Origins and Spread of Pastoralism in Africa," 128.
3. Pierre M. Vermeersch, "Out of Africa from an Egyptian's Point of View," *Quaternary International* 75, no. 1 (January 2001): 103–12.
4. Ibid.
5. Ibid.
6. Ibid.
7. Nicoll, "Recent Environmental Change and Prehistoric Human Activity," 558–61.
8. Ibid.
9. Ibid.
10. Kathryn A. Bard, "The Egyptian Predynastic: A Review of the Evidence," *Journal of Field Archaeology* 21 (1994): 265.
11. Ibid., 270.

12. Ibid.
13. Ibid., 271.
14. Ibid.
15. Ibid.
16. Ibid.
17. Donald B. Redford, *Egypt, Canaan, and Israel in Ancient Times* (Princeton, NJ: Princeton University Press, 1992), 5.
18. Ibid., 6–7.
19. Emery, *Archaic Egypt*, 38–39.
20. Christy G. Turner II, "A Dental Hypothesis for the Origin and Antiquity of the Afro-Asiatic Language Family," the Santa Fe Institute Seminar on Language, Genes, and Prehistory (March 1–3, 2004).

Chapter 8: Toxic Evidence for an Old Theory

1. *The Mystery of the Cocaine Mummies,* Equinox-Channel 4 and the Discovery Channel, September 8, 1996, documentary.
2. Ibid.
3. Ibid.
4. Ibid.
5. Ibid.
6. Lawrence Gustave Desmond and Phyllis Mauch Messenger, *A Dream of Maya: Augustus and Alice Le Plongeon in Nineteenth-Century Yucatán* (Albuquerque: University of New Mexico Press, 1988). (Web version available at: http://maya.csuhayward.edu/archaeoplanet/LgdPage/Dream/Start.htm.)
7. *A Dream of Maya* (quote from *Vestiges of the Mayas,* New York, J. Polhemus, 1881), 16.
8. Desmond and Messenger, *A Dream of Maya,* chapter 4.
9. Ibid., chapter 11.
10. *A Dream of Maya,* quote from "Mayapan and Maya Inscriptions," Proceedings of the American Antiquarian Society" (New Series) 1:246–82, 1881, 249–50.
11. Augustus Le Plongeon, *Queen Moo and the Egyptian Sphinx* (New York: Rudolf Steiner Publications, 1973), lv.
12. Ibid., liv.
13. Ibid., 21.
14. Ibid., 45.
15. Ibid., 46.
16. Ibid., 21.
17. Ibid., 150.
18. Ibid., 151–53.
19. Ibid., 39.
20. Le Plongeon, *Queen Moo and the Egyptian Sphinx,* 152–53.
21. Plato, *Timaeus and Critias,* translated by Desmond Lee (New York: Penguin Classics, 1977), 37–38.

22. Le Plongeon, 72–73.

23. Ibid., 73.

24. Gwendolyn Leick, *Mesopotamia: The Invention of the City* (New York: Penguin Books, 2002), 25.

25. Le Plongeon, *Queen Moo and the Egyptian Sphinx*, 45.

26. James Mooney, "Maya Indians," The Catholic Encyclopedia, online at www.newadvent.org/cathen/10082b.htm.

27. Le Plongeon, *Queen Moo and the Egyptian Sphinx*, xxx. Le Plongeon quotes Phillip J. J. Valenti, *Katunes of the Maya History*, 54.

28. Ibid., xxx. Le Plongeon quotes Juan Pio Perez, *Codex Maya*, U Tzolan Katunil ti Maya, 7.

29. Ibid., xviii.

30. Ibid., xli.

31. Ibid., 154. Le Plongeon cites Sir Gardner Wilkinson, *Manners and Customs*, vol. 3, 395.

32. Ibid., 154.

33. Ibid., 117. Le Plongeon cites Sir Gardner Wilkinson, *Manners and Customs*, vol. 3, chap. 61, 486.

34. Ibid., 156. Le Plongeon cites Champollion Figeac, *L'Univers, Egypte*, 261.

35. Ibid., 157.

36. Ibid., 158. Le Plongeon cites Christian C. J. Bunsen, *Egypt's Place in Universal History*, vol. 2 (London: Longman, Brown, Green, 1860), 388.

37. Ibid. 158. Le Plongeon cites William Osburn, *Monumental History of Egypt*, vol. 2 (London, Trubner & Co., 1854), 319.

38. Ibid., vol. 1, 311.

39. Ibid., 158. Le Plongeon cites Karl Richard Lepsius, *Letters from Egypt, Ethiopia, and the Peninsula of Sinai*, L. and J. B. Horner, trans. (London: Henry G. Bohn, 1853), 66.

40. Ibid., 160. Le Plongeon cites Plinius, *Naturalis Historia xxxvi*, 17.

41. Ibid., 160. Le Plongeon cites Clement of Alexandria, *Stromata v.*

42. Ibid., 160. Le Plongeon cites Piazzi Smyth, *Life and Work at the Great Pyramid*, vol. 1, chap. 12, 323.

43. Ibid., 160. Le Plongeon cites Landa, *Las Cosas de Tucatan*, secs. xx, 114, and xxxi, 184.

44. Ibid., 160. Le Plongeon cites Henry Brugsch-Bey, *History of Egypt under the Pharaohs*, vol. 1, Seymour and Smith, translation, 80.

45. Ibid., 162. Le Plongeon cites Samuel Birch and Sir Gardner Wilkinson, *Manners and Customs*, vol. 3, note, chap. 14.

46. Ibid., 162.

47. Ibid.

48. Ibid., 163. Le Plongeon cites Henry Brugsch-Bey, *History of Egypt under the Pharaohs*, vol. 2, Seymour and Smith, translation, 464.

49. Ibid., 163. Le PLongeon cites Herodotus, *History*, lib. ii, 144.

50. Ibid., 163.

51. Ibid., introduction, ubi supra, p. lix.
52. Ibid., 164. Le Plongeon cites Plutarch, *De Yside et Osiride,* sec. 25, 36.
53. Ibid., 165. Le Plongeon cites Herodotus, *History,* lib. ii., 42, 59, 61.
54. Ibid., 166. Le Plongeon cites Apuleius, *Metamorphosis,* lib. ii., 241.
55. Ibid., 166. Le Plongeon cites Diodorus, *Bibl. Hist,* lib. i., 27.
56. Ibid., 166. Le Plongeon cites E. A. Wallis Budge, *The Book of the Dead* chap. 110, verses 4–5.
57. "The Real Scorpion King," Providence Pictures, Providence, 2002, press release for History Channel documentary.
58. Ibid. See also John Noble Wilford, "Of Early Writing and a King of Legend," *New York Times,* Science Times, April 16, 2002.
59. Ray T. Matheny, "El Mirador, a Maya Metropolis," *National Geographic* (September 1987): 329. See also "Pyramids, Mummies, & Tombs," Discovery Channel Documentary hosted by Bob Brier.

Chapter 9: Egypt's Prehistoric Roots

1. Francisco García Talavera, "Relaciones Geneticas entre Las Poblaciones Canaria y Norte Africans." Online at http://personal.telefonica.terra.es/web/mleal/articles/africa/24.htm, accessed (1/15/2004).
2. O. Dotour and N. Petit-Maire, "Place des restes humains de la dune d'Izriten parmi les populations holocenes du littoral atlantique nord-africain," *Le Bassin de Tarfaya,* ed. Jean Riser (Paris: Harmattan, 1996).
3. Talavera.
4. Ibid.
5. Joel D. Irish and D. Guatelli-Steinberg, "Ancient Teeth and Modern Human Origins: An Expanded Comparison of African Plio-Pleistocene and Recent World Dental Samples," *Journal of Human Evolution* 45, no. 2 (2003): 113–44.
6. Joel D. Irish, "The Iberomaurusian Enigma: North African Progenitor or Dead End?" *Journal of Human Evolution,* October 39(4): 393–410, 2000, 395–97.
7. O. Soffer, M. Adovasio, and D. C. Hyland. "The 'Venus Figurines': Textiles, Basketry, Gender, and Status in the Upper Paleolithic," *Current Anthropology* 41, no. 4 (August–October 2000): 520.
8. Ibid., 518.
9. Ibid., 522.
10. Ibid., 524.
11. Marija Gimbutas, *The Age of the Great Goddess: An Interview with Kell Kearns,* Boulder, CO: Sounds True Recordings, 1992, audiotape.
12. Ibid., "Learning the Language of the Goddess," October 3, 1992, online at: www.levity.com/mavericks/gim-int.htm (accessed on 1/25/2004).
13. Ibid.
14. Ibid.
15. Gimbutas, *The Age of the Great Goddess.*
16. Ibid.

17. Ibid.
18. Ibid.
19. Ibid.
20. H.W. Fairman, "La Composition Raciale de l'ancienne Egypt," *Anthropologie* 51 (1947): 239–50.
21. John R. Baker, *Race* (Oxford: Oxford University Press, 1974), 519.
22. Ian Tattersall, *Becoming Human: Evolution and Human Uniqueness* (New York: Harcourt, Brace & Company, 1998), 10.
23. Ibid.
24. Ibid., 180.
25. Ibid., 99.
26. David Lewis-Williams, *The Mind in the Cave* (London: Thames & Hudson, 2002), 97.
27. Ibid.
28. Ibid., 98.
29. Ibid., 99.
30. Ibid.

Chapter 10: The Symbolist's Egypt

1. Chance Gardner, "Episode 1: The Invisible Science," *Magical Egypt: A Symbolist Tour*, Cydonia Inc., 2002, documentary series.
2. E. A. Wallis Budge, *Egyptian Ideas of the Future Life* (London: K. Paul, Trench, Trübner and Co., 1900), 17–18.
3. Moustafa Gadalla, *Egyptian Divinities* (Greensboro, NC: Tehuti Research Foundation, 2001), 17.
4. Gardner, "Episode 1: The Invisible Science."
5. Ibid.
6. Gadalla, *Egyptian Divinities*, 20.
7. Ibid., 100.
8. Ibid.
9. John Anthony West, *Serpent in the Sky* (Wheaton, IL: Quest Books, 1993), 32–33.
10. Ibid., 34–35.
11. Ibid., 35–36.
12. Ibid., 37–39.
13. Ibid., 40–42.
14. Ibid., 42–46.
15. Ibid., 47–50.
16. Ibid., 50–54.
17. Ibid., 41.
18. R. A. Schwaller de Lubicz, *Sacred Science* (Rochester, VT: Inner Traditions, 1982), 187–88.
19. Isha Schwaller de Lubicz, *Her-Bak*, vol. 2 (New York: Inner Traditions, 1978), 156.

20. R. A. Schwaller de Lubicz, *Sacred Science*, 192.
21. Lucie Lamy, *Egyptian Mysteries: New Light on Ancient Knowledge* (New York: Thames & Hudson, 1981), 9.
22. R. A. Schwaller de Lubicz, *Sacred Science*, 188.
23. Lamy, *Egyptian Mysteries*, 9.
24. John Opsopaus, *The Pythagorean Tarot*. Opsopaus cites Sextus Empiricus, Adv. Math. VII. 94–5, online at www.cs.utk.edu/~mclennan/BA/PT/, (accessed on 7/14/2004)
25. Moustafa Gadalla, *Egyptian Cosmology: The Animated Universe* (Greensboro, NC: Tehuti Research Foundation, 2001), 45.
26. Gardner, "Episode 1: The Invisible Science."
27. Ibid.
28. Ibid.
29. Timothy Freke and Peter Gandy, *The Hermetica: The Lost Wisdom of the Pharaohs* (New York: Jeremy P. Tarcher, 1999), 7.
30. Ibid., 19.
31. Ibid., 18.
32. Brian P. Copenhaver, ed. and trans., *Hermetica: The Greek Corpus Hermeticum and the Latin* (Cambridge: Cambridge University Press, 2002), 43.

Chapter 11: Bu Wizzer

1. Stephen S. Mehler, *The Land of Osiris* (Kempton, IL: Adventures Unlimited Press, 2001), 203.
2. Ibid., 11.
3. Ibid., 51.
4. Ibid., 116.
5. Ibid., 48.
6. Ibid., 77.
7. Ibid., 79.
8. Ibid.
9. Ibid., 92.
10. Ibid., 126.
11. Ibid., 140.
12. Ibid., 152.
13. Ibid., 185.
14. Ibid., 186.
15. *The Mythological Origins of the Egyptian Temple* was published by Manchester University Press, 1969.
16. Mehler, *The Land of Osiris*, 188.
17. Ibid., 189.
18. Ibid., 190.
19. Le Plongeon, *Queen Moo and the Egyptian Sphinx*, 215–17. See Le Plongeon's plate 23.
20. Ibid., Le Plongeon's plate 23.
21. Ibid., 57.

Chapter 12: Breaking into a New History

1. William Arthur Griffiths, "Malta: The Hiding Place of Nations— First Account of Remarkable Prehistoric Tombs and Temples Recently Unearthed on the Island," *National Geographic* (May 1920): 448.
2. Richard Walter, "Wanderers Awheel in Malta," *National Geographic* (August 1940): 272.
3. Ibid.
4. Ibid.
5. Griffiths, "Malta: The Hiding Place of Nations," 445–46.
6. Joseph S. Ellul, *Malta's Prediluvian Culture at the Stone Age Temples with Special Reference to Hagar Qim, Ghar Dalam, Cart-Ruts, Il-Misqa, Il-Maqluba, and Creation* (Malta: Printwell Ltd., 1988).
7. Kenneth J. Hsu, *The Mediterranean Was a Desert: A Voyage of the Glomar Challenger* (Princeton, NJ: Princeton University Press, 1983).
8. William Ryan and Walter Pitman, *Noah's Flood: New Scientific Discoveries about the Event That Changed History* (New York: Simon and Schuster, 1998), 88.
9. Ibid., 89.
10. Walt Brown, *In the Beginning: Compelling Evidence for Creation and the Flood*, 7th ed. www.creationscience.com, Center for Scientific Creation, 2001).
11. Ibid.
12. Ellul, *Malta's Prediluvian Culture.*
13. Vittorio Di Cesare and Adriano Forgione, "Malta: The Skulls of the Mother Goddess," *HERA* (June 2001).
14. Ibid.
15. Griffiths, "Malta: The Hiding Place of Nations," 449.
16. Correspondence with Stephen Mehler, July 12, 2004.
17. Griffiths, "Malta: The Hiding Place of Nations," 459.
18. Richard Ellis, *Imagining Atlantis* (New York: First Vintage Books, 1999), 28.
19. Di Cesare and Forgione, "Malta: The Skulls of the Mother Goddess."
20. Ellis, 233 (quoting Marinatos's 1950 essay, "On the Legend of Atlantis").
21. Ibid., 232–33.
22. Rossella Lorenzi, "Lost City of Atlantis Found in Spain?" *Discovery News* (June 8, 2004), online at: http://dsc.discovery.com/news/briefs/20040607/atlantis.html
23. Andrew L. Awler, "Rocking the Cradle," *Smithsonian* (May 2004): 40–48.
24. Steve Connor, "Does skull prove that the first Americans came from Europe?" *The Independent* (December 3, 2002).
25. Brophy, *The Origin Map*, 63.
26. John Major Jenkins, *Galactic Alignment* (Rochester, VT: Bear and Company, 2002), 99–101.

27. R. A. Schwaller de Lubicz, *Sacred Science*, 86.
28. Emery, *Archaic Egypt*, 192.
29. The original philosophical concepts of God and humanity's relation to God are from the ancient Egyptian writings of Thoth (whom the Greeks called Hermes), who was venerated from at least 3000 B.C.E. Portrayed as a scribe with the head of an ibis, he is accredited with the invention of sacred hieroglyphic writing. The writings of Thoth, commonly referred to as the *Hermetica,* set forth a foundation of thought that is apparent in Hebrew and Christian texts during later times.

    Remember that the biblical Moses was raised as a pharaoh's son—as royalty, he would have been educated by the wisest of teachers and exposed at an early age to Egypt's ancient history and philosophy. He is also credited with writing the first five books of the Bible, but that, of course, is another story.

30. Kuhn wrote numerous influential books and articles during his distinguished career. His most renowned work is *The Structure of Scientific Revolutions,* which he wrote while a graduate student in theoretical physics at Harvard. It has sold over a million copies in sixteen languages.

SELECTED BIBLIOGRAPHY

Baker, John R. *Race*. Oxford: Oxford University Press, 1974.

Bard, Kathryn A. "The Egyptian Predynastic: A Review of the Evidence." *Journal of Field Archaeology* 21 (1994): 265–88.

Brophy, Thomas G. *The Origin Map: Discovery of a Prehistoric, Megalithic, Astrophysical Map and Sculpture of the Universe*. New York: Writers Club Press, 2002.

Cesare, Vittorio Di and Adriano Forgione. "Malta: The Skulls of the Mother Goddess." *HERA* (June 2001).

Copenhaver, Brian P. *Hermetica*. Cambridge: Cambridge University Press, 2002.

Desmond, Lawrence Gustave, and Phyllis Mauch Messenger. *A Dream of Maya: Augustus and Alice Le Plongeon in Nineteenth-Century Yucatán*. Albuquerque: University of New Mexico Press, 1988.

Dunn, Christopher. "Advanced Machining in Ancient Egypt." *Analog Magazine* (1984).

———. *The Giza Power Plant*. Rochester, VT: Bear and Company, 1998.

———. "The Precision of the Ancient Egyptians." Online at www.gizapower. com/Advanced/Advanced Machining.html (March 2003).

Ellul, Joseph S. *Malta's Prediluvian Culture*. Malta: Printwell Ltd., 1988.

Emery, Walter B. *Archaic Egypt*. New York: Penguin Books, 1961.

Enoch, Jay M., and Vasudevan Lakshminarayanan. "Duplication of Unique Optical Effects of Ancient Egyptian Lenses from the IV/V Dynasties: Lenses Fabricated ca. 2620–2400 B.C.E., or Roughly 4600 Years Ago." *Ophthalmic and Physiological Optics* 20, no. 2 (15 March 2000): 126–30.

Fadhlaoui-Zid, K., S. Plaza, F. Calafell, M. Ben-Amor, D. Comas, and A. Bennamar-El Gaaied. "Mitochondrial DNA Heterogeneity in Tunisian Berbers." *Annals of Human Genetics* 68, no. 3 (May 2004).

Fermor, John. "Timing the Sun in Egypt and Mesopotamia." *Vistas in Astronomy* 41, no. I (1991): 151–67.

Freke, Timothy, and Peter Gandy. *The Hermetica: The Lost Wisdom of the Pharaohs*. New York: Jeremy P. Tarcher, 1999.

Gadalla, Moustafa. *Pyramid Handbook*. Greensboro, NC: Tehuti Research Foundation, 2000.

Gauri, K. Lal. "Geologic Study of the Sphinx." *American Research Center in Egypt Newsletter*, no. 127 (1984): 24–43.

Gimbutas, Marija. *The Age of the Great Goddess: An Interview with Kell Kearns*. Boulder, CO: Sounds True Recordings, 1992, audiotape.

———. *Goddesses and Gods of Old Europe, 6500–3500 B.C.: Myths and Cult Images*. Berkeley: University of California Press, 1982.

Gleadow, Rupert. *The Origin of the Zodiac*. New York: Castle Books, 1968.

Griffiths, William Arthur. "Malta: The Hiding Place of Nation's First Account of Remarkable Prehistoric Tombs and Temples Recently Unearthed on the Island," *National Geographic*, May 1920.

Harding, Arthur M. *Astronomy: The Splendor of the Heavens Brought Down to Earth*. Garden City, NY: Garden City Publishing Company, 1935.

Haynes Jr., and C. Vance. "Geochronology and Climate Change of the Pleistocene–Holocene Transition in the Darb el Arba'in Desert, Eastern Sahara." *Geoarchaeology: An International Journal* 16, no. 1 (2001): 119–41.

Hsu, Kenneth J. *The Mediterranean Was a Desert: A Voyage of the Glomar Challenger*. Princeton, NJ: Princeton University Press, 1983.

Irish, Joel D. "The Iberomaurusian Enigma: North African Progenitor or Dead End?" *Journal of Human Evolution* vol. 39, no. 4 (2000): 395–97.

Irish, Joel D., and D. Guatelli-Steinberg. "Ancient Teeth and Modern Human Origins: An Expanded Comparison of African Plio-Pleistocene and Recent World Dental Samples." *Journal of Human Evolution* 45, no 2 (2003): 113–44.

Le Plongeon, Augustus. *Queen Moo and the Egyptian Sphinx*. New York: Rudolf Steiner Publications, 1973.

Lehner, Mark. "Computer Rebuilds the Ancient Sphinx." *National Geographic* (April 1991): 32–38.

Leick, Gwendolyn. *Mesopotamia: The Invention of the City*. New York: Penguin Books, 2002.

Lewis-Williams, David. *The Mind in the Cave*. London: Thames and Hudson, 2002.

Malville, J. McKim, Fred Wendorf, Ali A. Mazar, and Romauld Schild. "Megaliths and Neolithic Astronomy in Southern Egypt." *Nature* (April 1998): 488–91.

Martin, Thomas R. *Ancient Greece*. New Haven: Yale University Press, 1996.

Matmon, A., E. Zilberman, and Y. Enzel. "The Development of the Bet-Ha'Emeq Structure and the Tectonic Activity of Normal Faults in the Galilee." *Israel Journal of Earth Sciences* 49 (2000): 143–58.

Mehler, Stephen S. *The Land of Osiris*. Kempton, IL: Adventures Unlimited Press, 2001.

Mellaart, James. *Earliest Civilizations of the Near East*. London: Thames and Hudson, 1965.

Nicoll, Kathleen. "Recent Environmental Change and Prehistoric Human Activity in Egypt and Northern Sudan." *Quaternary Science Reviews* 23, nos. 5–6 (March 2004): 561–80.

Osler, Sir William. *The Evolution of Modern Medicine*. New Haven: Yale University Press, 1921.

Petrie, William Matthew Flinders. *The Pyramids and Temples of Gizeh*. New York: Scribner and Welford, 1883.

Reader, Colin. "A Geomorphological Study of the Giza Necropolis, with Implications for the Development of the Site." *Archaeometry* 43 (2001): 149–65.

Redford, Donald B. *Egypt, Canaan, and Israel in Ancient Times*. Princeton, NJ: Princeton University Press, 1992

Ryan, William, and Walter Pitman. *Noah's Flood: New Scientific Discoveries about the Event That Changed History*. New York: Simon and Schuster, 1998.

Santillana, Giorgio de, and Hertha von Dechend. *Hamlet's Mill: An Essay on Myth and the Frame of Time*. Boston: David R. Godine, 1977.

Schild, Romuald, and Fred Wendorf. "Mysteries of the South Western Desert: The Megaliths of Nabta Playa," *Academia, Focus on Archeology* no. 1 (1) 2004.

Schoch, Robert M. "Geological Evidence Pertaining to the Age of the Great Sphinx." *Quaderni del Dipartmento di Matematica, Statistica, Informatica ed Applicazion, Serie Miscellanea* 3 (2002): 171–203

———. "Redating the Great Sphinx of Giza." *KMT: A Modern Journal of Ancient Egypt,* vol. 3, no. 2 (1992).

Smith, Andrew B. "Origins and Spread of Pastoralism in Africa." *Annual Review of Anthropology* 21 (1992): 125–41.

Soffer, Olga, M. Adovasio, and D. C. Hyland. "The 'Venus Figurines': Textiles, Basketry, Gender, and Status in the Upper Paleolithic." *Current Anthropology* 41, no. 4 (August/October 2000): 511–37.

Tattersall, Ian. *Becoming Human: Evolution and Human Uniqueness*. New York: Harcourt, Brace and Company, 1998.

Turner II, Christy G. "A Dental Hypothesis for the Origin and Antiquity of the Afro-Asiatic Language Family." The Santa Fe Institute Seminar on Language, Genes, and Prehistory, March 2004.

Vermeersch, Pierre M. "Out of Africa from an Egyptian's Point of View." *Quaternary International* 75, no. 1 (January 2001): 103–12.

Volney, Constantin-François. *The Ruins, or Meditation on the Revolutions of Empires and the Law of Nature*. New York: Twentieth Century Publishing, 1890.

Walter, Richard. "Wanderers Awheel in Malta." *National Geographic*, August 1940.

Wendorf, Fred, and Romauld Schild. "Nabta Playa and Its Role in Northeastern African Prehistory." *Journal of Anthropological Archeology* 7 (1998): 97–123.

Wenke, Robert J. "Egypt: Origins of Complex Societies." *Annual Reviews Anthropology* 18 (1989): 129–55.

West, John Anthony. *Serpent in the Sky*. Wheaton, IL: Quest Books, 1993.

INDEX